For
Whom
the Bells
Tolled

Tiomnaím an leabhar seo do mo thuismitheoirí uaisle oirirce, Matt agus Mary, ina gcuimhne agus le mór-bhuíochas, ar an gcéad dul síos; agus ar an dara, do mo chomrádaí dílse – atá imithe, atá linne anois, agus atá fós le teacht– sa Bhriogáid Múchta Dóiteáin, go háirithe, Michael O'Connell, Colm McGowan, agus Dick Beecher, a dhein an íobairt árdcheannasach.

FOR WHOM THE BELLS TOLLED

A HISTORY OF CORK FIRE SERVICES 1622-1900

PAT POLAND

Front cover image: Detail from Charles Vigor's painting *Saved*.
Reproduced by kind permission of T.L. Glossop O St J, QFSM, BSc,
MIFireE, Chief Executive and Commandant of the Fire Service College,
Moreton-in Marsh, England.

Back cover image: *The Fire at Cork Courthouse 1891* by Eugene McSwiney.
Reproduced courtesy of Mortimer Kelleher, President of the Southern Law
Association.

First published 2010

The History Press Ireland
119 Lower Baggot Street
Dublin 2
www.thehistorypress.ie

© Pat Poland, 2010

British Library Cataloguing in Publication Data.
A catalogue record for this book is available from the British Library.

ISBN 978 1 8458 8986 9

Typesetting and origination by The History Press
Printed in Great Britain
Manufacturing managed by Jellyfish Print Solutions Ltd

Contents

Acknowledgements 6

Abbreviations 9

Introduction 10

1 A Cork Gomorrah? The Great Firestorm of 1622 18

2 Chariots of Fire: Cork's First Fire Engines 37

3 Parish Pump Politics: The Role of the Established Church in Early Firefighting 46

4 Forged in Fire: The Insurance Brigades Make their Mark 65

5 Not Quite a Fire Brigade: The Indefatigable John Ring and his Pipe Water Men 102

6 Out of the Flames: The Cork Fire Brigade Emerges 145

7 The Thin Red Line: The First Cork Brigade 160

8 When a Cork Fire Inflamed Kipling's Wrath 192

9 O Captain! My Captain! The Long Reign of Alfred Hutson 200

10 Vigilantly Zealous for the Preservation of Life: The Street Fire Escape Stations 212

11 Working in Harmony under Intelligent Direction: The Cork Volunteer Fire Brigade 225

12 In the Line of Fire: Around the Clock with the Brigade 243

13 *Níl aon Tinteán mar do Thinteán Féin*: Station Life and Conditions *c.*1900 264

14 Fortune Favours the Brave: Some Profiles in Courage 278

Conclusion 291

Appendices:

1 Cost of Cork Fire Brigade from 1 October 1877 to 1 June 1880 294

2 Cork Fire Brigade Scale of Charges 1896 295

3 Nominal roll of members of Cork Fire Brigade 1877-1900 296

4 Chronology of Some Notable Cork fires (Earliest times to 1900) 298

5 Glossary of Cork place names mentioned in the text 300

Bibliography 301

Notes and References 307

Index 344

Acknowledgements

This book was only made possible with the help and support of a number of individuals. My first debt of thanks must go to my former supervisor at UCC, Dr Andy Bielenberg, whose encouragement was the impetus for further research. The staff at various local institutions could not have been more helpful, even though they surely must have heard the same questions many thousands of times during the course of their careers: Kieran Burke and staff of the Local Studies Department, Cork City Library; Tim Cadogan and staff of the Reference Department, Cork County Library; Brian McGee and staff at the Cork City and County Archives; and the staff of Special Collections (Q-1), UCC. Srs Pius and Joachim of the South Presentation Sisters, Douglas Street, kindly facilitated me with access to their archives, as did Sr Ursula at the Ursuline Sisters, Blackrock. A word of thanks must go to Dr Raymond Refauseé, Librarian and Archivist of the Church of Ireland Representative Church Body Library, Dublin, and his staff, for allowing me access to the old Vestry Minute Books of the Cork parishes.

I am indebted to the staff at the Reading Room, the National Library, as well as to the staff at the National Archives; in particular, Helen Hewson. Nearby, Siobhán Wynne, Head of Education and Training at the Insurance Institute of Ireland, kindly allowed me trawl through their archival documents. In England, special mention must be made of the staff at the National Archives, Kew, and to Sheree Leeds, Archivist, the Fire Mark Circle, for their unfailing forbearance in dealing with my myriad enquiries.

I wish to record my appreciation to the many individuals who contributed to the information gathered during the course of my research. The value of the help (and encouragement) received from each and every one is impossible to quantify. In alphabetical order, I would like to thank: Dr John Borgonovo, Ciara Brett, Con Buckley, Ray Canty, Stella Cherry, Dr Mary Clark, Dr Margaret Clayton, Richard T. Cooke, Tom Cotter, Donal Crean, Conal Creedon, Cmdr Alan Crosbie RN (rtd), Dr Dave Edwards, Ff. Las Fallon, Jim Fitzpatrick, Veronica Forde, Raynor de Foubert, Sgt Des Garrett, Tom Geraghty, E.H. Gledhill,

Richard S. Harrison, Richard Henchion, Ronnie Herlihy, Maureen Holland, Catherine Hudson, Stephen Hunter, Jack Irwin, Peter Lecane, Michael Lenihan, Jim Lynch, Nóirín Lynch, Denis Lynes, Esther Mann, Kevin Mahony, Antóin O'Callaghan, Sandra O'Callaghan Gerald P. O'Halloran, Kevin O'Halloran, Noel O'Keeffe, Canice O'Mahony, Denis O'Mahony, Michael P. O'Mahony, Stn O. Mick Meik, East Sussex Fire and Rescue Service, Comdt Tom O'Neill, Revd Brian O'Rourke, Lieut Col Brendan O'Shea, James O'Shea, John R. O'Shea, Liam Ó hUigín, Jim Murphy, John Murphy, Dr Seán Pettit, David R Pike, Noel Ross, Michael Rush, Ff. Ger Ryan and the committee members of the Fire Brigade Sports and Social Club, Chief Fire Officer John Ryan, Dr Colin Rynne, Revd Canon G.A. Salter, Revd Br Cathal Smiddy, Graham Smith, H.A. Smith, Tom Spalding, Bill Stewart, Alice Taylor, Kevin Terry, Niamh Twomey, Sgt Gerry White, Dr Roger Willoughby, Dr Denis Wilson.

I am forever indebted to Don Trotter who was frequently called upon to come to my assistance wearing one or other of his diverse hats: as a senior executive of AXA Insurance (formerly of the GRE and REA); as a member of the Select Vestry of St Anne's, Shandon; and as an officer of the Auxiliary Fire Service (AFS). Don always promptly produced the goods with his unfailing good humour and efficiency. The late John Higgins, Second Officer, Cork County Fire Service, provided invaluable details of the early brigade in which both his father and grandfather served. Similar information, not to be found in any published source, was afforded by the late Billy Ring, Third Officer, Cork Fire Brigade, whose father, Timothy, had served for twenty-seven years under Captain Hutson and became Chief Officer in his own right in 1928: the first Corkman to hold the post. Billy's fascinating anecdotes were received during many a late-night session in the Watchroom at Sullivan's Quay while waiting for the 'nines' (999) to 'go down' (ring) and the dawn to come up.

A special word of gratitude must go to Alan Crosbie, Chairman of Thomas Crosbie Holdings Ltd, for permission to use an image from the *Irish Examiner* photographic collection, and to Sir Kenneth Knight, CBE, QFSM, MIFire E, Commissioner of the London Fire Brigade, for permission to use an illustration from their archives. Peter Murray and Farrell Spence of the Crawford Art Gallery kindly facilitated me with an image of Hogan's *Minerva*. Researchers in Cork (and indeed elsewhere) will be forever in the debt of Dr Colman O'Mahony who was instrumental in locating, and saving, the ledgers containing the minutes of Cork Corporation Waterworks and Fire Brigade Committee which stretch from 1867 to 1929 and without which, it is no exaggeration to say, my research would not have been possible. My publishers, the History Press Ireland, and in particular, Ronan Colgan and Maeve Convery, have my sincere thanks for their counsel and support for the project.

Sadly, a number of people who provided advice and encouragement have passed away: my former comrades John Brennan, Denis O' Brien, Ken

O'Connell, Donal Moynihan, and Richard Walsh; Sr Angela Bolster; Annette de Foubert; Ken Greene; Richard I. d'Esterre Roberts, and Trevor Whitehead. As Yeats would have eloquently put it, 'I number you in the song'.

Finally, the book could not have been completed without the help and support (and, yes, Job's patience!) of my wife Elaine who encouraged me, with endless cappuccinos, when I was flagging, and to our four sons Greg, Ian, Pat, and Barry for their assistance with technical expertise when my own computer skills proved woefully inadequate.

Do cách, mo mhíle buíochas; go bhfaga Dia do shláinte agaibh.

Pat Poland

Abbreviations

Ald.:   Alderman
Aux. Fm.:   Auxiliary Fireman
BL: British Library
BPP: British Parliamentary Papers
CA: *Cork Advertiser*
CC: *Cork Constitution*
CE: *Cork Examiner*
CEE: *Cork Evening Echo*
CFB: Cork Fire Brigade
CJ: *Cork Journal*
Cllr: Councillor
CMC: *Cork Mercantile Chronicle*
DNB: *Dictionary of National Biography*
FDJ: *Faulkner's Dublin Journal*
Fm.:   Fireman
Ff.:   Firefighter
FMC: Fire Mark Circle
GRE: Guardian Royal Exchange
HC: *Hibernian Chronicle*
ILN: *Illustrated London News*
JCHAS: *Journal of the Cork Historical and Archaeological Society*

LFEE: London Fire Engine Establishment
MFB: Metropolitan Fire Brigade
NFBU: National Fire Brigades' Union
NFBA: National Fire Brigades' Association (Post 1918)
QCC: Queen's College Cork
RCB: Representative Church Body Library
REA: Royal Exchange Assurance
RHS: Royal Humane Society
RIC: Royal Irish Constabulary
RSPLF: Royal Society for the Protection of Life from Fire
SPLF: Society for the Protection of Life from Fire
SR: *Southern Reporter*
Vol.Fm.:   Volunteer Fireman
WNGA: *Waterford News and General Advertiser*
WWFBC: Waterworks and Fire Brigade Committee (of Cork Corporation)

Introduction

OLDE FLAMES.

'They marched escorted by fire'.

(*The Annals of the Four Masters,* on the Vikings).

In the grey half-light of early morning, a flotilla of ducks cruised peacefully across the broad expanse of the Cork river. Two snipe pottered with long, probing beaks among the marshes at the water's edge, and a stately heron perched on a nearby alder. They seemed quite unperturbed by the awesome sight unfolding in their midst. Barring the plaintive cry of a solitary curlew, only the splish-splash of the oars of the great fleet of Viking long-ships broke the silence as they rose and fell in perfect unison in the placid, peaty water, two men pulling on each shaft.

Days of hard rowing and hard tack had all but exhausted these hardy Northmen, who, their faces raw from the icy rain that stung like fish-hooks, in spite of the exercise, were chilled to the bone, their hands senseless with almost frozen water.[1] In an age when other mariners timidly hugged the coastline, with their single sails and navigating freely only with a following or quartering wind, they fearlessly steered their creaking wooden ships through ice packs and across the crashing seas.

Now, however, in anticipation of the coming action, their pulses quickening, energy-producing adrenalin streaming through their veins, all thoughts of the hardship of the long voyage to Ireland were forgotten. Suddenly, the endless matted greenery was broken by a spire of shining white masonry thrusting through the tree-tops.

Within seconds the dragon ships had beached. There was the quiet rasp of gravel, the clink of swords, the heavy breathing of the young warriors psyched up for action. They became taut as leopards about to spring. As they hopped over the gunwales into the chilly water and crept quietly up the gentle sloping hill towards the monastery of Cork, communicating by dumb show, the silence was broken only by the flapping wings of a startled waterfowl and the frightened bleating of a tethered goat. The phalanx of steel and fire was now unstoppable. As the community awoke, shrieks of terror and the cries of the dying resounded throughout the settlement. Monks, scholars and artists of renown, who had earlier congregated in the chapel for early-morning Lauds, having barricaded the doors, huddled around the altar chanting the great Kyrie Eleison – 'Lord have mercy on us!'. On the walls, purple hangings and gold ornaments in which precious stones glinted in the rush lights, vied for position with brightly-painted pictures of instructive scenes from the lives of Christ and the saints. Presently, the Vikings beat down the doors and swarmed in; but by now their blood-lust had cooled, the warriors realizing it was better to capture than kill, for slaves can be sold or ransomed.

Some hours later they left, carrying with them the monastery's most precious chalices and crosses worked in the finest gold and silver with beautiful intricate filigree. Priceless manuscripts, which took the monks years to illuminate, were trampled into the ground. Their final act, before they raced down the hill to their longships, was to put to the torch all the buildings in the settlement – the 'precious lamp in an era of darkness' – that tradition tells us was founded by Fionn Barra.

There can be little doubt that fire, as a terrifying weapon of war, played a major role in these attacks by the Norsemen. Indeed, the Irish Annalists described them as having 'marched escorted by fire'.[2] Chroniclers of Cork history, Fitzgerald, Edwards, and Tuckey, record additional fire raids by disparate groups of Norsemen on their Hiberno-Viking cousins in *Dún Corcaighe* in 833, 913, 915, 960, 978, and 995. In 1013, a year before the decisive Battle of Clontarf broke their power permanently, a great Norse fleet again sailed up the estuary of the Lee and later, as they beat their retreat, the attackers must have watched with some satisfaction at their handiwork, evidenced by a red glow in the western sky and an immense pall of smoke over the burning settlement. It is recorded, however, that on this occasion the aggressors didn't get away scot-free: prisoners were taken and subjected to unspeakable punishment.[3]

Other great fires ensued in 1064 ('Cork … and a great many churches were burnt that year'); 1080 ('Cork destroyed by fire'); 1089 ('Dermot, son of Turlough O'Brien, laid waste and plundered Cork, and sacrilegiously carried away the relics of St. Fin Barre').[4] A fire in 1087, not attributed by the Annalists to any attacking force, was probably accidental in origin.[5] During the great internecine wars of the early twelfth century, Cork suffered grievously. On *Lá Fhéile Bríd*, 1 February 1127, the *Árd Rí*, Turlough O'Connor of Connacht, laid siege to Cork and left it a blazing inferno. Evidence of considerable destruction by fire in the medieval city has been unearthed by archaeologists over the past twenty years or so. The wonder is that the early settlement managed to survive these frequent surges of attrition at all.

Cork city is, indeed, no stranger to the ravages of fire. Throughout its long and often turbulent history, the city has been visited by practically every calamity known to man. Plague, pestilence, pillage, war, famine, siege, flooding, tidal wave, and even earthquake. And fire. Fire knows no retreat. It is stubborn, ruthless, cunning, and totally unpredictable. It can move with incredible speed, or can lie dormant, smouldering for hours. Its method of attack is never the same; it thrives on the element of surprise. It is ruggedly independent, hovering somewhere between ally and enemy in humankind's endless fight to overcome a hostile nature. Down through the years, Corkonians have been constantly exposed to this ruthless destroyer. They have learned to respect its force, to know how quickly they must flee its path, what measures to take to confine it for their needs, and, at last, how to fight and extinguish it whenever it springs beyond bounds. Fires and firefighting in Cork are, without doubt, as old as the city itself.

EARLY FIRE HAZARDS AND BUILDING METHODS.

In early times, the smallness of the settlement put a limit to the scale of a fire and there was a fair chance of getting quickly into open country. But, as Cork developed on its familiar north-south axis, the fire risk became more pronounced. The single-storey buildings were not too difficult to get out of in a hurry, but they were built quite dangerously close to each other, and destruction of one almost always meant destruction of a 'neighbourhood'.

Excavations in recent years have revealed various types of housing construction in 'Viking Cork'. The walls were built with upright posts, interwoven with horizontal layers of hazel rods or wattles. Roofs were probably thatched and because of the wet Irish climate it appears that daub (clay-based plaster) was not widely used. A double wattle wall, filled with bracken, provided insulation for some houses. Bracken-filled side aisles, fronted by low wattle walls (perhaps covered with animal skins) were used as benches by day and beds by night.[6] Large timbers were of oak, wattle, and hazel. The houses were rectangular in shape, with a roof of straw or thatch. Doors were at either end. The central hearth between the doors released fire smoke through a hole in the roof – a considerable hazard in itself. Such houses needed to be replaced approximately every fifteen years. Open fires, rush lights, and later, candles and oil lamps, all added to the hazards. Fire was accepted as a periodic natural nuisance, to be endured philosophically. And throughout history, there has been renewed surprise each time it happens: surprise that so much chaos can come from such small beginnings.

THE ANGLO-NORMANS AND EARLY FIRE PREVENTION.

If the arrival on Irish shores of the fierce Norsemen had been a major culture shock to an earlier generation of Corkonians, then the advent of the first surge of Anglo-Normans under Milo de Cogan and Robert Fitz-Stephen, with their shiny armour and sophisticated ways, can have been no less so to those who inhabited the city in the latter half of the twelfth century. The newcomers undertook extending the Hiberno-Viking town, building a massive stone wall, on average eight metres high and three metres thick, around its perimeter, complete with sentry towers at regular intervals, about sixteen in all, which projected out from the wall in a 'D' shape.[7] Its stern sandstone and limestone walls rose to a defensive skyscape of turrets, towers and castellations. Cork began to take on the appearance of a medieval walled city complete with quayside, market place, and Main Street.

The Anglo-Normans introduced to Cork some of the rudimentary fire prevention measures which they had enforced in Britain from the time of William the Conqueror. Amongst these was the *couvre-feu* (fire cover) bowl from whence our word 'curfew' is derived. This was a special object, shaped somewhat like a bell with one side cut out. At sunset, and notified by the ringing of the church bells, every householder was obliged to place a *couvre-feu* or similar appliance over his fire to prevent the sparks from being thrown out and catching the building while the family was asleep. The fire would not extinguish completely but smoulder throughout the night, to be fully rekindled again in the morning. Lighting a fire was a tedious process, as, of course, no matches were available. Fragments of *couvre-feu* bowls were found during the late twentieth century excavations in Cork and Waterford. In Waterford, a section of one is on display in the excellent 'Treasures of Waterford' permanent exhibition. Householders, in bedding down their fires, had to ensure that no sparks or smoke could be seen issuing from the house, for in 1384 the corporation had made it illegal to leave one's fire burning all night.[8] The streets were patrolled by the night watchman who was entitled to demand one farthing from any householder disobeying the edict. The watchmen, apparently, were allowed to pocket any monies thus collected to supplement their meagre wages, which must have ensured no shortage of over-zealous early 'Fire Prevention Officers'! This tax was disparagingly referred to by Corkonians as 'Smokesilver'.[9]

A fire cover, or
couvre-feu.

This process of saving the fire from completely extinguishing was known in Irish as *'ag coigilt an teine'* and followed a set procedure. Last thing at night, the still-smouldering embers were covered in ashes and the curfew-bowl put in place. In the morning, the embers were raked out and put to one side while the night's ashes were disposed of. The glowing embers were then placed at the centre of the newly-laid fire, a draught was introduced and the fire quickly flared up. Evidence of the many years of adhering to this routine was unearthed during archaeological excavations in Cork between 1974 and 1977. O'Súilleabháin attributes some credence to the claim that many domestic fires remained burning for hundreds of years by this method.[10]

At some stage a short prayer was composed and invoked at night while bedding down the fire:

Coiglím an tine seo mar choighleann Chríost caidh;
Muire ar mhullach an tí, agus Bríd ina lár;
An t-ochtar ainglí is tréine i gCathair na nGrás
Ag cumhdach an tí seo agus a mhuintir thabhairt slán.

(I save this fire as noble Christ saves all;
Mary on the top of the house, and Brigid at its centre;
The eight strongest angels in Heaven preserving
This house and keeping its people safe).[11]

Punishment for causing fire, whether through accident or arson, was swift and dire. A charter of 1318 gave the Cork municipal authorities power to punish malefactors reserving four pleas – arson or incendiary, rape, forestalling, and finding of treasure.[12] A 1305 ordinance promulgated by the Dublin Common Council spells out, in no uncertain terms, what the retribution was for letting a fire get out of control:

For fire taking place in any house from which flames issue not, the householder, after the fire has been extinguished, is liable to a fine of twenty shillings. If the flames be visible externally the fine is forty shillings. Any person answerable for the burning of a street shall be arrested, cast into the middle of the fire, or pay a fine of a hundred shillings.[13]

Similar laws prevailed in Waterford city, with the additional proviso that should the perpetrator manage to flee the city, on recapture he or she was summarily hanged. There is no reason to suppose that Cork's 'fire laws' were any less draconian.

From earliest times, charms were regarded as having magical powers to thwart the depredations of fire. The so-called 'Fire Flower' (*Sempervivum tectorum*) or Common Houseleek, has a record of over 2,000 years of association with fire protection throughout Europe, where it was grown on house roofs as protection from fire or lightning. So effective was it held to be, that the Holy Roman Emperor Charlemagne ordered that every roof in his empire should be protected in this way. The Irish called the plant *Tóirpín* or *Luibh an tóiteáin*. Many regarded the thick, fleshy-leaved plant as having ideal 'fire-retardant' properties, believing that the sap-laden, juicy rosettes would actively discourage the spread of fire in a thatched roof.[14]

Pope John IX ordered church bells, when being cast, to be blessed to be invoked against fire and lightning. The bells were consecrated with imposing ceremony and sprinkled with holy water. The ringing of the church bells served two purposes: they served as a warning to citizens that an emergency was underway – they would run to the church and make themselves available to assist in the fire-fighting effort – and to appeal to the Almighty to 'quench the flames'. However, a special signal was needed to distinguish the fire alarm from 'ordinary' ringing and from very early times the warning consisted of 'ringing the bells backwards', or a reverse peal. This primitive, but effective, means of alarming citizens in times of emergency remained unchanged well into the nineteenth century.[15]

One of the towers on the western wall of Cork was designated a fire watch tower, complete with special fire alarm bell.[16] The sentry on duty, high up in his breezy station, on noticing any unusual fire or smoke emission would immediately ring the bell with great gusto and point in the direction of the fire to the alarmed citizens waiting expectantly below. Presently, it is assumed, the bells of St Peter's and Christ Church would take up the alarm with their reverse peal. The fire watch tower with its fire bell is clearly visible in the *Pacata Hibernia* map of Cork.[17] It stood on the city's western wall to the rear of St Peter's church in the (North) Main Street. Indeed, it was colloquially known as 'Peter's Tower'. Its position was on the eastern side of the present-day Grattan Street.

The 'Fire Flower'.

The firefighting equipment available during the Middle Ages appears, to our eyes, primitive in the extreme. A fourteenth-century edict of William II decreed that barrels full of water should be placed at strategic points for use in bucket chains and 'strong crooks of iron' with wooden handles be available. The purpose of these devices was to drag the thatch from a burning roof or to actually pull the house down to create a fire-break. Some of them were of great size, up to eight metres long and a third of a metre in the staff, and horses were sometimes harnessed to them to assist in the demolition of a building. The open space thus created would hopefully arrest the spread of fire.[18]

Long after people had mastered the various arts that made life more pleasant – even safer – and long after they had begun to weave intricate cloths, build fine houses, and print books, they were still helpless in the face of fire which, in a short time, could destroy what had taken years to create. Quick to organize for war and destruction, clever in the forging of weapons, people's only defence against fire was a few buckets of water, a pole with an iron hook on top, a few other rudimentary tools, and flight.

Map of Cork *c.*1600 based on that in *Pacata Hibernia* clearly showing the fire alarm tower (circled) on the western wall of the medieval city. The tower once stood to the rear of St Peter's church on North Main Street. (Courtesy of Cork City Libraries)

A catalogue of firefighting equipment from 1548. An illustration from Georgius Agricola's *De Re Metallica* showing a complete set of firefighting equipment in the workshop of a metallurgist. On the left-hand wall, from the top, can be seen three leather fire buckets, immediately underneath are two preventers, a sledgehammer, and a brass 'squirt'.

Narrow streets which had never heard of town planning made for congestion, and the extensive use of naked flames for lighting, heating, cooking, and trades added considerably to an already terrific fire risk. Once a fire started, it got quickly out of hand, flying brands setting alight thatched roofs and wooden beams. It was considered every man's responsibility to protect his own life and house, the lives of his family, and chattels, and while he could expect very little help from the authorities it was the custom, organized by the Church, to make collections for sufferers from fire and help them with clothing and furniture. These collections would, over time, evolve into the so-called 'fire briefs', whereby collections were to be made on the basis of parishes to assist those afflicted in another.

It was a cruel and relentless fate that doomed Cork to suffer the series of frightful fires that dogged her since the earliest days of her settlement. Fire had become the city's *leitmotif* in that it seemed new homes and stores had hardly been built on the ashes of one great fire when another even greater and more terrible would spread beyond all efforts to confine it. Records show that the city was 'burnt by the Irish' in 1378, and ten years later, so great was the destruction caused by the 'Irish rebels' who were making daily raids that many of the inhabitants decided to quit Cork city for good.[19]

But an even worse calamity was yet to come.

A Cork Gomorrah? The Great Firestorm of 1622

'This Year [1622] there happened a dreadful Fire in *Corke*, which consumed the greatest part of that City.'

(Richard Cox, *Hibernia Anglicana*).[1]

'The Citties of Sodom and Gomorrah were not more suddenly or more horribly consumed with fire from Heaven than this Cittie of Corke was this last of May'.

(From *The Most lamentable Burning of the Cittie of Corke, in the west of Ireland, in the Province of Monster*, (London, 1622)).[2]

Today, the expression would probably elicit a blank stare from the average teenager, but generations of Cork schoolboys in times past knew well how to frighten the wits out of dear old ladies living alone by means of a simple prank. 'Thunder up the gulley', they called it. By stuffing paper up a cast-iron down pipe (the 'gulley') of the targeted house and setting it on fire, a loud, roaring noise (the 'thunder') was produced. And in the lean days of the Second World War, and for a long time after when fuel was scarce, the housewives of Cork employed a not dissimilar phenomenon to get their weekly washing done.

For a few pence, a bag of sawdust was bought from Harte's Timber Yard on Wandesford's Quay or O'Shea's on Watercourse Road. A tin drum, with a hole made in the bottom to create a draught, was arranged on a number of bricks. A timber pole, or the handle of a sweeping brush, was held upright in the middle of the drum with the end protruding out through the hole in the bottom. The sawdust was then packed tightly into the drum, the pole withdrawn and the sawdust ignited from underneath. The resulting blaze provided sufficient hot water to do all the family's wash on Monday morning.[3]

In 1943, the British Prime Minister, Winston Churchill, paraphrasing the Biblical quotation from the book of Hosea,[4] vowed that 'those who sowed the wind shall reap the whirlwind', a reference to the *Luftwaffe's* bombing of British and other cities and the massive retaliation that the Allies planned. But how to carry it out with maximum and deadly effect?

Some faceless boffin, deep within the corridors of the British Air Ministry think-tank in Whitehall, probably first thought of it. Utilizing the same basic laws of atmospheric pressure that the Cork schoolboys used to frighten the old dears and the good housewives employed to do their weekly wash, namely that 'nature abhors a vacuum', the north German city of Hamburg, the beautiful 'Free and Hanseatic City', and now the second city of the *Reich*, was, in July 1943, selected for the Grand Experiment. Hamburg was ripe for burning on the clear night of 24 July 1943. Intelligence sources reported unusually high temperatures and low humidity readings that pre-heated the city. Shortly before midnight, American and British bombers began to sledgehammer the city and continued in waves, without let-up, for five days. Now, as the great armada of four-engined aircraft wheeled high overhead, their dreadful cargoes discharged, an awful, awesome sight, straight out of Dante's *Inferno,* unfolded beneath them. From east to west, and from north to south, as far as the eye could see, the whole world seemed to be on fire. With the orange glow reflected in their pale, oxygen-masked faces, the crews could only stare and marvel, hardly a word passing between them, at the hellish landscape far below. A phenomenon was occurring that had never before been experienced in a bombed city. What the aircrews were witnessing would, subsequently, add a new word to the lexicography of the Second World War: firestorm.[5]

The initial thermic firestorm phenomenon occurred when the many small fires caused by the deadly mix of countless incendiary and high-explosive bombs joined up, pulling in more and more oxygen. This increase in temperature caused a column of hot air to rise. In turn, this produced a tremendous updraught which created the atmospheric firestorm with its overwhelming force – the superheated rising air leaving to be replaced by fresh air at an ever-increasing rate and thus transforming the raid into a historic cataclysm. At its height, the 'artificial wind' at the epicentre of the firestorm reached a velocity of a Far Eastern typhoon, some seventy-five metres per second (160 miles per hour) – sufficient to uproot strong trees and fling cars into the air. More than 100,000 souls perished in that dreadful holocaust, up to 80 per cent of them from carbon monoxide poisoning infiltrating the air raid shelters which were designed to protect them.[6] Afterwards, most of Hamburg's 1.8million inhabitants fled, spreading the virus of panic throughout the country. The Third Reich itself teetered on the brink.

Did the conflagration that struck Cork on Friday 31 May 1622[7] develop into a firestorm? There is, of course, no way of knowing for certain that it did. But there are indicators to suggest that whatever visited Cork on that fateful day long ago was indeed of cataclysmic proportions; something so sudden, so totally unexpected in its frightfulness that the people could only react in total panic with no thought whatsoever given to any firefighting attempt. When the fire had sated itself after some hours, it seems that everything combustible within the city walls had been totally consumed with only the stone buildings still standing.

By comparing the report on the Cork fire with that published by the German authorities in the aftermath of the Hamburg catastrophe certain similarities emerge. The Germans concluded [8] that the firestorm was created by three specific factors. We may speculate that these ingredients were also present at Cork:

1. The first and most important factor was the weather. The raid occurred during an unusually hot and dry spell. Everything in Hamburg was tinder-dry. The Cork report observed: 'this last of May, being the most pleasant and delightful month of the year.' We may conclude that Cork had enjoyed at least a month of exceptionally fine weather, which ensured that many buildings, with their peculiarly fire-prone properties, including an abundance of thatched roofs, were also ripe for burning.

2. The second factor was the unusually concentrated marking and bombing. In the case of Cork, an analogy could be made with the fact that fires broke out in a highly-concentrated area practically simultaneously. The authors of the Cork report remark how the citizens:

Saw a dreadful lightning with flames of fire break out of the clouds and fall upon the Cittie at the same instant at the East and highest part of the Cittie. They were not run half the way when they heard a woeful cry behind them, for the West part was also set on fire.[9]

3. The third factor leading to the Hamburg firestorm was the absence of fire fighting formations[10] capable of launching a consolidated attack within the immediate area of the bombing, and their failure to harness the abundant natural water supply available in the city's two lakes – the huge *Aussenalster* and the smaller *Binnenalster*. Although some 41,000 firefighters had been drafted into the city from all over Germany at the commencement of the bombardments some nights earlier, they were largely concentrated on the western side of the city – the 'wrong' side – when the firestorm started.[11] By comparison, Cork in 1622, was surrounded by water, but had no firefighting equipment. The Cork report again:

Albeit they had a great abundance of water near at hand, there was no means to be had, nor any endeavour to be used to quench the flames.[12]

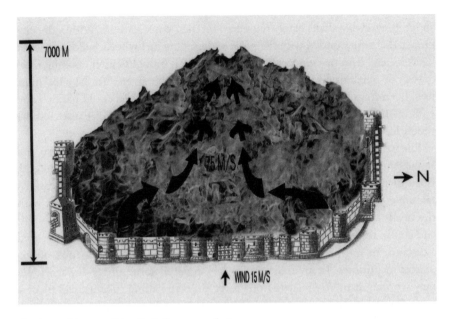

Conjectural image of the Cork firestorm of 1622.

Whilst important elements in the ultimate compound of ingredients, the first (the weather) and third (the dearth of firefighting equipment) factors would not, of course, of themselves constitute the catalysts to create a firestorm. The spark was provided by the, presumed, electrical storm at Cork, which caused fires to break out simultaneously at opposite sides of the town, creating, in effect, an enormous bonfire.

A PORTRAIT OF CORK AT THE TIME OF THE GREAT FIRE.

In order to assess the impact such a catastrophe had on a compact city like early seventeenth-century Cork, it is necessary to briefly re-acquaint ourselves with its topography.

An examination of the map in *Pacata Hibernia* affords a good idea of what Cork must still have looked like some quarter of a century later. The city is roughly rectangular in shape, surrounded by the great sandstone and limestone walls that had first been erected by the Anglo-Normans during the reign of King Edward I. In the many towers rising high over the city walls, bored sentinels gazed vacantly at the swallows flitting out over the great marshes and sandbanks, which stretched away to the east and west, swooping and diving in pursuit of mayflies. To their front, the only sound came from the plaintive cries of the waterfowl and the rustle of the wind in the rushes. Behind them, the low hum of the town going about its everyday affairs barely registered on their consciousness. Within the city proper, the air resounded with the noise of deafening cart wheels, bellowing street hawkers, and hammering coppersmiths, and winds brought either choking films of soot or pungent odours from nearby tanners and brewers. 'Traffic jams' must have been frequent as the narrow medieval lanes and streets could hardly cope with the horse-drawn traffic. Excrement from horses, dogs, and pigs spattered the streets, leaky dunghills abounded, and cess-pits were ever present.

The main street[13] lay on a north-south axis, culminating at the northern end at the North Gate Bridge, and at the South Gate Bridge at the southern end. Both bridges were complete with drawbridges and protected fortifications spanning the entrance. (These 'castles' later served as the city gaols, replete with the heads of executed misfortunates impaled on spikes, parboiled in bay salt and cumin to delay putrefaction). From the North to the South Gate measured a distance of some 630 metres. To walk the entire width of Cork took only a matter of minutes. In area, the entire city covered some thirty-six acres. We may wonder at the temerity of our forefathers in calling such a small place a 'city'. But then, and for centuries afterwards, most European cities were very compact. Writing in 1596, one London chronicler marvelled at the fact that the circumference of the walls of the city of London was all of two miles.[14]

At right-angles to the main street was the city quay, parallel to the present-day Castle Street. Here, at high tide, ships from far-off lands unloaded their exotic cargoes of silk, spices, and wines, their sailors lustily chanting work-songs as they passed the goods back along the quayside to the waiting carts. At the eastern end of the quay was the Watergate, flanked by the twin towers of the King's Castle and the Queen's Castle. The King's Castle, on the left of the Watergate entrance, was the power base of the English administration in Cork. At the junction of the quay end of the main street was the so-called 'Golden Castle' of the Roche family. This four-storey round tower was formerly known as 'Paradise Tower' (the spot to this day is called Paradise Place), or the 'Tholsel', wherein the corporation conducted its civic affairs.

The fashionable residences were situated in the many narrow lanes which intersected the main street, a maze of shadowy archways, cobbled courtyards and tranquil cloisters: some still remain to bear muted testimony to their former glory.[15] In their fine stone houses, with their courtyards and gardens under the shadow of the town walls, lived the 'merchant princes' of Cork. But if these mean lanes contained the 'upmarket' homes, they existed cheek-by-jowl with the more modest thatched-roof houses of the ordinary people. Those who lived in them were the carpenters, saddlers, masons, farriers, pewterers, butchers, bakers, silversmiths, goldsmiths, cordwainers, tailors, clothiers, coopers, bridlemakers, plumbers, tin-and-latten workers, founders, brasiers, glaziers, upholsterers, shoemakers, thatchers, and barber-surgeons of Cork. And down the years the cobblestones of these lanes have echoed with the footsteps of shuffling, cowled friars and clanking knights in armour; of the Pretender to the throne of England, the Flemish-born Perkin Warbeck; with those of the poet and Sheriff of Cork, Edmund Spenser (who, while in Ireland, advocated his own 'Final Solution' to the 'Irish Problem'); to the Adventurer and Mayor of Youghal, Walter Raleigh; and to the Spanish *Grandée* and vanquished of the Battle of Kinsale, Don Juan de Aquila. 'God's Executioner', the Lord Protector himself, Oliver Cromwell, has stalked these dark alleyways, as has the English monarch King James II, who, having deserted the Irish and fled from Kinsale after the Battle of the Boyne, was known to generations of Cork urchins only by the unflattering moniker of *Séamus a' Chaca*.[16]

Two parish churches were contained within the walls of the city. St Peter's, erected during the thirteenth century on the site of the present building (now the Cork Vision Centre), and Holy Trinity (aka Christ Church), first built in the year 1180.[17] Outside the city walls, on the north side, stood Shandon Castle, an Anglo-Norman structure; while on the south side Elizabeth Fort was located some 100 metres from the bridge.[18] As no reliable records are extant, it is difficult to gauge the population of Cork at the time of the Great Fire. Some twenty years earlier, the number stood at some 2,500, the vast majority of whom were Roman Catholics. A 1659 tally shows a practically unchanged figure of 2,403.[19]

The King was King James 1 of England and Ireland whom Cork had failed to proclaim on his accession in 1603. The Mayor of Cork was John Coppinger junior, scion of a dynasty of Roman Catholic public office holders that had served the city since at least 1319, and distantly related, on the distaff side, to Diana, Princess of Wales.[20]

GROUND ZERO: FRIDAY 31 MAY 1622.

The first to recognize the signs of oncoming disaster were the dogs of Cork. Mayor Coppinger had never seen his pet terrier in such a frantic state, scurrying about, barking, and yelping. He yapped to go out and yapped to come in; he dashed around, sniffing the ground. Coppinger was baffled, but resolved to forget it as he had important matters to attend to. Nobody in Cork realized what the dogs were trying to say.

The morning had dawned bright and clear with the swallows sweeping low over the city. It was another idyllic early-summer day. For weeks now, there had been no sign of rain, resulting in near-drought conditions: a constant source of worry to the folk living in the suburbs and liberties that depended on agriculture for a living. The gentle folk enjoying a game of bowls on the bowling green remarked on the extreme temperatures, which had brought with them a vague sense of unease, and which had turned Cork into a tinder-box; an accident waiting to happen. Coppinger stood back from the large looking-glass in the hallway to make some last minute adjustments to his dress. Straightening his stiffly-starched ruff collar, in his gaily-coloured doublet, white silken hose and patent, buckled shoes, he looked the very essence of an early seventeenth-century, sartorially-elegant gentleman. He liked what he saw.

John Coppinger had every reason to be pleased. His term of Mayor, thus far, had been uneventful. Much of the time of his council had been taken up with such mundane matters as agreeing rules and regulations governing the importation of wines into the city, like the Spanish dry white wine called Sack, and the sweet, fortified wine known as Oloroso. Giving his waxed moustache one last tweak, he decided he had better go, as he had some important business to attend to at the Tholsel – a short distance away – at twelve noon. Glancing at the lantern clock in the hall he saw that it was already ten to twelve. He could not know that, shortly, he would preside over a council that would witness the greatest fire disaster ever to befall the city of Cork.

Stepping outside the front door, Coppinger's nostrils were immediately assailed by the effect that the long, dry spell had had on the streets fouled with stinking refuse and dung, and gutters clogged with rubbish and ordure. Unscrewing the top of the vinaigrette, the small decorative bottle of scent that he carried to counteract such malodours, he took a good, long sniff before proceeding on his way. Rounding the top of the lane at its junction with the Main Street, there was a sudden, piercing cry of 'Gardyloo!'[21] from a window high above as a grinning, toothless old crone hurled the contents of the family chamber-pot into the street below, narrowly missing the First Citizen. Crossly glancing upwards to upbraid her, Coppinger was both amazed and disturbed to see that, all of a sudden, the clear, blue sky had been replaced with one so intensely black, so forbidding, so evil, that people had begun to light lamps and candles in their shops and homes just to be able to see. Living in an age before the Enlightenment, when much store was placed in symbols, portents, and superstition, when men and women were burned at the stake condemned as warlocks and witches, the Mayor now wondered whether the great Battle of the Starlings, fought over Cork just a year previously and reported in the London papers the following October – the very month when he had been invested with the Mayoral Chain of the Order of St Simplicius – had been some kind of supernatural warning that the Hand of God would fall on the city. On that occasion, thousands of starlings had gathered over Cork, arranged themselves into two 'armies' and, as if by a prearranged signal, suddenly attacked each other with shocking ferocity. For days the streets lay ankle-deep in numberless dead and dying birds. As he pondered on all of these things, the low-hanging, pitch-black clouds that had turned day into night began to boil and roll like the contents of some fantastic witch's cauldron, and with an ear-shattering clap of thunder, the very sky appeared to drip fire and fall upon the city on the eastern, Watergate, side – almost at the very spot where the Battle of the Starlings had raged a year before.[22]

Hundreds of men, women, and children spilled out of their homes and workplaces onto the streets, frightened out of their wits, and began to run, inexplicably, in the direction of the fire. Even as they did do, a second, almighty thunderclap was heard, and the thatched roofs on the western side also burst into flames. Prisoners in the gaols screamed to be released. The entire population was now trapped between two rapidly-growing, major conflagrations.[23] The deadly cocktail of ingredients necessary for a firestorm was fast falling into place. The immolation of Cork was nigh.

If a warning on the fire alarm bell on Peter's Tower was given, few must have heard it; in any case the fires spread so rapidly that any warning was futile. Neither was there any attempt to fight the fires even though the city was surrounded by water (shades of Hamburg again). Indeed, any such attempt would have been useless given the nature and rapidity of the fire spread. The woodcut from the report on the fire purports to show firefighting operations during the course of the conflagration. The illustration depicts a 'preventer' (a type of fire hook) at work and a bucket-chain working from a ladder. From the same house a child is being rescued by lowering-line. Nearby, the crowd stands behind a clergyman, reciting prayers. However, as the chroniclers of the account make clear, it appears that such was the rapid and overwhelming nature of the conflagration that no effective counter-measures were undertaken. Indeed, any such attempt made using the primitive fire fighting equipment of the period – leather buckets, preventers, sledgehammers, and squirts – would have been quite ineffective. This illustration must be treated with caution as patently it is a generic one of the period rather than an attempt to faithfully portray actual scenes from the Cork disaster. According to Blackstone, the same picture was used to illustrate a pamphlet on the Great Fire of Bury St Edmunds in 1608 and again, in 1612, for the narrative on the second Great Fire of Teverton in Devon entitled 'Wofull news from the West-parts of England'.[24] Fanned by the prevailing westerly wind, the process raced eastwards and soon joined up with the fires spreading westwards until the whole of the city within the walls was engulfed in flames. Roaring out of control with ever-greater strength, we may surmise that the artificial wind had developed into a storm with the violence and ferocity of a hurricane. Finally, the fires joined as one, and what previously had been individual fires now became a sea of fire with a temperature at its centre of up to 800°C.

When the fires commenced, many crowded into the city churches where they expected to be safe.[25] There, they crouched and prayed for deliverance, waiting for the horror to cease.

As the swift-moving fire ripped at the flimsy houses with the force of a hurricane, no doubt many prevailed on their wealthy neighbours who lived in their fine stone houses to open their doors and give them sanctuary. As the firestorm raged through the streets and lanes of thatched houses, the temperature in the churches and stone houses increased swiftly with the ingress of scorching hot air and smoke. The time had now arrived when the people had to decide whether to stay or leave and try to find safety elsewhere. Those who opted to try their luck indoors were in mortal danger either of suffering death from lack of oxygen and the severe heat, or of being buried alive beneath collapsing buildings above them. Many must have peered into the streets, saw that every-thing seemed to be on fire, decided they could not get through and withdrew indoors. As the conflagration consumed all the available air, it was replaced by smoke and deadly carbon monoxide. Lamps and candles lit during the initial darkness would not now stay alight. Many people lay on the floor of the churches to try to breathe in the slightest trace of clean, cool air. Those with the courage and strength made a last-ditch attempt to leave. To their horror they discovered that the lanes were impassable.[26]

At its zenith, the Cork firestorm would have caused temperatures to rise to an unbelievable level, without direct burning, and the heat must have caused bricks to burn slowly, turning them into ash, and limestone to decalcify. Objects made of metal or glass would have softened, and stained-glass windows in the

Woodcut from the report on the Great Fire of Cork in May 1622 purporting to show a scene from the conflagration. The illustration must be approached with caution as it is a generic one of the period used, as far back as 1608, to illustrate pamphlets on major fires.

churches melted. Only those who had the necessary will-power, courage, and luck, and who dared brave the flames, had a chance of surviving. Their way out of the burning areas was a race with death amidst fire, wind, and falling debris. The streets were gorges of pushing, struggling mobs, trying desperately to save something which would provide the basis of a new start. Adding to the confusion were maddened animals, which dashed about in a torture of pain from the red blizzards of hot cinders and sparks. The will of the human spirit to survive drove people to almost superhuman efforts. They had to run, gulping in the superheated air, trying to avoid falling buildings. In a world reduced to heat, noise, pain, fear, and despairing attempts to escape, many who hesitated met death on the spot. Showers of burning brands and sparks tumbled through the air like a blizzard of red snowflakes setting clothing and hair alight, burning through bare flesh, and searing into faces, necks, and eyes. In a frenzy, the tortured people smote at their faces and bodies; those who fell to the ground with sheer exhaustion spontaneously burst into flames.

Many of the luckier citizens waded through the marshy fens to seek refuge on an island in the channel[27] where they huddled, wet, shocked, and terrified, palms of hands pressed tightly over their ears to block out the awful sound of the holocaust emanating from the charnel-house that was Cork.[28] By late afternoon, most of the burned-out buildings would have collapsed and all the combustible material been consumed. The powerful artificial wind would have gradually dropped and here and there fires burned in a more conventional manner. A fire is dependent on three basic elements for its survival: heat, oxygen, and fuel. Remove any one side of the triangulation and the fire will go out. When all combustible material in Cork had been consumed, the firestorm, sated, lost its force. The heat decreased slowly. Those souls who had been lucky enough to escape through the gates, and the survivors on Island Negay, watched in awe as a great mushroom cloud of smoke, dust, and soot formed over Cork, blotting out the late afternoon sun.[29] It was probably nightfall on Saturday before the fires eventually began to die. By Sunday, the holocaust would have been all but over, the smouldering piles of goods in the city's cellars casting an unearthly red footlight on the panorama of ruin.

Gradually, hesitantly, as the survivors re-entered their burned-out city, what scenes must have presented themselves to their horrified eyes. Stark desolation met their gaze on every side. Everything was a burned, twisted mass, the streets and lanes full of dead bodies, many welded together by the heat and shrunken, like so many mummies, with skin resembling leather. Those who crowded into the churches had not escaped death either.[30] We may visualize with some degree of certainty, that some were found near the blocked exits, indicating that they had tried to escape. Others would have sat back in an attempt to conserve their strength, and, unknowingly, had begun to breathe the deadly, invisible, and odourless, carbon monoxide. Presently, they had fallen asleep and death had come painlessly from slow suffocation. No doubt, families were found grouped together with parents cuddling their children. We may speculate that the faces of the dead were mostly peaceful, showing no sign of suffering. Many would have been sitting upright or in positions they might assume while sleeping normally; the small amount of bright red-blood around their nostrils indicative of CO poisoning.

THE AFTERMATH.

The chronicle records that over 1,500 buildings were consumed by the flames, a figure which may be all-inclusive with lesser buildings such as out-offices being part of the final tally. The serious proportions the fire had assumed were immediately blamed on the blatant disregard for an existing bye-law which forbade the roofing of any new house with thatch.[31] Five months after the conflagration, Cork had a new Mayor, John Roche fitzPatrick, and on the night he was elected one of his first duties was to oversee the enacting of a new bye-law reaffirming the banning of thatch as a roofing material:

> Whereas the City of Corcke hath been often times afflicted by firings, and especially this Year of Our Lord, 1622, wherein near 1500 houses in the city and suburbs were consumed, and the whole city put in extremity of danger to be totally burned, which mischief hath arisen by thatch houses, for prevention whereof in part it hath been provided by former bye-laws, that no house newly built or re-edified should be covered with thatch, but for such as stood at the time of the said bye-laws so covered, being then a great number, no remedy was provided, but now, being truly enformed by the late grievous loss, and led by the example of the City of Limerick in the like case, and well weighing that the change unto the possessions will not be great in covering such thatch houses as stand within the city, which are but few in number, with stone or boards, or howsoever, a few particular men ought not to weigh against the common safety, it is, upon mature advice ordained and enacted by Maior, Sheriffs, and Citizens of this City, publickly assembled in the Tholsel of the City, upon the 10th October, 1622, that whatsoever thatch house within the walls of the City shall not be uncovered of said thatch before the feast of the Nativity of St. John the Baptist in the year 1623, it shall be lawful for such persons as be authorized by the Mayor, &c, to pull down all the thatch from any of said houses covered therewith within the City, and any person not reforming same before said feast, shall forfeit to the Corporation the sum of 40 pounds ster. For each house, the same to be recovered by action of debt in the Tollsel of the City, by the Chamberlayne for the time being.[32]

There is little doubt that the Great Fire of Cork in 1622 was the greatest fire disaster ever to befall the city. The record speaks of 'many hundreds [of people] … being consumed by the fire'.[33] What does this mean? Three hundred? Six hundred? As we have seen, the population of the city remained fairly static at about 2,500 over a sixty year period between 1600 and 1659. Assuming only 25 per cent of the population perished in the holocaust – a conservative estimate if one is to take at face value the horrors detailed in the narrative – this equates to a death toll of some 625 souls. Superimposed on the modern city with its population of 177,000[34] this percentage would translate into an unimaginable 44,250. Only then does the scale of Cork's worst ever catastrophe begin to sink in.

Little wonder that the report published in London in June 1622, likened Cork to the city of Gomorrah, the biblical city annihilated by fire and brimstone.[35] The code-name chosen by Air Chief Marshal Sir Arthur Harris, Commander-in-Chief of RAF Bomber Command, for the terrible attrition unleashed on Hamburg in 1943 was also 'Operation Gomorrah'.

In the weeks and months following the Great Fire of Cork, getting in out of the weather was undoubtedly the first priority of the people, and fire prevention protocols, we can assume with some certainty, were hardly given a second thought in the mad scramble for housing. Notwithstanding the fact that the thatch 'Fire Law' was firmly inserted in the local statute books, it seems that dwellings and shops were again built with little or no restriction on materials or methods. The rebuilding of Cork went aimlessly ahead. The outer walls of buildings often encroached upon the public street, their upper storeys protruding to such an extent that a person at a top window on one side of a lane could shake hands with someone leaning out on the other side. The outline of that narrow web may still be traced off the North and South Main Streets of today, now indicated by attractive bronze plaques set into the pavement.[36] The 'thatch' bye-law seems to have been little more than a knee-jerk reaction, an attempt to assuage the public outcry in the wake of the disaster, and to apportion blame on something (i.e. thatch), while at the same time appearing to be taking firm executive action to prevent similar occurrences happening in the future. It appears to have been little more than a seventeenth-century PR job. In the surviving corporation minutes, from the time the order became effective in 1623, and 1800 when Caulfield's transcription ends, there is not one entry concerning thatch being forcibly removed from a roof or of anyone being prosecuted for continuing to use the material. Building with slate and shingle, brick and stone, was still the domain of the 'comfortable' classes. No one would have dreamed of using the power to pull down buildings. Had they done so, many hundreds of Corkonians would have been rendered homeless.

The homes of the more well-to-do were often dual-purpose, with the merchants and shopkeepers living upstairs with their places of business and storerooms situated below. All householders required fire for cooking, lighting, and heating, but the gravest risk came from the many trades people – potters, bakers, blacksmiths, foundry men, coopers, goldsmiths/silversmiths, brewers, tallow-chandlers, dyers, soap-boilers, and so forth[37] – whose crafts demanded fires of great intensity to be kept going, sometimes around the clock, providing an unintentional, but grave, fire hazard. The hazard was further exacerbated by the prodigious piles of fuel kept in close proximity to their workshops. Many of their premises were built from highly-flammable materials, with inadequately constructed furnaces and ovens. The sparks from their fires, swept along by the wind, would drift into a nearby open window or land on a roof clad with organic material to start yet another blaze.

ASHES TO ASHES: ENTER 'CORPORAL JOHN'.

If the traumatic events experienced by Cork in 1622 (and during an earlier blaze in 1612) had been regarded as an 'Act of God', the reduction of the city towards the end of the century was very much the handiwork of man.

On 10 June 1688, Maria Beatrice Margherita Isabella d'Este, wife of King James II of England and Ireland (James VII of Scotland), gave birth to a son, James Francis Edward. The couple had hoped for such an outcome since their marriage in 1673 (James had two daughters from a previous union), and it now seemed the queen had finally produced a healthy male heir to ensure the continuity of the Stuart dynasty. But this happy event precipitated a political predicament that led to the removal and exile of James and his queen. James II was a devout Roman Catholic, but the vast majority of his English subjects were Protestant. The idea of a Catholic heir was too much. A group of peers, a bishop, and politicians (later called 'The Immortal Seven'), invited the Dutch *Stadtholder*, the Protestant William, Prince of Orange, to invade England. The crisis reached its apogee when, on 5 November 1688, aided by the so-called 'Protestant Wind', William landed in Devon with an invasion fleet four times the size of the Spanish Armada of a hundred years earlier. The next month, James left for exile in France, the *soi-disant* 'Glorious Revolution' having been achieved without bloodshed. The veracity of the adage, 'He, who England win, Must Ireland through come in', was about to be put to the test. The military campaign which William opened in Ireland in the summer of 1690 brought Europe's westernmost isle on to the centre of the European stage. Its success ensured the ascendancy of the Protestant landowning class in Irish social and political life for centuries.

The forty-year-old English general, John Churchill, Earl of Marlborough, (later, 1st Duke of Marlborough), the dashing 'Corporal John' to his men, arrived on the outskirts of Cork, having earlier disembarked at Passage West, on the morning of 23 September 1690 tasked with capturing the city for William.[38]

Setting up his main camp in the vicinity of the Lough, he quickly saw that the topography of Cork was a siege-maker's dream. But laying a siege was a complex operation. In the first instance, the enemy had to be forced into the area to be besieged. Then, the enemy forces were encircled by the besieging army facing inwards in order to keep them in. At the same time, an outward-facing ring had to be established to prevent reinforcements or supplies reaching the besieged. Following successful encirclement, the besieging commander had to decide upon the best method in which to proceed. His options were to starve the enemy into submission, blow the enemy into submission by sustained artillery bombardment, or to combine artillery barrage and an all-out assault on the city. Marlborough decided on the latter.

Equipped with some eighty ships (thirty-six of which mounted twelve guns each), forty-three cannon, and a 'coalition force' that would, at the siege's height, number almost 10,000 troops, he observed that the low-lying city was overlooked by hills on its northern and southern flanks: ideal vantage points for field-guns to mercilessly bombard the exposed target below. This Achilles' Heel in Cork's defences had been the subject of comment in an article written by an army officer sometime prior to the siege:

> Were it not for the Hills near it, which overlooks [sic] the City (in the same nature as at Kin-sale), it might be made a place impregnable, but the Hills has [sic] such a command of it, that a Battery from thence, would Beat the Town about the Ears of the Garrison.[39]

Defending Cork against this vastly superior force was a Jacobite army numbering less than 5,000. Despite the Jacobite Commander-in-Chief's, the Duke of Berwick, exhortations to burn down the city and withdraw into Kerry, the Cork Governor, Col Roger MacElligot, rashly decided to remain and try to defend the indefensible. He was ill-equipped with insufficient forces to man the defensive works, occupy the hills, and guard the Protestant citizens who were under arrest. To compound his problems, he now found himself face-to-face with the formidable and brilliant tactician, Marlborough.

Overwhelmed by the forces ranged against them, the small Jacobite garrisons abandoned Cat Fort (described by Ensign William Cramond of the Scottish regiment of Sir David Collier as 'a new outwork, not finished, on the top of a hill') on the south side, and on withdrawing from their positions on the north side, (including the old Norman fortification of Shandon Castle, now the site of the Firkin Crane building), set fire to the 'suburbs' in order to prevent the Williamite forces from investing them for strategic purposes in spite of an earlier assurance given by MacElligot that no such 'scorched earth' policy would be initiated. This action was recalled by eye-witness Joseph Pike, a Cork Quaker, who lived in the North Abbey:

In the 7th month,[40] 1690, Cork was besieged by the English; the Lord Churchill, afterwards Duke of Marlborough, commanded the siege, M'Gillicuddy [this is MacElligott], being then the Irish governor of the city. He was a rude, boisterous man, and gave out, that he intended to burn the suburbs; upon which, the inhabitants, English and Irish, treated with him to save them, and agreed to give him five hundred pounds in silver, most of which was gathered and paid to him; yet I could not trust his word, and removed the best of my goods, and thereby saved them. Notwithstanding which, he afterwards, without giving the least notice, burned both the north and south suburbs whereby not only the houses but much goods were destroyed. [41]

As the fires spread, the old Shandon Church and the Franciscan Abbey were consumed by the flames.[42] Now it was the city's turn to bear the brunt of the onslaught. With the evacuation of the hill forts (barring Elizabeth Fort, which, although surrounded and isolated, was not surrendered until the capitulation) Marlborough seized his opportunity. Assisted by his general staff, including Brigadier Charles Churchill (his brother), the Dutch generals Scravemoer, Ginkel and Tettau, the Duke of Wurtemberg and others, he quickly moved into the vacant forts, supplying each with several field-pieces. Free to reconnoitre the suburbs of the city at will, Marlborough selected the tower of the former Augustinian Abbey, the so-called 'Red Abbey', as his command post. In the abbey's gardens he located a battery of artillery.

Cork was now completely surrounded with batteries dug in at Fair Hill, Shandon, Gillabbey, and Red Abbey, as well as those in the captured forts. A ship landed with a new battery of artillery, which was set up near a tavern called the *Red Cow* situated on the quay (now George's Quay) under the Augustinian Abbey. Assisted by two newly-arrived gun ships, which levelled their cannon at the eastern wall (i.e. the Grand Parade side), Cork now lay in a pincer-grip at the mercy of the Williamite forces. Messages were sent to MacElligot, the Irish Commander, demanding his surrender. He answered by hanging out a blood-stained white flag, a symbol of defiance.[43] Presently, all along the line came the cries of 'Fire! Fire! Fire!' from the battery commanders as the bombardment commenced. At a given signal, mortars lobbed their bombs over the walls into the city. Soon the first flames appeared. Eighteen miles away, the nearest Jacobite troops, garrisoned in James' and Charles Forts in Kinsale, watched in trepidation at the glow in the northern sky blotting out the Plough and pondered their own ultimate fate.

In the several surviving eyewitness accounts of the Siege (weighted almost exclusively on the Williamite side), there is no mention of the firefighting effort within the city to counter the effects of the attack.[44] (Indeed, the only eyewitness testimony recorded from within the walls – that of Joseph Pike – is exasperatingly short on detail). This lacuna is, in my opinion, not unusual, and does not indicate that no such measures were in place. It would indeed have been an imprudent and foolhardy township, even by late seventeenth-century standards, that would not have organized some basic precautions against what, after all, were common-place occurrences – accidental fires.

Throughout that long night, the firefighting pickets must have worked feverishly, with their pitiful equipment, to try to stop the fires caused by the bombing spreading. Those citizens, still alive, who had survived the Great Fire some sixty-eight years before, must surely have urged the firefighters on to ever-greater effort, fearful of the terrible consequences of fires from two opposing sides joining up. The fire pickets may have included members of the Quaker community, who, while espousing the Williamite cause, played no part in the combat operations, being pacifists. We know that some were engaged in taking up the cobblestones in the streets to counter the deadly shrapnel effect of the mortar bombs.[45] It would have been particularly imperative that a fire-break was created between any buildings on fire on Main Street and Skiddy's Castle (aka the King's Storehouse), for that is where the defenders stored their dwindling supplies of gunpowder and ammunition. All would have been acutely aware of the consequences should the fires reach the magazine.[46]

We can only use guesswork to visualize the types of firefighting equipment available to the defenders, for no contemporary accounts from Cork are, to my knowledge, available. We can examine, however, the contemporaneous situation in other cities, including Dublin. It may be said with some degree of certainty that no fire engines were owned by the municipal authorities, for the first reference to such machines in the Cork Council records does not occur for another seventeen years.[47]

Engraving entitled 'Innemen van Corck' (the Capture of Cork) by Romeijn de Hooghe, from the annual newssheet *Hollanddsche Mercurius* for 1691. (Courtesy of Cork City Libraries)

Conjectural image of a 'fire squirt' being used to try to suppress the fires along Main Street, caused by the bombardment during the Siege of Cork, 1690.

Great emphasis would have been placed on bucket-chains. Leather fire buckets, some of which were beautifully decorated,[48] were usually stored in the churches along with ladders, and the fire hooks and chains used for pulling down roofs. Other implements consisted of 'fire scoops', large wooden shovels shod with iron, which were used to scoop up water from the gutter, or some other source. 'Fire squirts' (aka squrts) were also used. These were made from bronze or brass, resembled a huge hypodermic syringe, and took three men to handle. The nozzle of the squirt would be placed in a barrel of water which was kept topped-up by the bucket chain. The appliance was then filled by siphoning and carried as near to the fire outbreak as the heat and smoke would permit. With two men gripping the handles on either side, steadying, and taking aim, the third would shove home the plunger. The whole effort projected not much more than a decent well-aimed bucket of water onto the fire. Allowing for spillages, the jet falling short due to the distance from the seat of the fire, and the heat turning the water to steam ever before reaching its mark, one can well imagine the futility of the firefighting effort.

As is evident from later entries in the Council Book, nominally the Mayor, Aldermen and churchwardens were responsible as a body for such equipment. However, nobody was appointed whose duty it was to see that it was regularly inspected and serviced. Emergencies, such as the siege, often revealed that the fire buckets were leaky, the squirts rusty and inoperable, and lines and wooden ladders rotten.

With the night's blazes at last coming under control, Colonel Rycot, a Jacobite senior officer, stood on the eastern battlements of the city and swung his spyglass over to the right, picked up the dark bulk of Elizabeth Fort, and began another slow sweep of the horizon. Rags of mist drifted like shrouds across his view, interspersed with patches of shimmering moonlight reflected on the dark waters of the Lee below. Out there in the darkness, the night-long creak of wheels, the groan of tackle, and lines of flares told him that the Williamites were preparing their final, massive assault against the city. And then, in the early hours, quite suddenly, there was a great silence. Only the gentle murmur of the water as it crossed the weir disturbed the stillness. But neither he, nor anyone else in Cork, was under any illusion: it was the calm before the storm. All along the ramparts, cold, vigilant, anxious men waited for the dawn. In the early-morning light, low banks of fog swirled ghost-like from the waters, shrouding the valley of the Lee from view. The intermittent rain of the previous day now became a steady drizzle, soaking everything, much, however, to the delight of the exhausted firefighters.[49] *On this murky, grey morning, leaden clouds hanging oppressively from the sky, the brooding walls of Cork loomed up out of the mist, their massive red and white stones glistening with dampness, the smoke from the night's fires mixing with the early mist to create a cloying smog.*

A decision was made at the highest level to allow the 1,300 Protestant citizens, previously held under lock and key in the city's churches, free passage out of the gates, accompanied by Bishop Edward Wetenhall.[50] On Sunday 28 September, as the 6a.m. angelus bell echoed across the valley of the Lee and the weary Roman Catholic defenders prepared for Mass, the order was given for the bombardment to commence. As the priest intoned the Latin liturgy, the thunderous roar of the big guns and the incessant cackle of small arms must have grated harshly on their ears. They surely heard the cries of the Williamite officers as they worked the batteries. As the great cannons boomed and thundered, the old, Norman-built limestone and sandstone walls began to powder and flake. Blocks of stone fell away as heavy shot landed time and again on the same places. Soon, the walls on the eastern side (near today's City Library) eventually succumbed to the battering from the artillery at the *Red Cow* and a breach was effected.

Low water was in the early afternoon. One thousand Danish troops under the Duke of Wurtemburg crossed the river near the present Opera House, struggling over the sucking marshes to approach the breach and gain entry into the city. An hour later, the English, under Brigadier Churchill, crossed into the present-day South Mall area. Their guide was a Cork merchant, Nicholas Greene. With the water still deep in the centre of the river and up to the men's armpits, what a striking picture that crossing must have made! With scarlet tunics and picturesque costumes, the feathers of their broad-brimmed hats gently swaying in the afternoon breeze, swords, pistols, and muskets held aloft over their heads to keep them dry, each man had a 'bullet in the mouth' ready for immediate use.[51] As the columns forced their way through the cold, barren marshes, sustained fire was opened up on them by the defenders aligned along the city ramparts.

In the closing stages of the battle, one of the Williamite officers, the Duke of Grafton, was sent to reconnoitre the eastern marshes with a view to establishing a suitable site for yet another battery. Local legend has it that a canny Cork blacksmith, high on the battlements near the old Post Office area (opposite the present-day Sullivan's Quay), noticing him, took aim and fired, hitting him in the shoulder; in his splendid ducal uniform and hat he must have stood out from the ordinary rank-and-file foot soldiers like the proverbial sitting duck. The Duke fell, mortally wounded. The spot where it is believed he fell is still perpetuated in the name Grafton Street, a narrow thoroughfare linking South Mall with Oliver Plunkett Street (but in 1690, of course, a boggy marsh).[52]

At about three o'clock in the afternoon, with the Williamite forces closing ranks thirty metres from the city walls in preparation for the final assault through the breach, the Irish garrison, with ammunition stocks practically exhausted, beat a parley and a white flag appeared above the ramparts. An eerie stillness hung over Cork as the great guns fell silent for the first time in days. Presently, the lone figure of Colonel Rycot could be seen, white flag in hand, cautiously picking his way over the tonnes of crumbling masonry. MacElligot asked that the garrison be allowed to march out with all the honours of war; drums beating, colours flying, and troops with 'ball in mouth'. The English would have none of it, and, with further opposition futile, the city finally surrendered.

When Marlborough and his men broke camp on 30 September *en route* to their next encounter with the enemy at Kinsale, they left the city of Cork, not for the first time, nor indeed the last, a smoking, semi-desolate ruin. For the prisoners incarcerated on board the Williamite ship *Breda* in Cork Harbour, their torment by fire was not yet over. With a colossal detonation, which carried up the estuary to the city, the vessel blew up, instantly pulverizing almost everyone on board, including some 160 Jacobite prisoners of war.[53]

The reducer of Cork, John Churchill, Earl of Marlborough, (after whom, rather incongruously one imagines, an important city-centre street is named), to paraphrase his loquacious descendant, brought nothing to the city by the Lee but blood, toil, tears, sweat; and fire.

2

Chariots of Fire: Cork's First Fire Engines

'A little fire is quickly trodden out, which being suffered, rivers cannot quench'.

(William Shakespeare, *King Henry VI*, Part 3 – act IV, Scene VIII).

'Ordered, that two Engines for quenching Fire be provided, and the Mayor upon his going to Dublin is desired to enquire into it'

(Minutes of Cork City Council 29 October 1707).[1]

If the mantra of Fire Prevention Officers is, perhaps, the Irish proverb *'Ní h-é lá na gaoithe lá na scolb'*[2], it appears the inherent wisdom of the *sean-fhocal* was lost on the good Aldermen and Burgesses of Cork, for a full seventeen years after the reduction of the city by fire and bombardment passed before the council took the first tentative steps to acquiring its first fire engines.

Several factors appear to have been at work in stirring the city fathers from their lassitude. Firstly, the city was expanding inexorably outside the confines of the old medieval walls into the northern and southern suburbs, and new developments were also taking place on the east–west axis. Among the business community, the Religious Society of Friends (Quakers) and the French Huguenots were among those keenly eyeing the bleak marshes outside the city walls with a view to their eventual development. Indeed, as they acquired the various marshes, they called them after themselves: Fenn's Marsh, Pike's Marsh, Haman's (aka Hammond's) Marsh, Dunscombe's Marsh, etc. All this expansion and industry made it prudent that such assets should be covered by a modicum of fire protection. Secondly, it is patently obvious that fires, including those with fatalities – apart altogether from fires occasioned by war – were an ongoing problem in the crowded city. Thirdly, in the same year, 1707, the English Parliament had passed a law (6 Anne, *c.*58) entitled, 'An Act for the better preventing the mischiefs that may happen by fire'. The act made it mandatory for every parish (in London) to have and maintain a 'large engine' and a 'hand engine' (this was probably the ubiquitous 'squirt'), and also a 'leather pipe to convey the water without help of bucket into the engine'. The churchwarden of the parish had to see to it that stop-cocks were fitted on street water-pipes, where available, and to erect a plaque on 'the front of an house over against the place the stop-cock lies'.

The Act also imposed heavy penalties on those churchwardens who defaulted in their duties, and specified the sums of money that should be paid to the 'crews' of the first, second, and third parish pumps to turn up at the scene of a fire: thirty shillings for the first, twenty shillings for the second, and ten shillings for the third. As these were not inconsiderable sums of money in 1707, there was often much acrimony among the 'Keepers' of the parish pumps as to who exactly had arrived first on the fire ground, not always readily evident in the heat and confusion of the moment. These shenanigans and conniving may originally have given rise to the expression 'parish pump politics'.

The Act, however, had excluded the English provinces, and Ireland, and the parish councils, vestries, and churchwardens outside of London had no legal obligation to provide any fire equipment. Many municipalities and parishes, however, took on the task of providing some equipment voluntarily. It seems more than coincidence that the first reference to the acquisition of fire engines in the surviving minutes of Cork Corporation appears in the same year as Queen Anne's fire legislation of 1707.[3]

The early minutes of the city fathers' affairs are nothing if not enigmatic. The next reference to matters to do with fire protection (after the entry of 29 October 1707 directing Mayor ffranklyn to make enquiries into the types of engines available in Dublin) occurs almost twelve months later:

> 6th September 1708: On reading the presentment of the Grand Jury at the last sessions, touching the buckets and engines for extinguishing fire, agreed, that the same are necessary, and that the Corporation will contribute to the charge as soon as ascertained, and Alderman Goddard is desired to write to his friend in London touching the same.[4]

More enquiries! The frustrating thing is we do not know what, if anything, transpired following Mayor ffranklyn's and Alderman Goddard's investigations, for there is a gap of almost six years before the subject of fire engines is raised again, this time during Mayor Edward Browne's term of office:

> 26th October 1714: That in order to prevent the great danger of fire within the City or Suburbs the Mayor do send to Holland and purchase a good large pipe fire-engine of the best sort.[5]

Whereas the early eighteenth-century regulations relating to fire prevention measures applied only to London, the parliament in Dublin in 1715 enacted the first of several pieces of legislation applicable to 'The City of Dublin, or any other city or town corporate within this Kingdom'.[6] Thus, it seems that Cork Corporation was pre-empting its legal obligation by placing an early order for the fire engine that would ensure its compliance with the new legislation.

The most interesting aspect is that the engine is to be purchased in Holland, not, as one would have thought, in Dublin or England, for Dutch fire engineers under the inimitable Jan van der Heiden at this time led the world in fire engineering technology. His fame had spread far and wide including, apparently, to the banks of the Lee.[7]

Van der Heiden and his son, Jan junior, were the Fire Masters - General of the Amsterdam Fire Brigade (*Brandweer Amsterdam*). Due to its system of prompt alarms, rapid response, effective equipment, and sound tactics, it was regarded as the most efficient fire suppression organization Europe had witnessed since ancient times. In 1690, both men co-authored a book entitled *A description of fire engines with water hoses, and the method of fighting fires now used in Amsterdam*.[8] This treatise remains by far the most important source of information for researchers on the methods of fire extinction and the appliances employed in the late seventeenth and early eighteenth centuries. It remained unsurpassed until the mid-eighteenth century, when the fire engineer C.F.T. Young and fire officers Scotsman James Braidwood and Corkman Capt. Eyre Massey Shaw began to publish their theories. Of greatest value to us are the detailed analyses of their pumps, water supply systems, and hose.

The factory of the world-renowned van der Heiden fire engineers at Amsterdam.

We cannot be 100 per cent certain that the fire engine was purchased in Holland, as, once again, the trail goes cold, but the balance of probability dictates that it was, for within five weeks of the council directing the Mayor to buy a Dutch fire engine, a location was required in which to house such a machine. Not alone did the van der Heiden family run the Amsterdam Fire Brigade well into the eighteenth century, but they also secured their primary position as by far the most important and largest manufacturers of fire engines in Holland. Any engine that Cork Corporation bought from Holland almost certainly emanated from the van der Heiden factory at No. 5 Koestraat, Amsterdam.[9] Their machines were widely regarded as being vastly superior to anything made in these islands. Although Ireland had its own fledgling fire engine industry in the guise of John Oates ('Water-Ingineer to the Honourable City of Dublin, living in Dame Street, at the Sign of the Boot')[10], his appliances appear primitive when compared to the van der Heidens' ones. They did, however, share one technical detail. A poster issued in 1711 shows an Oates' fire engine with the branchman standing on top utilizing what appears to be a short length of delivery hose (a van der Heiden invention), rather than the fixed 'gooseneck' method preferred by English manufacturers. This indicates that, by this time at least, Irish fire engine makers were beginning to emulate some of their Dutch counterpart's inventions.

Two factors set the Dutchmen's apart. First, the introduction of the pump 'primer', where, by exhausting the air out of the pump and connecting lengths of specially-reinforced wired hose (to prevent it collapsing under the force of positive pressure),[11] atmospheric pressure raised the water from an open source, such as a river, up through the suction hose and into the fire pump.

The Dutch-made fire pumps could now tap into a virtually inexhaustible supply. For the first time in history the bucket of water was being superseded. The second factor which put the Dutch pumps streets ahead of the opposition was the invention of delivery hose, for the old problem of getting to close quarters with the fire had remained. The efficacy of the early engines was directly proportional to the distance they were placed from the building on fire. In the case of the smaller pumps, it meant bringing them practically right up to the burning building, and there are reports of appliances being burnt or crushed when part of the building fell on them (and burying the people operating them under the rubble). Firefighting had consisted of the so-called 'long shot,' with a fixed jet being directed from the fire engine some distance away from the building. Van der Heiden saw that the only really effective way to tackle blazes was to get to close quarters with them. To this end, he began experimenting with narrow strips of hide, which he sewed longitudinally using strong linen thread to close the seams. He called his new creation 'water snakes'; in English, the invention was dubbed 'hose', after the contemporary name for stocking. His hose was made in 15m (50 feet) sections with brass screw-thread couplings, which could be added *ad infinitum*. This meant that firefighters had now far greater flexibility in their attack on a fire, and their pumps could be set up quite a distance away. The Cork Council minutes contain a number of references to hoses being procured for the city engines; the leather work was carried out by local tradesmen:

30th January 1735: That £2.19s.9d be paid John Alleyn, Esq., for three hides for the use of the City Fire Engine.[12]

19th May 1740: That 19s 4 1/2d be paid Ald. Farren, having paid same to Jas. Supell for the leather pipes for the fire-engine.[13]

11th April 1759: That £1.13s.2d be paid Richd. Harrison, sadler, for leather work supplied for the City Engine.[14]

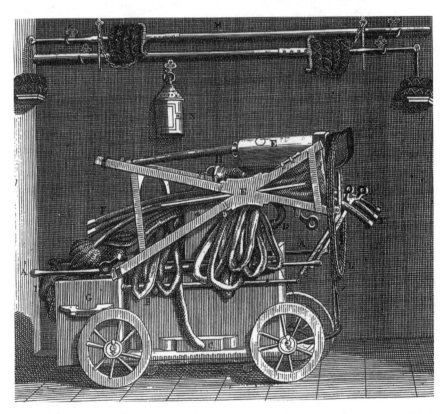

A typical fire engine made by the firm of van der Heiden. In October 1714, the Mayor of Cork was directed by the city council to 'send to Holland and purchase a good large pipe fire-engine of the best sort'. Note the delivery hose draped around the engine, which put Dutch-made fire appliances at the cutting-edge of early eighteenth-century fire protection technology.

CORK'S FIRST FIRE STATION.

For the first time in history, the city of Cork was legally bound to provide a firefighting appliance for the protection of its citizens. It had to be available at a central location and housed out of the weather. On 1 December 1715, the following entry appears in the corporation minutes:

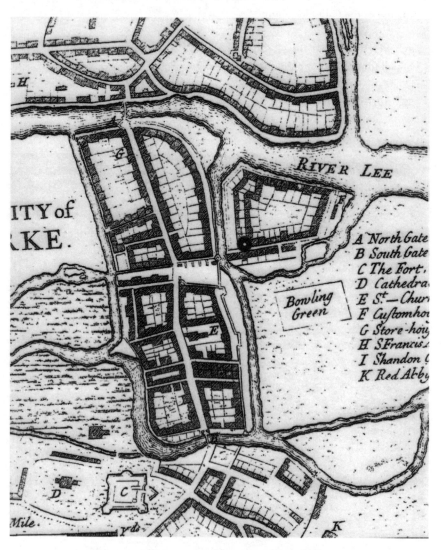

Story's Plan of Cork showing the location of the 'Corporation Yard on the Marsh' where Cork's first fire engine was housed (circled). The site approximates to St Paul's Churchyard on Paul Street, now incorporating the side entrance to the Cornmarket Street Shopping Plaza. (Courtesy of Cork City Libraries)

Ordered, that a convenient place be made in the South end of the lynny in the Corporation yard on the Marsh, according to the direction of Alderman Edward Browne, for keeping the water-engine, &c., which works Mr. Saml. Woodruffe, the City Surveyor, is to take care of.[15]

The 'Corporation yard on the Marsh' stood near the site of the present-day (deconsecrated) St Paul's church in Paul Street, now incorporated into a major shopping centre. The area comprised the former north-east marsh, also known as Dunscombe's Marsh after Alderman Noblett Dunscombe, a former Mayor of Cork, who leased it from the corporation. This marsh, and its intersecting channels, was among the first to be filled in outside the old city walls to create 'made ground'. The 'lynny' (aka a 'linhay'), a large, lean-to shed open to the elements on one side, was erected in the corporation yard in 1706, to accommodate the materials used in the building of the new Exchange at the junction of nearby Castle Street and Main Street. Thus, this humble shed, housing the city's first fire engine, may be loosely described as Cork's first 'fire station'.

Admirable as the developments in fire engine manufacture were, they alone were not the catalyst which eventually led to the formation of the first organized firefighting force in these islands. A catastrophe in London, caused not only Englishmen, but continental Europeans as well as us Irish, to take a painful interest in fire suppression. As a result, two lines of development began, both of which still have their place in present-day practice. These were, first, private and voluntary effort; and second, municipal and government provision. It also taught people one other enduring lesson at least: that wood burns more easily than brick. As we have previously noted, a fire requires only three things: heat, oxygen, and fuel to feed it. By the late autumn of 1666, a ten-month drought had turned London into a tinderbox. The city consisted largely of shanties and wood-framed buildings. The spark was provided in the early hours of the morning of 2 September, when a smouldering coal fell out of the fire of the King's baker in Pudding Lane. In the following four days 436 acres of closely-packed streets containing 13,200 houses and eighty-nine parish churches, including St Paul's Cathedral, were destroyed. Incredibly, the records state that no more than eight people lost their lives.

THE PHOENIX ARISES: NICHOLAS BARBON AND HIS 'FIRE OFFICE'.

'N. Barbon hath set up an office for Fire Insurance and is
likely to get vastly by it'
(Nathaniel Luttrell in *Brief Relation,* 1681).

The firefighting methods and equipment of modern times may be said to have been first conceived in London's vast acres of ashes. An air of melancholy hung like a chilly fog over the city. The passers-by hurrying down the half-deserted streets in their threadbare clothes had a bleak, morose look about them. Fortunes had been lost, businesses had been wiped out, and the debtors' gaols were full. A special stench, the odour of post-fire London, permeated the city. It was the smell of charred ruins drifting up like an autumn mist from thousands of burned-out buildings. The empty shell of St Paul's Cathedral echoed to the flapping of crows.

In a London side-street coffee house, a group of portly, bewigged investors sipped at their cups and puffed thoughtfully on their *meerschaum* pipes as they listened intently to the speaker at the top of the long table. Slowly, inexorably, the germ of an idea was planted in their minds. Fire insurance, he insisted, was the way to go. The only insurance at this time was marine insurance, whereby a ship and its cargo would be insured for a particular voyage. This was an altogether different matter to insuring a premises against the hazard of fire, an all too frequent occurrence for which they needed no reminding. As there was no previous experience of fire insurance, no one knew just how much capital would be required to finance such a venture, how much would be needed to settle claims, or the amount necessary to be invested to cover future claims. The wily businessman, however, had it all worked out. Supposedly christened at birth with the incredible moniker, 'If Jesus Christ had not died for thee thou hadst been damned'[16] by his fanatical father, 'Praise-God' Barebones of Oliver Cromwell's 'Little Parliament', Nicholas Barbon, for that is the name by which he was known, in spite of his supposed earlier appellation, grew up into an astute businessman renowned for sharp practice. Qualifying as a medical doctor at Utrecht University in Holland, it appears he never actually practised, preferring the cut-and-thrust of the world of commerce to the thrust-and-cut of surgery. Many of those who had lost everything in the Great Fire of London were only too anxious to liquidate the only asset they possessed: the plots of real estate their homes had stood on. Barbon soon bought up these sites at ridiculously low prices. With scant regard for the new building regulations, his only object was to put up as many houses as possible on any piece of land he could buy at the lowest rate, all in the shortest achievable time. In short, he was the original 'jerry builder'.[17] He acquired a reputation as a ruthless speculator, one who could turn his hand to anything where there was a profit to be made; and, inevitably, he made one. Now, in the aftermath of the Great Fire of London, yet another far-sighted decision was made by him.

A superb mathematician, he had worked out a scheme for fire insurance, launching his company from an office at 'the backside of the Royal Exchange'. He offered to insure the citizens against loss by fire, in return for premiums set according to the quality and size of their homes or businesses: 2.5 per cent for brick houses and 5 per cent for timber. Initially, the venture was known simply as The Fire Office, effectively the first fire insurance company in the world.

Printed at the head of its policy documents was the logo of a phoenix, the bird in Greek mythology that consumed itself by fire after 500 years and rose, renewed, from its ashes. It was an apt device for an insurance company founded in London after the Great Fire. The name 'Phoenix' was later adopted as the company's official title.[18] Other businessmen, stimulated by Barbon's success, appeared on the scene. In 1683, William Hale and Henry Spelman launched 'The Friendly Society for Securing Houses from Loss by Fire'. Barbon, not to be outdone, not only ruthlessly undercut the premiums of his competitors but also made a decision that proved to be one of the defining moments in fire-fighting history. He would provide, he announced:

> a group of men versed and experienced in extinguishing and preventing fire
> … servants in livery with badges who are watermen and other lusty persons
> who are always ready when any sudden fire happens, while they are very
> laborious and dextrous at quenching and not sticking in cases of necessity to
> expose themselves to very great hazards in their attempts.[19]

The first organized firefighting body these islands had seen since the days of the splendid Roman fire service, the Corps of *Vigiles*, set up under the Emperor Augustus some 1,200 years before, had come into existence.

But, true to form, Barbon's extravagant commitment was not made for any public-spirited or philanthropic reason. For a while, his Fire Office had performed very well, but over a period the large number of major claims began to make serious inroads into its reserves. Determined not to go under, he sought a way of keeping his losses to a minimum. No relief, he knew, could be expected from the parish beadles with their leaky engines and crews of untrained, callow youths. The only answer, he realized, was to give buildings insured with his company a special protection. Thus, he had initiated his own private firefighting force. The fierce competition for their fair share of the fire insurance market compelled new companies entering the field to also set up their own fire brigades, known as 'fire engine establishments'. As we shall see in Chapter 4, they were not to know that they were saddling themselves with an expensive responsibility, with establishments scattered the length and breadth of what were then termed the 'British Isles', including, in the course of time, Cork city, that would continue to plague them for nigh on 200 years.

Parish Pump Politics: The Role of the Established Church in Early Firefighting

'[Fires are extinguished] by the great number of admirable engines, of which, every parish has one … so that no sooner does a fire break out, but the house is surrounded with engines, and a flood of water poured upon it, 'till the fire is, as it were, not extinguished only, but *drowned*.'

(Daniel Defoe speaking of London in 1724).[1]

'The Fire Engines belonging to the several Parishes, which are now kept in such wretched condition, as not to be of the smallest use, when called forth, on any fire that happens, the Engine of St. Paul's Parish, only excepted'.

(Mayor of Cork Samuel Rowland, 1787).[2]

High over the roofs of Cork, from places of dust and pigeon-mess, where the wind howled through the slats, the church bells rang out across the frenetic streets below. They tolled in celebration of yet another royal birthday, of a victory over some now long-forgotten enemy, or to herald in the New Year, a custom which has continued down to our own time. They rang out to summon the faithful to church, they were rung, muffled now, to notify the citizens of the impending public execution of some unfortunate soul on Gallow's Green (later sanitized to 'Greenmount'), and frequently, they rang out to warn the parishioners of the imminent death of one of their neighbours. Traditionally, this 'passing bell' tolled nine times for a man, six for a woman, and three for a child, followed by one stroke for each year of their age.[3] But perhaps the sound that the people most dreaded to hear was the urgent summons of the reverse peal of the 'fire alarum', for, beginning early in the eighteenth century, the Protestant parish churches of Cork became the focal point of fire emergencies within the parish, each complete with its fire engine and 'Engine Keeper'.[4] In effect, each parish had its own community-based 'fire station'. As we have seen, Queen Anne took the first effective steps to try and stop the ravages of fire with her Act of 1707 which introduced that famous institution – the parish pump. Initially, this legislation was effective only in London, encompassing the area described as being 'Within the weekly Bills of Mortality'.[5] Not until 1715, during the reign of King George 1, was a legal onus placed on parishes in Ireland to provide firefighting equipment. A second Act, in 1719, specified the type of gear with which each parish was to be equipped, 'one large engine and one small engine' and also that, 'each parish shall provide, keep and maintain one leather pipe and jacket as the same size as the plug or fire cock'. Failure to implement the law could result in a fine of £10.

The parishes in question were those of the Protestant church, for by then, Catholic Ireland was suppressed in the deadly grip of the Penal Laws.[6]

From the beginning of the eighteenth century, the topography of Cork city began to change dramatically. Several new Protestant churches were erected during this period and older ones replaced. St Nicholas's, in Cove Street, was built in 1720 on the grounds of the ancient church of St Sepulchre. On 20 June 1726, it was struck by lightning and the east end damaged in the ensuing blaze (the present deconsecrated church was built in 1836). Christ Church on the (South) Main Street, built by the Anglo-Normans in 1180, survived until 1690, when it was badly damaged during the siege. It was replaced by a new building in 1722. The thirteenth-century St Peter's on (North) Main Street, having fallen into disrepair, was eventually demolished in 1782 and a new building erected on the site. The church of St Anne (housing the famous Shandon Bells) was also built in 1722 on the site of St Mary's, also destroyed during the 1690 siege.

St Paul's, in Paul Street (now incorporated into a shopping centre) was erected in 1723, and elevated to parish status in 1726 from the districts of the east marsh in the parish of Shandon and part of Dunscombe's Marsh in the parish of Christ Church. The site for the church was granted to Bishop Browne by the corporation (including part of the corporation yard where the city's first fire engine was housed). The medieval St Fin Barre's Cathedral stood on the same site, high on Gil Abbey rock outside the perimeter of the old city, as its illustrious Gothic successor. Of the aforementioned churches, only St Fin Barre's Cathedral and St Anne's are still open for worship, the others have long since been deconsecrated.

Each of the Established Church parishes had its vestry. With the decay of the old manorial courts, the vestry meetings attained a new significance, for whereas they had been initiated solely for the administration of ecclesiastical matters, they gradually began to take a hand in a number of parochial matters, such as Poor Law administration. The vestries became, *de facto* if not *de jure*, an early form of local government, supervising the maintenance of the parish infrastructure, taking responsibility for abandoned children ('foundlings'), feeding the poor, burying the destitute ('paupers'), and maintaining the parish pump, i.e., fire engine.[7]

These civic services were financed by a local tax called the 'parish cess'. After the abolition of the Penal Laws, the vestry included all ratepayers irrespective of religious affiliation although the officers had to be Anglican.[8] The eighteenth- and nineteenth-century vestry minute books of the Established Church parishes in Cork have survived.[9] All, without exception, contain many references to the upkeep and maintenance of the parish pumps (i.e. engines), payment to the Engine Keepers, building of sheds to house the engines, etc.

CHURCHES HAVING FIRE ENGINES.

As we have seen, several new Protestant churches were erected during the early years of the eighteenth century and older ones replaced. All had their quota of fire engines. In the 'flat' of the city, these included Christ Church (aka Holy Trinity), St Peter's, and St Paul's. The 'south suburbs' were served by fire engines housed in St Fin Barre's Cathedral and St Nicholas', while the northern side of the city depended on pumps located at St Anne's and St Mary's, at the east side of the foot of Shandon Street.

The North and South Main Street axis was still the main shopping thoroughfare. In this area, without doubt, the building with the greatest potential for disaster was Skiddy's Castle, close to the North Gate Bridge, wherein was housed the city's stock of gunpowder and explosives. For years, its very existence had given the City Fathers palpitations and frequently, they penned impassioned pleas to the Lord Lieutenant in Dublin to have the magazine

An early eighteenth-century Newsham manual pump being supplied by a bucket chain. The bewigged gentleman is standing on the air-vessel housing of the pump, while directing the branch which is fitted to a 'gooseneck' swivel. Other men are working the pump levers. To be effective, the engine had to be positioned in very close proximity to the building on fire, a stratagem fraught with danger to both operator and pump. Records remain of buildings collapsing and burying both.

Rocque's plan of Cork (1759) showing locations where the municipal and parish fire engines were housed. (Courtesy of Cork City Libraries.)

1. The municipal engine house situated near the City Courthouse adjacent to the Exchange.
2. St Fin Barre's Cathedral.
3. St Nicholas', Cove Street.
4. Christ Church (aka Holy Trinity), South Main Street.
5. St Paul's, Paul Street.
6. St Peter's, North Main Street.
7. St Mary's, Shandon.
8. St Anne's, Shandon.

removed to a remote location. A short time before the castle was removed, an eccentric young fellow named Jemmy Hudson, whose father ran a chemist's shop on the opposite side of the street, caught a rat in a trap one morning. Dousing the wretched rodent in turpentine, he set it on fire and released it. The rat scuttled straight across the street to the castle, where, in spite of the best efforts of the Redcoats on duty, it managed to enter a grating which brought it down into the magazine with its barrels of gunpowder. Fortunately for the inhabitants of Cork City centre, the rat expired before it reached the explosives, 'otherwise this entire quarter of the city would have been reduced to a heap of ruins'. Shortly afterwards, while hunting in Glanmire, Hudson was thrown from his horse and killed. His lifeless body was found the next morning, the horse having found its own way home.[10]

On paper, the parish pump system looked ideal: each neighbourhood church having a well-maintained fire appliance, ready to respond promptly to emergencies within its area of operations, or rushing to the assistance of contiguous parishes. The reality was somewhat different. By a strange oversight, the law which compelled engines to be procured and taken to fires did not provide for them actually being worked upon arrival, and as a rule the only object their custodians had in view was to secure the sum of money allowed to the Keeper of each engine that attended. At a time when Goldsmith's village preacher was 'passing rich with forty pounds a year', those entrusted with the (part-time) responsibility for the parish engines possessed a lucrative sideline to their ordinary living. Typically, at the end of the eighteenth century, an Engine Keeper's annual salary was about £5. This could be seriously enhanced where the Keeper was also in charge of maintenance and repairs. In 1800, Thomas Bennett's (who had a pump-making business in Brown Street) account for repairs to the St Fin Barre's Cathedral engine stood at £28.10s.7d.[11] At Easter 1816, St Mary's, Shandon owed Joseph Garde £103.14s.8d for fire engine expenses, plus another £100 'for necessary uses and repairs ... to be assessed on the inhabitants and Ploughlands'.[12] Sometimes the bills submitted were not accepted at face value and were set aside for further investigation. One such case involved Francis Geary, a maker of mathematical and optical instruments and a member of St Paul's Select Vestry with a shop in Paul Street. He had been appointed Keeper of the Royal Exchange Assurance's (REA) two fire engines in 1799. Their Engine House was in nearby Carey's Lane, off St Patrick's Street. At Easter 1807, he was confirmed as Engine Keeper (in succession to Thomas Blewit) to St Paul's at an annual salary of £5.13s.9d.[13] Twelve months later, he was enmeshed in controversy over an account he had submitted for repairing and painting the fire engine. The vestry minutes record:

> At a Vestry held pursuant to adjournment on May 9th 1808 for the purpose of taking into consideration the reports of the Committee that was appointed for inspecting the repairs of the Engine and Engine House, the Committee recommend the Parish to direct Mr. Geary to prove the several items of his Account, they also recommend the Parish to employ a reputable Sworn Measurer to value the Carpenter's work for repairing the Engine House. It was also agreed that forty feet of leather hose be provided in addition to the old one and that the old hose be repaired under the direction of Mr. David Sheppard and Mr. John Whitney.[14]

In the event, Geary's account was settled: £8.0s.4½d for the repairs to the engine and a further 3s.10½d for paint (which, compared with the accounts already mentioned, seem not unreasonable), but his position as Engine Keeper was abruptly terminated.

The job was given to Thomas Bennett, a member of the committee set up to investigate the account (and who had submitted his own hefty account to St Fin Barre's in 1800).[15] There is no explanation in the minutes as to the exact nature of St Paul's apparent animus with Francis Geary, but at Easter 1809, he surfaces as Engine Keeper in the contiguous parish of St Peter's at an annual salary of £5.[16] One can only speculate on what poignant human story lies hidden behind those quill-written, beautifully-executed, copperplate lines transcribed over 200 years ago. The episode, however, appears to confirm Dominic Behan's contention that there is no such thing as bad publicity – except, perhaps, one's own obituary!

Thomas Bennett went on to greater things. In 1812, he appears as Engineer in charge of the REA Fire Engine Establishment, a prestigious job, making a name for himself at city fires. When Sir David Perrier's corn store 'below the New Bridge' went up in flames on the night of 22 January 1812, the *Cork Mercantile Chronicle* noticed 'the promptness and extraordinary exertions of Mr. Thomas Bennett, Engineer, who on this, as well as on every other similar occasion, highly merited the approbation of his fellow Citizens'.[17]

By and large, the parochial system of fire protection was worthless. The engines frequently stood rotting in churchyards, the Beadle and other parish officials considering the attention that ought to have been paid to them to be the least important of their duties.[18] The ineptitude of the system was recalled by Charles Dickens, the famous novelist and one-time visitor to Cork, when he wrote:

> Such are a few traits of the importance and gravity of a parish Beadle – a gravity which has never been disturbed in any case that has come under observation, except when the services of that particularly useful machine, a parish fire-engine, are required: then indeed all is bustle. Two little boys run to the Beadle as fast as their legs will carry them and report from their own personal observation that some neighbouring chimney is on fire; the engine is hastily got out, and a plentiful supply of boys being obtained, and harnessed to it with ropes, away they rattle over the pavement, the Beadle, running – we do not exaggerate – running at the side, until they arrive at some house, smelling strongly of soot, at the door of which the Beadle knocks with considerable gravity for half-an-hour. No attention being paid to these manual applications, and the Turn-Cock having turned on the water, the engine turns off amidst the shouts of the boys; it pulls up once more at the workhouse, and the Beadle 'pulls up' the unfortunate householder next day, for the amount of the legal award. We never saw a parish engine at a regular fire but once. It came up in gallant style – three miles and a half an hour at least; there was a capital supply of water, and it was first on the spot. Bang went the pumps – the people cheered – the Beadle perspired profusely; but it was

unfortunately discovered, just as they were going to put the fire out, that nobody understood the process by which the engine was filled with water; and that eighteen boys, and a man, had exhausted themselves in pumping for 20 minutes, without producing the slightest effect![19]

When fire broke out in some stables in Knapp's Square on the morning of Thursday 11 January 1787, the only appliance of any use was the parish engine of St Paul's under its Keeper, Edward Sweeney. The incident prompted the Mayor, Samuel Rowland, to place a hard-hitting notice in the newspaper:

Cork.
The Mayor cannot avoid expressing his astonishment that in so extensive a trading city as this, a matter so obvious to the preservation of the Lives and Properties of all its inhabitants should be so shamefully neglected, and unattended to, and towards which he now wishes to excite their immediate serious attention, and that is, the Fire Engines belonging to the several Parishes, which are now kept in such wretched condition, as not to be of the smallest use, when called forth, on any fire that happens, the Engine of St Paul's Parish, much to the credit of the Person to whose charge it has been committed, only excepted, and to the assistance of which alone may justly be attributed the happily suppressing on Thursday last, a very dangerous Fire... which threatened destruction [of the] neighbourhood.

He went on to implore the church authorities to immediately put 'the Engines in complete order ... so as to render them of real use to the Public', and warned that, 'A neglect after this Public Notice must be considered as criminal in them, and they will be deemed by their fellow Citizens as highly accessary to any future losses they may individually or collectively sustain.'[20] This, less than thinly-veiled, threat prompted the vestry in at least one city church to urgently review their fire protection arrangements. The parishioners of St Nicholas's, Cove Street, assembled in vestry on 1 February 1787 and resolved:

That the engine the property of this Parish (now in very bad condition) be immediately repaired, an estimate having been given in to compleat the same, for four Guineas, we do hereby agree that the sum of four Guineas be raised on the Parish on Easter Monday next. Resolved, that Mr. Edward Swiney who has furnished the above estimate, is hereby appointed Keeper of the above Engine at a salary of five pounds per annum, to commence at and after the 25th March next, ensuring together with the sum of five shillings annually for the keeping the same in compleat order, with one coat of paint annually.
Resolved, that the Minister, Churchwardens, Mr. Clark, Mr. Hugh Lawton, Mr. Mansergh, Mr. Lamb, Mr. Bird and Mr. Bennett, be a committee for this

year to see the Engine, repaired properly, and to have it played in some public part of Cork, at least once in three months, and offtner if they shall direct. Henry Sandiford, Rector.[21]

This 'Edward Swiney' sounds suspiciously like the 'Edward Sweeney', Keeper of St Paul's engine, whose public persona was flying high in the aftermath of the Knapp's Square fire. Quite how he was supposed to be in two places at the one time in case of simultaneous emergencies is not explained!

DID THE ROMAN CATHOLIC CHURCHES MAINTAIN ENGINES?

With the relaxation of the Penal Laws and the gradual re-emergence of Roman Catholic churches, it may perhaps be assumed that these churches would have emulated their Protestant counterparts in the provision of fire engines. My research has unearthed no evidence to support this. The late Sr Angela Bolster, former Diocesan Archivist and author of the seminal four-volume *History of the Diocese of Cork*, advised me that in all her years of research she had come across no references at all to Catholic churches maintaining fire engines.[22] The daily accounts and inventories of two mendicant Orders of Friars having churches in Cork have survived. Neither House Books for the Augustinians[23] (1746- 1834) nor the Franciscans[24] (1764-1831), while minutely detailing, it seems, almost every single chattel contained within the walls of their respective monasteries, make no reference to firefighting equipment of any description. Contemporary newspaper accounts provide limited evidence. Other than acknowledging the attendance of one or more parish engines at a fire incident, the churches involved are not always identified by name. When they are, they are always Protestant. In light of the rebarbative Tithe Levy imposed on Catholics for the support of the Established Church, it may be adduced that through this tax Catholics were indirectly contributing towards the upkeep of the engines and were therefore entitled to their services. In any event, I have come across absolutely no evidence to suggest that Catholics were denied recourse to them in times of emergency. In the absence of any evidence to the contrary, I can only conclude that Roman Catholic parishes did not maintain fire engines. In this context, the theological maxim comes to mind: '*In dubio pro traditio*'.[25]

A TYPICAL PARISH ENGINE.

So far as I am aware no parish fire engine has survived in Cork city. However, at least two such examples are preserved in Dublin, and may be inspected at the Anglican church of St Werburgh. Both were constructed in accordance with the Newsham principle.

If the Dutchman Jan van der Heiden senior had earned the soubriquet of 'Father of Modern Firefighting', then the epithet 'Father of Fire Engines' must surely go to Richard Newsham, the son of a London button-maker, who patented his design in 1721 for 'A New Water-Engine for the quenching and extinguishing of Fires'. Newsham's design had re-introduced the concept of having an air chamber so as to equalize the pressure output from the pump. In this way, the jet was projected in an uninterrupted continuous stream, rather than in a pulsating fashion, as heretofore.[26] Newsham, did not, contrary to some accounts, 're-invent' the air chamber; some earlier engine builders had used air chambers on their pumps, but no one had done it quite so effectively as he.

For reasons that have never been fully explained, Newsham eschewed some of van der Heiden's earlier innovations, like the use of delivery hose, in favour of the old, discredited fixed-branch arrangement where the firefighter, standing on top of the machine, depended on the hit-and-miss capability of the 'long shot'. He was, however, the first to place long wooden pumping handles, called 'brakes', along either side of the engine. On earlier pumps, the levers were situated fore and aft, which restricted the number of pumpers that could 'bear a hand' at any one time. As many as ten persons could now stand side-by-side along each of the brakes, working them up and down in see-saw fashion. The brakes were made of oak, smooth, round, and just thick enough to permit a firm grip. A later design (1725) had both pumping brakes along the sides and treadles for extra men, standing on top of the engine, to use their feet in a rocking motion: 'to tread or dance in rhythm', according to a contemporary source.

Newsham built his models in six different sizes. Size No.6, the largest, had a discharge capacity of some 773 litres per minute (170 gallons, about one third of the capacity of a modern fire appliance) and was capable of throwing a jet of water some forty metres. This marque cost £70: a very substantial amount of money for which one could have bought a modest house. Perhaps the most serious drawback on Newsham's early models is that the handle for pulling the engine did not pivot. This is all the more surprising when one considers that such an oversight must surely have easily been rectified. However, pivot it did not, and in the narrow lanes and streets of Cork it meant that the firefighters, to turn a machine from one street into another, often had to physically lift it up and carry it around the corner. Christ Church (on the South Main Street) is credited with having the largest and most powerful parish engine in Cork.[27] These larger engines were not always advantageous in the spider's web of lanes and narrow streets that were a feature of old Cork. When the tallow house of Mr Hawkes off the South Main Street was severely damaged in a blaze on the night of 29 November 1800 and considerable time elapsed before firefighting water was made to bear on the fire, the *Hibernian Chronicle* censured the authorities for permitting such hazardous industries in built-up areas, surrounded by domestic dwellings, where the fire engines were unable to approach.[28] A similar situation prevailed, again off the South Main Street, when, on Sunday morning 9 January 1814:

> About 10 a.m., a fire broke out in the rere of South Main-Street and Tuckey-Street, among some poor persons' houses…the fire raged with considerable fury…and the engines were on the spot a long time before they could be of any service.[29]

Again, the larger engines could not be manoeuvred within their working optimum of the fire.

Notwithstanding, Richard Newsham's engines were a great success in these islands and in the British colonies (a number was bought by New York City in 1731), and his model, and not the van der Heidens', proved the blueprint for successive inventors in the years ahead. As one historian observed of him, 'He has given his country a nobler present than if he had added provinces to Great Britain'.[30] With the intensification of the trade wars between Britain and Holland in the eighteenth century, the great van der Heidens, their inventions, and their reputations were, for all intents and purposes, airbrushed from history in these islands.

CORPORATE AFFAIRS.

In 1753, Nicholas Fitton, who operated a foundry on Tuckey's Quay, made his own little bit of local history by becoming Cork's first (and perhaps only) fire engine manufacturer. Fitton claimed that his machines were every bit as good as any made in England, and reminded his clients that for all those times when one didn't actually require a fire engine, they were just the thing to have handy for watering the garden!

> Nicholas Fitton, Founder, on Tuckey's Quay, makes and sells all kinds of pewter, brass and copper work. Bells of all sizes which he hangs after the best and cheapest manner. He also makes all kinds of Water Engines for extinguishing Fires and supplying gentlemen's houses and gardens, which he will engage to be as good as any made in England.[31]

Some six years later, in January 1759, the Fittons' were awarded the contract by Cork Corporation for making a new, and repairing the old, fire engine, all for the sum of £17.17s.1d. This was certainly a bargain-basement price, for at that time a medium-sized Newsham engine ('Size No.4'), capable of discharging ninety gallons per minute to a distance of thirty-six yards, would have set the corporation

back some £40, plus the cost of importation from England.[32] The city's 'fire station' had, by this time, progressed from the 'lynny' in Paul Street to new premises
adjacent to the Exchange and Courthouse on (south) Main Street.

In 1708, arguably the most imposing building that Cork had seen in all its long
history was erected. This was the Exchange, built on the site of Roche's Castle. For
many years it was the hub of civic and commercial activity in the city. However,
the building jutted out rather incongruously across the Main Street, resulting in
the thoroughfare being divided into South Main Street and North Main Street.
Crofton T. Croker recalled this anomaly when he observed that the Exchange:

> Cringing from the northern blast,
> Hides half its ample front in Castle Street.[33]

The adjacent City Courthouse, also built during the early years of the eighteenth century, faced onto South Main Street. It was described as a fine two-storey
building, with steps leading up to the courtrooms. There were shops and apartments, situated on either side of the steps, which were let out to tenants; it was
then considered judicious for public buildings to generate their own income and
to be self-sufficient as far as possible. During 1739, James Piersey, a city elder and
wine importer with premises on Knapp's Square, had endowed the city with a
fire engine and buckets, which now gave the corporation a firefighting capability of at least two engines, several 'preventers' and innumerable buckets.[34] More
suitable premises had to be found for the growing stock of firefighting plant, and
on 14 January 1740, the council passed a motion requisitioning two apartments
under the City Courthouse 'wherein Mr Borson apothecary[35] lately lived, and
that now in the possession of Ellinor Soully'.[36] (What compensation was allowed
the discommoded Ms Soully for vacating her property is not revealed). Further,
it was resolved that Mayor Alderman William Fuller and Mr Thomas Browne
should oversee the work and 'employ proper persons' to look after the fire equipment. Thus, Cork's latest 'fire station' was located in the city centre at the very
heart of municipal affairs. One of the 'proper persons' may have included one
Ralph Vize, for on 20 November 1745, the council minutes recorded:

> In consideration of the necessitous condition of the Widow and children of
> Ralph Vize, dec., who was serviceable to this City in taking care of the Fire
> Engines, ordered, that £10 be given as charity to said widow, on giving up
> the materials belonging to said engines in her hands.

Members of the public who were so inclined could keep up to speed with
the very latest information on fire protection: what Dr Caulfield opined was
the very first public lecture delivered in Cork (in August 1769) embraced the
subject of fire engines:

The Cork Exchange, city council chambers, courthouse, and 'fire station' (to the right of the steps). In January 1740, the city council requisitioned two apartments under the courthouse to house the city's fire engines. The group of buildings shown in the illustration was removed in 1837 to facilitate the widening of the street when the new courthouse on Great George's Street (now Washington Street) was built. (Courtesy of Cork City Libraries)

Tomorrow will be read at the Cock Pit the Lecture on Hydraulics, illustrated by working models, all kinds of pumps, bucket-engines, water-engines, mills, fire-engines, and the celebrated Canal of the Duke of Bridgewater. Admittance, half a crown.[37]

In spite of the steadily growing number of fire appliances in Cork – municipal, parish, and private – the city suffered from calamitous fires at all too frequent intervals. Typically, when a fire broke out and was not immediately suppressed, there was very little the fire engines could do to stop it. The time lag between alarm call and the appliances actually delivering water onto a fire was just too great:

Cork, May 28th. 1727.
About 11 this forenoon a most dreadful fire happened in the south part of this city, occasioned by some sparks of fire which issued from a smith's forge. The fire seized on the upper part of the house which was thatched. A violent storm blew at North-West and continued so till the flames were extinguished. In about an hour's time 117 houses were burnt down. Most of the effects were lost, but we hear of no persons losing their lives except one child.[38]

John Fitzgerald's *Cork Remembrancer* (1783) recorded that, on 6 June 1762, a fire in Cat Lane consumed 150 houses. (That same afternoon, an unfortunate soldier belonging to Sir Ralph Gore's Regiment of Foot who 'was very active in suppressing the fire' decided to cool off in the river at French's Quay where he promptly drowned). A few years later, when fire broke out in a *thatched* cottage near St Fin Barre's Cathedral on the afternoon of Friday, 10 September 1766, yet another neighbourhood was wiped out in the space of a few hours:

Corke.

Friday afternoon between two and three o'clock a fire broke out in a thatched cabin in the South Liberties, situate between Bandon road and St. Finbarry's, which became so dreadful by the flames being driven by a very strong S.W. wind, that in less than two hours, that, and seventy-three others, that were roofed with straw, most of which were newly built, were consumed to ashes, by which there are at least 200 poor people reduced to the outmost want, having lost their little all.

A child about four years old perished in the conflagration; and a great many pigs, cats and dogs were burned in the houses. Two large ricks of hay that were made up at a little distance were set on fire by the flakes of burning straw which were driven about, and entirely destroyed; and but for the assistance of Nicholas Fitton, with his Water Engines, and the assiduity of the army and neighbouring inhabitants, the progress of the flames (which it was impossible to put a stop to till every cabin in that quarter, which was situated before the wind, was burnt down) would have extended much farther – It is truly lamentable to behold the devastation, and hear the cries of the poor unhappy sufferers, whose distress it is hoped will be relieved by the Charitable and Humane.[39]

The *Corke Evening Post* for Monday 15 September 1766 identified where the damage had been greatest:

Bandon Road 4 houses destroyed.
Piggot's lane 19 houses destroyed.
Coggin's lane 24 houses destroyed.
Kenry's lane 22 houses destroyed.
Crimmeen's lane 10 houses destroyed.

The careless inhabitants of the south side didn't have a monopoly on great accidental fires, however. In June 1775, 'A fire broke out this night in a house in Fair Lane, which burnt with great violence for some hours, whereby between 20 and 30 cabins were consumed.[40] The old bogey of fires in thatched houses densely packed together, frequently accompanied by high winds, was a losing combination; one which those early fire engines with their pitifully slow response times, untrained hands and lack of adequate water supply, could never hope to vanquish.

In the absence of proper statistics, it is not possible to quantify the number of fires which were caused maliciously. There is little doubt, however, that arson was feared every bit as much as murder. The tightly-packed lanes and streets of Cork were potential tinder boxes. As we have seen, whole districts could go up in flames in just a few hours. Some arsonists, it seems, were just expressing a grudge against society. Others, it was whispered darkly, were pioneers in the fire insurance business, punishing clients who had declined to pay their premiums. In an age of open hearths and thatched roofs, house fires were common even without arson, and a criminal subculture grew up around them. So-called 'fire priggers' specialised in stealing valuables on the pretence of helping burnt-out families retrieve their belongings. The authorities responded with their own terror tactics: the death sentence was frequently handed down for malicious burning.[41] But no deterrents worked. In the absence of a proper police force (the night watchmen were universally derided) darkness remained a separate realm, and criminals ruled it. The Council Book for 5 December 1730 recorded:

> Mr. Mayor communicated to this board a letter delivered him by Mr. Phineas Bagwell, Postmaster of this City, superscribed and wrote in the following manner:
> "To the Mayor of Cork" (on the back near the seal) –
> Postmaster, deliver this or weel burn your house –
> (Inside) – " Mr. Mayre, we are just come from England and cash is low, you must on Sunday nite put 50 gineays under Peter's Stocks[42] or you may depend if you fail the consequence will be Fire and Destruction, for we can't Starve. 'Your friends desire your Welfare'. – Philo."
> Resolved, that Mr. Mayor do by tomorrow's post send a copy of the above mentioned letter to the Government.

The English potential arsonists may not have been up to speed with their conventions, but appear to have been perfectly *au fait* with the writings of the first-century philosopher and historian, the Hellenistic Jew Philo. In any event, Cork avoided the threatened holocaust and no more was heard of the matter.

EARLY WATER SUPPLIES.

In contrast to modern fire appliances (present-day machines are called 'fire appliances' and not 'fire engines'), which carry 1,800 litres (400 gallons) of water on board, enabling them to launch an immediate attack on a fire while a more durable supply is being sourced, early engines relied completely on an external source, either 'open' (e.g. a river, lake, etc.,) or 'closed' (e.g. town water mains). And, prior to 1768, only the former was available to Cork firefighters.

This almost total reliance on the river for water created an unforeseen predicament for the city's firefighting services when, in the late eighteenth century, the culverting over of Cork's waterways began. Whereas previously, the engines could simply be brought to the water's edge – a readily available and unlimited source – in time of fire, suction hoses dropped in and pumping commenced, with the arching over of the channels this was no longer possible. Many areas of the city were now a considerable distance from a supply for the engines. Mayor Samuel Rowland was concerned enough to bring the dilemma to the attention of the wider public via a press announcement in the *Hibernian Chronicle* on 18 January 1787:

> [The Mayor] ... thinks proper to observe that Pumps for the accommodation of the Public, and to supply Water for the Engines in cases of Fire are much wanted in different parts of the City that are now arched over, and thro' which the River formerly flowed open and unconfined for their Benefit heretofore, and that some mode should be devised of raising Money for such purpose, either by the Assizes Grand Juries or otherwise.

An Act of 1762 had empowered the corporation to raise the necessary finance to install a pipe-water system in the city by issuing shares. This resulted in the creation of the Cork Pipe Water Company. But the new utility would prove to be the exclusive domain of those privileged enough to have a healthy bank balance: the vast majority of the citizens could not afford the annual charge of two guineas (£2 2s.0d) per household. These had recourse only to cisterns, public fountains, artesian wells, and the river, from which they would draw their water in buckets and carry it to their homes. Even as late as 1855, only 600 of the city's housing stock had water with an estimated 50,000 people still drawing their water from the river or public fountains.[43] Earlier artesian wells sunk within the old city had, due to its low-lying setting, required no great depth; many, however, were no doubt prone to contamination. Similarly, during the long months of summer when the dearth of water in the Lee caused the turbines to stop turning (thus disabling the supply) the people reverted to drawing their water from the river. Those who resorted to collecting it in this way were always in danger of slipping on the slime-covered steps and slipways, and falling in. Indeed, because of the number of fatal accidents at one such slip – Allen's Slip, near Crosse's Green – a contemporary observer cynically suggested it should be renamed the 'Drowning Slip'.[44] Many others, unwittingly, were putting themselves and their families in great peril by drinking the water straight from the river. John Wesley, leader of the 'Second Reformation' and founder of the Methodist Church, after a visit to Cork in 1756 recalled:

> I saw the plain reason why strangers usually complain of the unwholesomeness of the water in Cork: many women were filling vessels with river-water (which is that commonly used in the city for tea and most other purposes) when the tide was at its height. Now, although this is not salt, yet it cannot but affect both the stomach and bowels of tender persons.[45]

Even as late as 1782, unfortunates incarcerated in the notorious Debtors' Gaol, spanning the South Gate Bridge, were given salt water to drink due to the scarcity of fresh water, perhaps inadvertently hastening their early demise.[46]

The many-talented Nicholas Fitton of Tuckey's Quay, fire engine manufacturer and the official responsible for drilling the city's fire engines and taking
charge at fires[47] was, on 14 May 1768 awarded the contract for supplying Cork
with its first-ever piped water system. Work continued apace over the following years, supply being laid to the City Gaol, the Bridewell and the new
Mansion House, the official residence of the Mayor.[48] On 15 June 1774, he was
contracted to build a second reservoir, but by 1777, the corporation was dis-
satisfied with the progress being made and instituted legal proceedings against
him. However, independent arbitrators found in his favour, decided that he had
indeed honoured the terms of his contract and awarded him £1,500 – a prodigious amount of money. The early water mains laid by the Cork Pipe Water
Company were little more than tree trunks (hence 'trunk' mains) hollowed out
to form pipes. Larch, a member of the conifer family noted for its height and
valued for its durability, was the preferred medium.

In April 1970, when road works were in progress on the South Terrace, what
appeared to be just a baulk of timber came into view. An astute local resident recognized it for what it really was – a section of the original Pipe Water
Company conduit – and prevailed on the operator of the mechanical digger
to avoid making contact with it until the city's archaeological authorities had
been notified. About eighteen metres in all were exposed. The pipes which
could be removed measured 5.6m and 5.7m respectively. The diameter of the
bore was approximately 9cm. One end was pointed to form a spigot and the
other hollowed out for a socket, rather like the joints of a fishing rod. To prevent the joint from opening or loosening, the pipes were fitted with iron collars
and tightened with a nut and bolt.[49] The faint odour of larch could still be dis-
cerned after almost 200 years. Such trunk mains were capable of withstanding
only small internal pressures. Previous to the 1970 find, the only other known
piece of wooden main was presented to the Cork Public Museum in the 1930s
by Chief Officer Liam Monaghan of Cork Fire Brigade, having been excavated
in St Patrick's Street.

The original waterwheel and pump built by Nicholas Fitton raised the unfil-
tered water from the river to an open reservoir known as the City Basin situated
on the hillside above the Lee Road and thence by gravity fed through the
network of wooden mains to the city.[50] In time of fire, use could increasingly
be made of the growing new network of mains. The mains, however, had been
laid without hydrants (or 'fire plugs' to use the contemporary term). Therefore,
in order to gain access to the main it had first to be exposed by digging up
the road over it. This was not as difficult as may be imagined, as frequently the
pipes were not buried as deeply as modern mains, and, in any event, the streets
were not macadamed. After the main was uncovered, a hole was then bored in
it with an auger and the water flowed into the street. The hole in the roadway
was then made wider and deeper to create a 'basin' into which the suction hose

of the fire engine could be set. As may well be imagined, however, this practice played havoc with the water supply and pipe work, and did no favours to the city streets and footpaths which had to be filled in and made good after every fire.[51] Damage was often caused to the valves on the fire engines if the basin was particularly gritty or gravelly; in these cases, tubs which were carried on the 'tail' of the engine would be used to convey the water from the source to the engine. In an arrangement reminiscent of the modern 'sump' often found in industrial premises, which facilitates the use of suction hose by the fire service, the Council Book for 13 May 1760 recorded:

> That the Exchange slip lately covered be converted into a shop with a trap-door to go down to the water, and that same, when finished, be set for one year by public cant, and that three keys be provided to the door of said shop, one for the tenant, the other two to be deposited where the Mayor shall appoint, so that recourse may be had to the water in case of any accidental fire in the neighbourhood of said slip.

After 1826, another problem manifested itself in the mad scramble to expose the water mains in time of fire: the danger of being blown up from a gas explosion. There was always the possibility that the careless wielder of a pick-axe would sever the wrong main. When a fire occurred in Dublin, the *Freeman's Journal* for 2 January 1827 deposed how, 'The people exerted themselves with such impetuosity to find water, that two men had nearly lost their lives from breaking the gas pipe, the gas from which instantly exploded.'

Eventually, in order to protect the mains and streets from the damage caused by being regularly dug up during fire emergencies, 'fire plugs' were inserted at intervals along the network of piping. These consisted of wooden plugs driven into holes in the pipes and the protruding end cut off. When required, an auger was used to remove the plug and the tapered end of a wooden standpipe was driven into the hole, to which a hose was then attached. (The procedure of fitting the standpipe into the hole from which water was flowing under pressure invariably resulted in a good soaking for the hapless firefighter!) Thus, Cork's first 'fire hydrants' came into being. On 21 July 1772, the corporation ordered that:

> £200 be paid Ald. Millerd and Maylor, Mr. Burgess Morrison, Wrixon, and George Piersy, Esq., to be applied by them in erecting fire-plugs in convenient parts of the City and Suburbs, for extinguishing any accidental fires that may happen therein.[52]

During all the years of the Cork Pipe Water Company, there appears to have been no more than forty-five fire plugs in the city.[53] George's Quay and its immediate hinterland, with its plethora of mills and industries owned by the merchant princes, seems to have had more than its fair share. The main ran down Sullivan's Quay, George's Quay and along through the South Terrace (then 'South Parade') with spurs off to the side streets.[54] When fire broke out in the afternoon of Sunday 19 April 1840 in:

> the concerns of Mr. Edmond Goold, George's-quay, which for some time threatened to extend to the range of houses on the quay, and also to destroy a number of houses on Margaret-street ... it was perceived that the fire had originated in the kiln and that that portion of the mill would be impossible to save. The Atlas engine, under the superintendence of Mr. W.L. Perrier, being immediately on the spot, was worked with great effect upon the connection between the mill and flour stores ... by the active and well directed efforts of those present and it was confined to the building in which it originated and which it totally destroyed. The engines present were the Atlas, Royal Exchange, West of England, Scottish Union, and Christ Church and St. Nicholas' parish engines. The building and property are insured for £13,000 in the Atlas, Sun, West of England, York and North of England, and Caledonian Offices ... were it not for the great quantity of water supplied from the fire plugs, the conflagration would have spread through the entire range of buildings.
>
> Shortly after the roof of Mr. Goold's mill had fallen in, the flour-store of Mr. Herrick, on Charlotte-quay, at the opposite side of the river, was perceived to be on fire, when a number of gentlemen forced the gate, and having got on the roof, broke away the portion that was in flames. The fire originated by a spark from the burning mass at Mr. Goold's concerns falling on a tarred covering that was over the loft ... attached to the roof of the store.[55]

However, some months later, when fire broke out in the early hours of Thursday 2 July in the cooperage of Joseph Deyos in nearby Abbey Street, water for the engines of the Scottish Union, West of England, and the REA had to be supplied by the carts of the Wide Street Commissioners, the nearest mains, apparently, being on Douglas Street and Dunbar Street.[56]

As late as 1848, large swathes of the city remained inadequately covered with fire plugs, as Mr Coleman, owner of a small cabinet-making business in Grattan Street found to his cost. When, on the evening of 26 August, his premises caught fire:

> The engines arrived about 7 o'clock, but had to remain idle for a long time for want of a supply of water – it being ascertained that on the entire Marsh, there was not a single fire plug.[57]

This is very surprising when one considers that the area, including Grattan Street, was well supplied with water mains.[58] In the absence of any known deposited records, it is difficult to quantify the criteria applied to what seems to have been an abundance of firefighting water points in one section of the city to the exclusion of another (which contained, incidentally, one of Cork's most important buildings – the official residence of the Mayor of Cork, the Mansion House), although the conglomeration of industry along the south quays must have been a deciding factor.

For some inexplicable reason, the council at its meeting on 24 July 1781, decided to hand over the city's fire engine to the parish of St Nicholas and abolish the post of Engine Keeper: the minutes refer to the fire *engine* rather than *engines*, seemingly indicating that other equipment had already been disposed of.[59] In short, they appear to have closed down the city's official 'firefighting service'. No explanation is to be found in the official record for this extraordinary decision. Perhaps they thought that with fire engines now available in the various parishes (and, it is assumed, a small number held by various industries) the continued expenditure of (limited) city funds was both unwarranted and unjustified, and therefore municipal fire equipment was surplus to needs.[60]

And what of their obligation under the earlier 'Fire Acts'? In any event, there are no further references to fire engines or fire prevention measures being discussed at council meetings between this (1781) entry and 1800 when Dr Caulfield's transcription ends. By their remarkable action in abruptly terminating the city's fire service, the corporation had effectively abandoned the fire-prone streets of Cork to their fate, served only by the ill-organized parish structure, with its hastily-assembled volunteer firefighters and their leaky, ineffective equipment. Over eighty years would elapse before they took the first faltering steps to become involved in municipal firefighting again. In the meantime, as frequently happens on such occasions, private enterprise was waiting, in the wings, to fill the vacuum.

4

Forged in Fire: The Insurance
Brigades Make their Mark

'The Citizens of Cork … are respectfully informed, that for their Use the
Company have sent from London, at an heavy expense, Two very capital
ENGINES. One of the Engines is of the largest size, and is allowed to be
the first ever seen in this Kingdom'.

(Royal Exchange Assurance, 2 July 1799).

'Whenever our neighbour's house is on fire, it cannot be amiss for the
engines to play a little on our own'

(Edmund Burke (1729-1797), Irish-born Whig politician, man-of-letters, and kins-
man of Nano Nagle).

By the early part of the nineteenth century, the Cork citizenry were so long
used to the sight of the flashy uniforms of the Light Dragoon Guards or the
Regiment of Foot on their streets that they would hardly afford any newly-arriv-
ing swashbucklers a second glance. They were, however, full of curiosity now
at these, not military, but civilians, who suddenly appeared on the local scene
dressed in over-the-top flamboyant outfits. The name they gave themselves was
equally intriguing: 'Fire-men'. Novel though the notion was for the Corkonians,
the idea of insurance company firefighting teams was hardly a new one.

Fire insurance may be regarded as the product of a shift in attitude towards
hazard and providence beginning in the late seventeenth century. By mitigating
the fear of loss and diminishing uncertainty, insurance was recognised as acting as
an incentive for investment, innovation, and accumulation, as well as safeguard-
ing the value of property. In Britain, by the end of the seventeenth century, three
societies were actively engaged in the fire insurance business. They were The Fire
Office (later renamed The Phenix Fire Office), The Friendly Society, and the
Amicable Contributors for Insuring Loss by Fire (afterwards called the Hand-in-
Hand Office). As the idea spread, many more companies came into being, and by

1720, there were at least a dozen operating in London, including the Sun, the Union, the Hand-in-Hand, the Westminster, and the Royal Exchange.

But what of Ireland? One reason for the apparent reluctance of the various fire offices in extending their business across the Irish Sea was the difficulty of communication. The only means of travel between the different parts of what were styled the British Isles was by horseback, stagecoach, or sailing vessel. It may well be imagined, therefore, that little business was actually transacted outside the town or city in which a company's office was situated.

However, the author of the *History of the Royal Exchange Assurance Corporation in Ireland* suggests an additional, more sinister, reason:

> In 1681, a regular office was operating in a place described as 'at the backside of the Royal Exchange', and from that date onward England enjoyed the blessings and security of Fire Insurance. But not so Ireland. More than forty years elapsed before any company could be found sufficiently courageous to risk the doubtful prospects of an Irish connection. The troubled state of this country for many years, and the numerous incendiary fires, did not promise a very attractive field for the operations of an Assurance Company, and Ireland's past history was sufficiently lurid to give even the most enterprising Underwriters a pause ere risking their fortunes in the 'disthressful counthry'.[1]

Whatever the reason, the first 'sufficiently courageous' company to locate in Ireland was the Royal Exchange Assurance (hereafter REA). In 1722, it appointed its first Irish agent, Luke Gaven, with offices in Dublin's Abbey Street. The company had been granted its charter only two years previously, on 22 June 1720. In 1719, it had applied for a Royal Charter exclusively to underwrite marine risks. After many difficulties, it had obtained its charter on payment of £300,000 to the Exchequer to defray debts of the Civil List, an astronomical amount of money which, not surprisingly, they had considerable difficulty in raising following in the wake of the so-called South Sea Bubble fiasco when share values had plummeted.[2] The start-up of the company in Ireland was closely followed by the arrival, in the same year, of the London Assurance.

In Cork, it is evident that the concept of fire insurance was appreciated from its earliest days: an entry in the Council Book for 11 March 1724 reads, 'Ordered, that Mr. Masters insure Bretridge and Skiddy's Hospitals from fire having been built at the charge of the Corporation'.[3] (While the insurers are not named, only the REA and London Assurance were operating here at this time). The insurance companies had, naturally, a vested interest in ensuring that when a fire broke out, as little damage as possible was done in order to reduce the amount of a claim. In the absence of public fire services they set up 'Fire Engine Establishments' which were, effectively, private fire brigades, complete with premises, engines, equipment, and part-time firemen in distinctive uniforms. The system of local agents operated along the lines of today's franchise system, with provincial offices expected to embrace the 'corporate identity' of the parent body in matters such as rules and regulations, *modus operandi,* uniforms, etc. The engines and *matériel* were supplied by the head office of the company.

The REA lost no time in providing fire engines for their Cork office, the first company to so do, and they never lost an opportunity of reminding their rivals or the general public that they were the first to maintain, 'Fire Engines of various dimensions, at a considerable annual expense, for the general safety of the City'. Having established their Cork office in January 1799, by the following July an engine house had been located at Carey's Lane, off St Patrick's Street, where 'Two very capital ENGINES' were on stand-by. The 'Keeper of the Engines' was Francis Geary, an instrument maker with a shop in nearby Paul Street. (Geary was

A Royal Exchange Assurance poster dated 2 July 1799 advising Corkonians of the provision of 'Two very capital Engines ... [for] the Protection of this great Trading city'. At this time their 'Engine-House' was in Carey's Lane, off St Patrick's Street.

as we have seen, variously, Keeper of the parish engines of St Paul's and St Peter's).

It may seem strange that the REA, who, on the admission of their official historian, had tarried so long in coming to Cork due to the uncertain political situation outside the safety of the Pale, should decide to locate in the southern capital only months after the Rebellion of 1798. The Rebellion, however, had practically been a non-event in Cork City. With the exception of the lawyer brothers John and Henry Sheares, both hanged for their involvement, the city produced no notable rebel leaders. Indeed, mindful of the fact that local businesses depended to a great extent on the continued patronage of the Royal Navy and the large military garrison, the loyalist Mayor and corporation had railed against it and offered a reward to anyone who would inform on a rebel.

Revolution aside, for the vast majority of people, everyday life in Cork city at the dawn of the nineteenth century was grim. Sanitation was practically non-existent, and the disposal of human waste from the teeming lanes and streets posed a major problem. Bull-baiting in the streets, faction-fights, murderous attacks by gangs of cut-throats, and the unexpected appearance of the press-gang were common occurrences. Outbreaks of disease such as typhus fever, smallpox, and cholera occurred from time to time. Outbreaks of fire often spread from the building of origin, sometimes resulting in scores of people being made homeless. When fire broke out in a thatched house in Cat Lane, off Barrack Street, on the evening of 23 August 1800, fifty homes were 'reduced to ashes, and the unfortunate occupiers reduced to a state of great misery.'[4] Clearly, the use of thatch was still tolerated as a roofing material (in the suburbs at any rate), slate being beyond the pocket of the ordinary man in the street. In the south suburbs, the nuns of Nano Nagle struggled resolutely against the odds to impart an education to the daughters of the poor. (Another local street, Rutland Street, was once the home of Mary Aikenhead, a Protestant, who would later establish the Roman Catholic religious congregation, the Sisters of Charity). And as the curtain came down on the closing days of the eighteenth century, the south side would witness one of the biggest fires seen in Cork for years: a blaze recorded in some detail by the diarist of the Ursuline sisters from her convent situated practically across the road:

> On the night of the 8th of December [1799] while the nuns were reciting Matins the whole choir was filled with a glare of light, which every instant became more terrific. The alarm of course was great and but too well founded.
>
> The light proceeded from an immense fire which burst out in a large Sugar House built on the ground formerly occupied by an Augustinian Abbey, and which now shared the same fate as some other concerns erected there before, in consequence, as tradition says, of such buildings been [sic] raised on consecrated ground.
>
> The proximity of the Convent to the stores made the communication of

the fire from one to the other almost inevitable. The cry through the streets was – that all the waters of the Lee, could not extinguish such flames, an assertion which was easily credited by those who knew that beside the combustible nature of the sugar itself there was a paper manufactory attached to the stores, and within them at the moment no less than 1300 barrels of coals! The fire raged for some time without paying its respects to the Convent, otherwise than by an abundance of sparks. At last the chimney of the Infirmary was in a blaze, upon which the gardens were filled with the friends of the Establishment, nothing less was expected than the *rentrée* into the *beau-monde* of such of the Sisters as had no mind to become holocausts in the space of ten minutes!

Sr M. Magdalene Clarke mingled a little merriment with the dismay of that night's scare, and kept up the credit of the Convent, if not for courage at least for loyalty. One or two Gentlemen who got on the terrace to watch the progress of the fire towards the Monastery, and concert measures for its preservation were every instant entreated by Sr M. Magdalene, to "take care of the ships". They politely took great pains to convince her that the ships were in no danger whatsoever – that there was not one ship within reach of the flames.

She was not to be consoled – her lamentation over the ships continued to the great astonishment of the stranger Gentlemen who could not conceive, whence arose her extraordinary interest for his Majesty's Navy – but to the greater amusement of those who knew that Sr. Magdalene was only speaking her own language, and therefore could not make strangers comprehend, that her uneasiness was all occasioned by the chips in the Cooper's Yard which she naturally expected should every moment take fire!

Still neither the ships or chips or fire itself did any material injury here, the flames which caught the infirmary chimney were quickly extinguished – and the sparks though they fell thickly on the roof and walls did not spread owing chiefly to their having been thoroughly damped by the fire engines which played on them; or rather owing to the shield of Providence, that warded off the danger, and to the prayers of the glorious Protectress of this Monastery, on whose Conception the Calamity threatened the Monastery.[5]

At the time of the fire the sugar refinery was owned by Cork Huguenots David, George and Anthony Perrier.[6] Sugar refineries, with their giant boiling-pans, were notoriously susceptible to fire. The sugar, imported from the West Indies, would not have been easily ignited, but once alight as a result of the application of external heat, would have burned willingly and fiercely with great intensity and, being rich in carbon, produced volumes of thick, black smoke. If, as is likely, the sugar was stored in jute bags, spontaneous combustion may have occurred. Additionally, finely ground sugar and sugar dust can very easily give rise to dust explosions of great severity when dispersed in air. When sugar is bagged the sugar dust and lint on the bags, and the crevices between the bags assists the rapid spread of fire. The great quantities of black smoke and intense heat would doubtlessly have kept the firefighters, lacking even the most rudimentary breathing apparatus, back a respectable distance: small wonder that Tuckey recorded that the blaze 'raged with unabating fury until the next day, by which, property to a large amount was consumed'.[7]

On the cusp of the New Year the Cork fire engines were again in action. The *Hibernian Chronicle* for 30 December 1799 narrated how:

> Last Sunday a fire broke out in the house of Timothy M'Carthy, a very industrious poor man, in Broad Lane, which occasioned much uneasiness to the neighbourhood, but by timely assistance it was soon got under, and not before every article of this poor man's furniture was broken and thrown out of the windows, his bed and other articles burnt, which may be said to be his *all,* and he is thereby rendered an object for the commiseration of the Benevolent. Benefactions, towards his relief, will be received by the Printer hereof.

The advent of the war against the French under their Emperor, Napoleon Bonaparte, provided the fillip that the Cork economy so badly needed. The trade in provisions reached great proportions, and Cork's Butter Market, already famous by the dawn of the new century, steadily increased its business until its products were counted in millions. Much of this new-found prosperity was engendered through local businesses victualling the capital ships of the Royal Navy at Cove, then a major naval station on the Western Approaches. It seemed that with the passing of the 1800 Act of Union that prosperity increased nation-wide. A new air of hope and confidence was discernible and the time seemed ripe for economic expansion. This was reflected in the ever-growing number of insurance companies establishing offices in Cork.

John Connor's *Cork Directory* (1812) lists nine insurance companies as having offices in the city. These included the REA, the Atlas, the Westminster, the General or Phoenix Insurance Company of Ireland, the Dublin Insurance Company, the Globe Insurance Company of London, the Hibernian Insurance Company, the Eagle, and the British and Irish United Fire Insurance Office. By 1826, the same *Directory* shows the number had grown to twenty-one and the *Post Office Directory* for 1844 lists fifty-eight. However, during the greater portion of the nineteenth century when the insurance companies were associated with firefighting, it appears that no more than four maintained fire engines in Cork city. They were: the REA (the first), the Atlas, the West of England, and for a short period, the Scottish Union. As the focus of this research is on companies that participated in operational firefighting, these are the ones with which we are primarily concerned.

THE ROYAL EXCHANGE ASSURANCE (REA).

Prior to opening a dedicated office in Cork, their affairs were looked after by Messrs Hugh Jameson and Sons, from about 1781. From 1799, the company was represented by Austen Shinkwin and Sons. At this time, their office was on St Patrick's Street, with the engine house in nearby Carey's Lane. In about the year 1815, the company moved to 61 South Mall to a building formerly used as a barracks, from 1803, by The King's German Legion, a mercenary corps. Their engine house was in nearby Queen Street (A word of caution: it should be noted that the numbering of the South Mall was revised in the early 1840s. Nowadays, the street numbers run westwards on the south side, cross to the north side, and end at the corner of Parnell Place. Prior to the 1840s, the street numbers commenced at Grand Parade and ran eastwards on the Mall's north side. Thus the pre-1840s No.61 became No.5). In about the year 1824, the old structure was substantially rebuilt and a dedicated fire station opened. To mark the opening, the REA commissioned sculptor John Hogan to execute a statue in pinewood composite of *Minerva* (Roman goddess of Security, Wisdom, and the Arts), to be placed in a niche on the facade of the building, a work generally regarded as Hogan's first public commission. The old premises were demolished in 1889, the *Minerva* being acquired for the Crawford Art Gallery where it reposes to this day.

The Shinkwins were succeeded by John Leslie as Agent. Leslie died when his son was only nine years old and the Agency was held jointly by Robert Evory and the young James Edward Leslie until the latter completed his third-level education, when he was appointed sole Agent, which office he held until his death in 1888. The new Agents were Messrs Hussey and Townsend, 18 South Mall.[8]

One unequivocal indicator as to the performance of an insurance company was the amount of stamp duty paid to the government quarterly. The returns for the quarter ended 25 March 1822 show that the Atlas, with £909 18s.7d paid, was well in front of its nearest rival, the REA, which submitted £709 15s.9d.[9] By 1835, however, the REA had taken the lead with £4,721 submitted as against the Atlas' £4,000. (The National Insurance Company of Ireland was in second place with £4,337). A Mr Forde, who was Chief Clerk with Hussey and Townsend, recalled, 'During my time it was a race between us [the REA] and the Atlas, the Sun, and the West of England. I well remember how elated Mr. Leslie (our then Agent) would be when his quarterly payment was the largest.'[10]

Stamp duty, which had been introduced in Ireland in 1785 and was (unsuccessfully) petitioned to the Irish House of Commons in 1786, was eventually repealed in 1869. In 1968, the REA combined with the Guardian Assurance Company to become the Guardian Royal Exchange, which amalgamated with AXA.

The Royal Exchange Assurance fire station at 5 South Mall as drawn by architect Samuel Belcher *c*.1840. In the foreground is a uniformed member of the REA Fire Engine Establishment. (Courtesy of Don Trotter)

Minerva by John Hogan (1800-1858) which graced the front of the REA fire station on South Mall. (Courtesy of the Crawford Art Gallery)

THE ATLAS ASSURANCE COMPANY.

The Atlas had its origins in a meeting of businessmen at Will's Coffee House, Cornhill, London, on 19 December 1807. Agencies were established in Glasgow, Edinburgh, Manchester, and Ireland, and within two years the company was issuing policies on risks in the West Indies. An unusual feature of their fire policy was a Rent Clause, which for up to six months, paid a sum equal to any rent that one might lose following the loss of one's property in a fire.[11]

The Atlas lost no time in locating in Cork after its formation. In 1808, they appointed Edward Daly their Agent.[12] An advertisement in Connor's *Directory* for 1812 shows their 'Committee for executing Fire Policies' comprised Daniel Callaghan, Joshua Carroll, Henry Kellett, Abraham Lane, and Sir Anthony Perrier. The office at this time was on St Patrick's Street, where 'The public will please to observe, that the Atlas Office possesses the advantage of having a complete Fire Engine Establishment in this City'.[13] By the 1820s, they had moved to 'the corner of Cook Street and South Mall' (No.66 South Mall), with the fire station located at the top of Cook Street. One wonders how many people, waiting patiently in line to cash their cheques or carry out some other financial transaction, realize that the rarefied atmosphere of AIB's regional headquarters once echoed to the whinnying of horses and the clamour and bustle of a fire brigade turning-out? 66 South Mall was also the address of the Cork Pipe Water Company, of which Sir Anthony Perrier was Treasurer. The present magnificent representational building was erected during the early years of the twentieth century as Head Office for the Munster and Leinster Bank.

A fire policy for the year 1855 shows that the Agents in Cork were William Lumley and Anthony Perrier, and the 'Committee for the Management of the affairs of the Company with power to grant Assurances and to execute Policies' comprised Joseph H. Carroll, William Clear, Daniel Donegan, William Large, and Thomas Somerville Reeves.

The Atlas overall enjoyed rapid expansion, and from the mid-1880s, its overseas business was particularly successful. It made steady progress during the twentieth century, being acquired by its old rival, the REA, in 1959, which found its life business and overseas connections particularly attractive.

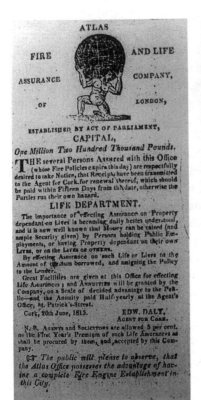

Above: A conjectural image of a fireman of the Atlas Fire Engine Establishment outside No.66 South Mall which housed the offices of the Atlas Assurance Company and the Cork Pipe Water Company. The entrance to the Atlas 'engine house' was just around the corner at the top of Cook Street. The representational building which stands on the site today is the regional headquarters of AIB.

Left: An advertisement in *Cork Mercantile Chronicle* for 26 June 1815 advising that 'The Atlas possesses the advantage of having a complete Fire Engine Establishment in this City'. (Courtesy of Cork City Libraries)

THE WEST OF ENGLAND FIRE INSURANCE COMPANY.

The West of England Fire Insurance Company was established on Christmas Eve 1807 with a capital of £600,000, after a town near Exeter in England was devastated in a major fire.

Connor's *Directory* for 1826 shows the West of England office situated at 5 Charlotte Quay where, 'In case of Fire, a most powerful Engine is always ready for the service of the Public, at the Company's Engine House'. The Agents were Thomas Harvey and Son of the well-known Cork Quaker family, later to be succeeded by G. N. Harvey.[14] Some years later the address of the office and engine house is given as 10 Charlotte Quay, now the site of the Capuchin Friary. *The Post Office General Directory* for 1844/45 lists them at 13 Anderson's Quay and by 1863, they appear in Robert H. Laing's *Directory* at 11 Anderson's Quay.

In 1890, their remaining fire engine was offered to Cork Fire Brigade, who declined to accept it, it being recorded, abstrusely, that it was then 'sent away'. In December 1889, the West of England engine in Limerick was offered to the municipal fire brigade there, who accepted it.

THE SCOTTISH UNION INSURANCE COMPANY.

Alexander Henderson, Lord Provost of Edinburgh, was the prime mover behind the formation of the Scottish Union Insurance Company in November 1824, with the famous novelist Sir Walter Scott as its first Governor. The company stationed fire engines at important centres and contributed towards the maintenance of the engines.

In 1833, the year it was granted its Royal Charter, the company opened its first Irish office, in the north, followed by Dublin in 1837.[15]

It seems the company located a fire engine in Cork within a short time of appointing an Agent. When fire broke out in the stables of James O'Neill in Pembroke Street in the early hours of 23 May 1837, the first insurance engine on the scene was that of the Scottish Union, followed closely by the West of England, the Atlas, the REA, and the Christ Church parish pump. However, the involvement of the Scottish Union in operational firefighting in Cork appears to have been relatively short-lived. An advertisement in the *Cork Constitution* on 2 January 1840 names the Agent as Eustace Harris, 50 George's Street (a premises now occupied by booksellers *Liam Ruiséal Teo.*) where 'a superior Fire Engine is kept in constant readiness'. By 1844, however, the *County and City of Cork Post Office General Directory* shows that the Agent is now S.P. Townsend, 9 South Mall, and the insurance offices maintaining fire engines are listed as the Atlas, REA, and West of England only. W. Forbes Gray, the company's historian, recounts that:

In 1848 there was much unrest in Ireland, and both Fire and Life business had to be temporarily suspended in the disturbed areas. Matters grew worse in 1849, which led first of all to the stoppage of Fire business throughout the whole of Ireland, and then to the limiting of life business to Dublin, Belfast and some northern agencies. There was a general resumption of business in 1856, tranquility having been restored.[16]

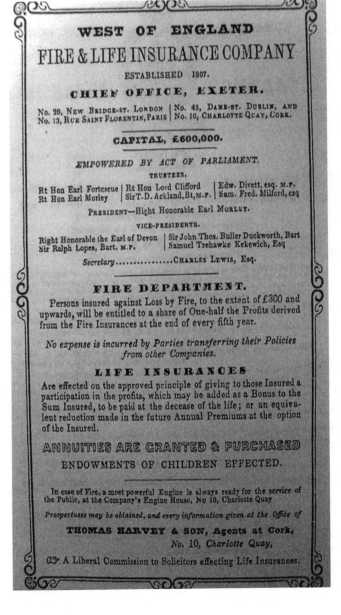

An advertisement from the *Cork Post Office Directory* (1844) for the West of England Fire and Life Insurance Company announcing that 'In case of Fire, a most powerful Engine is always ready for the service of the Public, at the Company's Engine House, No 10 Charlotte Quay'. (Courtesy of Cork City Libraries)

THE SCOTTISH UNION
FIRE AND LIFE INSURANCE COMPANY,
INCORPORATED BY ROYAL CHARTER.

CAPITAL—FIVE MILLION STERLING.

OFFICES in Edinburgh—No. 47, George-street. London—No. 449, West Strand. Dublin—No. 52, Dame-street.

Unquestionable Security, combined with Low Rates of Premium, calculated on Scientific Principles, are distinguishing features of this corporation.

IN THE FIRE DEPARTMENT

Losses by Fire are *immediately paid*; and property of every description is insured on the most advantageous terms. This Company pays annually to Government upwards of TWENTY THOUSAND POUNDS for Duty on Fire Insurances on Property in Great Britain.

IN THE LIFE DEPARTMENT

Assurances may be effected at Reduced Rates, without Profits, or at a higher premium with Participation in Profits, of which Two Thirds are retured at regular periods, *without being subject to any deduction for charges of Management.*

Prospectus, containing the Tables of Rates and Conditions of Assurance, may be had at the above mentioned Offices, or at any of the Company's Establishments throughout Great Britain and Ireland.

EUSTACE HARRIS, Agent,
50, George's-Street, Cork.

N.B.—A superior Fire Engine is kept in constant readiness. (937.) Dec. 28,

An advertisement from the *Cork Constitution* dated 2 April 1840 for the Scottish Union Fire and Life Insurance Company advising that 'a superior Fire Engine is kept in constant readiness' at their premises at 50 George's Street. (Courtesy of Cork City Libraries)

THE INSURANCE FIRE BRIGADES

THE FIREMEN.

The advent of the insurance brigades gave Cork City something which it had never had before: an organized approach to fire suppression. As reliance on the parish pumps diminished, the insurance brigades acquired a certain status as quasi-public institutions, with their firemen regarded as holding a kind of public office. Author Daniel Defoe, writing some years after the publication of his best-seller *Robinson Crusoe* (based on the adventures of real sailor Alexander Selkirk who departed Kinsale for the New World in 1703), observed that:

The several ensurance offices have each of them a certain sett of men, who they keep in constant pay, and who they furnish with tools proper to the work, and to whom they give jack-caps of leather, able to keep them from hurt, if brick or timber, or anything of not too great a bulk, should fall upon them; these men make it their business to be ready at call, all hours, and night or day, to assist in case of fire; and it must be acknowledged, they are very dexterous, bold, diligent and successful. These they call Fire-men, but with a kind of odd contradiction in the title, for they are really most of them Water-men.[17]

The London offices had, for years, when recruiting their part-time firefighters, given preference to men who made their living on the River Thames. These 'Watermen' were perceived as being used to long, unsocial hours and hard work, disciplined and unfazed in the face of danger. The insurance companies hired them on the explicit understanding that, on receipt of an alarm of fire, they could leave their place of work immediately and make straight for the fire station with all dispatch. It may be less than coincidence that the Cork 'fire stations' were all located within striking distance of the River Lee: the REA at Queen Street/South Mall; the Atlas at Cook Street/South Mall; and the West of England on Charlotte Quay/Anderson's Quay.

General employees of the insurance offices, such as porters and messengers, also acted as part-time firemen.[18] The firemen were under the direct control of the brigade's foreman or engineer, who, in turn, was directed by the Agent. (In some cases the post of engineer and foreman appears to have been amalgamated). He lived on, or near, the company's fire station. The *Cork Directory* for 1812 lists Thomas Bennett of Brown Street as engineer of the REA, whose station was then in nearby Carey's Lane (Bennett, as we have noted earlier, was appointed in 1808 to take charge of the St Paul's fire engine). An advertisement in the *Cork Constitution* in April 1838 lists John Cosgrave as resident engineer of the West of England Fire Engine Establishment at 5 Charlotte Quay; the *County and City of Cork Directory* for 1843 shows that D. Mc Carthy was engineer of the Atlas at Cook Street; and James Daly was now West of England engineer at Charlotte Quay, and in 1863 John Connors was resident engineer of the REA on the South Mall. These men were full-time employees, proficient in elementary hydraulics, pump operation, and firefighting techniques. They were selected by the directors of the insurance companies for their leadership qualities.

The offices required a substantial bond from prospective firemen (some English offices insisted on sums of up to £100), 'the bond of themselves and two respectable citizens for their good conduct and faithful discharge of the trust reposed in them.' In spite of this, there appears to have been no difficulty in filling positions. Panels were set up whence vacancies were filled. The competition for places was so fierce that the offices would hire only the best men. Each man was obliged to name two sponsors, one of whom was usually his full-time employer, the other some well-known man-of-affairs. Each recruit had to be of good character, literate, in good health, and under twenty-nine years of age at the time of joining. An examination of one such brigade, that of the REA for the year 1812, shows that the average height was 5ft 5in. In a brigade of thirty-two, the tallest man was 5ft 10¼ in. and the smallest 4ft 11½ inches. The average age was thirty-one, the oldest being thirty-seven and the youngest twenty-three.[19] While the exact number of firemen employed by the insurance companies in Ireland is unknown, Pearson estimates that the total number for Britain and Ireland in the 1820s was no more than 1,000. Generally, under an Act of Queen Anne (1707), the maximum number allowed in each brigade was thirty: the number of exemptions from naval impressment allowed by the Admiralty. [20]

The minutes of the Atlas Office for January 1809 record the rates of pay for their firemen:

> For attendance at Fires and Watches of six hours, each attendance:
> Five shillings, the Foreman.
> Three shillings and sixpence, the Engineer.
> Two shillings the Firemen.
>
> And for Chimneys:
> One shilling and sixpence, the Foreman.
> One shilling, the Engineer.
> Six pence, the Firemen.
> Not more than four men to attend a Chimney Fire.[21]

These were the agreed rates of pay for ten companies, including the REA. In addition, each member was paid an annual 'retaining fee', while the brigade that arrived first on the scene of a fire could expect a special payment from the company to be divided among the men. Unusually (for the period under review), at least one insurance company insisted on their men taking out insurance on their lives. From 1801, the REA required each man to affect a policy on his life for £100, the company making a contribution towards the premium.

On joining a company's 'fire engine establishment', the recruit was obliged to subscribe to its Code of Practice and discipline regulations. These rules and regulations were exact and detailed. One such set of rules is that of the Norwich Union. Because they run to several pages, of necessity they are condensed here:

RULES AND REGULATIONS TO BE OBSERVED BY THE FIREMEN BELONGING TO THE NORWICH UNION FIRE OFFICE.

A. That every Fireman shall appear on the first Tuesday in every month at the Engine-House, clean and in full uniform, at twelve o'clock precisely, when the roll shall be called; all absent at that time, or not appearing clean and in uniform, shall be fined One Shilling.

B. That any Fireman attending on the first Tuesday in every month in a state of intoxication, or discovered to be drunk at any time on duty, or when dressed in uniform of the Office, to be fined Two Shillings and Sixpence.

C. That any Fireman challenging another Fireman to fight, shall be fined Two Shillings and Sixpence; any one striking another to be fined Five Shillings; and if the man so struck returns the blow, they shall each be fined Five shillings.

D. That every Fireman shall attend a brother Fireman's funeral, clean and in full uniform, or forfeit Five Shillings.

E. That any Fireman absenting himself from any fire be fined Seven Shillings, unless he can produce satisfactory reasons to the Engineer for such absence.

F. That if any Fireman is observed throwing water or firebrands over another Fireman, or in any other manner annoying his comrade while on duty, he shall be fined Two Shillings and Sixpence for each offence.

G. That any Fireman ordered to turn-out and not immediately attending, shall be fined Two Shillings and Sixpence, and discharged.

H. That when the Firemen meet for any purpose, no stranger shall be admitted into the room without permission of the Engineer. The Fireman introducing him without such permission to be fined One Shilling.

I. That any Fireman cursing or swearing, or using obscene language at any meeting, or elsewhere, shall be fined Threepence for each oath, or each time he uses such language.

J. Every Fireman is at liberty to wear his uniform on Sunday, provided he wears the whole of it, but if he appears in part only, he will be fined One Shilling for the first offence and Two Shillings and Sixpence for the second.

K. On an alarm of Fire, every Fireman is to make the greatest haste to get on his jacket and helmet, and proceed to the Engine-House.

L. The first Fireman who gives the Alarm, and orders out horses, shall have Two Shillings and Sixpence over and above his wages.

M. So soon as one Fireman arrives with his jacket and helmet on, the Engine must proceed with the greatest speed to the premises on fire.

N. Whenever our Fire-Engine arrives first at a premises on fire, the Drivers will be paid Five Shillings each, and Ten Shillings will be paid into the Fund of the Office Firemen.

O. The Foreman being No.1, the Deputy No.2, the Engineer No.3, and in succession to No.24, the Fireman present having the lowest number on his hat or helmet is to take command of the Engine and Men until the arrival of a member with a lower number, or the Foreman.

P. Any Fireman disobeying the order of the member with the lowest number present, shall forfeit Five Shillings and be discharged.[22]

The story has been told that, in the very early years of the insurance fire brigades, if a brigade arrived at a fire and found that the property was not insured
with them, they would turn around and return to their station with no attempt
being made to extinguish the blaze. Another suggestion has been that the
'wrong' brigade, far from assisting the 'right' one on its arrival, would actually
hinder their efforts at firefighting by perhaps cutting their hoses or generally
causing mayhem. Where these stories originated no one has yet found out.
Bertram Williams thought he had traced it to an after-dinner speech towards
the end of the nineteenth century; this, in turn, was probably based on a report
in the newspapers some time previously of an altercation in the United States
between two volunteer fire departments, notorious for their rivalry, each of
whom claimed that they were entitled to extinguish a particular fire.[23]

When one considers it objectively, it stands to reason that no fire brigade
could allow a blaze to develop unchecked; the possibility being that their company insured, if not the adjacent property, then very likely the property next to
that. In any event, fire historians are highly sceptical of the 'rivalry' stories. For
my own part, I have found no evidence to suggest that by the time fire engine
establishments were set up in Cork (early 1800s) that any untoward behaviour
ever took place. On the contrary, there are many reports of fires where co-
operation between the offices appears to have been a foregone conclusion.

THE FIRE ALARM.

During the early years of the nineteenth century, Cork City had no regular police
force.[24] The magistrates were dependent on the military of the Cork garrison for
the preservation of law and order. In practical terms, this meant that the troops
turned out only where there was an extremely serious situation developing. In such
cases, the military would be drawn up in front of the crowd, arms at the ready, and
the magistrate or officer in charge would read the Riot Act, exhorting the people
to disperse peacefully. Additionally, the military frequently responded with the barrack fire engines to assist at large fires in the city. Notwithstanding, the various
General Officers Commanding objected to their men being employed on such
duties which they perceived, rightly, to be the responsibility of the civil powers.

During the hours of darkness, the city streets were patrolled by the night
watchmen, a corps of approximately fifty 'old, decrepit men on whom no
reliance could be placed', and who each received sixpence a week from the
corporation.[25] One commentator described them thus:

> Another peculiarity of Cork cannot fail to excite the astonishment of strangers
> – namely, the wholly unprotected state of the streets at night. The safety of the
> city is then intrusted to a few decrepit old men, armed with poles surmounted

by rusty bayonets. In leaving their lives and property thus exposed, the people of Cork evince a beautiful reliance on Providence, most affecting to contemplate in a distrustful and sophisticated age like ours.

The nightly "guardians" of the city, when they do not happen to be drunk or asleep in doorways, cry the hour in a manner which renders it impossible to understand them. They make use of a peculiar howl which baffles all description…Commencing in a key between a whine and an ullagone, his voice gradually swells into the following outlandish cry:- "Aw pa-haast alieavan a koolohawk, a fay-hay-hay-hay-hay hair noight, haw-haw-haw-haw-hawl's weigh-haw" [past eleven o'clock, a fair night, all's well], terminating the whole with a vicious yell, extremely startling, and even terrifying to nervous people who may happen to be awake, or be awakened by it.[26]

In any event, if the watchman discovered a fire, he was required to make his way as fast as his arthritic legs could carry him to the nearest engine house and alert the engineer. The following day, he would be rewarded by the insurance company with a small sum for his vigilance. A messenger, perhaps one of the engineer's children, would be sent off to summon the firemen from their homes or, if by day, their places of work. They were expected to report to the engine house without delay. Presently, if the fire was serious enough, the hue-and-cry would be taken up by other watchmen (and later, the police), by passers-by, by the church wardens of the various churches who would start ringing the church bells in reverse peal, and by the military in Elizabeth Fort or Cat Fort (both off Barrack Street) who would commence the 'beating to arms'. The parish engines, of course, also responded to calls of fire well into the nineteenth century.

The heavy, cumbersome engines were pulled to the scene of the fire by the firemen and hastily-recruited helpers. On the hilly streets of Cork, the only way to stop them when going downhill was to turn the engine abruptly at right-angles to the gradient: a manoeuvre fraught with danger for the men. Later, when the engines were modified to accept horses, the firefighters would proceed to the engine house, release the horses from the stables, tackle them to the engine, and turn out.

AT THE FIRE.

Charles F.T. Young, civil engineer and enthusiastic volunteer fireman, recalled the *modus operandi* for getting a manual fire engine to work:

On receiving a call for a fire the horses are immediately to be fetched – unless the engine is run out by hand – and put to; and whilst this is doing, the men belonging to the Brigade are to assemble in their uniforms, helmets, hatchets, and accompany the engine to the place where the fire requires their attention.

A conjectural image of the Atlas Fire Engine Establishment passing the statue of King George II on the Grand Parade *en route* to a fire breakout.

On arriving at the point where the fire is, take up a position within a convenient distance, so as to command both the fire and the water, whether it be a plug, a well or a pond, at the same time keeping the engine so placed that no injury may happen to it from falling walls or burning materials, as if these did not hurt the engine, they would be sure to inconvenience the men working it, which would by no means be desirable.

Next take out the horses and remove them to the nearest convenient place, and settle the engine in the position it is to occupy whilst at work, locking the fore carriage, to prevent it moving, by means of the pin supplied for this purpose, and when the suction hose is in place and in the water, and the delivery hose screwed on, and the man at the branch, the men at the levers may gradually begin pumping from slow speed at first, up to the best they can do.[27]

On arriving on the fire ground, each man knew exactly what his initial duties were. Again, we are indebted to the Norwich Union whose explicit directions to their firemen have survived:

NORWICH UNION FIRE ENGINE ESTABLISHMENT: INSTRUCTIONS FOR EXTINGUISHING FIRES.

1. Arrived at the premises on fire, the first object is to choose a situation for the Engine to play from, and on doing this, wherever it is possible, it is desirable to get to the windward of the premises on fire, the current of air greatly assisting the discharge of the water in a dense column, whilst playing against the wind scatters the water and greatly diminishes the force.

2. A canal, tank or reservoir are to be preferred to play from when the pipes or leather hose will reach; when they will not reach, recourse must be had to the plugs of the Water Works Company. The Fireman who arrives second at the Engine-House (always excepting No's 1, 2 and 3) should give notice of the Fire to the nearest Turncock.

3. The Foreman or Fireman in command of the Engine, should, as much as possible, recommend to persons dwelling in the vicinity of the fire, to fasten their doors and window-shutters: and to the next-door neighbours not to remove any of their Goods if there is a Party Wall between their dwelling-house or warehouse and the premises on fire. Should there be a Party Wall in which there are one or two doorways or communications with the premises on fire, two or three Firemen, with buckets, being stationed at such doorway or communications, may generally prevent the extension of the fire. Should the fire, however, not be adequately stopped by the buckets, the pipe of a fire engine, if it can be spared, should be directed to the communications.

4. The branchpipe of the leathern hose is at all times to be held and directed by No. 3, and one Fireman to assist him.

5. The Foreman should as early as possible send notice of the Fire to the Office, and obtain Copies of Policies as to any or what property is insured with the Company, and on receipt of the particulars must appoint a Guard or such other means as appear best calculated to preserve the stock, furniture, buildings, or other property, insured with the Company.

6. The Firemen are at all times to keep in view that the Fire Engine Establishment is the property of, and is supported at the sole expense of the Company, and therefore is not subject to the control or orders of the police, military, or any person or persons whatsoever – that the orders of the Foreman and in his absence, of the Fireman in command of the Fire Engine are at all times to be implicitly obeyed.

7. The Foreman, or Fireman, in command is to remember that when premises are on fire they are the property of the Office in which they are insured, and therefore he must act according to his own judgment as to the best means of preserving the property in danger.[28]

One of the first duties of the engineer after arriving on the fire ground was to select his pumpers from the crowd. None of the Cork brigades was large enough to provide men for the actual firefighting *and* manning the pumps. The engines required up to twenty men to work them, ten manning the levers on either side.

In 1861, when two insurance engines were contracted to draw water from the river to supply the city watering carts, eighty-eight men had to be employed, at two shillings per man, per day, to work the engines [29]. Only the strongest men were picked, for it was back-breaking work. The engineer would be careful not to choose any 'messers' or slackers, but this would not deter the mob from stampeding the fire engines in the hope of being selected. Even as late as 1863, a *Cork Examiner* editorial railed against the 'dangerous assistance of semi-drunken volunteers'. At the same fire, on Morrison's Quay, the mob attempted to throw the engineer *and* engine of the REA into the river after a dispute arose over the selection of pumpers.[30] The engineer then took up position at the head of the engine, and, with all eyes on him, gave the command 'Down with the pump!', indicating which line of men should start pumping first. (The command 'Down with the pump' survived the demise of the manual fire engine and was used well into the age of the motor appliance until eventually replaced with 'Water on!').

Manning the fire pumps was an exhausting job. Even a team of the fittest men required a relief after only five minutes at work; therefore a second team was also selected as back-up. This gave a total of forty volunteers needed for each twenty-man engine; there might be several at a fire, to say nothing of the insurance firemen who were engaged in the actual firefighting operation. It was a labour-intensive business, and a costly one for the insurance companies. Each volunteer pumper was given a token of tin or copper (called a 'ticket') which he handed in at the insurance office on the following day to secure his payment.

A typical manual fire engine used by the insurance 'fire engine establishments'.

A 'Black Jack' drinking vessel. Volunteer pumpers, recruited on the fire ground to work the insurance companies' fire engines, were issued with a beer ration, often served in 'Black Jacks'. Merryweather, the famous fire engine manufacturers, state in their 1906 catalogue that the company had issued 'Black Jacks' as part of the standard equipment on their fire engines for more than 200 years.

Because of the thirsty nature of the work, in the early years, the companies provided liquid refreshments for the volunteer pumpers. This was supplied during the five-minute break from pumping. As the men pushed the levers up and down, they frequently accompanied the rhythm with a monotonous chant of 'Beer, oh! Beer, oh!' If the supply of beer was slow in forthcoming, the chant could rapidly change to 'No beer? No water!' and the pumping would come to an abrupt stop. The men's beer was carried on to the fire ground from the nearest hostelry in enormous leather drinking jugs called 'Black Jacks'.[31] Merryweather, the famous fire engine manufacturers, actually supplied Black Jacks with each new engine ordered: they are listed in their early catalogues as part of the normal equipment of a fire engine! The largest Black Jack held six gallons (forty eight pints), and it was regarded as a sign of weakness for a man to use more than one hand while quaffing from it.[32] Merryweather's catalogue for 1906 claimed that the firm had made Black Jacks for over 200 years; they were made in tandem with other leather fire products such as hose, buckets, and helmets. The catalogue states that they were made of 'the best stout oak bark tanned leather, hand sewn, pitched within and blacked outside'.

The 'refreshment period' was often abused. In 1808, the secretary of one insurance company was moved to write, 'The Directors certainly will not pay the bill for repairing the pump; the charge is absolutely infamous. The guzzling bill is almost as bad. I must trouble you for the particulars of the amount of £16.2s.0d for men working the engine and for beer'.[33] (The directors had complained that the charge of twenty pence a gallon for beer was 'grossly extravagant'). For all that, it was vitally important that the volunteers working the engine did not get drunk. Steadiness of pumping was all-important. For the largest fire engines, forty strokes per minute were regarded as the optimum rhythm. This produced an output of some 170 gallons per minute (773.5 litres) throwing a jet to a distance of about 120 feet.

Reckless pumping by drunken men could damage the valves or pistons on the fire engine. Even when the men were sober, over-exuberance in working the levers could have the same effect. The consequences of this happening could be disastrous in a city the size of Cork with only a limited pool of fire engines. This lack of expertise was to be referred to on numerous occasions in the reporting of Cork fires. When Isaac Morgan's bake house and flour mill on George's Quay went up in flames on the night of 18 November 1802, the *Cork Mercantile Chronicle* documented how:

> About eleven o'clock last night a general alarm of fire was spread throughout the City, by the drums of the garrison beating to arms and the … bells ringing the customary warning. The new bake house of Mr. Isaac Morgan was found to be in flames, including the fine steam engine. The necessity of practicing occasionally the exercise of the Fire Engines was last night eminently conspicuous. There was a very material inexpertness which we lamented in the persons who worked them. No zeal was wanting – nor was any labour denied – but it was obvious that if more skill had been on the side of those good feelings, more service perhaps, might have been done.[34]

And again, when fire broke out in Lane's Porter Brewery in 'St. Fin Barry's' late at night on 26 October 1807, the entire concern and Walker's Distillery were seriously threatened with complete destruction due to the inept use of the fire engines. The *Chronicle* again:

> With respect to the Fire Engines, we have one more remark to make … they were not brought to the place on fire with that promptitude which we have observed on every other occurrence of a similar calamity; they arrived late; and when they did arrive, it was not known where to station them. One engine was obviously deficient in the force with which it should have discharged the water, and consequently inefficient in a proportionate degree. So much depends on the salvation of the city upon the proper use and readiness of the Fire Engines – that we have felt it our duty to notice them as we have done, and we trust so unpleasant a discharge of it will never again devolve upon us.[35]

Cork's First Citizen, Mayor Thomas Dorman, was not impressed at the standard of firefighting when O'Callaghan's Stores in the city centre went up in flames in January 1812. From his remarks it is obvious, in spite of the insurance establishments' undoubted increased sophistication, that standards still fell very short of what was expected:

The Mayor.
Having witnessed how very deficient in appointments some of the Fire Engines were on the night of 21st inst., when brought to the relief of Messrs. O'Callaghan's Stores when on Fire, begs to leave to recommend to the Proprietors of Insurance Companies, and the Keepers of Parish Engines, a Monthly Inspection of their Engines and Appointments, in order to be better prepared for such an exigency.
He also submits to their consideration whether Sucker Pipes should not be attached to every Engine, which when Fires take place so near the River as on the above Night, the more effectual relief may be afforded to avert the ravages of the destructive Element.
Thomas Dorman, Mayor.[36]

FIRE HORSES.

The Cork insurance fire engines were certainly capable of being horse-drawn. A photograph survives of the handing-over of the remaining REA engine (commissioned in 1858) to Cork Fire Brigade in 1888 and both horse-drawn engine and horse are clearly visible. Records remain of insurance engines responding to fires well outside the city limits where only the use of horse-drawn appliances would have been feasible. To quote but one example, when fire destroyed Marino House at Marino Point, opposite Passage West, on the morning of 14 May 1860, the Atlas brigade attended.[37] However, when the bakery and general provisions store of Jeremiah Buckley on Shandon Street went up in flames in the early hours of an August morning in 1859, the Atlas and West of England engines arrived at the foot of the steep incline and, 'there was a slight delay … by there not being sufficient aid on the spot to drag them up the street'.[38] It may be deduced from this that horses were only used when the distance was sufficiently great to warrant them. In any case, just any old horse would not suffice for fire duties. James Compton Merryweather, the renowned fire engineer, enumerated the qualities of a horse selected for fire duties in his handbook:

It should be active, prompt, docile, endowed with an instinct scarcely distinguishable from intelligence, free from vice and have at the same time the necessary qualifications to make it serviceable.
The head should be small, the forehead broad and flat, the eye kindly, strong and fiery, yet gentle looking, the ears thin, fine and often erect, the

nostrils circular, dilated, and red on the inside, the lips soft, thin and hairless, the cheeks well marked. The neck of a good horse will form an arch or agreeable curve, from the poll to the withers.

Horses that are fit for the fire service will have thick wiry sinews, distinctly felt as separate cords, running from the arm to the fetlock. As to wind and eyes, the fire horse should be legally and absolutely sound. The usual method of testing the wind, by punching the horse or pinching the windpipe, is not satisfactory; the horse should be galloped.[39]

A fire horse had to learn not to be frightened by the sudden blare of a military band starting up, the crowded pavements of the Grand Parade, or the impulsive dash of a child across its path. It had to learn to cope with the clatter and bustle of the hansom cabs and jingles on the South Mall, and, above all, to remain calm and sedate amid the din and clamour of the fire ground. An article in the *Cork Examiner* claimed that the average horse selected for fire work understood its duties 'pretty thoroughly at the end of two days, and the least intelligent never takes longer than a week to learn the ropes… the system of training is entirely that of kindness, and recourse to the whip is never necessary'.[40]

En route to the fire, the horses were allowed to adopt the gait best suited to them, with the bridle open and the head and neck free from checks and curbs. There was always the danger of a horse falling in the street, especially on the hills, in wet or frosty weather. To counteract this, the type of shoe recommended consisted of a narrow rim of steel, nailed or pinned to the outer edge of the hoof, thus allowing the frog of the foot to grow naturally forming a non-slip pad. If conditions were particularly slippery, coarse bags would be wrapped around the hooves.

The last fire engine of the REA Fire Engine Establishment being handed over to Cork Fire Brigade at the City Hall in June 1888. The engine was newly-acquired by the REA in 1858. In 1888, Cork Fire Brigade comprised six permanent staff: Firemen Michael Ryan, Michael Thompson, William Gloyne, and Keane Mahony. To the right of the engine are Supt Mark Wickham and Turncock Patrick Higgins (on right, wearing képi).

On arrival at the fire ground the horses were unharnessed and led away to a quiet corner, out of danger of crashing floors and collapsing walls, quietly accepting tit-bits from the crowd.

AFTER THE FIRE.

On arriving back at the engine house, the firemen's duties often took up almost as much time as they had actually spent on firefighting. Then, as now, every-thing had to be left in 'shipshape' order for the next call, which could happen ten minutes later or ten days later. The man responsible for the horse or horses was called 'coach', He saw to watering it, feeding it, and ensuring it had plenty of fresh straw. If brought back sweating, it was thoroughly cleaned down and dried. Nutrition was all-important. Hay was regarded as an inferior fodder for a fire horse, as it was not considered strengthening enough. It was given only sparingly and then made palatable by the addition of a sprinkling of salt water. Oats were much preferred – 'old, heavy, dry and sweet'. As a special treat, bran-mash laced with treacle would be given, which horses loved.

The fire engine itself was subjected to a thorough examination, especially when the pumpers recruited from the crowd had been particularly unruly and there was a possibility of valve or piston damage. Everything would be checked for 'soundness' and to ensure that the pump engine was quite dry. If it had been pumping dirty water, clean water was pumped through it. All the various small tools and items of equipment were cleaned down and replaced on the engine in an orderly fashion.

The leather fire hoses, used almost exclusively until the 1880s, required spe-cial attention. In order to give them a semblance of flexibility, they had to be greased down with a cocktail of tallow and cod-oil called 'dubbing' (aka 'dubbin'). Particular care had to be given to the seams in order to keep them watertight. Since the days of Jan van der Heiden, almost 140 years earlier, the method of making delivery hose had remained virtually unchanged. They were basically strips of hide sewn together, by hand, at the seams. In 1808, an American firm, Sellers and Pennock of Philadelphia, substituted rivets which proved a great success. But another eleven years were to pass before one Jacob Perkins introduced them into these islands.

Leather hose was made only from the best 'butts, tanned with oak bark, cut in lengths not exceeding 4ft 9in and only from the hind or prime parts of the butt, excluding all neck and belly'. It was very strong and durable and well able to withstand the rigours of the fire ground. Easily repaired, with due care and attention it was expected to have a lifespan of some fifty years. It did, however, have many disadvantages. On account of its bulk and weight, leather delivery hose was only made in forty-foot lengths with gunmetal couplings at either end. The weight of such a length of two-inch dry hose was 23.5kg. By contrast, the weight of a 25m length of modern 70mm delivery hose is about 14kg. Being so inflexible it was very difficult to handle and its bulk occupied much valuable space on the fire engine.

Because the leather was so thick with frequent seams, in long lines the flow of water was greatly retarded due to friction loss, resulting in a substantial difference between pump pressure and nozzle pressure. The coming of the steam fire engine saw its eventual demise due to its inability to withstand pressures greater than 120lbs per square inch (six bar). It was superseded by the invention of hose with a flaxen sleeve, known as 'canvas' hose, which was woven entirely by hand. Canvas hose was, at first, unlined, and relied on the swelling of the fibres when wet to give it a degree of water tightness. Later, a waterproof lining was added. If the hose rivets were dirty, they were scraped with a putty knife and finished off with a wire card. If required, couplings were highly polished with 'brick dust' or 'rotten stone', with particular attention being given to ensure that the leather washers on the female couplings were in place and clean and free from grit. The washers were rubbed with Neat's Foot oil to keep them supple. Both oil and dubbing could be purchased from Richard Stephenson's store on the North Mall.

Finally, when all was finished to the satisfaction of the Agent and engineer, the men would be dismissed. Tired and weary from the rigours and dangers of the night's firefighting, they would make their way home in the small hours through the deserted, gloomy streets of Cork. On occasion, an equally great, albeit different, danger was lurking, waiting, in the shadows:

> Impressment is carried out with far less discretion in Cork than in Dublin. Here sailors are seized quite openly in the streets.
> Charles Etienne Coquebert de Montbret.[41]

Impressment by the notorious press gangs had been an unsavoury feature of life in Cork and other ports for years. As a result of wretched conditions on board both naval and merchant ships, and often brutish officers, it is estimated that upwards of 40,000 men were lost to the British fleets up to 1801. In their frantic search for more sailors, liberal use was made of the press gangs. Men would be seized like common criminals, viciously assaulted if they resisted, hauled to the riverside followed by keening wives and lovers, and sent down in boats to Cove where the fleet assembled. By 1805, the year of the Battle of Trafalgar, it is thought that one third of the Royal Navy was mustered in this fashion. The great British naval commander, Horatio Nelson, was ashamed of it. He wrote, 'Something should be attempted to make our seamen, at the din of war, fly to our navy, instead of flying from it'.[42]

Insurance firemen, because of their importance, were spared impressment under an Act of Parliament (6 Anne, c.58). This immunity was conditional on the insurance Agents in each town and city providing an up-to-date list of the names and addresses, and a brief synopsis of the physical attributes, of their firemen to the Admiralty each year. Each man was then issued with a certificate called a 'Protector' which he was obliged to carry with him at all times, either on or off duty. The decree of the London Assurance in this regard was typical:

> The Firemen to wear their badges and have their certificate always about them to distinguish them; and if any happen to be pressed for want thereof, the charge that shall thereby be occasioned, such Firemen shall bear.

Clearly, should a fireman be impressed due to his own negligence in not carrying his certificate, his employers would be put to considerable expense and trouble in securing his release; a charge for which he would subsequently be docked.[43] In the early 1800s, with the United Kingdom in the throes of a deathly struggle with the French under Napoleon and with the outcome far from certain, the Cork press gangs were zealously pursuing their nefarious trade in acquiring cannon-fodder for His Majesty's Ships of the Line.

When a press gang was active in an area, the word would spread like wildfire and men would melt away from the docks. This made the gang's work more difficult. On such occasions, it had been known for them to throw caution to the wind and seize insurance firemen even in full uniform. On one occasion, woefully short of their 'quorum' after an afternoon's endeavours, one bright spark hit on a novel idea for making up their numbers: they would turn in a false fire alarm and ambush the firemen as they arrived.[44] Whilst I have come across no reference of an attempt to impress Cork insurance firemen, there is no doubt that the men were well acquainted with the machinations of the press gang, and may well have, on occasion, been saved by the timely production of their 'Protectors'. In any event, the practice was eventually abolished in 1815.

THE FIREMEN'S LIVERY: UNIFORMS, HELMETS, AND BADGES.

There was no possibility of a press gang mistaking an insurance fireman in full uniform for a civilian. Their uniforms were very distinctive and well-known to the public and the authorities alike. The offices took a great interest in how their firemen appeared in public; almost the first job after a company was formed was to agree on a logo and design a suitable uniform.

Some brigades issued top hats for 'undress' duty and helmets for operational work, others expected the men to manage with top hats only. (The earliest form of hat was known as a 'beaver'). The type of fire helmet used was made of horsehide with crossbars of metal. The interior was of leather, stuffed and quilted with wool, which was supposed to protect the skull from the impact of falling debris. This pattern was known as a 'quatrefoil' helmet. Tunics were made of the hard-wearing woollen fabric known as 'kersey', while the men's breeches consisted of a velvet-like material, noted for its durability, called 'plush'.[45] Outside of newspaper advertisements companies had few means of bringing their products to the attention of the public. An insurance fire brigade turn-out, an interesting diversion with the men clad in their colourful uniforms and the fire engines painted in distinctive livery (not always red), served the dual purpose of advertising the company and reassuring their watching customers, and potential customers, of their professionalism. As we have seen, the four Offices that maintained fire engines in Cork were the REA, the Atlas, the West of England, and the (short-lived) Scottish Union.

ROYAL EXCHANGE ASSURANCE UNIFORM.

Shortly after the company was formed, its firemen were issued with yellow tunics lined with pink. One can only imagine what these must have looked like after hours of hard firefighting, soaked through with sooty water and reeking of smoke. Later on the company relented and allowed their men to slip into something (marginally) more practical – a fetching pea-green ensemble. This was the type of uniform worn when their establishment was formed in Cork.

The outfit consisted of black top-hat with a broad gold band around the crown; pea-green tunic with large gilt buttons, plush green breeches, matching waistcoat with a double row of gilt buttons, white stockings, and buckled black shoes.

On the left upper arm was worn the badge of office bearing the company's logo, identical to that on the Office's fire marks. A white shirt and black cravat completed the uniform.

ATLAS ASSURANCE COMPANY UNIFORM.

The Atlas uniform comprised a long, bottle-green tunic, which stopped short some inches above the knee, tan breeches and waistcoat, black leather knee-boots, and a wide-brimmed hat with a buckle to the front. The badge of office was worn on the left upper arm.

WEST OF ENGLAND FIRE INSURANCE COMPANY UNIFORM.

The uniform comprised a single-breasted, dark-blue coat with red piping, red collar and epaulettes, a red waistcoat, light-blue trousers and black leather thigh-boots, and a brass badge showing the company's logo was worn on the left breast. Headdress comprised a black leather helmet with brass trimming, sometimes with the words 'West of England' or 'W E' embossed in gilt lettering across the front. Later helmets were made from brass.

Accoutrements of the West of England Fire Engine Establishment. From left: A copper and brass branchpipe, a fireman's leather helmet, and a fireman's personal axe. The company's Agents in Cork were the Harvey's of the noted Quaker family. Their 'engine house' was located, variously on Charlotte Quay (now Fr Mathew Quay) and Anderson's Quay.

THE DAY OF MARCHING.

The uniforms were very susceptible to wear and tear and were replaced on a yearly basis. This usually took place on the so-called 'Day of Marching'. The Day of Marching was an established fixture on the calendar of every Fire Office and was timed to coincide with the Annual General Meeting of the Board. On the day, the firemen would be given their new uniforms and, often accompanied by a band, would process around a town to advertise their company's products, handing out leaflets as they went. Later in the evening, the men would be each given a 'half-a-crown for walking' and treated to a slap-up dinner by the directors. In October 1811, the *Freeman's Journal* described one such 'Day of Marching' (except on this occasion the Dubs seem to have taken the easier option of hitching a ride!) by the REA firemen in the capital:

> There were two Engines, the first drawn by four horses, on the top of which sat twelve firemen and their Foreman dressed in pea-green, plush breeches and vests with gilt buttons. The men had two bugles on this Engine, and on arriving at Dublin Castle Yard played 'God Save the King' to the delight of the Viceroy and his family. The procession was followed by an astonished and admiring multitude.[46]

The minutes of the Atlas Office for 26 January 1809 record, 'Agreed, that the Firemen be distinguished by an Office Badge'. All the Offices provided badges for their firemen. The badge was a large oval, round, or octagonal plate with the company's logo or emblem embossed thereon. It was usually held in place by an armband on the left upper arm, except in the case of the West of England firemen who wore it on the left breast. Although fire engine establishments were maintained the length and breadth of the United Kingdom, it seems that only firemen located in the city or town of origin of a company were issued with the expensive hallmarked, sterling silver badges, while those in the provinces having to make do with badges of baser metals, like copper, tin plate, or brass. The last known example of a badge is one made for the West of England in 1836 by the badge and button manufacturers, Firmin. All are now highly prized by collectors.

FIRE MARKS.

By the year 1812, with Napoleon in full retreat from Moscow, Cork City had been laid out to the extent that, travelling back in time from our day, one would have little difficulty in finding one's way around. An edition of the *Cork Advertiser* for December of that year exhorted its citizens to:

> Behold the City of Cork and its present state compared with fifty years ago. At that period, and much later, unwholesome rivers ran through all those streets which now beautify the city; the Grand Parade, George's Street, Patrick's Street, the South Mall, were all rivers – with stores, cellars and little offices built upon the Quays.

If one stood in the middle of any of those thoroughfares in the early years of the nineteenth century and gazed up at the buildings, one would have noticed small, colourful metal plaques adorning the fronts of many. These plaques were called 'fire marks' and were a feature of the street furniture in Cork and other cities for many years. In much the same way as the distinctive and quirky shop signs had done in the previous century, fire marks must have added considerably to the picturesque effect of the streetscape.[47]

The firemark served a number of purposes: it marked the property so it was obvious to all that the building was covered by insurance, it acted as an advertisement for the insurance company, and it left firemen responding to a call in no doubt as to which particular building was insured with their Office. The earliest marks, as well as displaying a company's logo, also bore the customer's policy number. House numbering had been introduced in Cork in 1787. Previous to that, while traders could identify their businesses with colourful swinging signs, it was more difficult to locate a private house.[48]

By the time insurance fire engines appeared on the streets of Cork (1799), house numbering had been in vogue some twelve years. On completion of the transaction at the insurance office, a fireman would be sent round to the customer's property with a long ladder to nail the fire mark to the front wall, usually between the first and second floors – well beyond the reach of thieves who coveted them for their lead content. The building was only then declared 'marked'. Indeed, some companies did not regard the policy to be effective until the ritual of marking the property had been completed. Most companies charged half-a-crown for the policy and mark on top of the premium. In an 1803 advertisement for the REA, their Cork Agent, Austen Shinkwin, shrewdly waives this extra, unwelcome fee, 'No charge for Policy and Mark where the Sum Assured shall amount to £300 and upwards'.[49] Following on the introduction of the street numbering system, there was, in theory at any rate, no longer a specific need to mark insured property; the fire engines could simply go straight to a given address. However, the 'free advertising' factor still loomed large with the companies and also (as now) some householders neglected to put their house numbers on their front doors, so that there was always room for a degree of uncertainty. The practice of fixing marks on properties continued as late as the 1860s (the REA discontinued the custom in 1838) long after their original purpose had been forgotten.

To see a fire mark still in place on a building today is indeed a rare sight. At the time of writing I have identified just four examples of fire marks still *in situ* on Cork properties. Three are of the REA, in lead, and are on buildings at Camden Quay, South Mall, and George's Quay. Using the cataloguing system in Wright they are identified as pattern '10k', which dates them to about 1820. The fourth, on a house in Montenotte, is of the Protector Fire Insurance Company and is made of copper, issued between 1832 and 1835. (The company itself enjoyed a life span of only ten years, from 1825 to 1835 when it was amalgamated with the Phoenix Assurance Company). A copper mark of the Caledonian Insurance

Some early nineteenth-century fire marks. (a) Royal Exchange (b) Atlas (c) West of England. Aldwells's *County and City of Cork Post Office General Directory* (1844/45) lists fifty-eight insurance companies in the city of which thirty-two had their own distinctive marks.

Company is available for inspection at Cork Public Museum. The donor has stated that this was taken from a house on South Main Street in the 1950s shortly before its demolition. Caledonian marks are notoriously difficult to date, as the company used practically the same design and material from the time it was formed in 1805. Their Dublin branch did not open until 1834. As will be noted, it would be wrong to assume that only those offices that maintained fire engines issued marks: neither the Protector nor Caledonian had fire establishments in Cork.

For many years lead had been the preferred material for fire marks. It was durable enough to be impervious to the vagaries of the Irish weather and malleable enough to be stamped with the policy number and logo. As the wars against Napoleon Bonaparte dragged on, however, the price of lead began to rise due to an ever-increasing demand for its use in munitions. This set the companies casting around for cheaper, yet sturdy, materials. These included stamped copper, tinned copper, tinned iron, brass, zinc and, in some rare instances, terracotta. The lead marks were produced in cottage industry fashion by women in their own homes. The health hazard presented to them and their families by the boiling lead and fumes must have been considerable. The marks were hand-painted in bright colours with much use made of gold leaf. Today, only a very few still retain their original paint.

If a policy lapsed, a fireman would be dispatched to retrieve the mark from the building. It was not long before some wily insurance executive realized that the more marks his company had on buildings around town, the better it would appear to be performing. Henceforth, a mark was allowed to remain on a building even after the policy had lapsed to act as a 'free' advertisement. If the property owner decided to take out a new policy with a rival company, then, of course, the new company's mark would appear on the building too. Over a period of time, some buildings had several adorning their front walls. This phenomenon was alluded to in a poem of 1812 which compared the Prince Regent (later King George IV), due to his passion for wearing so many Orders and decorations, to one of these buildings:

For not e'en the Regent himself has endured
(Though I've seen him with badges and orders all shine
Till he looked like a house that was over-insured)
A much heavier burden of glories than mine.[50]

As time went by, it appears that the insurance brigades were prepared to turn-out to the houses of the poor and other uninsured properties on humanitarian grounds – and for any kudos that might accrue to them in so doing. When fire broke out in a dormitory of the Ursuline Convent on Cove Lane on the night of 4 May 1820, the latter concept was picked up, with shrewd perspicacity, by the community diarist:

Again we have to bless the Watchful Providence of an Almighty Guardian for our Preservation from the ravages of fire. Last night when the Mistress ... had sent her young to bed and was just in the act of following them up stairs, she was electrified by their all rushing down in a body with the comfortable intelligence that one of the dormitories was on fire, she ran up and perceived that in reality the upper end of the room appeared in a blaze, but on approaching nearer, she found that the flames were for awhile at least confined to one spot, that is to one of the windows of which the sash and the shutters were blazing furiously. It was unnecessary to call for help as the fire soon announced itself to the people in the street.

Many of our friends came to our assistance, among others some of the Insurance Companies arrived for *their own good as well as ours* [author's italics]. Fortunately the fire was soon got under and that owing to the presence of mind and activity of Sister Veronica, one of the Lay Sisters, who tore away the shutters of the windows and thereby prevented their spreading the flames. Had the accident occurred a few hours later, in all probability the consequence would have been dreadful as the children would have been [in] their first sound sleep and probably would not have been awakened until the flames had caught their beds! Upon investigation the fire was seen to have proceeded from the large kitchen grate where the immense and constant fires had heated the chimney flue to such a degree, that the heat gradually communicated itself to the timber which runs thro' the old wall and at length burst into flames. In consequence of this mishap there has been a general examination of all the walls through which any flues pass, that communicate with the kitchen chimney. Many of them were found in a very bad state.[51]

The insurance companies were effectively letting Cork Corporation off the hook by shouldering the responsibility for the public duty of fire extinction. This was never intended to be the case under their original charters and it would continue to vex them for many years. It was an expensive business to equip, maintain, and operate an insurance fire brigade: some of the larger Offices were expending up to 3 per cent of their annual income on them.[52] By the mid-1820s, several insurance companies had withdrawn from the fire insurance business altogether, as reported in the *Cork Constitution* on 13 January 1827:

It is stated as a proof that the present system of fire insurances is not profitable to the proprietors of Fire Offices, that the under-mentioned five Fire Offices have, within the last few months, entirely abandoned in the fire business, viz.– Hope, Eagle, Aegis, British Commercial, Southwark.

Two weeks later, which underscores the ruthless nature of the business, some of the bigger companies announced further incentives to prospective clients in the *Constitution* of 1 February:

The Royal Exchange, Sun, Globe, and Phoenix Insurance Companies are about to reduce the common risk insurance to 1s. per cent for the purpose of driving the junior offices out of the business.

THE FIRE IN THE NORTH CATHEDRAL, 3 JUNE 1820.

While each company constantly sought new ways and means to steal a march on their rivals in matters of generating business, the notion that their fire brigades operated an obstructionist policy towards one another on the fire ground seems little more than an urban myth. During the course of this research, when dozens of accounts of early fires were studied, no evidence came to light to suggest that the companies acted other than with probity towards one another.

On the other hand, there are many examples of co-operation between the Cork fire establishments. One classic example is the controversial fire which raged through the Roman Catholic Cathedral, known to generations as the 'North Cathedral' or 'North Chapel', less than a month after the fire in the Ursuline Convent. Built on a site high up over the city in the northern suburbs, it stands only a short distance from the world-famous 'pepper-pot' edifice of the Protestant St Anne's, Shandon. Building began in 1799 and was completed some nine years later. On the main altar stood a remarkable tabernacle almost three metres high, exquisitely carved from wood (and therefore highly combustible), and gilted, the work of Italian craftsmen. It cost £600. The architect of the Cathedral remains unknown, although the late Cork City Architect, T. F. McNamara, was of the opinion that it bore the hallmarks of Dublin architect Francis Johnston.[53] The *Southern Reporter* described how:

> About one o'clock this morning, this City was alarmed by the ringing of the bells, and loud cries through the streets, that the North Parish Chapel, the Roman Catholic Cathedral, was on fire. In an instant, crowds of persons of all ages and descriptions filled the streets, all hastening with consternation to the spot. The fire had burst through two of the windows, and on the doors being thrown open, the beautiful and costly Altar of this splendid and spacious Edifice was discovered in flames, and was already nearly consumed. The scene, combined with the exclamations of the immense crowd that had already collected, was awful and terrific, which was considerably increased when the grand and valuable Organ at the upper end of the building suddenly began to blaze. To save the Altar was impossible – but no time was lost in exertions to preserve the Building from destruction, which, happily, and by the indefatigable zeal of all present succeeded.
>
> In a few moments the Parish Engine arrived [not identified, but probably that of St Anne's Shandon], and was quickly followed by that of the Royal Exchange, accompanied by Mr. Evory, the Agent, those of the Atlas Company,

Messrs. Wise's[54], and several others, all of which being in excellent order, judiciously directed, and plentifully supplied with water, the fire that had caught the Organ in consequence of the intense heat, the peculiarly ignitable materials of the instrument, and from its being placed exactly opposite the Altar, was immediately extinguished, not, however, without, we fear, its being irretrievably injured.

At about half past three o'clock, after the Altar and all its sacred and costly ornaments had been reduced to a cinder, not a vestige remaining but the burnt fragments that strewed the floor, the fire was got under, and all apprehension of further damage or danger ceased. The multitude that had assembled then gradually dispersed. The Officer and attachment of military who attended... conducted themselves throughout the time with the utmost propriety and activity, in preserving order and a free passage of water, which was principally supplied by the poor women of the neighbourhood. Two High Constables and Peace Officers who were present also claim our notice, for their judicious and active regulations, which contributed considerably to the suppression of the fire and the preservation of good order.

How this fire originated has not with certainty been ascertained, but it is probable it was caused by a spark having fallen on the Altar on the preceding evening, when the candles were extinguished after the Vesper Service. An impression did prevail among many of the people, when the Organ was discovered on fire, and the distance between its situation and the Altar being so great, that it was not accidental; but when it is considered, in addition to the reasons we have already mentioned, that the immense body of fire on the Altar was directly opposite the Organ, and that a window behind it, being the only one in the Chapel open at the time, and the flame and smoke being of course drawn that way, it will be seen there can be no foundation for any such suspicion. We can ourselves attest, and many others can verify the fact, that even a considerable time after the fire in the Organ had been extinguished, and that of the Altar also, the heat of the walls and pillars immediately adjacent to the Organ was so great as to prevent the hand being placed against them for more than a moment.

We only notice the rumour now in order to point out its absurdity – we are sure it could not stand the test of a moment's inquiry.[55]

Though the newspaper report had gone to pains to suggest that the blaze was no more than an unfortunate accident, before the last embers were extinguished tongues had begun to wag. Subsequently, suggestions of malice were repeated in at least two published sources: in an poem written in Irish by the east Cork poet, Labhrás Ó Séagha, entitled '*Mo dheacairbhroid, mo léan*' (which loosely translates as 'My grief, my affliction'), and, much later, in an article on the history of the cathedral by Monsignor Patrick Sexton.

Mons. Sexton claimed that, following a provocative sermon on the Eucharist delivered by local curate, Revd W.J. O'Grady, the Catholic clergy of the parish only with difficulty dissuaded a mob from attacking and burning nearby St Anne's, Shandon. Some time later, the fire in the North Cathedral was discovered, the implication being that it was deliberately set by way of reprisal for the aborted attack on St Anne's. The theory that the fire was malicious may not be entirely without foundation for the following reasons:

1. During periods of social unrest in the late eighteenth and early nineteenth centuries, the burning of churches was, on occasion, resorted to as a means of expressing grievance.

2. The rooms of the cathedral were used for meetings by those who were opposed to the British Government's controversial ban on the appointment of Irish bishops.

3. The failure of several banks in Cork during 1820, some of which were controlled by Roman Catholics, was followed by an increase in tension throughout the city and indeed the country at large.[56]

In any event, the Roman Catholic clergy in general and the bishop, Dr John Murphy, in particular, were anxious to play down any suggestions of malice in order to diffuse tension in an already volatile situation. The cause of the fire was never ascertained.

This fire is but another example of the informal co-operation that existed between the various firefighting agencies in Cork during the nineteenth century: the insurance brigades, the parish engines and works fire engines, all working in tandem for the common good.

Useful and all as the insurance fire brigades were in the absence of government-sponsored bodies capable of reacting to civil emergencies, there was one notable deficiency in their make-up: they regarded the saving of human life from fire, or the amelioration of suffering during times of natural or man-made disasters, none of their business. While individual members of the fire brigades may have come to the aid of those in need of rescue, the official policy of the companies was that they were firefighting units only, not rescuers. This lacuna is perhaps best illustrated by two tragic incidents which occurred in Cork during the early years of the nineteenth century.

At 10p.m on Saturday 3 November 1810, a massive explosion occurred in Brandy Lane near St Fin Barre's Cathedral which reverberated all over the city. It appears that a man named Ellard, who worked in the gunpowder mills at Ballincollig, had secretly smuggled out gunpowder and was in the process of selling it to men who worked in a quarry near his home. Some of the powder had managed to get wet, and he put it in a kettle on the open fire to dry. It blew up, demolishing a number of houses, and killing eighteen people with many more suffering horrific injuries from which they later succumbed.[57] And on Saturday 8 June 1811, four people were killed outright and eight grievously injured in Cornmarket Street. The corporation, due to the derelict state of the Cornmarket, had employed contractors to demolish the building:

> While the labourers were at work on the roof, the projecting stone cornice … fell down suddenly while a number of persons were…immediately under it. Four unhappy persons of humble condition were killed instantly – some of them terribly mangled by the immense stones which formed the cornice.[58]

In neither case do the contemporary reports allude to an insurance fire brigade presence.

Not Quite a Fire Brigade: The Indefatigable John Ring and his Pipe Water Men.

'Ride a cock–horse to George's Street Cross,
To see Mr. Arnott atop of his horse,
With the fire escape, and the plugs, and the hose,
And he will have water wherever he goes'.

(John Fitzgerald, 'The Bard of the Lee', in *Gems of the Cork Poets*, 1857).[1]

'Mr Ring worked indefatigably, rushing about from hose to hose, directing the operations of the men, and labouring unceasingly at everything'.

(The *Cork Examiner* 10 June 1863)

The Christian name John seems, curiously, to be inextricably linked with the *dramatis personae* involved in the long struggle to establish a fire brigade in Cork in the mid-nineteenth century: Sir John Benson, pre-eminent in many of the major capital projects undertaken by Cork Corporation and the brains behind the new waterworks (later to become his *bête noire*);[2] Sir John Arnott, Mayor, wealthy entrepreneur, philanthropist, and responsible for raising the so-called 'Waterworks Fire Brigade';[3] John Francis Maguire, Mayor, prominent businessman, founder of the *Cork Examiner*, champion of economic nationalism, and long-time advocate of a city fire brigade;[4] and John Adams and John Ring, each of whom was in his capacity as Superintendent of the city waterworks, for all intents and purposes, the city's fire chief.[5] Each in his own way contributed, to a greater or lesser degree, to the gradual development of firefighting services in Cork.

The Cork Improvement Act of 1852 had given Cork Corporation sweeping powers. For the first time in its history it had the right to strike a rate, and was empowered to:

Cause fire-plugs and all necessary works … for securing an efficient supply of water in case of fire, to be provided and maintained … and … [to] mark on the buildings or walls near to such fire-plugs, to denote the situation thereof.

In 1856, a further Cork Improvement Act allowed the corporation to take over the affairs of the Pipe Water Company, and break its monopoly, which had effectively held the city to ransom for years, providing water only to those who could afford to pay for it.

Sir John Benson was engaged to design and oversee the building of a new waterworks and the laying of a new network of mains and fire hydrants, then called 'fire cocks'. The principal drawback of the old waterworks (built by Nicholas Fitton) had been the height of its totally inadequate reservoir. The so-called 'City Basin' was located in a field on the northern side of the Lee Road, some 3km from the city centre. At an elevation of only eighty feet and a depth of five feet, this gave a static pressure at the base of the hydraulic gradient of some thirty-seven pounds per square inch (2.5 bar). When factors such as variation in the size of the main, friction loss, sharp bends, deposits on the interior of the conduit (tuberculation), distance laid, and the actual opening up of the main for firefighting purposes were all taken into account, running pressure and volume of water available in the city centre were drastically reduced, hence the necessity for the fire engines maintained by the parishes and insurance companies.

Under Benson's plan, a new twin-cell open reservoir was constructed on Shanakiel Hill at an elevation of 180 feet (55m Malin).[6] Covering an acre of ground, it had a depth of fourteen feet and contained seventeen megalitres of water.[7] Later, a second, smaller, reservoir was built off the Blarney Road,

A 'Fire Cock' wall plate dated 1858, the year the new waterworks for Cork city was commissioned. Designed by City Engineer Sir John Benson, they were erected to mark the location of the nearest fire cock. Many are still *in situ*.

higher up the northern hills than the first. This was to serve the needs of the hillier areas of Cork, for in practice a water main is never laid so that any part is above the hydraulic gradient: there would be a partial vacuum in that part of the main, which would act as a siphon. Benson extended the mains network to about ninety-five miles (from the fourteen miles of the Pipe Water Company) to reach all parts of the city and suburbs.[8]

In February 1858, he supplied the council with a progress report on the new waterworks, which set down in some detail the layout of the cast-iron mains network:

> The mains to supply the city are completed into the reservoir with the neces-sary cocks, &c. The North main will be finished on to-morrow evening, from the Reservoir to the borough bounds at Silverspring, and to the East end of Penrose's-quay. This main passes through the grounds of Shanakiel, by Sunday's Well, Pope's Quay, King Street, and Lower Road to Silverspring. At Sunday's Well Avenue a branch main is laid through Blarney Lane to Mallow Lane.
>
> At North Gate Bridge a branch passes through Mallow Lane to the Guard-House at Blackpool. Branches are laid in Dominick Street, Church Street, &c. At Mulgrave Road a main runs by Upper John Street to the old Foundling Hospital. The Western main also runs by Patrick's Hill and Sydney Place to St. Luke's Cross. Also from the Tunnel steps by Summer Hill Road to St. Luke's Cross. This point being the highest level which the 180 feet reservoir commands.
>
> At North Gate Bridge a junction with the northern main will connect the main laid in the North and South Main Streets. The mains are continued across South Gate Bridge, the Bandon Road to Denroche's Cross, and Cat Lane to Friar's Walk. Mains are laid on Sullivan's Quay.
>
> At every 80 yards, hydrants or fire cocks are being inserted. These will also answer for street watering, as well as on occasions of fires. In addition to the above, service mains are laid in several of the cross streets, parallel to the large mains.[9]

By the summer of 1858, a minor miracle had been wrought in Cork. The new waterworks was finished, and water, for the very first time, began to flow into the homes of poor and rich alike. The people flocked in their droves to the Lee Road to gaze in wonder at Cork's new model waterworks. Out of 15,000 pipes laid, only five bursts were reported when the water was turned on, and not a single joint had failed – a remarkable achievement.[10] Because the water coming out of domestic taps was completely untreated, being drawn straight from the Lee and pumped up to the reservoirs (a system that prevailed until 1879), the corporation made it illegal to bathe in the river above the waterworks. People were prosecuted for allowing their dogs to swim above the weir. The total cost of the new waterworks and mains, including the purchase money to the old company, was £59,000.

The pressure in the mains could now throw a jet over the highest building in Cork, which was on the Grand Parade. The only thing needed now was a dedicated corps of firefighters to exploit the excellent new water system to full advantage. To this end, during the mayoralty (1859–1861) of Sir John Arnott, the corporation took the first faltering steps in that direction by the creation of a small 'fire brigade' from among the staff of the waterworks. It was the first time in over eighty years that dedicated public funds were expended on fire extinguishment. This 'Waterworks Fire Brigade' of four operated out of the municipal offices at 20 South Mall. It was under the direction of the Superintendent of the waterworks (first, John Adams, and after May 1860, John Ring). Their equipment consisted of a cart (called a van) on which was piled hose, standpipes, and branchpipes. When the furniture showrooms of Messrs Johnston's on Great George's Street went on fire on the night of Monday 24 January 1859, the new hydrants were used 'in anger' for the first time. The *Examiner* narrated how 'the [hydrant] most certainly did its work efficiently and instantaneously, to the surprise and admiration of all present'.

20 South Mall, Municipal Offices and 'Fire Station' of the Waterworks Fire Brigade. (1860–1877)

The 'firemen' reported for night duty following their ordinary day's work as water inspectors. Their *modus operandi* was outlined in a cynical editorial in the *Cork Examiner*:

> Say that an alarm of fire is given. The man on watch arouses the other men, who are in their beds by 10 o'clock, or thereabouts. He then runs off to call Mr. Ring [Waterworks Superintendent, living on Dyke Parade] and Mr. Walker [Town Surveyor, living on North Mall]. The three men take the van in which the hose is carried, and drag it to where the fire has broken out. The weight of the hose and van is not much under a ton. When arrived at the fire, two of this grand staff assume their duties as turncocks; and a very important and absorbing duty is theirs – for they have to regulate the pressure so as to bring the greatest possible force of water upon the burning and endangered building or buildings. One man remains to uncoil, to connect, and to manage the hose! Of course, one man can manage two or three hoses, and so point and direct the two or three nozzles as to command the flames in the most effectual manner. One man in Cork – he being an Irishman – is expected to do that which in London, Liverpool, Glasgow, and much smaller places, requires a trained, disciplined, and experienced, and therefore an efficient staff. Now as, in sober seriousness, this one amazing Irishman cannot perform prodigies, and do the work of a dozen men, he is obliged to obtain aid – and what aid! Suppose the hour to be eleven, and the night to be Saturday … the cry of fire has emptied the public houses in the neighbourhood, or, if the fire be on a grand scale, it has emptied the public houses of the city; and out of more than 500 tap-rooms rush the good, the mischievous, or the bad … many of the motley crowd are wholly drunk, or half drunk, or "elevated". And yet, [the firefighters] are expected to accomplish miracles with a staff of four men, the aid of the Police, and the dangerous assistance of semi-drunken and terribly officious volunteers.
>
> Turn and twist the subject as one may, to this conclusion we must unfailingly come – that if we want protection from fire, we must have a Fire Brigade, and that if we have a Fire Brigade, we must pay for it.[11]

The article had the fingerprints of the *Examiner's* owner, John Francis Maguire, stamped all over it. There was one other call the, presumably, exhausted dutyman had to make (not referred to in the *Examiner* editorial), and one of which everyone living in Cork must have been acutely aware. From Walker's house on the North Mall the hapless man had to proceed, as fast as he could, to the Waterworks on the Lee Road to get them to turn on the water for the appropriate area, for in the early years of Cork's new water system the supply was shut off at midnight, and, of course, there was no telephone, or any other communications system, to apprise them of an emergency. This may explain, to some extent, the frequent slowness of the 'brigade' in bringing water to bear on fires in the early hours.[12]

They received five shillings each for each fire attended, usually paid weeks behind time. If no fires occurred during their period on night-duty, no allowance was paid. When a major blaze broke out on the Grand Parade, the entire bill for the firefighting operation (which included paying the waterworks firemen and various helpers) came to £5.[13]

They frequently worked in atrocious conditions and often exposed themselves to great danger with only a suit of oilskins for protection. Unlike the insurance firemen who were issued with stout leather helmets, the waterworks men had to make do with sou'westers which afforded them no protection against falling debris. Later, they would bitterly complain that some of their members had died from wettings and other injuries received at fires. Despite frequent requests, their firefighting equipment was derisory. They received no proper training. The hoses were kept in an open yard exposed to all weather conditions and were so leaky that 'almost as much water passed out through the sides as through the nozzle'. Ring reported that the yard where the equipment was housed was so rat-infested that it was dangerous to leave the hose on the ground.[14] In spite of all its shortcomings, if the waterworks 'fire brigade' may not have been what the city actually required, it was a nod in the right direction.

For almost two decades, the head offices of the insurance industry in Ireland had badgered their respective British-based headquarters for funding for a more streamlined service along the lines of the London Fire Engine Establishment, without success. Now, as the nineteenth century wore on, a discernible change in attitude (as will become evident from a study of fires in the succeeding pages) with regard to their involvement in operational firefighting began to manifest itself. In 1860, W.N. Hancock, a pioneer in the study of economics, had shown that out of forty-five premises burned in Dublin during 1859, only twenty-six were wholly or partially insured, nine were uninsured, with no data concerning the remainder. Of the thirty-one companies with fire engines, six insured about half of the insured premises, but fought three-quarters of all the fires.[15] Assuming that all forty-five blazes were attended by insurance brigades, it was patently obvious that the days when they were a panacea for all emergencies of fire were numbered. As well as Hancock's analysis, a number of other factors fed into the eventual abandonment of the 'fire engine establishment' scheme.

In Cork, the commissioning of the new waterworks in 1858 was undoubtedly a major determinant. For the very first time, the city was no longer dependant on insurance, and other fire engines to fight fires. A powerful jet of water, drawn directly from the mains, could now reach over the highest building in Cork, to the extent that Sir John Benson had suggested to the Corporation Pipe Water Committee that 'the [assistance of] the engines could be done away with'.[16] The Perrier family, agents for the Atlas, had been heavily involved in the Cork Pipe Water Company, of which, Sir Anthony, who died in 1845, had been treasurer. Now that, finally and irrevocably, their monopoly had been broken and a corporation waterworks fire brigade formed, it is likely that the Perriers unobtrusively reverted to their establishment's original *raison d'etre*: to attend fires only in premises insured with them. If such was the case, their insouciance may not have been atypical of their fellow agents' attitude post-1858.

The year 1860 had been a disastrous one for fire insurance companies in general. In the case of one company, the Patriotic, although there was new fire insurance business, losses were almost double those of the previous year and completely out of line with the losses sustained during the previous eight years.[17] In quick succession, in 1861, came the great fire of Tooley Street, involving multiple vast warehouses in London's dockland, which brought the insurance industry to its knees. The huge fire, which claimed the life of the famous commander of the LFEE, James Braidwood, continued to smoulder until 22 July – exactly one month – before it was finally extinguished. The bills for claims totalled more than £2.5million, an unimaginable sum of money by 1861 standards.

The immediate reaction of the insurers was to treble the cost of premiums, an action which elicited howls of indignation from already hard-pressed merchants. It also brought into sharp relief the long-felt conviction among insurers that the days of providing a 'free fire service' for all were numbered. The insurers put the civil authorities on notice that they were no longer prepared to fund and maintain fire services that were increasingly perceived (by the general public as well as the industry) as a facility to be provided, like the police, out of the public purse. Finally, an Act of Parliament in 1862 established the Dublin Fire Brigade, which heralded the end of the insurance fire brigades' operations in the capital.

A survey of a cross-section of notable fires that occurred in Cork during the course of the nineteenth century reveals, from the early years when the insurance engines could be expected to attend in some strength, to a time, post the late 1850s, when their attendance was no longeer guaranteed and eventually ceased altogether.[18]

REIGN OF FIRE:
HISTORIC BLAZES THAT SHAPED A CITY.

1840: A NIGHT OF MELODRAMA: THE CURTAIN FALLS AT THE THEATRE ROYAL.

When the great Hungarian composer and virtuoso pianist, Franz Liszt, arrived in Cork for a series of concerts at the end of December 1840, it would have been expected that his engagements would be held at the city's premier entertainment centre, the Theatre Royal on George's Street (where the celebrated violinist and composer Paganini had earlier performed). His concerts, however, took place in the Clarence Hall of the Imperial Hotel on the South Mall, for

Depiction of a theatre on fire, mid-nineteenth century. A fireman and a turncock (on left) are connecting a standpipe to the town's main while (on right) two manual fire engines are being worked by teams of volunteer pumpers who were paid for their services on an *ad hoc* basis. The firefighters have obviously decided that the theatre is beyond saving as the greater effort seems to be concentrated on protecting the buildings on the opposite side of the street. When Cork's Theatre Royal went up in flames in April 1840, five manual engines were brought into operation. (*ILN* 15 March 1856.)

the nearby theatre had burned down in a spectacular fire in the previous April.[19]

The second Theatre Royal to stand on George's Street opened its doors to the public in July 1760. It was situated three blocks east of its predecessor which bore the same name and which stood at the corner of George's Street and Playhouse Lane (now Prince's Street). (The old theatre was often referred to as the 'Theatre Royal on Dunscomb's Marsh' and opened in 1736).[20] The new theatre was erected between Morgan's Lane (now Morgan Street) and Five-Alley Lane (now Pembroke Street) on the site now occupied by the General Post Office. Its postal address was 29 George's Street. With an impressive colonnaded facade, the building measured 42m by 19m, dimensions which ensured it was the largest theatre in Ireland outside of Dublin. During the following eighty years, it was Cork's principal centre for the performing arts.[21] In 1827, it was closed for a time for refurbishment, and the *Cork Constitution* of 24 April of that year gives us a brief insight into what the theatre may have looked like on the night of its burning some years later:

Last night the Theatre opened under the direction and management of Mr. Macarthy, and we were highly pleased to observe the improvements. This

Theatre is now one of the neatest and most compact in Ireland, and little inferior to many of note in the Metropolis of the Sister Kingdom. All the Boxes are newly molded in gold, and tastefully festooned with pink satin – the seats are newly covered, and backed most comfortably. The seats in the Pit are also covered with green cloth, which, together with the light appearance of the House, and the brilliancy of the Gas, has a very pretty effect indeed.

Fires in places of public entertainment in Cork have been few and far between. In the past 170 or so years, just six have been recorded: the Theatre Royal (George's Street) 1840, the Lee Cinema (Winthrop Street) and the Imperial Cinema (George's Street) both in 1920, the Pavilion Cinema (St Patrick's Street) 1930, the Washington Cinema (Washington Street) 1938, the Opera House (Emmet Place) 1955, and the AOH Hall (Morrison's Island) 1956. Thankfully, Cork has been spared the horrors so often associated with such fires elsewhere in that none was attended with loss of life.

Even after the widespread use of thatch and timber as building materials had been supplanted by brick and slate, the old style of theatre buildings were still notoriously susceptible to fire. With little or no effective fire separation between the stage and auditorium, a common or continuous roof extending over both areas and their high, cavernous interiors packed with highly-flammable materials (with no special facilities for storing scenery, costumes, curtains and paints, to say nothing of permanent fixtures like seating, galleries, and tinder-dry timber flooring), all contributed to a cocktail of materials that could prove deadly in the event of an outbreak of fire. Lighting in 1840 was by way of gas, but supplementary lighting in the form of hanging lamps, sconces, and candles was not unknown. Limelight, used to create brilliant effects on stage, was created by heating pure lime by means of the constant application of gas-fired burners. The swirling skirts or prodigious costumes of the actresses on stage were only inches away. The local authorities paid little heed to the obvious dangers, as they were far more concerned with any hint of sedition or an actress showing a naughty glimpse of leg than with public safety. Galleries were constructed with no alternative means of escape; dark, tortuous passages and steep, obstructed narrow stairs, down which the public were expected to flee in their hundreds in an emergency, were the norm. Architects of the day saw nothing wrong with incorporating low roofs and small exit doors in their plans. Firefighting appliances, other than water buckets (which more often than not were full of rubbish) were usually non-existent.[22]

The majority of theatre fires had their origin on the stage side: the stage, flies, and back stage were all areas of high risk. The invention of the proscenium wall and arch, with a non-flammable safety curtain (a concept developed by Capt. Eyre Massey Shaw about whom we shall hear more) was a major step forward in reducing the number of injuries and fatalities in fires in theatres. The safety curtain (Shaw insisted that the curtain could be dropped and fully in place in less than twenty-one seconds), completely and effectively cut off any chance of flames reaching from one part of a theatre to another. Prior to the invention of the safety curtain, stage curtains were frequently made from highly-flammable green baize.[23]

Cork's Theatre Royal was totally destroyed by fire in the early hours of Palm Sunday, 12 April 1840; it was the last performance before Easter. The curtains had been drawn around midnight following a 'benefit for Mr and Mrs Wood'.[24] The fire was discovered just after 2a.m when flames were observed bursting through the roof, having 'previously ... traversed the entire interior of the building'.[25] Then:

> The engines (West of England, Scottish Union, Atlas, Royal Exchange, and subsequently St. Paul's) arrived ... about half-past two, the roof on the first discharge of water fell in, the flames ascended with a power, a brilliancy, and a variety (the latter property arising from the colours employed in the paint-ing and decorations) which, had it been unattended with danger, would have rendered the spectacle magnificent. For miles around, the city was, we may say, *illuminated,* and the property destroyed is considerable.
>
> As nothing could be done to save it, the efforts of the engines were directed to the protection of the surrounding buildings. The West of England took up its station opposite Austen's Tavern, and to the vigour with which it was worked the preservation of the Tavern is attributable. The same service was rendered to the Savings' Bank, the Dublin Coach Office ... by the Atlas, the Exchange and the Scottish Union. After the first quarter of an hour the supply of water was abundant, and to this, and the stillness of the night ... we owe it, under Providence, that we have not to announce ... one of the most extensive and calamitous fires with which the city was ever visited.[26]

By five o'clock in the morning the building was a heap of smouldering ruins, along with the wardrobes, orchestral instruments, a valuable collection of old music, and three pianos, two of them of considerable value. Neither the building nor its contents were insured.[27] Frank Seymour, proprietor of the nearby Theatre Royal Victoria in Cook Street, offered the use of his theatre 'in the most liberal manner' to the dramatic company of the, now-destroyed, Theatre Royal.[28]

On 8 June 1853, the building was re-opened by Mr R.C. Burke, 'its popular and genial owner during the last years of its existence'.[29] It was refurbished in 1867 under the direction of Sir John Benson. Sold to the Post Office in 1875, it opened as the Cork General Post Office in 1877.

1848: A BRACE OF BLAZES: CROSSE'S GREEN AND CITY CENTRE.

The eve of a St Patrick's Day is invariably a busy one for the people of Cork. Band rooms and clubrooms of the various voluntary and sporting bodies are veritable hives of activity, all making last-minute preparations for the national feast day. That day in 1848 should have been no different; except that parades and demonstrations all over Ireland had been proscribed by order of the Lord Lieutenant.

The year 1848 has been called 'The Year of Revolutions'. In that year, established orders in Austria, Hungary, Germany, and Belgium were toppled like ninepins in a bowling alley. The overthrow of the so-called 'Citizen King', Louis Philippe of France, with a Republic being proclaimed again, was greeted rapturously in Ireland by adherents of the Repeal movement. Dublin Castle, ever vigilant for the slightest rumblings of unrest, could detect the national barometer rising inexorably and was extremely jittery. The 'usual suspects' were rounded up, including leaders of the Young Ireland movement like William Smith O'Brien, Thomas Meagher, John Mitchell, and their followers. Many were later transported.

With tension rising all over the country, Cork city was in a state of high alert in the week preceding St Patrick's Day. Because of its symbolic nature, the 'Castle' was scared it might be used by disloyal subjects to have yet another go at Perfidious Albion. The local militia was embodied and horse-drawn artillery, complete with full ammunition limbers, rattled across the cobblestones of the city on the long haul up to the barracks. All leave was cancelled and the garrison confined to barracks. Four field guns were placed across the main entrance on the Youghal Old Road, and the authorities waited.

Suddenly, sometime after two o'clock in the morning, the urgent galloping of a horse could be heard coming up the hill, and a breathless policeman dismounted at the barrack gate calling for troops. The bugle sounded, the stand-to turned out, and in a short while, every man-jack in the barracks was dressed and ready for action. The cavalry mounted up and artillerymen stood by their guns. Only then did it become apparent that, in one sense, it was a false alarm. When the policeman finally managed to get his breath, he explained that the assistance of the garrison was required, not to quell an uprising, but to help at yet another major fire down town:

> Yesterday morning, about two o'clock, the watchman at Crosse's Green discovered that the extensive steam mill and concerns of Mr. William Lane were on fire; he immediately gave the alarm, but before any effectual means were taken to arrest the conflagration the whole building was wrapped in flames. The police, under the command of Sub-Inspector Walker, a company of the 44th Regiment, under Lieut. Colpoys, adjutant, and a number of civilians, were quickly on the spot, together with the fire engines of the Atlas, Royal Exchange and West of England insurance companies. The new engine of the Atlas, a powerful and most efficient one rendered valuable aid being worked … in the rere of the concern, and pouring in a copious and continuous body of water, which

checked the flames, and saved the building which contained the machinery.

Those of the Royal Exchange and West of England worked across the river to the north of the building. The Mayor was present, with Messrs. Perrier [Atlas], J. Leslie [Royal Exchange], Walter Ronan [Minerva Insurance], James Adams [engineer of the Atlas, and Pipe Water Company] and others who rendered efficient assistance. At one period considerable apprehensions were entertained for the safety of the Police Barrack at Elizabeth Fort: sparks of flaming embers were falling so thick on the yard and sheds, that wet blankets and other appliances were put in requisition to prevent ignition to the surrounding buildings. The property was insured for £3,500 with the Royal Exchange and West of England, but the greater portion of this was on stock and machinery.

The £1,800 insured on the premises will scarcely cover half the damage. From circumstances which have come to the knowledge of the authorities, it is expected the origin of the conflagration may be traced to incendiarism. Three months ago the extensive stores adjoining these premises belonging to the same firm, and which were not insured, were totally destroyed by fire, the occasion of which still remains a mystery.[30]

Barely three months after the big fire at Crosse's Green, the city centre itself was threatened by a conflagration that destroyed much of the block bounded by Cook Street, St Patrick's Street, Robert Street, and George's Street, where Penney's department store now stands.[31]

On Sunday 11 June, at about 1.30p.m., 'while the greater portion of the citizens were at Divine Service', someone noticed smoke coming from a premises in Cook Street. This housed the businesses of Messrs McSwiney (sugar and tea dealers), O'Hara (haberdashers and silk merchants), and O'Boy (furniture dealers). Within five minutes of the alarm being raised, the flames and radiated heat were so intense that the Victoria Hotel on the opposite side of Cook Street was in grave danger of being engulfed. The *Cork Constitution* takes up the story:

The Chamber of Commerce, Victoria Hotel, and the houses on that side of Cook Street, were saved from destruction entirely by the efficient working of the Atlas, Royal Exchange and West of England fire engines. When it became evident that the west side of Cook Street was saved, the police and firemen turned their attention to cutting off communication between the concerns on fire, and the houses on Patrick Street, to which it formed the rere. At this time the 26th Cameronians, under arms, commanded by Major Whittingham … arrived from the barracks with the garrison engine and were most useful in protecting property, working the engines, etc. It was discovered that the house of Messrs. Pericho and Guissani in Cook Street, and the reres of the houses of Messrs. O'Hara, Fitzpatrick, Tangney, Gordon, O'Boy and Roche in Patrick Street were on fire and it was by the most daring exertions ... and the efficient working of the engines, with a plentiful supply of water from the company's water pipes, that the fire was stayed, but not before the properties of all were seriously injured.[32]

The editor of the *Examiner* was not quite as complaisant as the *Constitution* hack. In a stinging editorial on the day after the fire, he lamented, among other things, the lack of water:

Water was more valuable than gold; and we learn that, even in one of the houses damaged by fire – that of Mr. Pericho – the agent of the Water Company would not suffer a pipe to be broken, though its timely rupture might have saved a large amount of property!

Damage was estimated at £20,000, a colossal sum. The *Constitution*, whose offices in Marlborough Street were only a stone's throw from the fire ground, now changed tack and joined in the clamour for a proper fire brigade:

Fire Brigade.
Well, are we to go in the old way? Are we still to continue without an effec-tive force for the suppression of fire? Are life and property still to be left at the mercy of an element that destroys without distinction? Are we to run the risk of another such fire such as that which raged on Sunday, and which had it occurred at night, would probably have laid the whole square in ashes? And are we all the time to see the moneys collected by the Corporation appropri-ated to purposes of far less interest to the heavily taxed contributors?
   We have so often referred to the necessity of providing a Fire Brigade that we now content ourselves with calling attention to what we suffer from want of one. If the citizens choose to let the want continue, of course they can do so; but if they do not, they must awake the Corporation to their duty. This is the more imperative because the assistance of the Parish Engines can no longer be commanded, the rate raised for those engines being disallowed, in consequence of the complaint of the Council and its 'liberal' supporters that the collection of it was an obstruction to the franchise. For every sacrifice to 'popular' clamour the public, in one way or another, are made to suffer.[33]

Faced with ever-growing public agitation, the corporation agreed to set up a sub-committee to look into the whole matter of forming a fire brigade. The committee reported that the old manual engine belonging to the Atlas (the new one had made its debut at Lane's fire) would be available to any proposed municipal fire brigade; the Mayor would simply have to make a formal applica-tion to secure it. The corporation, however, would need to contribute £100 a year towards the upkeep of the brigade, and the other civic bodies, including the Harbour Commissioners and the Wide Street Commissioners, would be expected to contribute an equal amount. The *Cork Examiner* for 12 June 1848 documented how:

> The subject of a Fire Brigade was again brought before the Board [of the Wide Street Commissioners]. Alderman Dowden proposed that 20 of the most active men in the employment of the Board should be enrolled to form a Brigade, and that they should each get a shilling a week additional wages for their services. There were already four parish engines, and five men to each would be able to manage them efficiently. According to his plan, the whole of the establishment would not amount to more than £200.

However, board member Mr Roche reminded the commissioners that a similar motion had come before them previously, in November 1846, and was abandoned for want of co-operation from the other municipal bodies as well as opposition from the insurance companies, save the Atlas. The insurance companies feared that if a public fire brigade were formed the people would feel so secure that they would not insure their property. The commissioners quickly concluded (with some degree of relief, one suspects), that it was not within their power to grant any monies for such a purpose and the whole subject disappeared from the public radar.[34]

As far back as 1828, an Act of Parliament entitled, 'An Act to make provision for the lighting, cleansing, and watching of cities, towns, corporate and market towns in Ireland in certain cases' (9 George IV., Cap.82) had empowered the corporation to purchase:

> One or more Fire Engine or Engines, with all necessary apparatus, and to make and appoint ... a proper Person or Persons as may be necessary to work such Engine or Engines, with such Salaries and Allowances ... and to hire or rent any convenient House or Houses for keeping such Engine or Engines.

But this Act, like all such subsequent Fire Acts throughout the nineteenth century, merely allowed, rather than compelled, the corporation to make provision for fire protection, and nothing was done. The City Fathers were well aware that few Irish cities and towns had any municipal firefighting arrangements. In the case of Dublin, for instance, firefighting was still the preserve of the parish pumps, the insurance brigades, and the Dublin Metropolitan Police 'Fire Brigade'. Their 'fire station' was at the Police Training Depot at Kevin Street, where there was, 'a magnificent engine, under the special direction of a ... Sergeant, fourteen firemen (from the mounted police), and twenty of the recruits to work the pumps'.[35]

1850: A DRAMATIC END TO THE TROUBLED CORK SAW MILLS.

At an early hour on Tuesday morning, the premises known as Dixon's Patent Saw Mills, King Street were discovered by the police patrol to be on fire. Though the engines of the West of England and Atlas Offices, in addition to one from Mr Hewitt's Distillery [on the Watercourse Road] were speedily on the spot … as were a large body of the 40th and 41st Regiments under the command of Col. Beresford, and a large body of the constabulary … in consequence of the dryness of the timber stored within the premises, in less than two hours the entire building was consumed. The premises were insured in the National and Patriotic Offices, and the property destroyed amounted to between £800 and £1,000.[36]

The proprietor, Henry Dixon, publicly thanked those in charge of the fire engines for coming to his assistance, including, 'the Agents of the West of England and Atlas Companies, who, although the premises were not insured with them, sent their powerful Engines'.[37]

For the weary James Adams and his firemen, there was to be no respite that Christmas of 1850. The day after St Stephen's Day, another big fire broke out in Cork. This was at the business premises of W.J. Tomkins in Winthrop Street in the heart of the city. The building was extensively stocked with casks of fine old port, sherry, and whiskey, which had been bought in for the Christmas and New Year trade. The fire was discovered by the son of the owner, who, throwing open the front doors at 6.30a.m., was at once assaulted by a terrific blast of heat. The fire instantly spread with great fierceness.

Once again, the insurance brigades quickly responded to the alarm, as did the engine from Cork Barracks. The *Cork Examiner* reporter observed that:

> The preservation of the adjoining premises is to be attributed to the judicious disposition of the Engines … one of which was retained in Winthrop Street, another in Robert Street, another in Old George's Street and the fourth in Patrick Street, and thus completely hemmed in the conflagration. Messrs. Perrier and Tivey rendered very efficient service in directing the operations of the Firemen.[38]

The fire was not without its moments of drama – and sheer entertainment:

> A number of persons who were on the roof of the adjoining building, having perceived what they considered to be a pile of priceless ledgers in the loft of the building on fire, lowered themselves by ropes into the burning building and succeeded in saving the books.[39]

The 'priceless ledgers' turned out to be nothing more than bundles of waste paper. Then, much to the delight and glee of the watching crowd, as the foolhardy duo made their way back up the rope, 'While engaged in this perilous undertaking, a hose was directed on them to keep them cool and the rope from burning through.'[40]

Meanwhile, at ground-floor level, the highly-flammable whiskey was presenting its own special problems. As cask after cask was engulfed by the flames, the heat caused the spirit to vaporize and burst the casks. To the great dismay of the disbelieving mob, a fireman directed a jet of water on to the spirit flowing from the burning building to make it too watery to burn. Chuckled the *Examiner*, 'Many were the laughable but unsuccessful attempts to obtain a can or two of the scalding liquor, which was to be seen on all sides pouring into the gutter.'[41] Presently, a number of firemen, having cautiously entered the building after the main body of fire had been extinguished, soon felt distinctly happy and euphoric as inhalation of whiskey vapours produces practically the same effect as actually drinking it.

The spate of fires at Christmas 1850 prompted what may well qualify as one of the briefest (and most waspish) editorials in the history of the *Cork Examiner:*

A Fire Brigade.
Will Cork ever have a Fire Brigade? Two formidable fires in one week! What next? As the last sufferer is a member of the Corporation perhaps the matter is not hopeless. We shall see.[42]

1858: MAJOR FIRE AND NEEDLESS FATALITY ON GRAND PARADE.

Tom Rogers felt on top of the world. A fine, strapping, tee-total lad of just eighteen summers, he was well-liked by his elders, and because of his roguish devil-may-care charm, his company was much in demand among his peers, particularly by the girls. Only the previous evening, his employer, builder Edmund Murphy, had confirmed the great news that Tom was to be indentured to him as an apprentice. He could hardly wait to get home to break the story to his widowed mother. What a difference full-time, gainful employment would make to their frugal circumstances!

Tom had begun his day by attending early Mass at the South Chapel on that cold Wednesday morning, 6 January, the Feast of the Epiphany. Now, as he left his home in Grafton's Alley off the South Mall, his cap set jauntily at an angle, he had the shining, eager face and mischievous grin of a young man ready to take on the world. He thought about the many tasks that lay ahead of him in the decrepit old building they were renovating close to the Queen's Old Castle on the Grand Parade. Tom wasn't bothered; he had never been afraid of hard work. Life was good. He could not know that, sadly, this day would be his last on this earth.

Young Tom and his boss, Edmund Murphy, beavered away all day until the fading winter daylight made it too difficult to continue. As the street lamps of the new Cork Gas Consumers' Company twinkled on, like so many fairy lights, they decided to call it a day. In the next-door premises, Mr Hayden, the silk-merchant and linen-draper, had gathered his family together for their evening meal on an upper floor: it was the era of 'living over the shop'. The Cork Examiner for 8 January takes up the story on what happened next:

> On Wednesday evening a fire of extraordinary fury broke out in the establishment of Mr. Hayden, Grand Parade, which resulted not only in the complete destruction of that and an adjoining building, but also, we regret to say, in the death of a young man named Thomas Rogers, and in an accident of a very serious nature to a member of the City Constabulary, Constable Phelan.
>
> The shop was closed about six o'clock, and Mr. Hayden's family...were assembled in one of the upper apartments when an alarm was given that the first floor was in flames. The fire seems to have originated in the shop ... the stove kept there [appears to have] become over-heated, and the flue ignited the ceiling. The flames spread with such rapidity that the inmates of the house were obliged to get out through one of the windows onto the ledge ... from whence they were taken down by means of a ladder after undergoing great danger. The fire quickly mounted to the upper floors, and in a little more than half an hour from the time the alarm was given, the whole building, including the roof, was enveloped in flames, which shed a strong lurid light down Patrick Street and along the Parade.
>
> A strong party of police soon arrived under Sub-Inspector Brew and Head-Constables Crowley, Roe and Hayes ... and about seven o'clock the engines of the Atlas, West of England and the Royal Exchange Insurance Companies began to arrive, and were worked as quickly as the confusion that prevailed and the inexperience of those who volunteered their services would allow.

Among those who volunteered their services were Tom Rogers and builder Murphy. With the arrival of the military fire engine, worked by a party from the Royal Elthorne and Leicester Militia, all efforts were now directed at saving the adjoining buildings, including the large retail premises of the Queen's Old Castle:

> Two of the engines played freely on it [and] so great was the alarm felt for its safety, that the young men employed there commenced removing the goods ... had there been proper order and regularity preserved in the efforts to extinguish the flames, it is the opinion of a great many that the damage would be far less. The only fire engines in the city are those belonging to the insurance companies and the military, and we have no fire brigade as most large cities have. Had the fire occurred later in the evening, or had the wind blown with any violence from the south or east, it would have been impossible to save the Queen's Old Castle and the whole range [of buildings] as far as Castle Street. Some of Mr. Hayden's family would no doubt also have lost their lives, as there is not a single fire escape in the city.[43]

About midnight, as the fire was at last being got under control, tragedy struck. Tom Rogers, accompanied by the policeman and a night watchman, entered the building under repair to check the extent of the damage caused by the fire next door. As they reached the top floor in the pitch-black building, the whole front of Hayden's fell into the street without warning, bringing down the adjacent building with it. The trio was buried under mounds of rubble. Constable Phelan and watchman Collins were removed, unconscious, in a few minutes, but the rescue of the young man was a different matter.[44] The greater portion of the debris had fallen on him. In a long and painstaking operation, the next-door premises had to be shored up and secured before his body was found and removed.

The next day, the inquest on the deceased was held in the Bridewell. Hardly had the proceedings got under way and the first witness Edmund Murphy been called when the redoubtable John Francis Maguire was on his feet. He wished to avail of the opportunity, he said, to make a statement on behalf of the newly-established Cork Gas Consumers' Company, which had only commenced supplying gas through their new network of mains during the previous fortnight. He was anxious to dispel certain malicious rumours going around town that the cause of the fire could be attributed in some way to a leak of gas from the new pipes. He wished to make it clear that Mr Hayden had, in fact, declined to take his gas from the new company, and 'no matter whose gas it was, it had nothing to do whatever with the fire, one way or another'.[45]

In that year, 1858, Cork was in the unique position of having two rival companies supplying gas to the city, each with its own plant (on adjacent sites) and network of pipes. A bitter and sometimes acrimonious battle had been fought between the old monopolistic United General Gas-Lighting Company (which had provided Cork with gas since 1825) and the new Cork Gas Consumers' Company for the hearts and minds, to say nothing of the wallets, of Corkonians. The new company was deeply suspicious of *agents provocateurs* spreading malicious rumours about their professionalism and the safety and quality of their pipe network.

Back in July of 1824, the Wide Street Commissioners had awarded the English-based United General with the contract to light the city of Cork for twenty-five years. Under the terms of the contract, Cork Corporation was forbidden to negotiate with any other company for the supply of gas. The United General set up its gasworks on Monarea Marsh, off the Old Blackrock Road. In 1845, their contract was renewed for a further thirteen years. With the passing of the Cork Improvement Act in 1852, the Wide Street Commissioners were abolished and the corporation were, at long last, masters of their own affairs. They at once sought ways and means of breaking the crushing monopoly of the English company. The price of gas in Cork was dearer than anywhere else in the United Kingdom. The breakthrough came in 1856 with the adding of the Joint Stock Companies Act to the statute books, and the Cork Gas Consumers' Company was incorporated on 18 September 1856.

The United General tried in vain to meet the challenge by cutting the price of its gas drastically, but the people had had enough. Over 1,000 consumers agreed to take their gas from the new company from New Year's Day 1858. Under its first secretary, the popular Denny Lane, poet, businessman, and Young Irelander who had been imprisoned in the aftermath of the 1848 Rising, Cork Gas Company commenced operations. On Christmas Eve 1857, the city was illuminated by the new gas under contract from Cork Corporation.

Then, Hayden's fire intervened and those antagonistic to the new company had a field day. Because the fire was by far the biggest seen in Cork for several years, they decreed that it had to be the fault in some way of the new pipes being laid by the inexperienced and unproven fledgling company. A couple of days later, another opportunity for scare-mongering presented itself to the enemies of the Cork Gas Company. In the early hours of Saturday 8 January, fire broke out in the premises of James Reidy in Cook Street. Once again, the family lived overhead. Once again, the family was trapped. Unable to find the keys of the front door to let themselves out onto the street, fortuitously, some late-night revellers happened to be passing and kicked in the lower panels and by this means the family made good their escape, but only by the skin of their teeth. The *Cork Examiner* reporter was soon scribbling furiously in his notebook:

> The fire had now extended over the entire of the upper floor and burst out through the front windows, illuminating the entire street. The engines of the Atlas and West of England companies quickly arrived, but in the confusion that prevailed the fire-plugs could not be come at, and it was found necessary to tear up the pavement in Old George's Street and on the South Mall to obtain a supply of water, so that they could not be set to work for an hour after their arrival, during which the fire continued to rage with great fury, a strong gale blowing at the time.[46]

That 'the fire-plugs could not be come at' is surprising. The Atlas fire station was only a few metres up the street from the fire ground and one would imagine that the engineer and firemen would be well acquainted with the location of the fire plugs in the immediate vicinity of their own station. Indeed, the County and City of Cork Almanac 1843, which included the locations of all thirty-nine plugs in the city at that time, lists a plug at the junction of Cook Street and South Mall.

As the fire raged out of control and unchallenged, the next-door Royal Victoria Theatre seemed in imminent danger of being involved. The owner and staff started to remove anything they could lay their hands on, including the scenery and props.[47] Then, no sooner had the fire plugs been located and a supply of water laid down to the fire engines, than another problem presented itself: there was a shortage of manpower to work the pumps:

Owing to the lateness of the hour, not many people had assembled around the place, so that there was a want of persons to work the fire engines, and some of the police were asked to give their assistance, but they refused, stating that it was not their business.[48]

Such were the vagaries of firefighting operations in nineteenth-century Cork! Eventually, the police relented and agreed to man the pumps, and with the arrival of the REA (who were instrumental in saving the theatre), the fire was suppressed at about 4a.m.

This time, there was a connection with gas, albeit a tenuous one: James Reidy was a gas fitter and subscribed to both companies. Those who were keen to exploit the situation for their own nefarious purposes were quickly silenced when it was established that it was the United General's gas which was supplying the interior of the premises where the fire had started, a fact not lost on the *Cork Examiner*, whose proprietor was, of course, John Francis Maguire, the primogenitor of the Cork Gas Company. In yet another hard-hitting editorial, it deplored the state of preparedness of Cork to deal with emergencies of fire:

> There is not a more helpless community in the world, or one less prepared to deal with a calamity of the kind. Our engines are mostly in a deplorable state of asthma, and the best are only good 'squirts'. [In a few months] we shall have fire-plugs in every street, to which hose can be attached, and a pressure which will drive a stream or streams of water over the tops of the highest houses. In March we shall have a supply of water at our command which will make us altogether independent of an ordinary burning, and able to cope with the very worst.
>
> Perhaps it may be no harm to state, for the benefit of all gossips, that the 'new gas' had nothing whatever to do with the fire. The fire commenced inside, and therefore the new gas, which was outside had nothing to do with it … the 'new gas' is as innocent as a babe of all harm in the matter.[49]

In spite of many difficulties, the Cork Gas Company prevailed, the United General finally capitulated, and in July 1859, the new owners took possession of the plant and works of the monopoly which had held the people of Cork in thrall for some thirty-three years.

THE (NOT SO) GREAT ESCAPE:
CORK'S FIRST FIRE-RESCUE APPARATUS.

'We've a Fire Escape, when our houses are lightin',
But where to look for it would puzzle the D....'

(John Fitzgerald, in *Cork is the Eden for you love, and me*).

Cork's first wheeled fire escape was purchased following the public outcry in the aftermath of Hayden's fire. It cost the corporation £58 10s. 0d and the *Cork Examiner* for 12 April 1858 related how:

> This engine [sic], which was so much needed in Cork, has been brought over from London, free of expense, by the Cork Steam Ship Company. It has not been yet decided upon what part of the city to place it. Some members of the Council suggest the Bridewell yard, whilst others are in favour of putting it in a more conspicuous place.
>
> Whatever its situation may be, its arrival ought to be a source of congratulation, for no other city in the Empire, of equal extent, was so ill-provided as ours against fires.

And would be. From the time of its arrival, there is only one reference to it having being extended to see how it worked. After that, no one was ever trained in its use, and, consequently, it was never brought into operation at a fire. With no dedicated fire brigade, it seems the city fathers didn't quite know what to do with it. It was shunted around the city from post to pillar, first to the yard adjoining the Bazaar (on Cornmarket Street), then to the corporation yard on Western Road near the Lancasterian School, and finally, in 1877, to the fire station yard on Sullivan's Quay, as it grew increasingly decrepit.

The Sub-Inspector of Police had declared that he would 'practice his men daily on it until they become proficient in its use', but nothing appears to have come of this well-intentioned aspiration. Only when Cork's first fire chief, Mark Wickham, arrived to take up his appointment almost twenty years later and declared the, by then, rotting escape 'totally useless' was it disposed of.

The coroner at the inquest on Thomas Rogers had thought it, 'most reprehensible on the part of the authorities not to have them [escapes]. There is hardly a street in London in which they have not them.'[50]

The 'fly ladder' escape (the telescopic escape was still in the future) was the invention of one Abraham Wivell, a member of the RSPLF. Mounted on a spring carriage with large road wheels was the main ladder, thirty-five feet long, made of fir on account of its lightness, and capable of reaching to second floor windows. Ten feet from the top of the main ladder was a twenty-foot fly ladder, also made of fir, hinged on a bracket. When not in use, the fly ladder hung, head downwards from its hinges, along the rounds of the main ladder.

When the window to be reached was higher than thirty-five feet, the head of the fly ladder was swung through the arc of a circle by a guy-line attached to a lever at the base, the head of the ladder coming to rest against the building ten feet higher than the head of the main ladder. If still too short to reach those trapped, a sixteen-foot extension ladder could be added to the fly ladder, giving an overall height of sixty feet. To the underside of the carriage was fixed

A 'fly ladder' wheeled escape
in action, similar to the one
acquired by Cork Corporation
in 1858 following on the fatal fire
on Grand Parade.

a chute made from stout sail cloth, strengthened by copper-wire netting, by means of which trapped people could slide to safety: not unlike the idea of the escape chute in modern airliners. The canvas chute, however, being nearest to the burning building, was very susceptible to catching fire, and the soaking of the cloth in alum was recommended to make it fire retardant to some degree.

The main disadvantage of the fly ladder escape was that in order to elevate the 'fly', the main ladder had first to be resting against the building on fire. In narrow streets and lanes it was frequently found impossible to throw the fly ladder over. Despite the drawbacks, fire escapes of this type continued in use for more than forty years, and the numbers manufactured increased along with the number of people who were saved by them. Poor Wivell, whose idea it had been, was never to benefit financially from his invention. He died, destitute, in the workhouse.

On 11 April 1858, the council members met to pass a vote of thanks to the Cork Steam Ship Company for having transported the new fire escape, *gratis*, from London. Well, perhaps not quite so *gratis*; later the same day, two senior executives of the company, Ebenezer Pike and L. W. Glover waited on the corporation 'to request permission to put a tramway across the road from the yard of the Cork Steam Ship Company to that of the Great Southern and Western Railway for the conveyance of goods'. Their application was granted.[51]

1861: A NIGHT TO REMEMBER: SEVEN SOULS PERISH ON GEORGE'S STREET.

Since Martin Millerick had turned in for the night, he had found it impossible to get to sleep. His stomach was giving him hell. He was sure it was the result of a bad pint of porter – a 'caskey' pint, as Corkonians called it – which he had downed earlier on in the night at Long's public house across the street. To add to his misery, the caterwauling of the pesky streetwalkers entertaining their sailor friends from the docks, right under his window, was totally seeing him off. Only when Sub Constable Fitzgerald had arrived on the beat and moved them on could he begin to relax. He pulled his nightcap well down over his ears on that frosty Tuesday morning, 26 February 1861, and mercifully drifted off to sleep.

Sometime later he awoke. Thankfully, his stomach had settled down, but it was the renewed screeching in the street that had jolted him from his slumber. By the ghostly-green glow of the hissing gas lamp outside his bedroom window, he peered at the pocket watch he always kept by night on his bedside locker. It was half past one. Where was the bloody policeman now? So like the police – never around when you need them. He would have to deal with the revellers himself. Grumpily, he pulled on some clothes as the screaming persisted, and sleepily glanced out of the window. To his horror, he saw thick, brown smoke pouring out of the upper windows of Long's premises. Little knots of people were beginning to gather on the street. By the time he had awoken his son and collected a ladder, which he kept in the hall, John Ring, the waterworks Superintendent, and his men had arrived and begun to play a hose on the burning public house. Millerick felt he had to do something other than just be a passive spectator at the unfolding drama. Accompanied by Head Constable Roe, he entered the house by an upstairs window, but they were soon driven out by the choking smoke and intense heat.

For a time, confusion reigned as to whether the members of the Long family had made good their escape. Beyond pouring water in the windows of the premises from the street, nobody seemed to know what to do. The waterworks 'brigade' had arrived in George's Street promptly enough from their base on the South Mall and made down a standpipe to a hydrant in Cook Street. When their superior, John Ring, arrived, he opened a second hydrant on Elbow Lane, near its junction with George's Street.[52] Soon, two good jets were working on the fire. So far as the waterworks men were concerned, their duty ended there. Rescue, or entering buildings on fire, was no part of their brief. No one knew where the wheeled fire escape – purchased by the corporation three years earlier after another fire tragedy – was kept, save a small boy who said that it was housed in the corporation yard on Lancaster Quay, a distance of about a kilometre away. When Sub Constable Fitzgerald, who obviously hadn't the faintest idea what a fire escape looked like, heard this, he asked the little boy, in all seriousness, if he would go and fetch it: a piece of equipment weighing up to 655 kilos and normally requiring the efforts of five men to handle it properly.[53] Someone asked another policeman if he would enter the house with him to attempt a rescue, but the policeman replied he was afraid of getting his feet wet as he was only wearing his slippers. When asked later for the policeman's number, the man replied that he could not tell 'for I am no scholar'.[54] Not one of the civic authorities – the corporation, nor its waterworks 'brigade', nor the police – emerged from that unhappy night with enhanced reputations.

On that terrible February morning in 1861, seven souls lost their lives: publican Eugene Long, his wife Catherine, four of their children, and Catherine's aunt, Mary-Anne Crowe. All had been overcome by the effects of smoke, and when the bodies were recovered the following morning, all were largely unmarked, save Mrs Crowe. Only one member of the Long family survived: a baby who was out at nurse. Margaret Buggy, the servant girl who first discovered the fire, was the only one to come out of the house alive.

At the coroner's inquest the next day, the corporation was roundly condemned by the jury. They found that, 'the corporate authorities, who have charge of the fire escape, were much to blame in not having the machine ready to be availed of and in a central position'. They recommended that the standpipes used by the waterworks men should be kept in the same place as the escape, and they should always 'accompany each other to fires under the supervision of a properly-organised fire brigade, and that each police station be supplied with two or three ladders of different lengths'.[55] Outside of Long's, three other premises were destroyed that night. When the unfortunate homeless and destitute people presented themselves at the corporation offices seeking some relief, they were curtly asked to leave the premises by an official who told them corporate funds could not be diverted for such purposes.[56]

In the aftermath of the tragedy, once again the cry went up for the establishment of a proper fire brigade. Once again, the moneyed citizens chanted their mantra: the extra taxation required would pose an undue imposition on the rates. The corporation did, however, make an attempt to implement at least one of the jury's recommendations. The police were approached to see if they would allow ladders and fire equipment to be stored in the yards of the various city stations, which they could use in times of emergency. The reply was swift, polite, and firm: the police would always render any assistance they could at the scene of a fire, but they were peace keepers first and foremost, not firefighters and that is how they intended to remain. The corporation's suggestion, however, was not at all out of order. Belfast had a combined Police and Fire Brigade under Corkman, Capt. Shaw, and Dublin had its Metropolitan Police Fire Brigade with headquarters at Kevin Street. Many British cities and towns had their Police Fire Brigades also, a situation that prevailed well into the twentieth century.

The tragedy at Long's public house was notable for the number of lives lost, the greatest fire tragedy in Cork within living memory.[57] But it is also striking for one other reason: the non-attendance of the insurance fire brigades who were conspicuous by their absence. All three engine-houses were located but a short distance from the scene of the fire: the REA on South Mall, the Atlas on Cook Street, and the West of England on Anderson's Quay. This fire, probably more than any other, serves to illustrate the marked shift in emphasis that was beginning to manifest itself with regard to their *modus operandi*.

1862: *GAUDEAMUS IGITUR*: THE COLLEGE IS IN FLAMES!

The fire at Queen's College, Cork (hereafter QCC; now UCC) in the early hours of 15 May 1862 was certainly, if not the largest, the most controversial fire experienced in Cork in years, the repercussions from which would continue to smoulder long after the last glowing embers had been extinguished.

There is no doubt that the fire was the work of an incendiary or incendiaries. In the weeks and months after the fire, the theories on who the culprits might have been ranged from the ridiculous to the sublime and, like the chief suspect in some fantastic Agatha Christie whodunit, each could be shown to have had a motive. They included the college steward, a porter, Roman Catholic zealots, and perhaps most bizarre of all, even the President of the college himself, Sir Robert Kane. To compound the air of mystery, even the accused in a contemporaneous murder case was woven into the web of intrigue. But more of that anon.

At about 5.30a.m. on Thursday 15 May, a woman living across the river from the college on the heights of Sunday's Well was up attending to a sick child. Drawing back the curtains, she looked across the valley of the Lee at the university, distinctly visible in the distance with no suspicion of anything being amiss. A few minutes before six she again happened to glance out of the window and was shocked to see smoke belching out of a chimney, quickly followed by flames.[58] Not long after, just over the wall from the college in the County Gaol, some warders going about their early morning business had noticed 'a great smoke arising out of the west wing' of the college and immediately raised the alarm.[59] A messenger was sent round to rouse the college staff. The Vice-President, Dr Ryall, and the President, Sir Robert Kane, were both asleep in their apartments in the East Wing, a short distance across the quadrangle from the building on fire.

Dressing hurriedly, even as they stepped out onto the lawn they could see the building opposite in flames with the fire beginning to break through the roof. The affected wing was a large cut-stone building, approximately 36m long by 9m wide, with a corridor running along its length on each floor communi-cating, on the west side, with the various lecture rooms. Here were housed the chemistry, pathology and *materia medica* departments. When the building was originally erected, little or no thought was given to the problems of internal fire spread. Additionally, the building had a common roof void, unbroken by fire stops, which allowed the fire to spread laterally very quickly.

In those pre-telephone days, the only means of summoning firefighting equipment from the city was either by runner or by horseback. It is not clear which method was employed, but while this was underway some members of the college staff, including Sir Robert, warily entered the ground-floor corridor, where half-consumed matches were discovered under each of the doors leading to the lecture rooms. The incipient fires had burned themselves out under three doors, but at the fourth, which led to the *materia medica* room (wherein were stored pathological specimens preserved in flammable methylated spirits), a sub-stantial fire was in progress. As the fire took hold they made good their retreat.

The news spread rapidly throughout the awakening city. The first fire engines to arrive were from local industries: Beamish and Crawford's brewery on South Main Street and Richard Perrott and Sons, Founders and Millwrights, of the Hive Iron Works on Hanover Street. Given the level of communications, the time lost in mustering staff and the fact that the heavy engines had to be man-ually hauled to the fire ground, some considerable time elapsed before their arrival. Then, the discovery was made that the college authorities had neglected to install fire hydrants within the grounds, 'but Mr. Perrott having discovered the locality of the water pipe, tore up the ground over it, and immediately cut a hole in it' to obtain a water supply.[60] As this was being done, the 'water-works brigade' arrived under their Superintendent, John Ring, having pulled

The fire in the West Wing of Queen's College, Cork, 'spiritedly drawn by Mr. Stopford'. Curiously, Stopford seems to have depicted a night scene, whereas, in reality, the fire took place on a bright May morning. (*ILN* 24.05.1862).

their 'van', top heavy with hose, branchpipes, and fittings all the way from their depot on the South Mall. Their standpipe was wedged into the break created by Richard Perrott and the hose 'was played actively on the building'.[61]

All thoughts now turned to averting total disaster by trying to stop the fire from spreading to the north and east wings. The *Cork Examiner* narrated how:

> The flames quickly extended themselves to the lower part of the wing, and rapidly approached the end where it joins the main building, with which it communicates by a single door, the division between them being a good stone wall … a large iron plate was placed up against the door communicating with the burning wing, and this and the playing of the hose prevented the fire from extending, and confined it altogether to the wing in which it had originated.[62]

At around 8a.m, two hours after the initial alarm, the men of the REA arrived with their engine. There are no reports of any other insurance engines in attendance at what was undoubtedly the most significant fire in Cork that year. No insurance had been taken out on the college, which may have played a major part in the tardiness of the REA in responding and the non-attendance of the others. Five hours after the call for assistance had gone out, a party of military, in the charge of Colonel Smith, appeared, having dragged their two engines all the way from Victoria Barracks. Inexplicably, only then it seems that anyone thought of harnessing the river as a means of fighting the fire: a readily available and inexhaustible source for the pumps only a short distance down an embankment from the burning building. Relays of soldiers were put to work drawing buckets of water from the river to supply the engines, but by then it was too late to make a difference. With a final resounding crash, the remaining portions of the roof fell in, and eventually, the fire, sated, burnt itself out. The departments affected consisted principally of the *materia medica,* pathology, surgical and midwifery museums. A 'collection of cinchone [sic] plants made for the late Emperor Napoleon' went up in the flames, as did 'the herborium [sic] … considered to be one of the finest in Great Britain'.[63]

The fire in QCC was widely reported. The *Illustrated London News* carried the story in its edition of 24 May, accompanied by a depiction of the fire 'spiritedly drawn' by 'Mr. Stopford of Cork'.[64] The House of Commons in London was awash with rumours about 'the three train loads of explosives' that had been taken right up against the college by dissidents and blown the place to smithereens. John Francis Maguire, Mayor of Cork and MP, happened to be in the House and quickly scotched that absurdity. Now the hunt for the perpetrator began. Later the same day, the college authorities launched their investigation, a search that would take numerous twists and turns over the course of many months. Almost immediately, the spotlight fell on the college staff themselves.

QCC first opened its doors to fee-paying students in 1849. Enjoying a handsome setting at the western edge of Cork, it is dominated by a wooded limestone precipice overlooking the Lee's meandering south channel. Perched on the cliff top is the three-sided, Gothic quad of white limestone quarried from the escarpment. The complex (for which the template appears to have been Magdalen College, Oxford) is the earliest large work of local architectural team Deane and Woodward, which went on to design the legendary Oxford museum under the influence of John Ruskin. Building commenced as the effects of the disastrous potato blight were beginning to become manifest, and, during the subsequent years of the Great Famine, the employment available, both to artisans and labourers must have proved a godsend to those desperately seeking work.

Sir Robert Kane's term of office was marred by internecine disputes with his fellow academicians. So much so, that by the year 1865, almost 50 per cent of the original professors had been dismissed or had left of their own volition. Such a man had enemies waiting in the shadows, patiently biding their time for him to let his guard slip. To compound the fledgling college's problems, the Roman Catholic Church was antagonistic towards the Queen's Colleges, set up in Cork, Galway, and Belfast. The form of organization and the character of the colleges were felt to be out of accord with Catholic educational principles, and after a storm of public controversy, they were condemned by the Hierarchy. Regarded as 'Godless places', in 1847 the Holy See had condemned the Queen's Colleges with their 'grievous and intrinsic dangers'.[65]

In the feeding frenzy after the fire, for a time attention centred on two Roman Catholic priests, who only two weeks previously had spoken out against the college system. Suspicions were raised that 'Ultramontane' extremists might be to blame.[66] Then, it must have been Williams, the steward; or perhaps Reynolds, the porter. All could be shown to have had the motive, the ability, and the wherewithal to set the fire. But the most outlandish claim of all was made by a senior member of the academic staff, Professor Denis Brenan Bullen, who held the Chair of Surgery.[67] The culprit, he intimated, was none other than President Kane himself, suggesting Kane may have engineered the fire in order to divert attention from his many absences from his duties on campus, a major bone of contention among senior staff. Bullen, who desperately coveted the college presidency and (obviously) would go to extreme lengths to discredit Kane, must have taken momentary leave of his senses to make such an audacious claim, for under examination his contentions utterly collapsed. He later declared that he was completely mistaken, withdrew unreservedly his accusations and tendered his profound apology; to no avail. The debacle, not surprisingly, ended in his resignation in 1864 and almost ruined his professional reputation.[68]

And what of the story of the man who was later hanged for the murder of his wife? On the day after the fire in the college, the *Cork Examiner* carried a report with the headline 'Committal of Mr. Burke, Clerk of Waterford Union, on a charge of poisoning his wife'.[69] This concerned the celebrated case of Richard Burke, who was later indicted at Clonmel Assizes on 2 July 1862 for the murder of his wife, Johanna, and subsequently hanged. Several versions of the story have been promulgated down the years, among the earliest being Tim Healy's account in his autobiography.[70] Healy's narrative, which contains several inaccuracies, has been taken at face value by some subsequent chroniclers. The story, gleaned from contemporary newspapers (principally, the *Waterford News and General Advertiser* and the *Cork Examiner*) is briefly as follows:

On Tuesday 13 May 1862, an inquest was held at Clogheen, Co. Tipperary, into the death of local woman, Johanna Burke, whose husband Richard was Clerk of the Waterford Union (i.e. the Workhouse). Mrs Burke had died in agony at her home on the night of 14 April 1862, after taking some 'medication' sent to her from Waterford by her husband. In her dying moments, the poor woman whispered to her sister, Alice, 'Oh, Ally, Ally! God forgive them that caused it – God forgive them!'[71] It emerged that Richard Burke had been 'seeing' the schoolmistress of the Union for some time.[72]

Evidence was heard from the local physician, Dr Walshe, that he had performed a post-mortem on the deceased on 15 April, detached her stomach and a small portion of her intestine, sealed them in a jar and given it to the police.[73] Constable Hatton testified that he had brought the jar to Cork on 24 April and handed it over to Dr John Blyth, Professor of Chemistry at QCC.[74] Blyth confirmed that he had received three items from Hatton:

A bottle containing a fluid which was found to contain 'harmless Essence of Turpentine'

A paper packet containing a white powder which he analyzed as 'a mixture of Epsom Salts, Carbonate of Magnesia and the deadly poison, Strychnine'.

The stomach and part of the intestine of the dead woman, contained in a jar with five seals.

Strychnine was found in the viscera. Dr Blyth remarked that the items were deposited in his private laboratory in the college, which was in the West Wing. The jury withdrew, and returned in a short time with their verdict, 'That the deceased Johanna Burke came by her death from the effects of Strychnine, which she received from her husband, Richard Burke, from Waterford.'[75] Burke was immediately taken into custody and transported to Clonmel Gaol.

Although Burke had been arrested, Dr Blyth's forensic analysis concluded and verbal evidence given at the inquest, the substantive evidence – the jar containing the dead woman's stomach – still reposed in the doctor's laboratory in QCC. The conspiracy theorists argue that the accused might have had a slim chance of escaping the gallows if the damning evidence could have been destroyed. The suggestion is that Burke, who apparently had 'pleasing manners, a large amount of good nature and a warm readiness to oblige'[76] had a large circle of friends, some of whom may have engineered the fire at the college in a last desperate bid to save their pal. Undoubtedly, they knew that the damning jar reposed in the doctor's lab, for he had said as much at the inquest. But whether the short window of opportunity, from the proceedings on Tuesday to the early hours of Thursday morning, can be reconciled with the organizing of an arson attack on the college is another matter. If, indeed, they did succeed, they must have been shocked to discover that their efforts were in vain; Dr Blyth, only the very evening before the fire, had removed the jar from his laboratory and sent it to Waterford, as reported in the *Cork Examiner* on Saturday 17 May 1862:

Curious Coincidence.

The chief evidence connected with two charges of murder now pending had been entrusted to Dr. Blyth, Professor of Chemistry in the Queen's College, and narrowly escaped destruction in the recent fire. One was the stomach of the deceased Mrs. Burke, supposed to have died of poisoning by strychnine. It had been in the laboratory of the College, and had only been sent off to Waterford the evening before the fire. The other was the bloody knife and clothes which had been found after the murder of Maguire, and had been entrusted to Dr. Blyth for the purpose of detecting blood upon them. They, too, had been in the laboratory and were there during the progress of the fire. In the confusion, we are informed, they were torn out of the place in which they had been deposited and flung upon the lawn. They were first observed by Dr. Blyth himself, who recognized them at once, and put them in a place of safety.

On 24 July 1862, Richard Burke was found guilty and on Monday 25 August was publicly hanged in front of Clonmel Gaol. The perpetrator of the fire at QCC was never brought to justice. Many of the ordinary Cork people, to whom the college was a remote and arcane place, learnt of the fire with apathy and indifference. To them, Queen's College was an irrelevancy. In fact, in his report on the blaze, Constable Goulden deposed that 'amongst the lower order of people ... there is no feeling of regret. Some say it is a pity any of the buildings escaped'. The last word on this extraordinary episode in the college's history must surely go to the head of History and English Literature, Professor Rushton. When asked to report on the state of his department in the aftermath of the blaze, his riposte was singularly apposite, brief, and entirely fact-filled: 'Burnt'.[77]

Poster offering a reward for information leading to the arrest of the person(s) responsible for the college fire. It was never awarded.

1863: A HARD DAY'S NIGHT: TWENTY-FOUR HOURS OF DESTRUCTION AND TERROR.

ST PATRICK'S STREET.

In June 1863, within the space of twenty-four hours, thousands of pounds (many millions of euro today) worth of damage was caused in two major fires in Cork. Both fires were discovered by the night watchman on his beat; and both were discovered at exactly half-past one in the morning. Sadly, the second fire was attended by loss of life.

The four-storey premises of W. and H.M. Goulding, 'Druggists and Dispensing Pharmaceuticals', occupied 108 St Patrick's Street, now the site of the Savoy Shopping Centre. The Goulding brothers, William and Humphrey Manders, were heavily involved in the business affairs of Cork, and as well as their extensive city centre outlet, owned a fertilizer factory at Blackpool, the Goulding's Glen Chemical Works, covering an area of eight acres. Their St Patrick's Street premises extended almost to Drawbridge Street at the rear and to William Street on its western flank, and, according to the *Cork Examiner*, 'contained drugs, oils, chemicals, etc – every article being more or less combustible and suited exactly to feed flame, amongst the rest being large quantities of vitriol [sulphuric acid], oils of all kinds and cotton waste'.[78]

The fire was discovered by the watchman at 1.30a.m. on the morning of 10 June 1863. While passing on his beat through William Street, he perceived thin streams of smoke and flame issuing out under the side door of the building. The alarm was at once given, and soon after a large party of policemen arrived from the St Patrick's Hill station. A mounted policeman was dispatched to alert the various firefighting agencies and the other city police stations. John Ring and the men of the waterworks arrived and by 2a.m. had two good jets working on the fire, ably assisted by Sub-Inspector Channer, the senior policeman, who, 'worked as hard as any labouring man on the spot, with his coat off, working and directing one of the hoses himself', but:

> Considering the exceedingly inflammable nature of the materials … it soon became plain that no chance whatever existed of saving [the premises] from utter destruction. The streams of water from the hoses, which were of great volume and strength, soon smashed the windows in the upper storeys; but here an unexpected disadvantage arose. When the windows were broken, a free current of air began to pass through which greatly fostered and extended the flames.
>
> At this point few views could be conceived grander than that presented by the scene. All Patrick Street, down to the bridge, and far up in the opposite direction, was rendered almost as clear as day, and the roaring and hissing of the flames in which numerous columns of water buried themselves, the anxious and terrified aspect of the spectators, and all the surroundings of the scene imparted to it an interest of the most remarkable description. At 3a.m., the roof and all the internal portions of the building fell in with a tremendous crash. We are informed that the hydrants discharged no less than two million gallons of water in the course of the night.[79]

Presently, the engine of the REA arrived, as did, at 3.30a.m, the barrack engine and detachments of the 99th and 57th Regiments under Capt. Chamberg. They found themselves with little to do, however.[80] There were only two fire hydrants at a convenient distance to the fire ground (in spite of Sir John Benson's prediction, in 1858, that there would be a hydrant at every street corner in Cork), and these were already in use by Ring's men. In any event, such was the pressure and volume of water now available in the 'flat' of the city that, increasingly, the insurance and barrack fire engines found themselves redundant at fires. The jets worked directly from the water mains were far more powerful than the manual engines could produce.

At one point during the course of the night consternation was caused when a rumour circulated among the crowd that Richardson's, only two doors away from the building on fire, was full of gunpowder. This transpired to be a few packets, stored in a desk, which was rapidly removed after the initial alarm. The *Cork Examiner* was loud in its praise for John Ring and the waterworks firemen:

> Mr. Ring worked indefatigably, rushing about from hose to hose, directing the operations of the men, and labouring unceasingly at everything. One gentleman, living very near the scene of the fire, informed us that were it not for Mr. Ring's exertions he believes the greater part of the block would have been burned.[81]

Alas, *Sic Transit Gloria Mundi*. Presently, Ring's tiny force of water inspectors-cum-firefighters would find themselves fighting a rearguard action in consequence of the opprobrium heaped upon them for their incompetence. Spontaneous combustion was mooted as the cause of the fire.[82]

All that day, John Ring and his men worked hard at the scene of the fire on St Patrick's Street, damping down and turning over, and generally making the gutted premises safe. As dusk fell, Ring handed over responsibility for the building to the police and returned, with his little band, exhausted, to their base on the South Mall.

The *Cork Examiner* opined that fires in Cork seemed to come in twos, and frequently in threes.[83] Many now had a presentiment that another bad fire was imminent. They were not to be disappointed.

NORTH MAIN STREET.

The night watchman was an old man. After a lifetime of hard graft and now crippled with arthritis, he still worked long, unsociable hours to provide himself with a few hot meals a week, washed down with a couple of pints of porter, his only diversion. Tonight, he was particularly tired. Having discovered the fire in St Patrick's Street the night before, he had generally helped out as best he could, pulling a hose here and taking a message there for Mr Ring. Now, having finished his 'beat' in the vilest weather seen in Cork in weeks – the rain was incessant – he settled back, soaked through, in his little hut close by the works for the new North Gate Bridge.[84] Reaching in his coat pocket for his most prized possession, a tortoiseshell snuff-box sent him by his married daughter in America, through the dancing flames of the brazier he imagined he could see a strange light coming from the top of the North Main Street: something other than the yellow, singing glow of the street lamp whose bouncing reflection lit up the puddles. Shuffling, he set off to investigate. What he had secretly feared was soon realized. He was horrified to see flames belching from the windows of Shea's grocer shop and, frighteningly, no sign of activity within.

Groping his way through the thickening smoke, he began hammering on the front door and shouting at the top of his voice. The din echoed eerily along the deserted street and whipped back in his face. Presently, the commotion alerted the Shandon Street watchman on the other side of the timber bridge, who now joined his colleague. At last, the occupants of the house began to stir.

William Shea had gone to Doneraile that day on business, leaving his wife, four young children, a servant girl, and an apprentice behind. In the dead of night a fire broke out in a downstairs room. In three minutes, temperatures in the room had reached a lethal 260°C. Other rooms downstairs began to fill with noxious fumes. In four minutes, the upstairs and downstairs hallways, and the stairs were impassable. The apprentice, Jeremiah Barry, was asleep on the top floor when he was awakened, not by the smoke rolling up the stairs, which would have anaesthetized him, but by the din created by the watchmen in the street. He made every effort to get down the stairs to assist the family but was driven back by the heat and smoke billowing up from below. Light-headed from the fumes he had inhaled, he managed to get out onto the roof and, precariously, made his way to the next-door skylight where he dropped down into the attic, and thence out onto the street. Reported the *Examiner*:

> As usual, the first step taken by the persons in the street was to burst in the front door, and, fanned by the draught thus created, the flames which were then raging in the shop and kitchen, burst up through the ceiling ... the family thus were cut off from all means of access to the street through the lower part of the house.[85]

The servant girl, Hannah Fleming, her frightened face momentarily framed in the window like some grotesque cameo of Munch's haunting *The Scream*, now began to do the unthinkable: she started to throw the children out of the third-storey window, beginning with the five year old little girl. Even though mattresses had been placed in the street for just such an eventuality, little Rose landed with a thud on the pavement and was rushed to the North Infirmary, gravely ill.[86] What happened next was worthy of a well-trained troupe of circus performers, and kudos must go to the police for their imaginative thinking. Several ladders had been rushed to the scene by neighbours, but none was long enough to reach the trapped people. (Nobody thought of the fire escape, purchased some five years before after a similar tragedy, locked away on Lancaster Quay a couple of hundred metres from the scene). Eventually, a ladder about twenty feet in length was procured, but it still fell short of the window where the trapped people huddled, about thirty feet from the ground. Then:

Under the direction of Constables Moloney and Fahey, it was raised on the shoulders of two men, and while held in this position as securely as was possible, it was placed against the wall beneath the window at which the inmates of the house were. But even then the ladder did not reach quite up to the sill of the window, and Mrs. Shea had to let herself down by her hands to gain the upper rungs. She was received by the constables, who had mounted the ladder and was safely handed to the ground. In this way, two children and the maid were saved. Not seeing anyone else at the window, the constables came off the ladder, the flames by now bursting out fiercely from the windows of the first floor. The appalling fact became known that one of the children [Mary Ellen, aged eight] had been left behind in the burning house. The fire had by that time spread from the top to the bottom of the house, and was bursting out from all the windows.[87]

By the time the waterworks men under John Ring arrived, a full hour had elapsed, and by then the fire had spread to three adjacent premises: Falvey's spirit stores, Harley's provision stores, and D'Arcy's confectioners. The flames threatened to extend to Hifle's Public House on Phillip's Lane:

> Mr. Ring, although nearly exhausted by his efforts on the previous night, was most efficient in the direction of the hose, and was ably assisted by Mr. Walker [Town Surveyor] and a party of the Corporation policemen and turncocks. The Constabulary party, under the command of Sub-Inspector Channer ... were indefatigable in their exertions, and but for the services they rendered at the commencement of the fire the whole of the female inmates of the house might have been lost. The heat from the burning houses was sufficient to wither up the paint on the houses opposite.[88]

Although all the affected premises were insured (the relevant companies are not specified in contemporary reports), no insurance fire brigade was in attendance.

Once again, the appalling shortcomings in Cork's firefighting and rescue capability had been highlighted in the worst possible way: the loss of human life. Great destruction of property had been visited on the city centre in the space of twenty-four hours, and, although abundant pressure and volume of water were now available from the new mains, as long as it could not be harnessed advantageously it could serve no useful purpose for firefighting. Even when the waterworks men arrived at North Main Street (an unacceptable sixty minutes after being called out), the fire hydrant opposite Phillip's Lane, close to the blazing buildings, could not be opened due to lack of maintenance: it had to be broken open with a pick-axe.[89]

Yet again, the jury at the inquest on the little girl castigated the corporation 'for not having fire escapes for such emergencies, and also for not having ladders at the different police stations of the city'.Yet again, the *Cork Examiner* under its editor, the young Thomas Crosbie ('a brilliant and powerful prose writer,' who would, on the death of Maguire in 1872, purchase the newspaper), was vociferous in its condemnation of the apathy attending the formation of a fire brigade:

> A fire escape has been purchased.They [the corporation] have been assured by their officer [John Ring] that the escape is useless without the aid of a trained fire brigade, and they cannot fail to be aware that the appointment of such a body is an absolutely necessary precaution for the preservation of human life.This subject has been brought before their attention by the Mayor [John Francis Maguire, the owner of the newspaper]; it has been pressed on them in this journal repeatedly; it now remains to be seen whether the force of public opinion, excited by the horror of this late occurrence, will not coerce the adoption of some speedy and decisive measure.[90]

A correspondent to the *Examiner,* who signed himself 'An Assurance Agent', recommended 'a far better way' of saving life from fire than escapes. He suggested each police station be equipped with ladders 'similar to those used in London [by the LFEE], made in lengths of 12 feet, fitting into each other.These are cheap, light and easily managed by anyone, and would be far more useful than fire escapes'.[91] Such ladders were called 'scaling' or 'military' ladders.A scaling ladder was a tapering ladder, some 6ft 6in long (not twelve feet as the writer stated) with two steel sockets outside the strings at the head and with two similar sockets inside the strings at the heel for the purpose of shipping another length at either end. Five ladders thus coupled together would produce a ladder some twenty-nine feet long, the optimum height recommended.

On the face of it, 'Assurance Agent's' suggestion had a degree of merit.What, obviously, he was unaware of is that members of the LFEE did not use such ladders (which required a high degree of dexterity and training to use) as rescue ladders, expecting members of the public to descend them. Rather, they were used for a variety of general purposes, such as communication between floors where staircases had been burned away, for entering the holds of ships, to form small bridges providing access from one wall or building to another, or, as an improvised stretcher, lowering an injured person from a height.The corporation, to its credit, did act on the jury's recommendation and provided the city police stations with extension ladders and ropes: a move which was directly responsible for saving the lives of fifteen people in Shandon Street before the year was out.

Meanwhile, back on St Patrick's Street the theatrics were not yet over.With all available policemen and the waterworks men concentrated at the fire on North Main Street, Constable Maher, finding himself all alone on duty at Goulding's, spotted some glowing embers (known to firefighters as 'bull's eyes') in a corner of Sheehan's Stores, next door to the gutted premises. Picking up a hose which had been left on the street for such a purpose, the good constable, who may have provided the inspiration for Hilaire Belloc's mischievous firemen who, 'took Peculiar Pains to Souse, The Pictures up and down the House.'[92] took to his new-found role with *élan,* or, as the *Cork Examiner* diplomatically put it, 'with a hearty good will'. In consequence of Constable Maher's over-exuberance, whose zeal, sadly, was greater than his skill, Sheehan's, who had recently stocked up with the best of 'China, Cut-Glass, Lamps, Parian, French and Bohemian Vases', were obliged to have a great clearance sale of water-damaged goods.

The arcane 'Fire Brigade Committee' was roused from its torpidity and dusted off in the aftermath of the two big fires and asked to provide yet another report to the City Council on the setting-up of a brigade. This report, which took all of a week to prepare, was laid before council on 18 June 1863 in the following terms:

Proposed Fire Brigade.

* Mr Walker to select eight men from those in the employment of the Corporation, for the purpose of working the fire escape, in addition to the four men now under Mr Ring for working the hoses.

* Premises to be taken – say one or two houses – as near as possible to the Bridewell, to be given rent free to the eight men under Mr Walker. Mr Ring's four men to remain as at present, at the Pipe Water Office, South Mall.

* One man to be required in regular turn to watch all night and take charge of the fire escape, which should be placed every night as near the Bridewell as possible; his duty would be immediately to call his comrades and proceed with them at once to any place where their services may be required, on the first intimation of a fire in the city.

* The eight men to be occasionally exercised with the fire escape in the evenings; when so employed to receive each a quarter of a day's pay.

* Each of the men to be entitled to at least 5s. for every night or part of night their services are engaged in working the escape, with power to the committee to increase the amount according as they consider it may be merited for special services.

* One man to be dispatched immediately from the pipe-water station to inform Mr Ring and also one from the Fire Brigade to inform Mr Walker on the first intimation at either station of an outbreak of fire in any part of the city.

* It shall be the duty of Mr Ring and Mr Walker to attend immediately when called, and each to do his best to preserve life (in the first instance) and to prevent the spread of fire, with power to employ any additional hands they

may require under special circumstances, who shall be entitled to be paid such sums as the committee may direct, according to their services rendered.

* The remuneration to Mr Ring and Mr Walker to be such as they may from time to time be considered entitled to by the committee.

* That for the protection of life at fires that ladders of such length and description as should be approved of by Sir John Benson be supplied to each police station in the city immediately.

* A rope, say 30 yards, to be always at the pipe-water and fire-escape stations. It shall be one man's special duty at each station to have the rope ready for use, if required, at the fire.

* The police stations to receive intimation as soon as possible on the outbreak of fire in any part of the city.[93]

In time-honoured fashion, that report was destined to go the way of all the others that had gone before it: 'referred back to a special committee'.

BLACKGUARDISM AND DEATH OF A FIREFIGHTER ON MORRISON'S QUAY.

The year 1863 in Cork would end, literally, in a blaze of publicity. In a month where the newspapers' column inches vied with each other for different angles on news from the American Civil War – then in its twentieth bloody month – the *Cork Examiner's* theory that Cork fires seemed to come in threes would soon be realized. That month of December saw John Ring and his men tackle three more blazes, two serious and one major. The latter was every bit as destructive as the fire in Goulding's of St Patrick's Street, and is notable for the death of a firefighter: not one of the waterworks brigade, but a supernumerary who was assisting them.

The major fire occurred at Messrs Power and Gamble's stores on Morrison's Quay, and was discovered at 10p.m on Friday 4 December 1863. It very soon spread with alarming rapidity, and in a short time the blaze could be seen in the night sky from all parts of the city. As word of the conflagration spread, the public houses all over town emptied and a great throng assembled along the quays to watch the late-night spectacle.

Within twenty minutes, the brigades of the REA (whose fire station, on the other side of the block at 5 South Mall was itself threatened by burning embers carried over the roofs by the superheated air currents) and the Atlas were on the scene, and 'a number of men in the crowd promptly volunteered to work the engines which they did most heartily'.[94] The single jets from the engines, however, made little impression on the growing inferno. Morrison's Island with its old, close-packed buildings and narrow streets had an assortment of stores and warehouses through which flames could race unhindered by fire-resisting doors or walls. Soon, the houses in Queen Street were under threat, as were those in Keeffe Street and Catherine Street. The adjoining warehouse of Messrs Hall, full of corn, burst into flames. It was not until 10.45P.M., three-quarters of an hour after the alarm was raised, that the waterworks men arrived from their base on nearby South Mall and got a jet to work. Fumed the *Cork Examiner*, 'It is much to be regretted that with so admirable a supply of water power as Cork possesses, not a single hydrant was turned on the fire until a very considerable period after it broke out'.[95] The military engine turned up to add its contribution to the firefighting effort.

Sometime after midnight, Thomas Geany, one of the waterworks firefighters, was being assisted by twenty-seven-year old Jeremiah Duggan, an employee of Perrott's Foundry. Together they had managed to procure a ladder and began working a branch from the roof of a building in Catherine Street. Someone – it was never discovered who – came along and wandered off with the ladder. The pressurized hose, unsupported now by the ladder, took charge and propelled the unfortunate Duggan from the roof. He was rushed to the South Infirmary where he died from massive internal injuries.[96]

On the quayside, the mood of the mob now turned distinctly ugly. Stones were thrown at the police and soldiers. A policeman was struck in the eye, grievously wounding him. The engine of the REA was rushed by a drunken horde who demanded 'tickets' from the engineer, John Connors.[97] On being refused, they attempted to throw the engine, and Connors, into the river. The police had had enough. They baton-charged the mob, isolated and arrested the ringleaders, and order was restored.[98] Sighed the weary *Examiner* editor, 'These acts of misconduct were exceptional, as on the whole, considering the hour and the night [a Friday – pay night], the immense crowd behaved itself very well'.[99]

Some weeks after the conflagration, the widow of Jeremiah Duggan applied to the corporation for some relief. Her letter was accompanied by certificates of her late husband's good character and sobriety. A number of Councillors corroborated this. A sympathetic member took the view that because the deceased man 'held the Corporation hose' at the time of his death, he should 'be considered for the time as a Corporation officer. It was in saving property for which they were responsible, that the accident occurred. The Corporation, therefore, were bound to come forward in the matter (hear, hear)'.[100] Others strenuously objected to corporation funds being appropriated for such a purpose. They were adamant that it was a matter for the insurance companies to sort out. In the event, the matter was referred to that great Limbo of Corporate Affairs, the Standing Committee, which effectively did nothing for the disconsolate woman. Pierce Power (the co-owner of the warehouse in which the fire originated), took it upon himself to open a public Subscription List with a personal pledge of £5. Robert and Henry Hall contributed an equal amount.

When the list closed in January 1864, a total of £19 5s 0d had been pledged.[101] (At the same time as the relief fund was launched for Duggan's destitute widow, contributions were invited for a 'Testimonial' for a retiring local bank official. When the fund closed some weeks later, £166 had been subscribed).[102]

The two serious fires occurred in Nelson's Place and Shandon Street. The coach factory of James Johnson on Nelson's Place went up on the night of 21 December 1863 and, one week later, in the early hours of 28 December, No.87 Shandon Street, occupied by Sexton's public house, and the adjoining house, were burned to the ground. The nearby RIC barracks were also threatened. In scenes reminiscent of the tragedy on North Main Street, fifteen people were brought to safety, one by one, from the upper floors by ladder by one plucky individual. Fortuitously, on this occasion, there was no loss of life:

> The fire was discovered by the watchman for the locality, Patrick Desmond, about 1 o'clock [a.m]. He immediately gave the alarm at Shandon Street police barracks. Head Constable Carey and all the men in the station at once came out, and finding that the fire was in the underneath part of the house, burst in the front door ... in less than five minutes after, so fierce and rapid was the fire, the [families] were entirely cut off from communication with the street.[103]
>
> A brave fellow named Arthur Cogan ascended the ladder, and with considerable difficulty and no small danger to himself ... succeeded in rescuing a man suspended from a window-sill, thirty feet from the ground. The women and children ... stood at the windows, crying bitterly, and a scene of the greatest compassion prevailed.
>
> Cogan ascended the ladder again and again, each time bringing with him some of the persons above, nor did he desist until he had succeeded in rescuing every one of the inmates from the terrible fate which a few moments before appeared to be so imminent. The poor families residing in the upper part of the house lost everything they had in the world.[104]

The ladder was procured from the RIC barracks, a consequence of the jury's recommendation after the North Main Street fire that the city's police stations should be supplied with ladders and ropes by the corporation. John Ring, Robert Walker, and the waterworks men appeared soon after, but so far had the fire progressed by then that Sexton's premises suddenly collapsed into the street.

The outcry for the formation of a fire brigade was now reaching a crescendo. Members of the public, coroners and juries, a small number of insurers, and a few of the City Fathers, led by Mayor Maguire, were all singing from the same hymn sheet, but the majority of Aldermen and Councillors still baulked at the concept. With so many capital projects in hand at the one time – the new waterworks and all that that entailed (a project as big in its day as the Main Drainage Scheme of the early 2000s) – new bridges, etc., they argued that the anticipated cost of a brigade (estimates varied from £100 for the most basic outfit to £500 for a brigade incorporating a night watch[105]) would simply be too great an imposition on the already over-burdened ratepayers. Clearly, however, the firefighting arrangement under the aegis of the waterworks department was not working well.

At a council meeting following the Morrison's Quay fire, the exasperated Maguire launched an uncharacteristic attack on the untrained, ill-equipped, and over-worked men of the waterworks fire crew:

> Everything that could be consumed was destroyed before the fire brigade had drunk its last cup of tea and eaten its last slice of bread and butter. I have heard of a parson who could not preach on a certain Sunday because his congregation, which consisted of his clerk, was unwell. I have heard also in the early history of a local institution where there was a certain class of such small proportions that when someone asked if the professor attended his class, his answer was that the class had a tooth-ache and couldn't attend. Well, now, if the parson couldn't preach to his clerk it would be no national disaster, nor if the professor had to wait until his class recovered from the tooth-ache, but I say it is a serious thing for a man, with life and property involved, to have to wait until men with the duty of public protection think fit to finish their tea. Such a state of things is a disgrace.[106]

Ring was not prepared to take the biting criticism lying down. In a statement issued to the press, he patiently explained that he had done all he could with only four men at his command:

> Mr. Ring left his house on the Mardyke at half-past ten o'clock, about five minutes after he was called, or less. He must have been therefore at the fire at twenty minutes to eleven. Two hydrants were laid on, and of one of these, which was at full work, Mr. Ring took charge, Mr. Walker being at the other, arranging ladders, &c. Mr. R. Scott and Mr. Jameson, and several other gentlemen, as also Constable No. 51 can confirm the statement that the hydrant was at full work at the time stated. There are four pipe-water men on the South Mall ... With such means what is the cause of the delay at fires? It is mostly caused by the confusion and the trouble of keeping the crowd at a distance. Where is there any city in which more is done to confine a fire in a manufactory to the premises first on fire? This has been done at all times in Cork; it was done at the fires at Messrs. Gamble's and Hall's, as well as Messrs. Goulding's and Mr. Russell's, at which the hydrants were at work long before the fire-engines.[108] [The latter claim was not entirely correct. In the case of the conflagration on Morrison's Quay, the *Examiner* reported that the REA brigade was on scene at 10.20p.m., whereas the corporation men opened their first hydrant at 10.45p.m.].

Aggrieved by the Mayor's disparaging remarks, the waterworks' men too were determined to have their say. On the basis that people were expecting too much of their limited capability, they objected to being referred to, by some politicians and in the newspapers, as 'the fire brigade'. They were water inspectors. In fact, at the inquest into the George's Street fire in February 1861, Cllr Julian had objected when reference was made to the 'fire brigade'. There *was* no fire brigade attached to Cork Corporation, he insisted.

The corporators listened, and then referred the whole matter to the Standing Committee, whose solution was to issue each man with a second set of oilskins.

Mayor Maguire felt it was now incumbent upon him to take matters into his own hands to try to advance the process. He knew he had to get professional advice, and there was only one person he knew well enough to turn to. He remembered that, while passing through the Reporters' Room in the *Examiner* Office, a small single-column news snippet had caught his eye:

Captain Sir Eyre Massey Shaw, MA, KCB the first and most famous commander of the London Metropolitan Fire Brigade. Shaw penned the 'birth certificate' of Cork Fire Brigade at Monkstown, Co. Cork, in 1864. (Painting by Henry Weigall (1833-1876) ARA).(Courtesy of the Commissioner of the London Fire Brigade)

Captain Shaw. – Her Majesty the Queen visited on Monday afternoon the Dowager Duchess of Sutherland, at Stafford House, and kindly enquired after Captain Shaw, the Chief of the Fire Brigade, who is but slowly recovering from the effects of the accident he recently met with at a fire. Mr. Hewitt, who is attending to the dowager duchess, was instructed to make known to Captain Shaw (on whom he is also attending professionally) her Majesty's kind inquiry.[108]

Capt. Eyre Massey Shaw had replaced James Braidwood, killed at the great fire in London's docks in June 1861, as commander of the London Fire Engine Establishment. Shaw was born at Ballymore, outside Cove, Co. Cork, on 17 January 1828, to Robert and Rebecca (*née* Reeves, of Castle Kevin, Killavullen) Shaw of Glenmore Cottage, a substantial Georgian house, still occupied. His family was connected to the aristocracy. His father carried on a provisions business in Fish Street (now subsumed into the Merchant's Quay Shopping Mall) in Cork. His grandfather, Bernard, had been Comptroller of Customs in Cork and lived, variously, with his wife, Jane (*née* Westropp) at the Cork Custom House (now the Crawford Art Gallery) and Monkstown Castle.

Educated at Trinity College where he received his BA (1848) and MA (1854), Eyre was commissioned in the North Cork Rifles and rose to the rank of Captain. In 1860, he was appointed Chief Constable and Chief Fire Officer in Belfast (a dual post), and following Braidwood's untimely death, was successful in his bid for the post of Superintendent of the LFEE. Shaw's personality could not have been more different to his quietly efficient, unassuming predecessor. If the taciturn Scotsman had preferred the quiet shades of relative anonymity, the new incumbent heartily enjoyed the bright lights of fame. Although they differed in almost every respect, both men shared at least one critical characteristic: consummate professionals, they were totally committed to providing the best possible fire service to the citizens of London.

Maguire lost no time in enquiring after Shaw's progress, and was delighted to learn that he intended, early in 1864, to spend some time recuperating at his parents' home at Monkstown, not far from Maguire's own residence 'Ardmanagh' in Glenbrook. Some weeks later, over lunch in the Imperial Hotel, Shaw readily agreed to prepare a report for the council on the formation of a fire brigade. Furthermore, he would personally deliver it to the City Fathers to discuss its implications.

6

Out of the Flames: The Cork Fire Brigade Emerges

'The cost of [a fire brigade] would be a mere trifle for such a city as Cork'

(Capt. Eyre Massey Shaw, Chief of the London Fire Engine
Establishment, February 1864).

'For the credit of the city, and in order to do away with standing
disgrace, that the minutes of the Committee [re the establishment
of a fire brigade] be adopted'.

(Ald. Nagle, October 1877).

Capt. Shaw's report was delivered to a specially-convened meeting of the city
council on Friday 4 March 1864. It read:

Monkstown,
February 24th, 1864.
Sir,
In compliance with your request, I beg to give you the following summary of
my suggestions regarding a Fire Brigade for Cork:-
    With such a water supply as you have, you will not need a large force of
steam and manual fire engines, as elsewhere; but I do not think you would
be safe without at least two good manual engines, with seven-inch cylinders,
and eight-inch stroke, to be worked by 28 men each. You should also provide
six hose reels, each mounted with 400 feet of hose; a standpipe, branches, and
a few small tools, and one large tender to hold about 1000 feet of hose; with
ladders, standpipes, crowbars, saws, heavy axes, and all the usual appliances.
The hose reels should be distributed through the town, and the tender and
engines should stand in the central station, or depot, in which also it is essential that the superintendent should reside. This distribution of your force into
districts will be a much better arrangement for Cork than massing the whole

in one central station, as, in consequence of the short distances, the firemen with the first reel may always be expected to arrive within five or six minutes of the discovery of a fire, and may therefore often save much valuable property, which would be completely on fire, or, perhaps, totally destroyed, before the arrival of men and engines from a distant central station.

With regard to the men, I should say a force of 12, with a competent superintendent, would be sufficient for your ordinary requirements. One man should have charge of each of the hose reels in the outlying districts, and the remaining six should reside in, or as near as possible to, the central station, in which, as I have previously mentioned, I think it most important that the superintendent should have his quarters.

The cost of this organization would be a mere trifle for such a city as Cork. Indeed, many private firms go to much greater expense for protecting their own property. The whole of the appliances, if purchased new, would not cost a thousand pounds; but, in your case, the expense would be much less, as I understand you have some already.

The annual expense may be estimated somewhat as follows, viz:

Annual Estimated Expenses.
Superintendent: £100.
12 Firemen, at £5 each: £60.
Clothing: £40.
Incidental expenses: £100.
Total annual expenses: £300.

Under the head of incidental expenses I include gas, coal, repairs, and pay for drills at the rate of 2s. per man, as the men should be drilled once a fortnight, and, of course, could not be expected to give their time for nothing.

In addition to the above, which includes only the permanent staff and plant of the brigade, there would probably be an extra expense for assistance and refreshments at every fire, which should be otherwise provided for.

Before concluding, I would suggest that immediate steps be taken to provide a large number of additional fire-plugs or hydrants, as the present ones are much too far apart. Indeed I think you will find it the best economy in the end to lay them down at distances not exceeding one hundred feet apart, at least in the principal streets and business parts of the town generally. I would also mention that there is great room for improvement in your present standpipes, branches, etc., but these, as well as the discipline and training of the firemen, are rather matters of detail, on which, however important, I think it better to avoid entering more fully at this stage of your deliberations, when a simple statement of my suggestions of yesterday is probably all that you require. On the mode of raising the funds for carrying out the project, I do not presume to offer any opinion further than this, that I think it will greatly tend to the efficient and harmonious working of the Fire Brigade to allow the Insurance Companies which subscribe to be in some way represented on the committee or board of management in charge of this department of the business of the Corporation.

I leave this to-morrow; but if I can further assist you in your laudable undertaking, pray write to me in London, and it will give me great pleasure to do so in any way you can point out.

I have the honour to be, sir, your obedient servant,

Eyre M. Shaw,

Chief of the London Fire Brigade.

J.F. Maguire, Esq., M.P., Mayor of Cork.[1]

The report was debated at length and Maguire made an impassioned plea to the council for its adoption. He thought the plan would involve very little cost to the city. He envisaged allowing the insurance companies to have representation on the fire brigade committee in return for an annual subscription. (Shaw's brigade was still wholly maintained by insurance companies, and, although he had signed his report 'Chief of the London Fire Brigade', strictly speaking, its official name was the London Fire Engine Establishment). The Mayor went on:

Two or three of the agents – confidential gentlemen – may represent the insurance offices of Cork upon the Fire Brigade Committee, and if we get £100 or £150 from the Insurance Companies, and if we spend £200 a year more, that £200 a year will only amount to ½d in the pound in the rates. ('hear').

That is a matter which should be known, and it is right that this should be known also – that more damage has been caused at fires by drunken, incapable men rushing to grasp the fire-engines than would have been done had there been no-one present at all ('hear, hear').

What we want is a trained, drilled body of men, and I tell you that it is discreditable to the city of Cork that there should be in it no protection, not for property but for life ('hear, hear'). If you adopt the report you will do a great deal of good for you will then have a drilled force – a body of cool, active honest men for the protection of the lives and property of the citizens ('hear, hear').[2]

Maguire thought Shaw's suggestion of recruiting their firemen from amongst the ranks of the corporation's own tradesmen deserving of consideration, but then came the matter of pay. Shaw had recommended '12 Firemen, at £5 a year each'. 'We may find', opined the Mayor, 'that £6 or £7 a year would be nearer the mark [and] 2 shillings a day while training'. It is difficult to imagine how both men arrived at these figures: they appear to have greatly underestimated the real cost of wages.[3]

Shaw's report was enthusiastically and unanimously adopted and at last the long-awaited breakthrough seemed imminent. For a time, it was jostled about from committee to sub-committee, to eventually drop from sight, pigeon-holed, along with all the other previous reports. And when, in the fullness of time a brigade would be established, it would be a very much scaled down entity to what Shaw had proposed.

Some weeks later, on 23 March 1864, the spectre of incendiarism again, briefly, reared its ugly head when fire broke out at QCC, only to be dispelled (and with great relief) when it became obvious that the blaze, on this occasion, was entirely accidental: the result of a hearth fire. The fire engulfed a room in the West Wing which was still under repair since the major blaze almost two years before:

> The joists of the flooring of the room which was burned run almost into the fireplace of the next room. In this fireplace, in which there is no grate, a fire had been lit for the last few days by some cabinet-makers who are at work in the room and who required the fire for melting glue, etc.
>
> Had there not been such a copious supply of water at hand [from a hydrant and hose installed since the previous blaze], or had not the fire been so early perceived, not only would the whole wing have been destroyed, but all evidence of its origin would have been lost, and the fire would have been wrapped in the same mystery which enveloped its famous predecessor.[4]

It appears that Professor Bullen was not satisfied with the explanation of this latest blaze at the college, for the same day's *Cork Examiner* reported that he had 'a private interview at the Police Office … with Messrs. J.L. Cronin, R.M., and W.L. Perrier, and that a further information was sworn by him in reference to the burning of Queen's College in 1862'. However, at the triennial Visitation of QCC in the following month, Bullen announced that he would not proceed and withdrew his earlier statements. He resigned his Chair and was withdrawn from office.[5]

Expecting the insurance companies to subscribe to the upkeep of a municipal fire brigade was also a non-starter. This matter with the companies would continue to rankle, on and off, for many years until local authorities finally got the message. Upon each and every application the answer was in the negative. William Coote, in his article, 'Fire Extinguishing in Ireland' expounded the insurance companies' perspective. He argued:

> 1. That the cost of the brigade would have to be paid for out of premiums, and that, as the brigade is bound to give its services to every one within its proper district, those who do not insure would also be entitled to its use; thus the provident would have to pay for the improvident. No matter how much the efforts of the brigade reduced the cost of insurance, the fact which I have stated would still remain.

2. A first-class brigade protection naturally induces a large number to do without the aid of insurance companies, so that the companies, by supporting the brigades, would be acting against their own interests.

3. Most fire brigades have fire escapes and other appliances for saving life, and in many cases where life is at stake the efforts of the brigade are concentrated upon saving life, while the ravages of the fire are unheeded.

As matters stand, therefore, it would be as unreasonable to expect fire insurance companies to defray the cost of fire brigades as it would be to expect the life assurance companies, or even the accident companies, most of whom now include fevers under the category of accidents, to contribute towards the maintenance of boards of public health, or to debit those companies which transact burglary business with the cost of the upkeep of the Dublin Metropolitan Police and the Royal Irish Constabulary.[6]

The subject of the formation of a public fire brigade again entered the public domain with the passing of the Cork Improvement Act of 1868 when, under the heading of 'Part X – Fire Brigade' it was enacted that:

The Corporation may from time to time purchase by agreement, or take on lease, any buildings within the Borough for Fire Brigade Stations, Engine Houses, and Firemen's Dwellings, and any other buildings necessary for Fire Brigade purposes, etc., etc.

The Corporation may provide and maintain such engines for extinguishing fire, together with water-buckets, pipes, water carts, and appurtenances for such engines and such Fire Escapes, and other implements for safety or use in case of fire, as they consider necessary, and may purchase, keep, or hire horses for drawing such engines, etc., etc.

And so on for a further eleven paragraphs, encompassing such diverse matters as the appointment of a fire chief ('an Inspector of Fires'), water supplies, and the right of fire brigade members to 'break into any building within the limits of this Act being or reasonably supposed to be on fire … without the consent of the owner or occupier'.[7] But the common denominator in every paragraph was the word 'may' rather than 'must': an exclusion that was seized upon by the parsimonious City Fathers as an escape route for shirking their responsibility to the citizens. They knew very well that Cork was not unique in having no municipal fire service. Apart from Dublin and Belfast, great swathes of the country were without even the most rudimentary fire cover.[8]

Early in 1870, some council members made an effort to resurrect interest in the matter. The Fire Brigade Committee was re-formed and representatives from the insurance industry were invited to its inaugural meeting. Only one turned up.

Another attempt was made some weeks later, with a similar result: no business was transacted for want of a quorum. Then, something happened in June of 1870 that shook the Cork establishment to its very foundation and served to underscore the city's glaring lack of preparedness when confronted with emergencies of fire.

THE RIOTS OF 1870 AND THE 'NIGHT WATCH'.

During Easter Week 1916, troops of lancers made repeated charges along Dublin's Sackville Street in the face of withering fire from the insurgents ensconced in the General Post Office. While the gesture may have been magnificent, *mais ce n'est pas la guerre*. Many believed that the sight of cavalry, in full battle order, charging down a principal thoroughfare in a city of the United Kingdom in modern times was unique, but for a precedent one must turn the clock back by some forty-six years to the troubled streets of Cork in that summer of simmering social unrest of 1870. The disturbances have been described as the worst the city had experienced since Marlborough's siege of Cork, and the London *Times* thought they were reminiscent of Paris on the eve of a revolution.[9]

What had started as a fairly low-key strike amongst the tailors of the city soon mutated into a hydra with a life of its own, with business after business becoming embroiled in a bitter general strike and even the seamen on the ships in port joining in. The *Cork Examiner* called it a 'contagion'. It was the first general strike in the country. For night after terrifying night, fierce running battles were held in the pitch-dark 'flat' of the city (the rioters had taken the precaution of breaking the street lamps to thwart identification of them by the RIC), between a stone-throwing mob of hundreds (most of whom had nothing to do with the strike) and the police armed with rifles and bayonets fixed and cavalry with sabres drawn. Skulls were cracked open and bones broken, with many serious injuries on both sides. The infirmaries were full with the wounded. Police cells bulged to capacity. In a week not renowned for its lighter moments, there were one or two gems:

> Several ludicrous circumstances occurred during the disturbances. At the corner of Winthrop Street an energetic constable having dispensed a suspicious group, was returning to his party, who happened at the moment to be approaching at the *pas de charge*. Finding a stone on the pavement, he stooped to remove it, and both his person and attitude being mistaken in the gloom, the officer in command of the advancing party called out to 'Strike that ruffian!', an order which was zealously obeyed by a comrade, who bestowed on the stooping constable a buffet of his baton which will probably render a sitting posture rather uncomfortable for some time.[10]

Sadly, the *Examiner* man failed to record for posterity the stooper's retort.

On what would prove to be the penultimate night of general unrest, the rioters added an ominous new weapon to their arsenal: incendiarism. At 2a.m.on Sunday 26 June, the stables of Edward Daly, proprietor of the Albert Bakery at Cross Court Lane off the North Main Street, were torched.[11] The police concentrated on trying to rescue the terrified horses from their ordeal, in which they were successful, but the premises continued to blaze. Then a curious turn of events took place. As the fire spread towards the houses in Cross Street, the fire-lighters now became the firefighters, as they realized to their dismay that if left unchecked, the flames would consume their houses, too. Bucket-chains were frantically organized, and eventually, with great difficulty the fire was subdued. There is no mention of any firefighting units – corporation or insurance – being mobilized during the disturbances. It may be that their personnel, too, were caught up in the general strike.

The whole shattering experience was enough to send the City Fathers scurrying back to their pigeon-holes to blow the dust from the shelved plans for a fire brigade. This time, they decided that Capt. Shaw's ideas were not far-reaching enough. They would institute a Night Watch, which could also double as a fire brigade.[12] An advertising campaign was launched to attract a suitable candidate for the office of 'Chief Constable of the Borough of Cork Night Watch'. Fifty-one applications were received. The preferred applicant, Robert Gifford, certainly came with an impressive array of trophy positions on his C.V.: ex-Chief Constable of Kent, ex-Chief Constable of Berwickshire; ex-London Metropolitan Police; and latterly, Chief Officer of the Devonport Police Fire Brigade.[13] Mr Gifford thought the proposed Night Watch about sufficient for Cork's needs, and that it could indeed 'be utilized for the purposes of the much-spoken of, and much needed, Fire Brigade'.[14]

It was proposed to divide the city into three districts, with a staff of forty-four: the Chief Constable, three sergeants, and forty constables.[15] As usual, however, the devil was in the detail. The corporators turned a paler shade of white when they hurriedly did their sums and realized that their grandiose plans would cost, for the personnel alone, some £2,036 in the first year to implement:

Salary of Chief Constable: £120.
3 Sergeants @ £1 per week: £156.
40 Constables @ 15 shillings per week: £1560.
Clothing: £200.[16]

Such a scheme would require a rate of four pence in the pound to realize, whereas Shaw's proposal had only accounted for a half-penny in the pound. Exit, stage left, Mr Gifford; 'don't call us, we'll call you'! That was in October 1870, and no more was ever heard of the idea of a Night Watch. Some among the council would later live to regret allowing a man with such an excellent pedigree to slip through their fingers.

In spite of this latest turnabout, the consensus for the formation of a brigade was gaining momentum. But every time it seemed a breakthrough was imminent, something else always cropped up to divert the City Fathers' attention. The proposal to build a foot-bridge from Sullivan's Quay to the Grand Parade, for example. (The bridge was built, 111 years later, in 1985). All that it now required was one final, concerted push. That too, would come; but before it happened, two more fires – one serious, one major – lay in its path. Sadly, the serious fire was attended, yet again, by tragic loss of life.

'O DARK, DARK, DARK, AMID THE BLAZE OF NOON'. HIGH DRAMA ON DAUNT'S SQUARE.

Mary O'Callaghan was a worried woman. As she hurried along Brunswick Street on her way to the courthouse, accompanied by her lodger, Hannah Flint, she wore a deep frown. Just one week since, two soldiers from the 25th Regiment at Cork Barracks had entered her draper's shop at Daunt's Square – close to Woodford, Bourne's – and while one had kept the staff distracted, the other had been busy helping himself to some items of clothing. They were spotted and ran off, the shop assistants pursuing them hot-foot along St Patrick's Street. Some policemen took up the chase, and the duo was hauled, kicking and screaming, along Cornmarket Street to the Bridewell. It took six policemen to subdue them, and as they were dragged past O'Callaghan's shop they cursed and swore revenge. If they were gaoled, they shouted, their comrades would avenge them.

Thus, on that Friday morning, 16 October 1874, she quickly blessed herself passing St Augustine's, head bowed against the bitter wind blowing down the Western Road from the Boggeragh's, and fervently whispered a quiet aspiration to her late husband to give her the strength to carry her through the day.

As the morning's court cases wore on, the sheer tediousness of it all did nothing to pacify her state of mind. She had to force herself to avert her eyes from the malevolent glare of the two accused, seated between two policemen. And then, just as the case was about to be called, she jumped, startled, as a policeman tapped her urgently on the shoulder. Would she mind stepping outside for a minute?

Standing on the top of the courthouse steps, she gazed in dismay at the roiling clouds of dense, black smoke gathering over the northern end of the Grand Parade, which told their own story. As she ran like the wind back to her blazing premises, the frightful curses of the two soldiers rang in her ears. She was only vaguely aware of the Angelus bells booming out their call to prayer across the noonday city.

Daunt's Square was a bedlam of confusion, shouting, screaming, and the crackling of flames. The crowd, already thirty deep, stood as if riveted, watching the flames spectacularly leaping from window to window up the facade of O'Callaghan's. And then, to their utter disbelief, a little old lady appeared at a window of the third floor and began to climb out. Recounted the *Examiner*: 'Exclamations of horror and prayers for her safety burst simultaneously from the crowd below'.[17]

The fire was first discovered sometime after 11.30a.m. by the shop assistants. Investigating the strange smell, they opened the door of the ground floor 'oil room' adjacent to the stairs, and were immediately confronted by a mass of flames. Not alone did they not take the simple precaution of closing the door to the room on fire, but they made another fatal mistake. Reacting automatically in the way that they had done a thousand times before when leaving the shop unattended, they locked the door onto the street while making good their own escape, thus sealing the fate of some of the five people still remaining on the upper floors of the building.[18]

In that room an insidious, deadly transformation had occurred. The fire in the closed room had, without sufficient air, burned quietly for a time, during which it gradually heated the contents to their ignition temperature. When the door was opened, the fire, suddenly saturated with life-giving oxygen, quickly spread over the whole room in the dreaded phenomenon known as a flashover. As the flames, toxic smoke, and superheated gases raced up the narrow funnel of the stairs, Arthur Flint, a thirty-nine-year-old marine dealer, swiftly considered his terrible position. Gathering up his little daughter and son under his arms, and grabbing Mary Walsh, Mrs O'Callaghan's elderly servant, by the skirt, he decided to make a dash for it down the stairs. It was a fatal mistake. Meanwhile, on the top floor, Eliza Grogan was climbing out onto the window-sill.

Alderman John Jones was among the first to spot her predicament. Calling on some men to help him, he sprinted down the Grand Parade to the English Market to procure a ladder, fear pounding in his veins that he would be too late. But the ladder, when fully extended, fell five feet short of Mrs Grogan's window. Quickly sizing up the situation, a young slater (and thus well used to heights) from Douglas Street, named William Kavanagh, skillfully and quickly climbed the ladder and guided the old lady's feet onto the uppermost rounds, and, amid great cheering, brought her to safety. (Eliza Grogan was the only one of the trapped occupants to escape entirely unharmed. She later testified that at the first sign of trouble, and realizing that the stairs were impassable, she had closed her bedroom door – thus inhibiting the ingress of poisonous smoke and gases – and gone to the window to cry for help. Although she had to wait some fifteen minutes for the ladder to arrive, her actions saved her life).[19]

The Flint party was less fortunate. Poor Arthur, who had sucked flame and superheated gases down through his bronchial passages, on reaching the foot of the stairs with his charges – all hideously burned – found the hall door locked. All collapsed, unconscious, just feet away from the street. There they lay, their lives ebbing away, until corporation Street Inspector Denis Lyons kicked in the door and they were dragged out. Arthur Flint, his son, and Mary Walsh all succumbed from their awful ordeal. (In the confusion the little boy was initially missed. His charred remains were later discovered by the Mayor himself. The little girl lay critically ill at the North Infirmary).

It was the single greatest loss of life from fire in Cork for many years, made all the more shocking by virtue of the fact that it had taken place in broad daylight with the drama unfolding in front of thousands of spellbound Corkonians. Previous fatal fires had all occurred late at night or in the early hours of the morning, witnessed by only a few dozen people at most. The building was totally gutted, later demolished, and the cause of the fire was never established. The fact that the soldiers had sworn revenge was taken seriously, but nothing was ever proved.[20]

One interesting theory came from a correspondent to the *Cork Examiner* writing some days after the fire. He had served in the Royal Navy, he said, on board HMS *Liffey* on station in the Mediterranean. One night, the fire alarm bell was sounded after the ship's watch smelled smoke. 'The slightest hint of fire in a ship causes great alarm', he wrote. On investigation, it was found that some oil-soaked cloths, used by the seamen, had been discarded in a locker and were smouldering. When the door was thrown open by the Master-at-Arms, the smoking mass burst into flames: a classic example of spontaneous combustion. He concluded:

> We know that the cheaper waterproof garments are mainly composed of strong calico saturated with some oily substance, and it would be well for manufacturers and dealers in these articles to know that they are very likely to take fire if packed together or kept in a close [*sic*] room.[21]

The correspondent, who signed himself 'W.B.', may have been nearer the mark than realized. If the oily material was near some source of heat, the danger of ignition would have been greatly increased. Not only would the heat generated be unable to get away, but additional heat would have been supplied by the secondary source. And the kitchen, complete with stove, was directly over the oil room. Was this the cause of the fire? Perhaps. And perhaps not. We shall never know.

Of firefighting, there was the usual interminable delay while messengers were sent, first to the Corporation Offices at 20 South Mall, then around the city to inform the water inspectors-cum-firefighters who were engaged at their ordinary work. When, eventually, three hydrants were got to work (from Grand Parade, St Patrick's Street, and Paul Street) the pressure was so poor that all the water did was to splash uselessly off the windows of the burning building. A volley of stones and broken bottles was directed at the windows to break them, and the desired result was very soon accomplished with 'the able assistance of a few Cork marksmen.'[22]

As on all previous occasions, no rescue attempts were undertaken by the 'pipe-water' men.

William Kavanagh, who had acquitted himself so tirelessly throughout the day (he made several sorties off the head of the ladder trying to locate the victims), applied to the corporation for compensation for his destroyed clothing, boots, and personal effects to the amount of £6 16s. 0d. Rather than lauding the young man for his commendable efforts in doing his best to save human life (in fairness, the Mayor and some councillors did) an undignified, ill-advised public wrangle among the City Fathers ensued, a number of whom deprecated the awarding of any such *ex gratia* payments. Still others invoked the old chestnut: tell him go to the insurance companies for his money. Grudgingly, Kavanagh was given £5.

Hardly had the latest pathetic victims of Cork's shameful legacy of negligence been cold in their graves than we had disgraced ourselves again.

A LEAGUE OF EXTRAORDINARY GENTLEMEN: FIRE AND FROLICS ON DUNBAR STREET.

It was the biggest and costliest fire in Cork since the burning of Goulding's on St Patrick's Street in 1863 and it was the talk of the town for weeks afterwards. Not only on account of the many men who had been thrown out of work with no means of putting bread and butter on their tables, nor the by now legendary tardiness of the waterworks men in getting to work on the fire; rather, the talk centered around the unseemly shouting match between the Mayor, Sir George Penrose, and the owners of the premises, and the disgraceful scenes which accompanied the puny firefighting effort by elements of Cork's 'gentry'.

The extensive five-storey premises of Joseph William McMullen's Cork Steam Mills was located between Dunbar Street and White Street (to the rear of St Finbarr's South Chapel), and stood at right-angles with a corn store, capable of holding 10,000 barrels, which faced onto George's Quay.[23] McMullen's occupied the site of the earlier William Dunbar Mills, and was regarded as an ideal spot for a flour mill, standing in close proximity to both the Corn Market (on the site now occupied by City Hall) and the river. McMullen's Mills were among the largest steam mills in Cork, and with Furlong's on Lapp's Quay, the first to embrace the new 'roller' process. Rollers produced a fine white flour, rather than the coarser grades turned out by the traditional millstone process.[24]

The fire was first spotted at around 10.45p.m. on Monday 1 May 1876 when flames were seen on the top floor at the White Street side of the building. (This cannot be taken as a firm indication that the fire actually started on the top floor. In tall buildings, the staircases and 'opes' for hoists, etc., often allow smoke and superheated gases, via convection currents, to rise from basement to roof, where, unless they can escape, 'mushroom' out. Heat can cause secondary fires at this and, subsequently, other levels). Shortly:

> It made a magnificent blaze. The fire spread downwards with great rapidity from floor to floor, and the flames ... rose in immense volume, completely demolishing the roof and bursting through the fifty windows. A terrible

grand spectacle was thus presented to the huge crowd of spectators who were attracted from all parts of the city by the glare.[25]

Among the crowd was a gaggle of frock-coated, stovepipe-hatted toffs, who earlier, having all night imbibed not wisely but too well, staggered out of the City Club on the Grand Parade.[26] Now, still on a high and unsteady on their feet, they watched the proceedings unfold through rheumy, jaundiced eyes. They found the whole episode hilarious. So well they might. The corporation men, although arriving early on the fire ground, had taken an unimaginable one and a quarter hours before the first jet was turned on the fire. Another full hour elapsed before they managed to bring a second into play. In the meantime, the complex blazed out of control, threatening Sutton's Coal Yard on White Street, the Confraternity Rooms of the South Chapel, and scorching the houses near the entrance to the mills on Margaret Street.

The mill owners were beside themselves with rage, watching their premises, in which they had heavily invested in new technology only two years before, go up in smoke. The Mayor, representing the corporation, became the object of their opprobrium, and 'in the excitement of the moment hot words were exchanged'.[27] With the situation becoming ever more farcical, the gentlemen from the Club decided that hot words needed a cool remedy, and, seizing the hoses from the waterworks men, gleefully turned the water on the great throng of people (including the firefighters), among which were 'many respectable citizens. It was a melancholy sight while the man's property was being ruined', sighed the *Examiner*.[28] The fire effectively burned itself out, the destruction being complete with over £15,000 worth of damage done, many millions in today's currency. The *Cork Constitution* now took up the cudgel:

> When Patrick Street, Grand Parade, Great George's Street and the South Mall have become a heap of ruins by fire, the Cork Town Council will face up to the fact that a proper fire-extinguishing apparatus with a thoroughly competent, trained Fire Brigade are imperatively necessary to the safety of the city. Is there a city or town in England or Scotland where such gross negligence exists in regard to provision for fire extinction?[29]

Sadly, the short answer to their question was no.

THE END OF THE BEGINNING.

John Ring, Superintendent of the waterworks since 1860, rose to his feet, weariness etched across his rugged features. Determined to bring matters to a head once and for all, he took his pince-nez from his top pocket, and, carefully adjusting them to the correct place on his nose, made an impassioned address to the assembled corporators:

I beg to lay before you the following remarks with respect to the Fire Brigade. I hold it simply the duty of the Waterworks Committee to keep their mains ready to supply water for the suppression of fires.

I implore you to keep my men free for more requisite duties. The attendance of my small staff at fires completely upsets all my arrangements for the proper working of my department and causes many things to be delayed which ought not ... it indirectly costs the Corporation nearly as much as would enable you to have a staff accountable for the duty [of firefighting] under the orders of a proper and trained man. Any assistance, as far as my head goes, I will with pleasure give him.[30]

Ring expostulated that it was not the business of a waterworks department to be an operational fire brigade; its only function at fires should be to ensure an adequate supply of water from the mains for such a service. He pointed out that his tired, small staff, reduced from a high of twelve in 1869 to, now eight years later, a mere six, was snowed under with their own work without having to perform firefighting duties as well.[31]

Incredibly, in light of all the long years of procrastination, events now began to move swiftly. Even seasoned council-watchers, who had seen many false dawns, were impressed. Alex McCarthy, the Town Clerk, was directed to approach the Chief Officers of the Dublin (Capt. Ingram) and Metropolitan (Capt. Shaw) Fire Brigades with a view to them recommending a suitable officer to undertake the establishment of a fire brigade for Cork. Curiously, Shaw's reply is not recorded in subsequent minutes, but Capt. Ingram recommended Mark Wickham, a member of the Dublin Fire Brigade (hereafter DFB) for some fourteen years.[32]

Mark Wickham was thirty-nine years old and had joined the DFB in 1863, a year after its inception. On 12 June of the following year, he married Mary McDermott in St Nicholas of Myra church in Francis Street. They had nine children in all, eight of whom were born in Dublin, and the last, John Thomas, in Cork (he died in infancy) in 1878 when his father was then chief of Cork Fire Brigade.[33] There is anecdotal evidence to suggest that, prior to joining the fire brigade, Mark had served some time as an 'escape conductor' with the Irish Society for the Protection of Life from Fire. As a member of the fledgling DFB rostered for practically continuous duty, he may well have 'cut his eye-teeth' at such notable Dublin fires as the tragedy in Westmoreland Street in 1866 where six people lost their lives, and the great whiskey blaze at Malone's Bonded Warehouse in 1875 when thirteen unfortunates died in agony from drinking the contaminated, filthy, full-proof spirit as it flowed down the gutters from the fire-ravaged buildings.[34]

Invited to Cork to be interviewed and to compile an audit for the Waterworks Committee of Cork Corporation (under whose aegis the new brigade was to function), Wickham delivered his report on 23 February 1877. It is worth reproducing in full, as it contains a full inventory of the firefighting equipment then under the control of the city:

> To the Waterworks Committee,
> Gentlemen,
> In compliance with your order, I have met with the kind assistance of Mr Ring and one of his men, and examined the various apparatus in use at present for extinguishing fires in the Borough of Cork with the following results.
>
> There are 650 hydrants distributed throughout the city, so as to command nearly every house and building within the Borough with a pressure of water sufficient to reach the roofs of the highest buildings.
>
> I find that all the apparatus are very suitable and in good condition. I would recommend that one "Hose Reel" be provided which will make your plant complete. To insure efficiency, the Brigade should reside in one House situated in a central position, with good yard and stable attached where the reels and apparatus etc., with a Horse Reel will be kept in readiness at all times, day and night.
>
> Mr Ring has furnished the following priced list of the present "Plant":

650 Hydrants, cost:	£6825.0.0.
47 lengths of leather hose; about 2000 feet:	£394.16.0.
6 Brass stand pipes:	£40.0.0.
6 Brass hand-pipes:	£18.0.0.
3 Hand reels:	£54.0.0.

A cartoon of Cork's first fire chief, Mark Wickham, attributed to Cork political caricaturist and lithographer Stephen O'Driscoll (c.1825–1895). O'Driscoll's silhouettes depict Superintendent Wickham (on right, with red shirt and képi) and an Alderman of the corporation. The cartoon is titled 'Our Plucky Alderman: The Fire at Brown's Mills'. (King Street, February, 1887).

Hammers, chisels, etc (in reels):	£27.0.0.
Fire escape:	£50.0.0.
Ten sets of ladders:	£75.0.0.
	£7483.16.0.
Provide one Horse reel at a cost of:	£50.0.0.
	£7533.16.0.

The Brigade will consist of:

1 Superintendent, yearly:	£100.0.0
1 First-class Assistant @18/ weekly:	£46.16.0
3 Second-class Assistants @ 16/ weekly:	£124.16.0.
4 Supernumeraries, at say, 30 fires @ 5/	£30.0.0.
Horse and harness:	£50.0.0.
House and premises for staff:	£50.0.0.
Incidentals:	£100.0.0.
	£501.12.0.
Say in round numbers:	£500.0.0.

Mark Wickham,
Cork, 23rd February 1877.[35]

There was a delay while the corporation made a last-ditch effort to induce the insurance companies on board. In return for a total contribution of £250 from the forty-four companies in the city, they would be allowed representatives on the committee having control of the fire brigade. As on every previous occasion, the proposal fell on deaf ears. Then, at the Waterworks Committee meeting on 24 September 1877, Cllr Daly proposed the following motion: 'That we recommend to Council to forthwith proceed to establish a Fire Brigade for the City of Cork pursuant to Mr. Wickham's Report, irrespective of the subscriptions in aid of expenses to be given by Insurance Companies.' Mark Wickham's report was formally adopted by council on 28 September, and on 1 October Ald. Nagle moved, 'For the credit of the city, and in order to do away with standing disgrace, that the Minutes of the [Waterworks] Committee be adopted.' Ald Dwyer seconded the proposal. Mayor Barry Sheehan put the resolution, and declared it carried.

After all the frustration throughout the greater part of the nineteenth century, of costings, debate, discussion, delay, deferment, dawdling, estimates, reports, and general apathy, to say nothing of heartbreak and bitter tears, the final passing of the motion was almost an anti-climax. One fact, however, was incontrovertible. The Cork Fire Brigade was, if not quite yet 'open for business', at long last, a reality.

7

The Thin Red Line: The First Cork Brigade

'The fire brigade deserve immortal credit for their superhuman efforts …
they proved simply invaluable'.

(The Mayor of Cork, 29 March 1878).

'The fire brigade should be disbanded'.

(Councillor Julian, 23 April 1891).

Mark Wickham arrived in Cork on Friday 12 October 1877 to take up his appointment as Superintendent of Cork Fire Brigade (hereafter CFB) deriving his authority from the Cork Improvement Act 1868 (31 & 32 Vic., Cap 33).[1] So far as the corporation was concerned his duties were crystal clear:

> To Superintend the Fire Brigade, all men employed at fires to act exclusively under his superintendence and that he take no order at a fire from any person but the Mayor, but act on his own responsibility.[2]

Unlike Chief Fire Officers today, he was expected to attend at each and every incident, no matter how trivial, in person.

Among the many pressing tasks facing him were the selection of suitable premises as a fire station, along with the recruitment, equipping, and training of staff. The council had fixed the number of permanent men to be engaged at a derisory four, the same figure that the so-called 'waterworks brigade' had had to contend with through all the long years of incompetence, and only a third of what Capt. Shaw had recommended as a minimum in 1864. Such a minuscule outfit, of course, did not deserve the accolade of 'brigade' at all, but four is the number suggested by Wickham himself in his report. From day one, the fire brigade would be run on a shoestring, the Cinderella of municipal services, a situation which would prevail up to relatively modern times.[3]

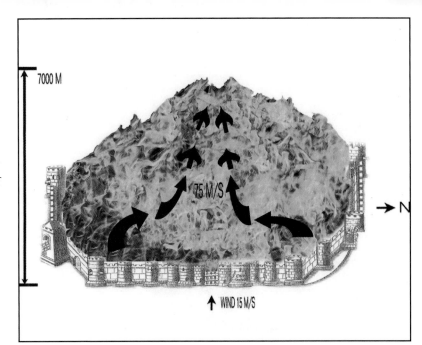

Conjectural image of the Cork firestorm of 1622.

A cartoon of Cork's first fire chief, Mark Wickham, attributed to Cork political caricaturist and lithographer Stephen O'Driscoll (c.1825–1895). O'Driscoll's silhouettes depict Superintendent Wickham (on right, with red shirt and képi) and an Alderman of the corporation. The cartoon is titled 'Our Plucky Alderman: The Fire at Brown's Mills'. (King Street, February, 1887).

Atlas fire mark.

Reverse of the bronze medal
of the Royal Society for the
Protection of Life from Fire.
(Courtesy of Dr R. Willoughby.)

The Royal Exchange Assurance fire station at 5 South Mall as drawn by architect Samuel Belcher c.1840. In the foreground is a uniformed member of the REA Fire Engine Establishment. (Courtesy of Don Trotter.) Note Hogan's *Minerva* in its north-facing niche.

Tóirpín – The 'Fire Flower'. A plant with a record of more than 2,000 years of association with fire protection throughout Ireland and the continent of Europe.

An Irish Fire Service rank-marking, incorporating *Tóirpín* in the design.

Brass helmet issued to members of Cork Fire Brigade 1877-1935. The helmet was first introduced to London Metropolitan Fire Brigade in the 1860s by Captain Shaw. The model he chose closely resembled the helmet worn by the *Regiment de Sapeurs-Pompiers* of Paris.

Detail of the Cork Fire Brigade helmet plate incorporating a design of flaming torch, crossed axes, and branchpipes.

Detail of the 'fire-spewing' dragon embossed on the comb of the helmet. Legend has it that Capt. Shaw's little daughter, Anna, found the drawings of the new helmet on his desk and added her own inimitable touch, the ferocious dragon.

The silver helmet presented to Alfred J. Hutson by his Brighton colleagues in July 1891. The inscription on the peak reads, 'Presented to A.J. Hutson by the officers and men of the Brighton Volunteer Fire Brigade as a token of their esteem after 16 years' service July 1891'. (Courtesy of Raynor de Foubert).

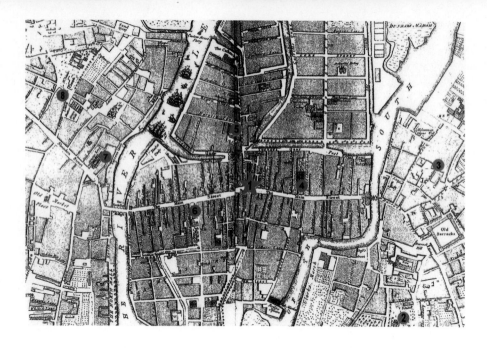

Rocque's plan of Cork (1759) showing locations where the municipal and parish fire engines were housed. (Courtesy of Cork City Libraries.)

1. The municipal engine house situated near the City Courthouse adjacent to the Exchange.
2. St Fin Barre's Cathedral.
3. St Nicholas', Cove Street.
4. Christ Church (aka Holy Trinity), South Main Street.
5. St Paul's, Paul Street.
6. St Peter's, North Main Street.
7. St Mary's, Shandon.
8. St Anne's, Shandon.

Conjectural image of a 'fire squirt' being used to try to suppress the fires along Main Street, caused by the bombardment during the Siege of Cork, 1690.

Conjectural image of the drama unfolding at the fatal fire at Alcock's in the early hours of 27 November 1900.

A conjectural image of a fireman of the Atlas Fire Engine Establishment outside No.66 South Mall which housed the offices of the Atlas Assurance Company and the Cork Pipe Water Company. The entrance to the Atlas 'engine house' was just around the corner at the top of Cook Street. The representational building which stands on the site today is the regional headquarters of AIB.

An illuminated address presented to Alfred J. Hutson by the 'Officers and Men of the Brighton Volunteer Fire Brigade' in July 1891. This was one of three such addresses presented to Hutson upon leaving Brighton to take up his Cork appointment. (Courtesy of Raynor de Foubert).

Captain Sir Eyre Massey Shaw, MA, KCB the first and most famous commander of the London Metropolitan Fire Brigade. Shaw penned the 'birth certificate' of Cork Fire Brigade at Monkstown, Co. Cork, in 1864. (Painting by Henry Weigall (1833–1876) ARA). (Courtesy of the Commissioner of the London Fire Brigade).

His first duty was to reconnoitre his 'ground' and thoroughly familiarize himself with the city of over 80,000 souls for whose fire protection he now shouldered the burden of responsibility. He would have found that, for all intents and purposes, Cork was a thriving, burgeoning place. The centre was dominated by business activities with many fashionable stores lining the main thoroughfares of St Patrick's Street, King Street, George's Street, and Grand Parade. The South Mall, then as now, was reserved almost exclusively for the banks, insurance offices, and real estate agents. Modern transport in and out of the city was via several railway stations servicing the different approaches from the four points of the compass, and by the popular cross-channel Steam Packet. The motor car was still in the future, and the streets echoed with the clop of horses' hooves, the creak and roll of carriages, carts, 'jingles' (the forerunners of our modern taxis), gigs and broughams, and the crack of drivers' whips. The hissing lamps of the Cork Gas Company illuminated the houses and streets after dark.

For those fortunate enough to have a job, the breweries, distilleries, flour mills, the docks, and a myriad smaller industries all provided steady work, while the world-famous Cork Butter Market, close by the equally-famous Shandon Bells was still a highly desirable job. Across the city, on the south side, the new St Fin Barre's Cathedral was nearing completion. A few weeks before, the new Cork Opera House had opened its doors with a performance of 'Our Boys'.[4] On the north side, the redoubtable and much-loved, Br James Dominick Burke of the North Monastery was, yet again, revealing the power of scientific marvels to an enthralled populace, this time by a demonstration of the magic attributes of electricity by flashing beams of light (by way of 120 Callan electric cells) in the night sky – two years before Thomas Edison invented the light bulb. In George's Street, the Theatre Royal, purchased by the Post Office in 1875, had morphed into Cork's new General Post Office.

The British Empire was at the apogee of its power. *Pax Brittanica* reigned supreme. Much pride was generated, in certain quarters, by the knowledge that the empire was four times larger and more populated than its Roman forerunner, and that it was expanding at a far quicker rate, at an average of 100,000 square miles a year: that was 270 square miles a day or an area the size of Dublin's Phoenix Park every thirty minutes. For centuries, apart from the occasional revolt, the majority of the population took the conditions of everyday life as given and the possibility that any of this was under threat was rarely considered. High up over St Patrick's Street for all and sundry to see, the Union Flag, with its saltire cross of St Patrick in place some seventy-six years, buffeted by the prevailing westerly wind, slapped its cords against the flag-pole outside Government House proclaiming in no uncertain manner that Cork was firmly every bit a part of the United Kingdom as Coventry, Chester, or Cheltenham. Or was it? The tiny British queen, Victoria, was known to many in Cork as *Banríon an Ghorta Mhór* – The Famine Queen.[5] Cork Fenian Brian Dillon might be in his grave some five years since, but the aspiration for national self-determination had never quite gone away, and already a charismatic new leader had emerged to inspire many among the Nationalist movements of the day. That man was Charles Stewart Parnell, 'The Chief', who was elected MP for Cork in 1880.

Globally, vast land areas of the planet, including the North and South Poles, remained unexplored. Rule by imperial dynasties was still very much the order of the day. A handful of European countries controlled the continents, in which most lands were colonies, not countries in their own right. Just one year previously, on 4 July 1876, the United States of America had celebrated the 100th anniversary of the signing of the Declaration of Independence. The US Army was still pursuing Native Americans in the northwest, and in June General George Armstrong Custer and units of his Seventh Cavalry made their Last Stand at the Battle of the Little Bighorn. Electricity and telephones were in their infancy.

In 1877, a mirage of prosperity concealed the reality of Cork. The lush green sweep of the South Mall, the broad elegance of Great George's Street, and the handsome shops of St Patrick's Street – 'Pana', to Corkonians - were only a surface veneer, a facade as false as a film set. Behind them were crowded the festering tenements of the Marsh, with the dense patchwork of the south side and north side slums stretching up the hills on either side of the river. It was a complex, fissured society, divided by religion, politics, and class. The monied classes had long eschewed the by now unfashionable city centre lanes for the genteel, leafy suburbs of Sunday's Well, Tivoli, Montenotte, and Blackrock, where they resided in substantial houses with finely-manicured lawns protected by high walls, cocooned from the crime and ill-health associated with the hoi-polloi.

Beneath the thin veneer of prosperity, lay a parellel, twilight world, so graphically described by Dr Colman O'Mahony in his book, *In the shadows: life in Cork 1750 – 1930* (Cork, 1997). It was a realm of chronic unemployment, grinding poverty, destitution, lack of education, disease, alcoholism, and desperate slums. The terrors of cholera and tuberculosis were rampant. In the month after Mark Wickham took office, a public inquiry was held to identify the cause of typhoid fever in the city. It deduced that bad sanitation was a principal factor. City Surveyor Robert Walker testified that of the 10,000 houses in the city, 2,500 had no 'privies or ash-pits', 5,000 had no water-closets, and 2,500 lacked sewerage connections. In other words, not a single house within the Cork borough boundary conformed to sanitary 'best practice' of the time. Overcrowding was a major problem, with thousands of families having to live in one room. The city's infrastructure was ancient and sclerotic. Effluvia from the north side, south side, and city centre were discharged, untreated in any way, straight into the river, where hordes of youngsters swam during the summer months.

Such was the Cork into which Mark Wickham, accompanied by his wife

Mary and their five young children arrived.[6]

'ONWARD, THE LIGHT BRIGADE': THE GALLANT FOUR GO INTO ACTION.

Supt Wickham did not have long to wait for the first test of his officership. For the fledgling fire brigade there was to be no honeymoon period. The unit's very first operation was a humdinger, a conflagration that, even today, would tax the resources of the brigade. Exactly one week after his arrival in Cork, on Friday 19 October at 10.30p.m., fire broke out in the provision stores of John F. Cunningham on Merchant's Quay, an extensive concern covering almost an acre of ground stretching back to North Street and Warren's Place, an area now included in Merchant's Quay Shopping Mall.

The fire, which began in a loft on the North Street side, quickly ran along the open roof void towards the quay:

> making a brilliant blaze which was seen all over the city and attracted a large crowd of spectators. The Corporation Fire Brigade – the appellation is now for the first time used with some propriety – were on the ground some twenty minutes after the fire was discovered, and under the intelligent direction of Mr Wickham … they set to work with energy … to extinguish the fire.[7]

In marked contrast to previous firefighting efforts in Cork, the new firemen now did something rarely before seen at a fire in the city: they entered the burning building to seek out the source of the fire, their noses close to the nozzle of the branchpipe to avail of the cool air sucked in by the low-pressure region created by the vortex of the water jet.

The untried firemen, who, after all, can have only received the very rudiments of basic training, responded to their Superintendent's orders quickly and efficiently. They breathed the first whiffs of the poison generally referred to by the innocent-sounding name of 'smoke', little realizing that they would soon get to know it as well as a doctor knows death. He showed them the importance of keeping close to the ground to take full advantage of the layer of relatively clear air left as suffocating smoke rises. As they advanced up the stairs, they hugged the side nearest the wall where, he pointed out, it would be strongest. In the heavy smoke they pursued the fire from room to room, now on their stomachs, now on their knees, advancing a few inches at a time like supplicants approaching a holy shrine. They watched, awe-struck, as the fire slithered up the walls and, mushrooming across the ceiling, advanced on them. They listened, in wonder, for the first time at the strange, groaning, ominous sounds that only a doomed building on fire makes. Under Wickham's direction, the doughty quartet mounted quickly to the roof, cutting away the burning portion while at the same time allowing the fire to vent. Eventually, utilizing the excellent water supply available to them, the fire was completely extinguished at all points.

Early on in the incident, Supt Wickham had liaised with the senior RIC officer on the fire ground, Sub-Inspector Potter, and a large force of police sealed off the area on all sides allowing the brigade to apply themselves to their work unhindered by the unruly interference of the mob, which had been a feature of Cork fires on so many other occasions. Concluded a delighted *Cork Examiner*:

> The loss would certainly have been much larger but for the activity, intelligence and discipline which characterised the operations of the Fire Brigade. In this respect the scene at the fire was in striking contrast with what we have been accustomed to witness on such occasions in this city. The water supply on the occasion was most abundant, and the hose was in perfect condition.[8]

The brigade's performance was closely monitored by Mayor Barry Sheehan and a number of prominent officials including the City Engineer and the Harbour Master Capt. Byrne, the latter keeping a weather-eye out for his wooden and canvas cargo-laden charges, moored cheek-by-jowl all the way up to St Patrick's Bridge and separated from the conflagration only by the width of the quay. All were in agreement that the CFB had come through its first major test with flying colours.

The succeeding weeks were busy ones for Mark Wickham as he set about moulding his tiny force into an effective firefighting unit. They were taught that the essence of firemanship is to work as a team, self-reliant but interdependent. As they drilled along the quayside under the critical gaze of their fellow citizens, they quickly acquired the cynical soubriquet of 'The Gallant Four', a nickname that would stick for years.[9] On 15 November 1877, the council confirmed the appointments of the four firemen: John Walsh as '1st Class Assistant' at 18 shillings a week and three '2nd Class Assistants' at 16 shillings a week each. They were Patrick Ellard, James Sheriff, and Michael McCarthy. In keeping with the tradition begun in the Metropolian Fire Brigade under Capt. Shaw, the previous occupations of the three Second Class Assistants were listed as seamen; that of Walsh, curiously, was not recorded.

Accommodation was acquired on Sullivan's Quay to house the brigade. Numbers 15 and 16 were rented from one Michael O'Leary, a cork-cutter who lived at No.18, at a rent of £50 per year. The four firemen and their families occupied No.15, previously the quarters of the County Inspector of the RIC.[10] Henceforth, this would be known as the Fire Brigade Residence. Supt Wickham and his family lived next door at No.16. Both addresses are now subsumed into the 'Government Buildings' complex.

Further up the quay, at No. 24, stood an open yard behind a high wall accessed via an arched gateway with limestone pillars.[11] In this 'fire brigade station' were housed the two hose reels (for the time being, still pulled by hand), all the fire-fighting equipment, life-lines, jumping sheets, and two-wheeled escapes. One was the old fly ladder escape purchased (and never once used at a fire) back in 1858 and now decayed and useless, the other a brand-new 60ft telescopic escape purchased on the fire chief's recommendation from Clayton and Co. of Dublin for £90.[12] All the equipment was stored in the open at the mercy of the weather. A major disadvantage soon proved to be the arch over the gate, for in order to get the functioning escape away, it had first to be modified into 'bridged' mode to allow it to be run horizontally. In this way it would be trundled along the streets to the scene of the outbreak where, if required, it had to

An illuminated address presented to Sergeant Michael Ryan, Cork Fire Brigade, on the occasion of his retirement in 1891. It depicts the original fire station on Sullivan's Quay (top left). Two wheeled fire escapes are seen resting against a wall in the yard. In the bottom left corner is a fireman wearing the distinctive shirt of the period which led the men to be known as 'Redshirts'. The scroll is signed by (left column): Mark Wickham, William Gloyne, Keane Mahony, Patrick Higgins, Jeremiah Crowley, Michael McCarthy, and (right column): William Purcell, James Keating, Nicholas Butler, Philip Lecane, John Murphy, and Alfred James Hutson, Superintendent.

be re-adjusted back to vertical mode before it could be used. All this was time consuming when seconds counted. Following representations from the chief the archway was eventually removed.

An out-office was provided for the station 'watch', as the dutyman was called. All calls were 'running' calls, where the alarmist had to report a fire verbally and in person directly to the fire station. Neither the brigade nor the police had telephones; the fire station was not connected by telephone until 1885.[13] When the brigade's first horse was purchased in February 1878 for £40, a stable was added to the yard. Finally, to ensure that the public at large knew that the CFB was now officially 'on the run', a red lamp was placed over the station gate.[14] One can only trust that the colour wasn't misconstrued by the denizens of the nearby quays!

THE BRIGADE UNIFORM.

The same uniform was adopted for the Cork firemen as that worn by their Dublin colleagues. This differed substantially from firemen's 'undress' (i.e., operational) uniform issued throughout the rest of the United Kingdom. With the exception of the brass helmet, it had more in common with the US firemen than their UK counterparts. J. Robert Ingram, the first Chief Officer of the DFB, had served as a volunteer fireman in New York and equipped his men in the style of uniform worn by his former corps. Unlike their counterparts in Belfast and Britain where the double-breasted lancer tunic with high Prussian collar was favoured, the Dublin and Cork brigades' undress uniform consisted of a heavy-duty, double-breasted, bib-front red shirt, known as a smock, with brass buttons, navy kersey trousers, and high leather Napoleon boots.[15] Napoleon boots reached in front above the knee, unlike 'Wellington' boots – favoured by London firemen – which reached above the calf and below the knee. Both types were made of the best grained leather, special care being taken to render them waterproof. The mode of uniform led to the firemen being referred to as 'Redshirts'.

The waist belt was of black leather with a large brass buckle. A fireman's axe encased in a black leather pouch hung on the wearer's left side, while a combined hose wrench and nozzle spanner was carried in a pouch on the right-hand side. In later years, with the growing danger of electrocution at fire incidents, the wooden-handled axe – which provided no protection against electric shock other than the limited insulation properties of the wooden handle – was withdrawn in favour of a model with a rubber-insulated handle. The trainee fireman was shown how to make best use of his axe in a number of ways, including how to make a forcible entry by snapping a padlock with a quick twist of the pointed side.[16]

The hose wrench and nozzle spanner (aka a hose key) was another essential piece of a fireman's personal gear. Delivery hose has to be connected length for

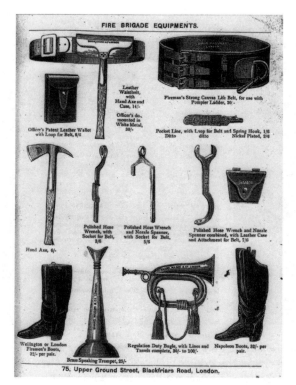

A page from the Shand, Mason & Co. Firemen's Outfitters catalogue. Shand, Mason were suppliers to Cork Fire Brigade.

length until the required number is attained to complete the line. Nowadays, each length has a male and female instantaneous coupling, and it is a straight-forward matter to 'marry' one to the other by simply clicking them together. In 1877, however, with such couplings in their infancy and still something of an unknown quantity, fire brigades invariably favoured couplings with either round or 'V' threads. (Cork had 'V' threads). Each length of hose had to be laboriously screwed on to the next, thus the necessity for each man to carry his own hose key in order to ensure the joints were complete and watertight. The nozzle spanner side of the wrench was used for changing nozzle sizes on the fire ground as the situation demanded.

The 'dress' (i.e. non-operational) uniform consisted of cap, navy-blue, single-breasted patrol jacket and navy-blue, heavy-duty trousers. The records make no mention of a cap-badge being issued at this stage, but this was not unusual for early municipal fire services. The firemen's cap was known as a Nelson cap, and was loosely based on the Royal Navy ratings' head-dress. Supt Wickham wore a 'képi' type cap, then favoured by principal fire officers. In keeping with the practice at the time, it is most likely that the fire chief's helmet and uniform 'furniture' (i.e. buttons, buckles, epaulettes, etc) were finished in silver in con-trast with the brass used for the other ranks, but I have been unable to verify

Above left: Brass helmet issued to members of Cork Fire Brigade 1877–1935. The helmet was first introduced to London Metropolitan Fire Brigade in the 1860s by Captain Shaw. The model he chose closely resembled the helmet worn by the *Regiment de Sapeurs-Pompiers*.

Above right: Brass helmet (1855 model) of the *Regiment de Sapeurs-Pompiers,* the Paris Fire Brigade.

Below left: Detail of the 'fire-spewing' dragon embossed on the comb of the helmet. Legend has it that Capt. Shaw's little daughter, Anna found the drawings of the new helmet on his desk and added her own inimitable touch, the ferocious dragon.

Below right: Detail of the Cork Fire Brigade helmet plate incorporating a design of flaming

this as the records are not specific enough. His immediate successor, Alfred J. Hutson, certainly had silver accoutrements; some of his personal equipment has survived, including his magnificent silver helmet.

The fire helmet differed only from the DFB pattern in the helmet plate, the large badge worn on the front of the helmet. Whereas Dublin had an imposing, specially-struck plate incorporating the Dublin City Arms, the Cork brigade, being a much smaller entity, had to settle for the standard plate which came attached to the helmets purchased directly from the Shand, Mason catalogue. This model comprised a design of a flaming torch, two crossed axes, two branchpipes, etc, and remained unchanged during the sixty years that the brass helmets were in service.

The helmets, belts, pouches, axes, and hose keys were purchased from Shand, Mason and Co. Firemen's Outfitters, London. The bill for equipping the entire brigade amountied to £9 17s 4d. James Sugrue, Merchant Tailor of 94 South Main Street, submitted his account for tunics, trousers, and caps which came to an additional £24, while John O'Connell of 91 George's Street was able to supply first-class Napoleon fire boots, made on his premises, for £1 7s 6d; a saving to the corporation of 4s 6d a pair over the same boots advertised in the Shand, Mason catalogue. The heavy-duty, red shirts with which the firemen were equipped for fighting fires were purchased on the open market but when tenders were again invited in July 1878, James J. Hurley of 75 South Main Street was successful with his tender of £1 each.

Initially, each fireman received one set of uniform only. This meant that they frequently turned-out in clothing still ringing wet from the previous fire. In spite of repeated pleas from Mark Wickham for a second set of undress uniform for his men, the matter was continuously deferred. Only when the Town Clerk, Alex McCarthy, made a personal appeal to the Mayor was authorization given for a spare uniform. In April 1878, he reported that, 'having seen the firemen after attending at a recent fire, in such a condition, owing to the saturated state of their clothes ... it is necessary for the preservation of their health, and perhaps their lives, to provide them at once with a change'.

ON THE RUN: THE BRIGADE'S FIRST APPLIANCE.

The issue of *The Fireman*[17] for 15 February 1878 recorded:

A New Fire-Reel.
Mr Wickham, the energetic Chief of the Cork Fire Establishment, has recently received a new fire-reel, known as a 'One-Horse Fire-Jumper', and had a turn-out of his staff for the occasion. The new Fire-Reel has been constructed from the patent of Captain Ingram, Chief of the Dublin Fire Brigade. It is designed to carry four or more men, with [up to] 440 feet (132m) of hose and all necessary fire appliances.

Ever since the days of the 'waterworks brigade', the men had to haul the heavy 'van', laden with firefighting equipment, to any part of the city to which they might be called. This situation still prevailed for the first three months of Cork Fire Brigade's existence. Then, undoubtedly to the great relief of the firemen, a special hose reel, to be horse-drawn, was purchased at a cost of £52.14s.2d. The horse, a chestnut mare, accounted for an extra £40.

The hose reel was an American invention and was first introduced into the UK in 1837 by William Baddeley CE and used in Birmingham.[18] The horsed hose reel – the 'jumper' – was designed in 1861 by William Roberts and adapted for use in this country by Capt. Ingram who was familiar with them from his service in the United States. Their *modus operandi* was straightforward. The jumper was driven to the hydrant nearest to the fire ground. A crew member jumped off, connected a standpipe (onto which the delivery hose on the reel was already connected) and, as the horse galloped off to the fire with the remaining members on board, the hose line was paid out behind until the required length was reached. When this was achieved the line was disconnected from the reel, a branchpipe inserted, the signal given to the man at the standpipe for the water to be turned on, and the crew was ready to tackle the blaze. A box under the crew's seat carried an array of small gear – branches, nozzles, axe, lines, etc. In 1900, a second jumper, a four wheeler, was added. This was built by Jessop Browne and Co., Carriage, Cab and Car Builders of Brunswick Street, Dublin.[19]

The famous Cork firm of coach builders, Johnson's of Nelson Place – 'Carriage Builders by Special Appointment to His Excellency the Lord Lieutenant' – was also in the business of manufacturing horsed hose reels for fire brigade use. When a deputation from Cork was invited to partake in the International Fire Brigade Tournament and Exhibition in London in 1893, James Johnson promptly offered to contribute £25 towards their expenses and placed his 'Patent Combined Horse-Reel and Side-Car' at their disposal. Although his offer was accepted by the corporation, and the team was proudly photographed in London on Johnson's appliance (later appearing in the *Fireman* journal), there is no record of any firm orders being placed as a result of the exposure.[20]

The weeks and months following the brigade's establishment were extremely busy for the hard-pressed unit. Hardly a day went by without some urgent call on their services, leading one Town Councillor to complain that 'it was a remarkable fact that fires had increased in the city since the fire brigade was established'. When this silly observation was received with hoots of laughter from his fellow City Fathers, he retorted, huffily, that it was no laughing matter at all, but 'a plain fact' (more laughter).[21] As fire followed fire, accolade followed accolade. After a blaze in the stores of Garrett Russell in Cotter Street on Sunday 3 March 1878, the *Cork Examiner* reported that, 'the brigade under the able superintendence of Mr Wickham worked splendidly ... and is further

A 'Jumper', made by Johnson's. In the driver's seat is Supt Alfred J. Hutson. The team consisted of Auxiliary Fireman James Keating and Volunteer Fire Brigade members Mahony, Murphy, Sullivan, and McNamara. (London, 1893).

proof of the efficiency of our new fire brigade'; and on 9 March, 'owing to the energetic action of the fire brigade, the flames were soon extinguished' after an outbreak in Mahony's Basket Factory in Brunswick Street.

The next great test of the brigade's capability came on the afternoon of Friday 22 March 1878. This major fire involved, ironically, the remainder of the block that the brigade had saved during the first call to Cunningham's Provisions Stores on Merchant's Quay. The *Cork Examiner* headline ran:

> Great Destruction of Property: Four Business Houses Burned.
> One of the most disastrous fires that has occurred in Cork for many years broke out yesterday, and resulted in the destruction of a considerable portion of the block of buildings lying between Maylor Street and Fish Street. The fire made a small beginning in the paper store of Mr. D O'Reilly, paper man-ufacturer, 3 Maylor Street, a few doors from Patrick Street. The store at the rear immediately adjoins the Royal Billiard Rooms of Mr P.J. Farrell, which readily caught the flames and extended it back to the premises behind Messrs Wright Bros., Grocers, The London House, and the grocery establishment of Atkins Brothers. In an incredibly short space of time the flames completely enveloped the two latter houses, both of which were stocked with highly ignitable material – The London House laden with fancy articles and Atkins' with wines, whiskey, brandy, candles and oil. [22]

Supt Wickham and his staff responded promptly 'at the first alarm of fire, between 1.30 and 1.45p.m', and as they arrived found the blaze extending to the roof of William Banks and Co. (which they succeeded in saving) whose premises stretched from Maylor Street to Fish Street. For the first quarter of an hour, the water supply was very poor and for a brigade totally dependent on the mains the consequences of this could be dire. With no fire engine to pump water from the limitless supply of the River Lee, gallingly only a stone's throw away, it was tantamount to sending a company of soldiers into battle without ammunition. (Coupled with the paucity of personnel this was a lacuna that would continue to hinder the operations of the brigade. In spite of Wickham's exhortations, the council continued to baulk at providing the relatively small sum required to purchase a steam fire engine. When eventually ordered in 1905, it still only cost £295. The value of Cork property that such an appliance might have saved in the intervening twenty-eight years is incalculable).[23]

As the turncocks of the waterworks went efficiently about their business, the water supply gradually improved until, with the dubious help of 'supernumer-aries', untrained men from the crowd who volunteered assistance in return for payment, six jets were in operation. By 3p.m. the whole block was one mass of flame. Shortly afterwards, two companies of the 87th and 16th Regiments arrived from Victoria (now Collins) Barracks with their manual engine, but their suction hose was too short to reach down to the water from the quayside. The soldiers, helpless, had to contend themselves with assisting the police to hold back the vast crowd which thronged the streets from St Patrick's Bridge to Winthrop Street. By six o'clock, the fire was surrounded, but a pall of thick black smoke hung over the city centre for hours.

The newspapers were generally sympathetic to the firefighting effort but noted, 'the smallness of the brigade and the impossibility of three or four men being in half-a-dozen or more places at the same time'.[24] It was also observed with satisfaction that, in spite of the enormity of the task facing them, that no loss of life or injuries of note had been sustained.

At the height of the fire the chief had directed some of the hastily-recruited supernumeraries to go to the fire station on Sullivan's Quay to fetch the wheeled escape which he urgently required. While rushing back up Prince's Street with the unwieldy, unfamiliar apparatus, they inadvertently hit a signboard project-ing from the premises of a Mr Lee causing him to later complain bitterly to the corporation. The escape, he said, had been handled with extreme carelessness and was in the charge of a disorderly gang of roughs. Patiently, Mark Wickham explained that he had been unable to spare a fireman to go with the supernu-meraries to the station to collect the escape. The signboard had projected five feet out over the street and the escape had to be negotiated past a horse and cart parked on the opposite side, and in any event only the tip of the spear on the sign had been bent. This particular incident led to more control being exercised over the supernumeraries. From now on only trusted men from the crowd, men who the Superintendent or a brigade member could vouch for, would be hired. They were also to be issued with 'medals' – not unlike the tickets once given by the insurance companies to volunteer pumpers – which they would produce after the fire in order to be paid – 2s 6d for each fire. The account for the supernu-meraries was then passed to the appropriate insurance company who reimbursed the corporation. This was the only concession made by them in subscribing to firefighting operations. When the corporation continued to press the insurance companies to subscribe to the brigade's upkeep even this was withdrawn.

Another off-shoot of this major fire was that the firemen were issued with a second uniform. The Mayor said that by Saturday (the day after the fire), the men 'were all quite saturated with water, and it was really a manifest injustice, a crying evil' that no change of uniform was provided. Sir George Penrose said that, 'when he saw the state of the men on Saturday' he determined, 'to put an end to it at once' and went straight to the Town Clerk (Alex McCarthy) to get a requisition for a temporary second uniform. But Cllr Creedon thought the very idea of circumventing the official tendering process was 'monstrous'. Cllr Banks said that there was disquiet amongst the general public about the size of the brigade; it was simply too small for what was expected of it. He was, 'not suggesting that the permanent staff should be increased' but a trained auxiliary corps should be formed from men in the corporate staff – a suggestion that would ultimately bear fruit.[25]

The acclaim continued. The Mayor said he, 'never saw men working like the fire brigade did, and they deserved immortal credit for the superhuman efforts they used in putting a stop to that dreadful fire ... the brigade proved simply invaluable.'[26] Ald. Nagle said he, 'had some experience of fires, and never saw anything like the way the new brigade worked.'[27] One week later, shortly after midnight on Saturday 30 March, the city centre experienced another serious outbreak. This time Lynch's Oil and Colour Warehouse on Great George's Street was engulfed. Mr Lynch, his wife and family, seven persons in all, were asleep on the premises when the fire broke out. All managed to escape with their lives. The fire brigade 'were on the spot without delay and the hydrants brought into requisition ... but due to the inflammable nature of the stock they had little effect'. By 2a.m. the fire had extended back to Tobin Street and seriously threatened Cleburne's Outfitters, but was eventually contained by 'the men of the brigade [who] worked with great energy and skill to check the advance of the flames'.[28]

A respite from large fires was now given the brigade, a luxury it had hardly known since its inception, allowing it to take stock and settle down to an ordinary working routine (if fire brigade duties can ever be classified as ordinary and routine). But for some among the council, the notion of members of the brigade, as they saw it, now sitting around all day with nothing to do except play cards and drink tea while awaiting an alarm call which may or may not come, was anathema. The concept of an immediate-response emergency service, able to scramble at a moment's notice, was unheard of. Milton may have considered that, 'they also serve who only stand and wait', but the councillors were having none of it. If the firemen had nothing to do between answering calls then they would find plenty to occupy them.

The traffic on the new Parnell Bridge badly needed to be regulated, so two firemen were dispatched there on traffic duty, 'their helmets, belts, and axes to be deposited in the Corporation Offices on the South Mall'.[29] And how about the usual chaos in Winthrop Street caused by the 'jingles' (horse-drawn cabs) milling about? A man in uniform was badly needed there! As for the cattle-market, miles from the fire station on the north side of the city, that surely could do with a fireman or two early in the morning to put manners on the farmers coming in from the country with their herds of fractious cattle! One alderman, passing the fire station one day, was incensed to see the brigade's chestnut mare, on which £40 of ratepayers' money had been lavished, standing placidly in her traces, playfully flicking her tail at him, awaiting an emergency call. Not good enough! A disgraceful waste of corporate funds! The dusty streets badly needed watering and it really was too much to expect the hard-pressed corporation to buy a second horse for such purposes when, clearly, the fire horse was under-utilized. And so, with the protestations of the fire chief going unheeded, the brigade horse was sent off around the city pulling the watering cart. To add insult to injury, even some of the scarce new fire hose was requisitioned for this purpose. Suddenly, every alderman and councillor seemed to have his own pet project at which a fire brigade presence was essential. The station was now manned only by Supt Wickham and, at best, two men, with the others on bridge duty, traffic duty, or market duty, everywhere except where they should have been. In the event of a fire call, the hose reel had, in the absence of the horse, to be once more pulled by hand to the scene. The situation was inexorably returning to the bad old days of the 'waterworks brigade'.

Inevitably, it was only a matter of time before this unsatisfactory state of affairs would rebound on the corporation; complaints of delays in the time it took the brigade to turn up at fires started to arrived on the mayor's desk. After a fire at Hill Lane, Pope's Quay, in January 1883, Cllr Lane complained of the, 'apparent tardiness in the arrival of the brigade' at the outbreak. The only concession made was, from then on, the RIC was authorized to hire a cab so that a constable might give an alarm of fire at the fire station. Supt Wickham, also, was at liberty to hire a cab to, 'accelerate his arrival at the scene of a fire occurring at any considerable distance' from the station. Incredibly, the dispersal of the firemen on extra-curricular duties remained common practice.[30]

SUPERINTENDENT MARK WICKHAM: 'INSPECTOR OF EXPLOSIVES'.

On 11 May 1882, the Under-Secretary at Dublin Castle forwarded the report of Her Majesty's Chief Inspector of Explosives, Colonel V.D. Majendie, to Cork Corporation. Majendie had complained of the non-administration of the Explosives Act in the city. Britain was in a state of high alert with the Fenian campaign of dynamite attacks on government and other high-profile buildings in full swing. Although Gladstone's second Irish Land Act had become law in the previous year, promising the so-called 'Three Fs' – Fair rent, Free sale, and Fixity of tenure – it failed to placate the extreme element in the Fenian movement who maintained that violent revolution was the only means of gaining independence. The corporation's response to Col Majendie's admonition was to give Mark Wickham an additional title, 'Inspector of Explosives', *sans* training or extra remuneration. So far as they were concerned, the matter was now disposed of. One of Wickham's first 'finds' of explosives was in a workshop in Blackamoor Lane right behind the fire station: Mr Allport, the proprietor, had 110lbs more of gunpowder on his premises than he was entitled to have.

When, after some months had elapsed and, not unreasonably, the fire chief sought some remuneration for this extra extremely dangerous duty, the corporators quickly decided that he had, after all, no technical knowledge of explosives and released him from the responsibility, which they then promptly foisted on the hapless City Engineer (*sans* training or remuneration).

SPARKS FLY ON KING STREET AND ON SULLIVAN'S QUAY.

Head Constable Patrick Cantillon was determined to put an end to it, once and for all. For the past few nights now, he had been receiving reports on his desk from a 'concerned citizen' about the shenanigans and clandestine drinking in that shebeen on King Street. Waiting for the weekend in order to maximize the number of 'found-ons' that he might nab, he decided the time had come for the raid. Calling on a number of policemen assembled in the day-room, he collected his spiked helmet with its large pewter-coloured 'Crown above the Harp' helmet plate, and stepped outside the door of St Patrick's Hill RIC station into the balmy night air. At that precise moment, 1a.m on Monday 28 May 1883, he heard a distant shout which sounded like 'Fight!' Adrenaline flowing now, fight-or-flight response shifting into top gear, Cantillon set himself a brisk walking pace down the hill. 'Never run into danger', the words of his instructor in the Depot rung in his ears, 'and always maintain your dignity'.

With the station party trooping dutifully behind, one of the younger members began, cheekily, to whistle 'The Bright May Moon' in time to the click of the Head Constable's heels. A withering backward glance from Cantillon told him his sense of humour was misplaced. As they turned the corner of St Patrick's Hill into King Street they noticed a crowd had gathered outside Dobbin and Ogilvie's 'Monster Warehouse', from which a lurid glow emitted. With mixed relief, Cantillon now realized that the cry which had shattered the stillness of the night had not been 'Fight!' but 'Fire!' All thoughts of the raid on the pub now gone, he ordered one of his men to hot-foot it to Sullivan's Quay to summon the fire brigade.

Dobbin and Ogilvie's handsome block of buildings had been built some five years before in the classic High-Victorian tradition. The buildings, three in number, comprised a block known as Hibernia Buildings with a frontage of 125 feet and a depth of 153 feet.[31] The central building consisted of the warehouse and counting-house, the eastern building comprised a tobacco and snuff factory, while boiled sweets and other *bon-bons* were manufactured in the western building. The walls, floors, and staircases were composed of brick, iron, stone, and concrete, all of them substances which from time immemorial were looked upon as materials best adapted to resist fire. The front walls, fully twenty inches thick, were gracefully faced with limestone, with the windows – comprising up to 80 percent of the frontage – encased in elegant limestone frames, divided by pillars and surmounted by carved capitals. Unsprinklered, such a building was regarded as 'fireproof' and then the owners began to fill it with a huge mass of goods of the most flammable description.[32] Almost 200 people were employed there.

Now, as the fire took hold, the fierce exothermic reaction was for a short time penned into what was practically a huge retort. Even as Head Constable Cantillon gruffly ordered the growing throng of people to go back a safe distance from the building, the huge build-up of heat shattered the glass in the front windows with explosive force, sending scores of deadly flesh-ripping shards in every direction and belching an enormous mass of flame across the street. The shutters on the buildings opposite began to smoulder. Only as the *Cork Examiner* reporter was about to leave the scene to file his story did the fire brigade arrive. He narrated how:

> The flames cast a lurid glare which illuminated King Street along Camden Quay, and stretching across imparted a peculiar tint to the river; and even far down Patrick Street the houses were tinted with the great light caused by the conflagration. The appearance of the sky all over the city was singularly affected by the fire – like a beautiful sunset with the warm glow struggling against the approaching dark hours. For miles around the city the fire was perceptible.[33]

The tardiness of the brigade now came in for scrutiny. The newspaper reporter alleged that there was no sign of the fire brigade 'for fully thirty-five or forty minutes' from the time the blaze was first noticed, and even when they did arrive:

> Persons who were present do not speak in terms of approbation of the working of the Fire Brigade. It is certainly a very grave reflection upon the efficiency of this corps that they should have brought with them a quantity of hose which must have been rotten.

(From being constantly abused on street-watering duties, perhaps?) The report continued, 'It is felt, too, that there was a lack of intelligence in dealing with the fire at the outset'. This last remark was prompted by 'several of those present' advising the fire chief on how best to deploy his meagre resources. Wisely, he decided to fight the fire on his own terms. Later, the tone of the article ameliorated somewhat, for by 3a.m., 'the members of the Fire Brigade are working with a will and the supply of water is now copious'.

In the bowels of the huge cauldron of fire, the stone staircases keyed into the walls cracked through and came down with an almighty crash, while the lintels to the windows began to calcine and fly to pieces. The iron girders, twisted and warped under the influence of the tremendous heat, brought down the floors; and elsewhere, the girders and ties, as the water from the firemen's jets came in contact with them, strained the walls and eventually caused them to fall. The military engine arrived about 3.30a.m. and it was directed by Supt Wickham to Wellington Road, at the rear of Dobbins', to afford some protection to the buildings there, principally Dr Knight's Academy, which was in grave danger. By 5a.m. the fire was virtually under control but not before the principal warehouse and the sweet factory lay in ruins. The tobacco factory, 'after an hour's continuous hard work by the Brigade', was saved and suffered only some water damage. Damage was put at approximately £25,000 and the reliable old chestnut of 'spontaneous combustion' was trotted out as the likely cause.

In contrast to its earlier approach, when the fire brigade could do no wrong, the *Cork Examiner* (which for years had campaigned long and hard for the setting up of a municipal fire service) was now not slow in putting the unit under the spotlight. For, by 1883, it was increasingly evident that the brigade had a problem, one that had neither been foreseen nor anticipated, and one that would blight its formative years. It was a difficulty concerning neither lack of funding nor equipment (although these things were problematical in their own right), but of discipline, or the want of it. In truth, if Mark Wickham had been a good Conductor of Fire Escapes he was a poor conductor of men. Following his initial successes, he gradually began to lose the earlier esteem in which he had been held. Turmoil and ineffectuality became the hallmarks of his governance. Initially, he had had the public backing and the goodwill of the council to implement a new kind of firefighting system for Cork, but he failed to deliver. In spite of a strict code of rules and instructions which he had composed and promulgated, it was manifestly apparent that he was unable to maintain the high ideals he had set himself. Eventually, like many a new broom, he was worn down by apathy and indifference.

The number one cause of indiscipline was the tacit toleration of the abuse of alcohol, an attitude which seemed endemic then in the Cork, if not indeed the Irish, psyche. Father Mathew's great temperance crusade had taken place well within living memory.[34] In an era when diversions were few, *ennui* was often fuelled by the long dreary periods of inertia on duty, only infrequently interrupted by calls to action. There was no leave in the accepted sense. Any request for leave had to be laid by the Superintendent before the Waterworks and Fire Brigade Committee who considered each case on its merits. Only if a very special family event warranted it would leave be granted. Annual leave was unknown. It is, perhaps, not stretching the imagination too much to visualize why some men, on continuous duty for virtually months on end, might occasionally turn to alcohol as a form of escapism. When poet Dryden asserted that, 'drinking is the soldier's pleasure' he perhaps, by extension, included all those serving, long hours, in uniform. [35] Additionally, the firemen's red shirts were not waterproof and regularly they had to work for many hours at incidents soaked through to the skin. What better antidote to the freezing cold than a pint and a hot toddy (a remedy with which the medical profession concurred; many nineteenth-century doctors prescribed alcohol as a remedy for the firemen's traditional ailments of bronchitis, arthritis, 'flu, and even TB)?

In fairness to Mark Wickham, another predicament for him was, as the *Cork Examiner* had put it, 'the smallness of the brigade'. In such a small outfit, respect and authority had become personalized. Unable to keep his distance and maintain his mystique as an authority figure, the confined nature of the brigade's cramped quarters meant that he was increasingly perceived and judged solely on his qualities as a man. When his successor, Alfred Hutson, succeeded in having a new central fire station built, one of the first things he included in the plans was a dedicated 'Chief Officer's residence', erected next door to the station at 23 Sullivan's Quay. This was a luxury denied the first fire chief.

Less than two months after the King Street fire the whole question of discipline was again to the fore; only this time the recommendation was that Mark Wickham himself be dismissed. The weary members of the Waterworks and Fire Brigade Committee heard how a complaint had been preferred by Fireman John Walsh against the Superintendent for abuse of authority. In his defence, the chief outlined how he had directed Walsh, the dutyman on the evening in question, to explain the workings of the fire escape to some visitors to the station. Walsh, he maintained, had done so only very reluctantly and in a manner disrespectful to him. Later, when he visited the watchroom again (in company with the civilians) he found Walsh absent from his post and on his arrival, gave him a dressing-down and 'said more than I ought'. One of the visitors corroborated the Superintendent's evidence as to the want of discipline displayed by Walsh; but the other backed Walsh's version (as did Fireman Ryan and John Moore, the foreman lamplighter, who happened to be in the station) including the coarse language used by Wickham, his challenge to Walsh to fight, and, damningly, that 'the Superintendent was under the influence of drink'. [36] Finding in favour of Walsh (who, curiously, seems to have escaped censure for his initial insubordination), the committee unanimously agreed to recommend to council that Mark Wickham should be dismissed. However, at an assembly of the full council on 17 August 1883 the recommendation was amended: Wickham was fined £2 with a stern warning that any repetition would lead to his immediate dismissal.

During the following years the discipline problem continued to fester with only limp-wristed attempts made to come to grips with it. Nobody seemed to have the answer as to how to solve it. Eventually, one exasperated public representative, Cllr Julian, seriously suggested dismissing the entire brigade and starting all over from scratch, and, indeed, one by one, the four who had initially made up the unit in 1877 were all dismissed, until by 1891 only Mark Wickham himself remained.

THE GREAT BLAZE AT ST DOMINICK'S MILL AND REORGANISATION

With the expansion of the city outside of the confines of the medieval walls, one of the first places to be industrialized was Crosse's Green, itself only a stone's throw from the walls.[37] Over the years, a range of industries had been established in the area, notably distilling, brewing, and flour milling; and the district had become notorious for some of the most devastating outbreaks of fire ever witnessed in Cork. Chief amongst these were: Walker's Distillery (28 April 1804), Lane's Porter Brewery (26 October 1807), Lane's Corn Store (9 December 1847), Lane's Steam Mills (17 March 1848), and St Dominick's Flour Mills, operated by Robert and Henry Hall, on 13 January 1872. When the rebuilt St Dominick's was again destroyed by fire in controversial circumstances on the night of Saturday 19 June 1886, the corporation, under pressure from the business community and the general public, determined that some reform of the city's capacity to tackle major fires was overdue.

A number of Cork flour mills had been destroyed by fire during the latter half of the nineteenth century, for with the advent of new technology came new risks. The *Fireman* (reproducing an article from the *Miller* journal) enumerated some of them:

> Flour mill fires have a habit of breaking out in the evening shortly after the shutting-down of the mill. Bearings will get hot, while the friction caused by pulleys, conveyors and other parts of machinery getting out of place and rubbing, is necessarily liable to cause serious mischief, especially when the mill is freed from the care and control of the operative staff.[38]

S.G. Gamble, Second Officer of the London Fire Brigade, agreed, adding that:

> The unobserved overheating of machinery is a risk, which, with proper attendance and supervision, should never take place, but is not an uncommon cause of fire. Long shafting, bearings hidden from general view or not necessarily accessible, enclosed bearings, and those working in a dusty or gritty

atmosphere, form the most likely sources of trouble. Accumulations of dirt, waste materials, and grease on the shaftings, bearings and brackets, facilitate heating and feed a starting fire.[39]

The *Miller* advocated that each mill should be patrolled by a vigilant night watchman who should remain on duty for some hours after a mill had stopped. Because:

> a fire generated by friction will smoulder and smoulder, sometimes for hours, before breaking into a flame, it is essential that the watchman be constantly on the move, keeping his eye, as it were, all over the mill, and ready to detect with his nose the first faint indications of fire.

But Gamble asserted that in his experience night watchmen were frequently a source of danger in themselves due to the high incidence of smoking he had observed among them:

> Invariably watchmen never closed doors behind them on their rounds. If they did so, fires would probably be limited in their destructiveness to the room or section in which they originated. Unfortunately, the average man will take neither of these simple precautions.[40]

St Dominick's Mill stood on Crosse's Green on the site of the ancient Dominican Priory, known as St Mary's of the Isle, founded in 1229 by Lord Philip de Barry.[41] The mills were divided into three compartments: the new mill (built after the 1872 fire), the old mill, and 'the backs'. Both the new and old mills had their main entrances on Crosse's Green. The new mill was a large limestone building of four lofts with an extensive side front to Proby's Quay from which it was separated by the mill stream. The old mill was to the north of the new mill and adjoined it. The entrance to 'the backs' was via Convent Lane, which led to the back entrance of the convent of the Sisters of Mercy. 'The backs' consisted of an engine-house and the screen-house, a building also with four lofts, which stood immediately to the rear of the new mill and connected with it by 'iron, fire-proof doors'.

The *Cork Examiner* reported that the fire first showed itself at 10.50p.m. on the night of Saturday 19 June 1886 when some local men, employees of the mill, saw flames bursting through the roof of the screen-house. (A corporation inquiry subsequently established that the fire was spotted as early as 10.15p.m). Battering on the mill door they were let in by the night watchman who was quite unaware that the premises were on fire. Foolhardily, they made their way up through the darkened building until they reached the room on fire, almost at once doubling back on their tracks until they had located a fire hose, which they proceeded to connect to a hydrant in the yard. Dragging the heavy, charged hose up through the four floors of, by now, smoky lofts they were horrified to find a wall of fire advancing down the stairs on them and dismayed to find that, 'the force of water was weak and would not reach the fire'. Sensibly, they dropped the hose and beat a hasty retreat.[42]

Only at 11p.m was the fire brigade station (a few hundred metres from the mill) notified by the police and they arrived in less than five minutes. By the corporation's own estimate, fifty minutes had by now elapsed since the fire was first noticed. The firemen at once made down to the street main, but, even while doing so, they realized they were already fighting a losing battle. They knew the water main on Crosse's Green was a puny four-inch one which, for all intents and purposes, was useless for tackling a fire of such magnitude. The *Cork Examiner* echoed the sentiments of many, including the fire chief, when it declared:

> The fire would have been … confined to the loft in which it had originated if the head of water was sufficiently strong at the beginning, but it was a repetition of the old story in cases of fire in Cork – no water power. We understand that the main laid down in Proby's Quay is only a four-inch, and this limited service, together with the deficient power, enabled the flames to gain very rapid headway.[43]

With the lofts falling in with thunderous roars, the *Examiner* noted that one could easily have read a newspaper on the South Gate Bridge so great was the glare from the conflagration. Mark Wickham summoned the turncock, Jeremiah Crowley (an elderly man seconded to the brigade from the waterworks) and directed him to take all necessary steps to concentrate the pressure onto the fire ground. Crowley proceeded to the Grand Parade where, following instructions he had received from the waterworks engineering staff in 1882, he shut down the ten-inch cocks outside Nos 8 and 78. This manoeuvre, however, made no difference to the men waiting for water on Crosse's Green.

The *Cork Examiner* took up the story, describing how:

> A very startling and dangerous incident [then occurred]. Firemen Ryan and Mahony were in one of the lofts of the screen-house (which had not at this time fallen) with the hose, and Mr Edwin Hall, one of the proprietors of the mill, was with them. Wickham seeing the fire spreading in the new mill, thought their position dangerous, as in a few moments their retreat might be cut off, and went in on a lower loft into the screen-house. Ascending the ladder to the loft which the firemen and Mr. Hall occupied, he informed them of their position, and got ready to assist them in dragging out the hose.
>
> Just then the floor of the loft suddenly burst into flames, and the fine loose flour on the floor instantly shot up in fiery particles, burning the faces of the men and clinging in their nostrils and eyes. They could not see one

another. Wickham, standing near the top of the ladder, stretched out his hands and caught his fellow brigade-men, and, drawing them to him, they threw themselves down together to the next loft, Wickham falling on his head. He, however, was saved from a fractured skull by his helmet. It was afterwards found that Mr Hall, knowing the mill thoroughly, had escaped unhurt. The hose, owing to the accident, had to be abandoned. Within a few minutes… the fire showed in front of the new mill … in a great sheet of flame.[44]

After this unnerving incident, Mark Wickham had no time to feel sorry for himself or to reflect on his near-miss; he still had a major fire on his hands with no water at his disposal. With the blaze now running completely out of control he sent for Turncock Cantillon of the waterworks, whom he thought would have a more intimate knowledge of the complicated system of valves and cocks. Cantillon at once went to Sullivan's Quay where he shut the ten-inch cock outside No. 36, thereby isolating the flow to Blackrock, by which tactic, he later asserted, the pressure of water on Crosse's Green should have doubled. The chief later repudiated this claim and insisted it had made no difference. In any event, he said, the fire had made such headway by then that the premises were beyond saving.

Sometime around 1a.m., one hundred men of the Suffolk Regiment, in the charge of their Colonel, arrived with the barrack engine but found, 'there was not a sufficient depth in the mill stream to work their engine satisfactorily'.[45] (The efficacy of the military engine is doubtful. Sir George Penrose, a member of the corporation, remarked that, 'You might as well be playing a syringe as the military engine. It would put out a little fire but not a large one.'[46]) With the feeble jets making little or no impression, the fire effectively burnt itself out in the early hours of the morning. Only the massive stone walls of the mills saved surrounding property from being engulfed too. Twenty thousand pounds worth of damage had been caused to buildings, plant, and stock. The mills were insured with the 'London, Liverpool, and Globe Insurance Company'.[47]

The shortcomings in the city's firefighting service (or, perhaps more correctly on this occasion, the water service) were once more catapulted into the public eye. The *Cork Examiner* fired off a highly-critical editorial, and public indignation soared high. A week after the fire, 'a large and influential deputation' of the city's establishment – household names like Beamish, Day, Lunham, Scott, McMullan, Cade, Ledlie, Newsom, Haughton, Dobbin, and Atkins – waited on Mayor Paul Madden and the council. They were there 'to impress the necessity of increasing the efficiency of the Fire Brigade. They were a business deputation – and they meant business'.[48] They railed at the fact that the city, 'when a large outbreak of fire took place, was left absolutely at its mercy. The Superintendent of the Fire Brigade should be perfectly acquainted with all the details of his work and of the water system in the city, and from what had appeared on the papers they thought such was not the case'.[49]

A member of the deputation, Robert Scott, thought the present system in Cork was an utter failure. People might imagine that the losses all fell on the English and other insurance companies, but, 'these companies did not come to Cork to do business at a loss, and although they gathered an enormous sum of money from Cork in fire premiums, if they found themselves losing by it, they would be sure to recoup themselves by increasing the premiums for insurance'.[50] He recalled that he had visited a small town in south Wales recently, a place of only 6,000 souls, but they had a full-time fire brigade of twelve men, assisted by a volunteer reserve and, 'the brigade were constantly about the town exercising themselves and learning how to be prepared for fires when they would break out'. He thought Supt Wickham should take a leaf out of their book. The Mayor, in defence of the firemen, retorted that he personally attended all the large fires in Cork and his experience was that the brigade, 'considering the smallness of the numbers, always worked very efficiently and intelligently'. The corporation, he said, had carried out all the recommendations proposed by Capt. Shaw of the London Fire Brigade; but the Town Clerk quietly interjected to remind him that this was not quite true.[51]

In the face of the trenchant criticism the corporation decided to set up its own inquiry into all aspects of the working of the fire brigade and water supply with the following terms of reference:

> To what extent ought the corporation to undertake to provide for the suppression of fires in the city?
> Are the present means sufficient for that purpose?
> If not, what further provision ought to be made in the matters of (a) water supply (b) fire brigade (c) engines and appliances?
> Is the supervision of the fire brigade satisfactory?
> If not, what changes ought to be made therein?
> The estimated cost involved in any recommendations the committee may make.[52]

The special sub-committee deliberated on these points for more than six months, submitting their report on 10 March 1887 on, 'The circumstances attending the fire at St Dominick's Mills and the failure of the Fire Brigade to extinguish it'. They concluded that, under the terms of the Cork Improvement Act of 1868, the corporation had no statutory obligation to maintain a fire brigade at all. The Act merely authorized them to provide a service, not required them.[53] While repudiating any express obligation on the part of the corporation in the matter, they recognized, 'the expediency of making reasonable provision for the protection of the lives and property of the citizens'. The ratepayers, however, should not be asked to incur any serious addition to the present cost of the brigade of about £600 a year. In this connection, they noted that repeated efforts and inducements to get the insurance companies to subscribe to the brigade's upkeep had been in vain.

They regarded the firemen as being, 'well up to their work, and had acquitted themselves most creditably of a very arduous and perilous duty'. On the night of the fire in question they had 'exerted themselves with characteristic energy and daring, and at no slight peril to themselves, but they were absolutely powerless to deal with the fire.' The committee felt bound to point out the really effective service rendered in numerous instances by the brigade for one of its extent and resources. In almost every instance, it had confined a fire to the building of origin, 'a task rarely accomplished by the largest and most efficient Brigades in the kingdom'. Hastily-recruited supernumeraries, with no training, were of little or no value, but notwithstanding this, they could not agree to recommend an increase in the permanent staff of four. Rather, they were suggesting the creation of an auxiliary corps of six men who would be recruited from other departments of the corporation and be, 'properly trained in the skills of firefighting'.

In the matter of the water supply, they found that there was an abundant supply of water in the reservoirs on the evening of the fire; in fact, one of the pumping engines had had to be stopped at 11p.m. to prevent overflow. They regarded the inadequacy of the pressure in the hydrants to be due to one or both of two causes: the insufficient size of the main from which the hydrants were supplied or the inadequate steps taken by Turncock Crowley for the purpose of concentration. The insufficiency of the main in that locality was only brought to their knowledge by the inquiry. This they attributed to the fact that, 'there has never been prepared a proper map showing the situation and size of the water mains in Cork City'.

The sub-committee decided to conduct their own experiment by replicating, in so far as was possible, the circumstances prevailing on the night of the conflagration. They noticed that the jet attached to the principal hydrant, when the two ten-inch cocks on the Grand Parade were closed, only reached the first floor; but when the ten-inch cock on Sullivan's Quay was also shut, the jet reached to the top of the building. They qualified this observation, however, by pointing out that during the course of the fire, several hydrants were drawing from the one four-inch main, thereby probably negating any benefit that may have accrued from the shutting down of the Blackrock main. The discovery of the insufficiency of the main at Crosse's Green led the committee to speculate that other areas of the city might have 'like defects' and Resident Engineer James O'Toole was directed to report on the size and sufficiency of the mains in the vicinity of all churches, mills, public buildings and 'other large establishments'. The engineer recommended the substitution of all three-inch and four-inch mains by six-inch ones, a suggestion with which the committee agreed.[54] The failure of the supply from the hydrants had, 'brought prominently into view the advantage of having a Steam Fire Engine', but only if the insurance industry could be persuaded into buying one for the brigade!

The focus of their attention now shifted to the hapless fire chief. The committee regretted that he did not consider it his duty to be personally acquainted with the, 'proper process of concentration' and appeared to have thrown all responsibility for this on Turncock Crowley, 'a man who is too old and feeble to be solely relied upon for so critical a duty'. They continued:

The Committee cannot refrain from expressing their strong disapproval of the want of care and forethought displayed by the Brigade Superintendent ... his omission to study the water supply arrangements is evidence of a lack of zeal and industry on his part which we regard as simply lamentable. The Superintendent should be not only a practical fireman but a man of superior intelligence and conduct whose personal influence and capacity for controlling those under him would at all times ensure prompt and strict obedience, as well as general respect for the authority with which he is invested. The Committee have had great difficulty in arriving at a definite conclusion as to the remedy that should be applied to the weakness in this respect; but they have taken steps in that direction which they hope will lead to a better state of things in future.

What those steps were was not spelled out, but one thing was certain, Mark Wickham's imbroglios with the Waterworks and Fire Brigade Committee were far from over.

SUMMARY OF RECOMMENDATIONS

* The three-inch and four-inch mains in certain localities, mainly near public buildings, to be replaced by six-inch ones at a total cost of £727.

* More hydrants to be added to the system.

* A Code of Instruction to be made up and printed in book form for members of the fire brigade, to assist them in concentrating pressure at the scene of a fire.

* It shall be the duty of the Superintendent at a fire to dispatch one or more firemen with specific instructions to concentrate the pressure of water to the locality of a fire.

* The brigade is fairly equipped in the matter of engines and appliances [the brigade did not possess any kind of engine], but an auxiliary corps of six men to be set up from corporation employees. These auxiliaries to be drilled on Saturday afternoon, and to be equipped with the same uniform as the regular firemen – brass helmet, red shirt, long boots, and belt and axe. They will be paid a retainer of two shillings per week on top of their current wages, and a premium of between two shillings and sixpence and

ten shillings for each fire attended. The auxiliaries are required to reside within 500 yards of the fire station [later reduced to 300] and, on being summoned to duty by the sounding of a large bellows Fog Horn, will proceed at once to the station and obey the orders of the Superintendent.

* Firemen Michael Ryan and Michael Thompson, being the senior men, to be promoted to Sergeant.

On 20 August 1888, the following men were selected for training as auxiliary firemen: Michael McCarthy, William Purcell, and Nicholas Butler, all of the City Engineer's Department; James Keating, Lighting Department; John Murphy, Sanitary Department; and Philip Lecane, Cleansing Department.

The report was submitted to council by Mayor John O'Brien on 29 April 1887. The councillors were keenly aware that reorganisation, invariably, means more outlay and thought that the ratepayers should not be asked, 'to incur any serious addition to the present expenditure of about £600 a year'. The setting-up of the auxiliary corps and other improvements were put in abeyance while the insurance agents of the city were again approached (as the corporation was entitled to do under Section 122 of the Cork Improvement Act of 1868) to bear the additional costs. Replies were received from the Liverpool and London and Globe, Commercial Union, County Fire Office, Hand-in-Hand, National Assurance of Ireland, Scottish Provincial, Guardian, and the Mutual Fire Insurance Company. The first three suggested the corporation should approach the Fire Offices' Committee, the London-based umbrella body for fire insurance companies, to adjudicate on the matter. Of the remaining, the Hand-in-Hand refused outright to contribute in any shape or form, while the others vaguely suggested more meetings or requested to know what the other companies were doing. The corporation decided to approach the Fire Offices' Committee. Their lengthy reply, dated 29 June 1887, was in the negative. The Fire Offices' Commitee secretary, one H. Ernest Hall, emphasized that:

The Fire Offices' Committee maintains that fire extinction is a public duty similar to police protection, which ought consequently to be paid out of the rates, for the levying of which Statutory powers are given to local authorities. The function of Insurance Companies is simply to indemnify their policy holders against loss by fire – to take risks as they find them, and rate them accordingly, and experience shows that if owing to improved fire extinguishing arrangements, or to any other cause, fires diminish either in number or in magnitude, it is the public, not the Insurance Companies, who benefit in the long run, because the result is that either premiums decrease, or property is insured for a small amount, the insured reaping the benefit in either case.

I may add that the propriety of the principle contended for by the Insurance Companies is now fully recognized by the Legislature, and that of late years the numerous attempts which have been made by local authorities to impose, either directly or indirectly, upon the Companies any share of the expenses of fire extinction have invariably failed.[55]

As a result of the Fire Offices' Committee's rebuff (they also recommended to the local Agents to cease forthwith subsidizing the cost of supernumeraries and alarmists) the council huffily rejected the reorganisation report and specifically forbade Mark Wickham from hiring any more supernumeraries at fires. Henceforth he would have to make do with his staff of four, irrespective of the size of the outbreak.

The Waterworks and Fire Brigade Committee members interpreted this as a vote of no confidence in their management of the brigade as:

such an instruction would make the unit less efficient than heretofore ... as it would be impossible for the four firemen to convey the escape and apparatus to the scene of a fire without much loss of time'. They went on to say that they now declined 'all further responsibility for the management and control of the Fire Brigade and request the Council transfer same to some other Committee.[56]

When the corporation, who had harboured some fanciful notion that the place of supernumeraries at fires might be taken by the police was emphatically rejected by that body, they realized they had been hoist on their own petard. Begrudgingly, the report was adopted, complete with the recommendation for the auxiliary unit. Financially, they would have to dig deeper into the municipal pockets than ever before. The councillors now breathed a collective sigh of relief, safe in the knowledge that the whole fire brigade question had been finally resolved and put to bed. Unhappily, any respite from the controversy which seemed to bedevil the unit was to be short-lived, in fact, worse was yet to come.

During the months when the sub-committee's report was in the process of preparation, the night skies over Cork were illuminated by the glare of two of the biggest fires of the decade, both occurring during the month of February 1887. These were the major fires at St Luke's church (Church of Ireland) early on the morning of 9 Wednesday, and Browne's Mills on King Street on the night of 23 Wednesday.

Fires in Cork city churches, although very infrequent, are not entirely unknown. In the past 275 years, just seven have been recorded: St Nicholas', Cove Street (C.O.I.) in 1726; St Finbarr's, Dunbar Street (R.C.) in 1727; the Cathedral of St Mary and St Anne (R.C.) in 1820; St Mary's, Pope's Quay (R.C.) in 1846; St Francis', Broad Lane in 1866; St Luke's, Summerhill North (C.O.I.) in 1887; and St Michael's, Blackrock (R.C.) in 1962. While all were damaged to a greater or lesser extent, the destruction of St Luke's and St Michael's was complete.

The church was the second to stand on the site. In 1837, a beautiful little Gothic building of white limestone with two porches on either side of a slender spire had been consecrated by Bishop Kyle. The architects were the famous brothers James and George R. Pain.[57] It was to act as a Chapel of Ease to St Anne's, Shandon, the renowned 'pepper-pot' church. In 1872, St Luke's was elevated to parish status, the first incumbent being Revd Mervyn Archdall (later Bishop of Killaloe) and he succeeded in building a fine new church on the same site. The plans were executed by Sir John Benson and W.H. Hill and it cost £11,000 to build. The style of architecture was North-Italian Romanesque, with seating for 1,000 people. It had the distinction of being the first Protestant church built anywhere in Ireland after the passing of the Irish Church Disestablishment Act in 1869.[58]

At 6a.m. on 9 February, as a Mr Buttimore made his way up through Mahony's Avenue on his way to work, he was startled to see dense smoke issuing from the windows of the infants' schoolroom, located under the south-western corner of the church. He went at once to the house of the Rector, Mr Archdall, and then to alert the Sexton, Mr Bonchier. The RIC at St Luke's was alerted. In the confusion, the keys of the church could not be found, and a large form was used as a battering-ram to break in the main door. The massive inrush of air which resulted sealed the fate of the already-stricken building. They were confronted by what a fire brigade member later described as 'one sea of flame'. Someone suggested that it might be a good idea to call the fire brigade and they were notified at 7.10a.m.

As the brigade clattered along the cobblestones of the almost deserted quays, the crew contemplated the glare in the sky to the north-east and knew, instinctively, that the task which lay before them was hopeless. The St Luke's area was, at the highest level, commanded by the 180ft reservoir and the consequent lack of head, coupled with small diameter mains, would mean feeble firefighting jets. The church was a complete write-off, save for the vestry room and the belfry tower. By virtue of the saving of the vestry room, the church plate, registries, and parochial records were removed, unscathed, by a Mr Richard Doyle.

The cause of the fire was immediately suspected to be the heating furnace situated underneath the floor of the church, where a large boiler was fixed, in which coke was burned. The *Cork Examiner* speculated that the fire may have been underway since midnight, a suggestion not entirely without merit: concealed roof spaces, organs, and belfries often enabled church fires to reach large proportions before discovery, while the lofty form of church construction with wide spanned roofs ensured a ready air supply to feed a fire. The cost of the damage was put at £16,000, but the church was insured for only £9,300. The third church on the site (also designed by W.H. Hill) was rededicated on 8 February 1889. Due to falling congregation numbers, the final service was held on Sunday 2 March 2003 by Revd Brian O'Rourke. It was later purchased by Cork City Council.

Two weeks later, another well-known Cork landmark fell foul to the, to use the *Cork Constitution's* habitual phrase, 'all-devouring element'. The extensive five-storey flour mills of Browne Brothers at 46 King Street were completely

Above left: Elevation of St Luke's church, St Luke's Cross, from *Irish Builder* (No.14, 1873). The church was completely destroyed by fire on the morning of 9 February 1887. (Courtesy of Cork City Libraries)

Above right: The remains of St Luke's church on the morning after the fire. (Courtesy of Don Trotter)

gutted in an outbreak first noticed at 9.45p.m. on Wednesday 23 February by some policemen on beat duty on Wellington Road. Although the brigade was in attendance quickly and, 'worked with great energy',[60] once again such a great area of fire was quite beyond the capacity of four men, with limited equipment, to control effectively. As the whole of King Street and the surrounding area was enveloped in the conflagration the *Examiner* journalist waxed lyrical, 'The sound of crackling timbers, the loud orders of the firemen to one another, and the wind rushing through the windows and fissures and adding to the strength of the fire, all mingled together in curious fashion'.[61] With all hope having evaporated of saving the mills, the firefighters turned their attention to the adjacent premises of Cade's mineral water factory. Two hundred men of the 11th Devon Regiment and the 93rd Highlanders assisted the RIC in holding back the enormous crowd.

As the buildings began to disintegrate the huge coping stones on Browne's crashed to the ground and two firemen escaped certain death only by dropping their branch and fleeing for their lives. In a passageway between the blazing building and the eastern side of the mill a third fireman, and some civilians who were assisting him, evaded being crushed only by the skin of their teeth when massive chunks of brickwork and masonry, without warning, toppled into the lane and shattered the arch over the gateway a split-second after they had made good their escape. The *Examiner* thought there was no doubt as to the origin of the fire:

It broke out in a place known as the silk machine room, of which there are a very large number situated on the top loft. Owing to the delicate nature of these machines they require constant overhauling and repair…and some men had been engaged in repairing them … [for which] they were obliged to use a candle to give them light. The theory is that a snuff of this candle accidentally got on one of the machines, and that it smouldered before it burst into flames. The men are steady men, teetotallers, and they deny the suggestion that they had been smoking.[62]

The machinery destroyed was put at £12,000 and the cost of rebuilding at £18,000.[63]

The two major fires had been tackled by the brigade in an efficient manner. St Luke's, on an island site, was already doomed even as the fire was discovered, and there was no suggestion from any quarter that the firemen had done anything other than their best. Browne's had, at least, been confined to the building of origin. The unit certainly had internal difficulties, but these had mostly been confined to closed quarters. That was all about to change on the evening of Saturday 28 May 1887 (a month after the adoption of the special report on the brigade when things were only meant to get better). The *Cork Examiner's* headline on the following Monday morning was easily the most humiliating ever composed in connection with the CFB. It lamented, 'Disgraceful Conduct of the Fire Brigade'. If a budding Mack Sennett had been on hand to direct an episode of his whacky Keystone Cops, he could hardly have done better.

The paper described how, about 6.30p.m. on the previous Saturday, fire had broken out in the stores of McCarthy Brothers, Ships' Chandlers, on Albert Quay. Mr McCarthy, the co-owner, had locked up only half an hour earlier. The blaze was noticed by some sailors working on a ship lying at the quay and they informed the police at nearby Union Quay barracks. As the police under Sergeant Meehan, assisted by some sailors, attempted to salvage goods from the burning premises the fire rapidly intensified. The fire brigade was called. What happened next became the subject of, yet another, wearisome inquiry for the dispirited City Fathers. The *Examiner* documented how:

> The Fire Brigade arrived about ten minutes to seven, but it soon became evident that something was wrong with them. On their arrival they had a preliminary row about arranging the hose. Having got it in order, Mr Wickham, the Captain, took up the hose with the intention of having it applied on the side.[64]

On seeing this, one of the firemen 'quietly shoved' the chief and took the hose from him. The fire was raging on the first floor, and as the firemen brought the hose up the wheeled escape they were slagged and jeered by the goading mob.

This only served to raise the hackles of the firefighters who turned the hose on the disbelieving crowd, soaking many. The *Examiner* report continued:

> Mr Wickham contented himself with walking about and blowing his whistle every ten minutes; but now the men had some rows among themselves and used the hose on one another. The fire reached its height about 7p.m and declined from that time, a fact for which the Brigade deserve little credit. They amused themselves at times, or avenged themselves for the derisive shouts of the crowd by now and then turning the hose on them in pure wantonness, Mr Scanlan, insurance agent, and Mr Milling [RIC District Inspector] having it turned on them individually at times. A little after eight, the fire was put out, and the Fire Brigade men found all excuse for further amusement gone.[65]

The upper floors of the building were badly damaged and the loss was estimated at £2,000.

At the inevitable post-mortem, Mark Wickham denied the newspaper report. No man had disobeyed his orders, he insisted, and it was untrue to suggest that any of the firemen had personal disputes. As the men went about their work, he thought someone in the crowd must have deliberately slashed the hose, and it was the spray from this that had soaked the civilians and police. The firemen concurred, claiming the press report was grossly exaggerated, and added that they were greatly impeded in their duties by the behaviour of the mob. The police, the proprietors of the business, and insurance agents having given their evidence, the corporation concluded that the allegation that the firemen had deliberately and wilfully mishandled the firefighting equipment was not substantiated. They did, however, find that the man who had 'quietly shoved' the fire chief was guilty of insubordination; and the latter was himself, 'guilty of a grave dereliction of duty by suppressing from his report all mention of such insubordination'.[66] The Superintendent was fined £1 and the fireman ten shillings. As historian Richard Henchion concluded:

> It had been the distinctive fate of Mark Wickham, Superintendent of the Fire Brigade, to be ever and always, wittingly or unwittingly, at the receiving side of verbal criticism or physical abuse during the greater part of his working life. Few of the services overseen by the Council aroused greater discussion and encountered more widespread obloquy than the Fire Brigade. The irony of this is that the Brigade comprised no more than a staff of four and a Superintendent.[67]

8

When a Cork Fire Inflamed Kipling's Wrath

'Sit down! It is only a chimney fire!'

(Judge Monroe at the burning of Cork Courthouse, Good Friday 1891).

'That a new Superintendent be appointed, applications to be invited from the principal Fire Brigades of the United Kingdom'.

(Minutes of the Waterworks and Fire Brigade Committee, 29 April 1891).

Rudyard Joseph Kipling, staunch imperialist and great 'Poet of the Empire', whose stanzas on the holy abstractions of honour, patriotism, and duty were framed into set-piece epitaphs and carved on numberless gravestones, was incandescent with rage. Mr Kipling, who made exceedingly good poetry, was, like his beloved queen, most definitely not amused.
He had read in the newspaper of how, at a fire which consumed the Law Courts in Cork City:

Above the portico a flag-staff, bearing the Union Jack remained fluttering in the flames for some time, but ultimately when it fell the crowds rent the air with shouts, and seemed to see significance in the incident.

'Significance, indeed!' he fumed. Dipping his favourite pen into the ink-well on his desk he sent it scuttling across the blank page:

The English Flag.
Winds of the World, give answer! They are whimpering to and fro,
And what should they know of England, who only England know?
The poor little street-bred people that vapour and fume and brag,
They are lifting their heads in the stillness to yelp at the English flag!

And so on for a further sixteen verses, making it one of his longer poems, and almost certainly the only poem in the English language composed in the aftermath of a Cork fire by so famous a personage. The blaze in question destroyed the Courts of Justice on Great George's Street on the evening of Good Friday, 27 March 1891.[1]

Throughout the course of many centuries the judicial centre of Cork lay in that rectangular piece of real estate which lies between St Augustine's Street and Castle Street. As far back as the early years of the seventeenth century, during the reign of King James I (James VI of Scotland), Courts of Justice were conducted in the King's Castle there; an icon which tradition holds is still commemorated on the Cork Coat-of-Arms. The last trial of note to be held within its walls was that of the accused in the so-called 'Doneraile Conspiracy', so ably defended by Daniel O'Connell and so eloquently described in Canon Sheehan's *Glenanaar*.

In that same year of 1830, the authorities decided that the courthouses were inadequate for their purpose, and at the following Spring Assizes the city and county Grand Juries agreed to a presentment of £18,000 to erect a new court-house fronting on to the new street called Great George's Street, 'between Cross-Street and the turn leading to Hammond's Marsh'. The Court of D'Oyer Hundred, representing the corporation, agreed to co-operate with the Grand Juries and to pay the sum of £2,000 towards the purchase of the site. On 1 July 1831, the contract for the completion of the building was awarded to the firm of George R. Pain with the sum of £16,000.[2]

Before long, a dispute arose between Pain and the Cork Stonecutters' Society. Pain intended using a terracotta composition for the capitals on the Corinthian intercolumnations of the portico, as, he insisted, that Cork limestone could not be used. The stonecutters maintained otherwise, and, in a deposition composed at the society's rooms at Ellis's of Capwell, they stated that they were more than capable of executing the work in locally-quarried limestone. The Grand Jury took the side of the stonecutters, and the delicately-carved capitals are still *in situ* all those years later, a permanent tribute and credit to the skill and talent of gifted Cork craftsmen of long ago.[3] Indeed, Lord Macaulay, the English historian, politician, and poet, considered the finished portico, 'worthy of Palladio'.

In the ensuing years, many Irish nationalists stood in the dock as judge after judge sat on the bench, robed in their imperial red, and harangued them for their disloyalty. In September 1890, the infamous Crimes Court, set up under the Coercion Act in an effort to break Parnell's National League, had imposed prison sentences on William O'Brien MP, John Dillon MP, and nine others for conspiracy. Outside the Tipperary courthouse the RIC panicked when followers of the accused tried to force their way into the already-packed building. The fracas, and the charges that followed, became known as 'The Tipperary Riot' case. Due to the highly-charged atmosphere in Tipperary town and its hinterland the authorities decided to transfer the trial of the five men charged with rioting to Cork, where it was scheduled for Holy Week 1891.

IN THE HEAT OF THE NIGHT: KIPLING SEES RED.

On the fourth day of the hearing, 27 March, the Court did not sit until 2p.m. on account of it being Good Friday. Sometime after 3p.m. several people in court remarked that they thought they could smell burning wood, but no investigation was carried out. As the evening wore on, and the first shadows of the late spring evening began to fall, the closing speeches for the prosecution and the defence had been delivered and Mr Justice Monroe began his address to the jury. A hush came over the thronged courtroom and, bar the odd cough and the rustle of a crinoline-clad lady shifting in her seat, the only sound was the drone of the judge's voice echoing across the chamber. Then another, quite distinctive, sound was heard: the unmistakable crackling sound of burning timber.

The sub-sheriff whispered urgently in the judge's ear and an uneasy murmur rippled across the body of the court. Hesitatingly, deferentially, one by one the people began to get up from their seats to leave. 'Sit down!' snapped the judge, impassive and stern, 'it is only a chimney fire!' A frightened exclamation, and all eyes were focused on the circular glass roof over the courtroom where the supporting woodwork had suddenly burst into flames. Stubbornly, only when the molten lead from the window frames fell into the room in hissing drops, did the judge authorize the sub-sheriff to announce, 'This Court stands adjourned for half an hour. God save the queen!' As he rose from the bench Monroe glanced at his pocket-watch. The time was 6.15p.m. Four years would elapse before a Court would again sit in the building.

As a member of staff put through an urgent telephone call to the fire brigade, frantic efforts were being made by others to save priceless records. Included in these were the ancient records of Cork city and county which had been transferred from the former courts. Sadly, their efforts were only partially successful.[4] William O'Brien and John Dillon (who attended as witnesses for the defence under a writ of *habeas corpus*) were ushered out through a side door onto Courthouse Street and, under mounted police escort, conveyed in sidecars to the County Gaol on the Western Road. The *Cork Examiner* described how the fire brigade was on site and made down within twenty minutes of the discovery of the fire.[5] For the first time at a major fire in Cork, Mark Wickham had a tolerable number of trained men under his command. In addition to the four permanent members, he now had the six auxiliary firemen as well: Michael McCarthy, William Purcell, Nicholas Butler, James Keating, John Murphy, and Philip Lecane. A concerted effort was made to tackle the fire at its source and to this end:

> A hose was brought in through one of the windows at the Nile Street end
> of Courthouse Street and was carried along the top of the gallery, and from
> a position over the door the [firemen] began to play on the flames, which at

this time were vigorously breaking out at the top of the roof. The water was turned on but had very little effect. The supply of water was very weak. This was a distinct failure, the water not rising more than twenty feet.

The fire now began to make headway with tremendous velocity, and with a north-westerly wind blowing diagonally across the building the flames made great headway…the County Grand Jury room was a mass of flames, which burst through the windows, thus admitting the strong breeze prevailing and sweeping the conflagration inwards.[6]

Meanwhile, outside Dwyer and Co. across the street, twenty-five-year-old Eugene McSwiney, who lived in nearby Grattan Street, deftly captured the animated scene in superb detail in his sketchbook, later to be committed to oils.[7] In the City Grand Jury room the timber statue of King William III (actually a statue of King James II with the head supplanted by a loyalist corporation) which occupied a place of honour, burst into flames and was immolated in the whirling vortex of fire. An urgent message for assistance was relayed to Victoria Barracks, and within the hour 250 men under arms of the Berkshire and Shropshire Regiments under Major-General Davies, were on scene with their fire engine. A ring of steel was thrown up around all approaches to the building, allowing the firefighting operation to proceed unimpeded by the massive throng of spectators which had gathered from all points of the city to watch the late evening spectacle.

The Cork Courthouse, Great George's Street, in flames on the evening of Good Friday, 27 March 1891. (*Black and White* journal, 4 April 1891)

The inside of the building was now one cauldron of fire:

> When the flames rushed from the Grand Jury room to the staircase, which
> gave way in a moment, several brigade men narrowly escaped with their lives.
> The debris blocked their escape route through the corridor, and the hose
> had to be abandoned. A burning rafter fell between two firemen, fortunately
> without injuring either. The intrepidity with which they acted throughout
> and the degrees to which they freely exposed themselves was most com-
> mendable.[8]

The firemen with some difficulty made their way out of the doomed building
and all efforts at suppression were now concentrated from outside. The water
supply had improved immensely, but even in the comparative safety of the
street danger was imminent:

> By 7.30p.m. the heat became so great that it began to tell on the limestone
> facade ... the supports inside having been taken away the weight of the
> stonework outside caused the cornice to give way and the enormous mass
> of stone fell with a tremendous crash into Courthouse Street. The shock was
> terrific as might be expected from tons of stone falling from such a height
> into a narrow street. Several windows in the houses opposite were shattered
> ... the stones [fell into the street] up almost to a height of twenty feet. The
> Fire Brigade suffered severely, losing almost £100 worth of hose.[9]

As the flagstaff on the roof was seen to fall back into the flames, a colossal cheer,
which so enraged Rudyard Kipling, went up from the crowd far below. But the
crowd might have saved its collective breath, and Kipling his spleen, for in fact
the Union Flag was still intact. Although having disappeared from view when
the flagstaff fell, it was retrieved, practically unharmed, from the roof on the
following day by County Surveyor, Samuel Kirkby. By midnight the inferno,
sated, was subdued.[10]

The following morning, even as the fire brigade was still in attendance
damping down and turning over, City Sheriff John Roche announced that
the Assizes would reconvene in the Model School on Anglesea Street. The
Crown Prosecutor, one Edward Carson Q.C. (a name that one day would be
on everyone's lips in Ireland), failed to convince the special Cork jury ('eleven
Protestants and one Catholic') of the accused's culpability. After an absence of
an hour and a quarter, they acquitted three of the defendants and could not
agree in the case of the two remaining. O'Brien and Dillon, the two Members
of Parliament, were spirited away through the school yard and into the adjacent
Union Quay police station. Later, when the jubilant crowd had dispersed they
were returned to the County Gaol under escort. No sooner had the court

risen, than Edward Fitzgerald (later Sir Edward), well-known local builder and council member, moved in with his staff of workmen to convert the school into a temporary courthouse.[11]

The *Cork Constitution*, ever ready and willing to bad-mouth the nationalist population, darkly insinuated that the fire may have been an act of incendiarism. There was not a jot of evidence for this suggestion and it was conclusively put beyond dispute when the cause was traced to the flue of the hot water furnace having caught fire.[12] The courthouse was rebuilt by Samuel Hill, to the design of William Hill, and opened in March 1895. The cost was a little under £25,000.

Today, completely restored inside and out, it is a building striking in its architecture with its ten fronting columns, solid and graceful. The figure of Justice , flanked by Law and Mercy, replete with her scales, is mistress of all she surveys on her lofty perch. During the troubles of June 1917, her scales were removed by an intrepid rioter and were only restored when the Irish tricolour flew over the building. The courthouse, which was originally erected during the reign of King William IV, still bears the name of the king carved on the limestone facade.[13]

A NEW BEGINNING.

Although the fire brigade was not able to prevent the courthouse from being burnt out, its standing soared high in the aftermath of the fire. Many agreed that the firemen had given their all in trying to save the building and had risked life and limb in the process. At a meeting of the Law and Finance Committee of the corporation on 31 March 1891, the High Sheriff, Mr J. Pike, declared that he,

> wished to say that from beginning to end the Cork Fire Brigade used every possible exertion under the circumstances. He would like if the Corporation got a better fire engine. The Brigade men did their work splendidly, and showed the greatest pluck, but they had not a sufficient supply of water.[14]

Cllr Crean agreed, and remarked how early on in the evening he had climbed onto the roof of the courthouse to gauge the extent of the fire for himself. If an engine had been available the fire could have been cut off from the unaffected part, he said.[15]

Others were less sanguine. There were dark mutterings in some quarters that the fire brigade had failed in its duty to stop the fire and the head of the brigade was Mark Wickham. The Town Clerk deplored the fact that the fire chief 'appeared to work as one of the men instead of superintending them'.[16] No matter that a comparable conflagration in Dublin would have warranted a full muster of its entire firefighting force of some forty-odd men and their appliances, or, in London, a 'District Call' from the first attending officer would have brought a response of up to eight steam engines and their crews, the fact remained that one of Cork's best-known representational buildings had been destroyed and the evidence was there for all to see in the great, grey smoking hulk on Great George's Street. The spotlight fell, once again, on the unhappy fire chief who now became the lightning-conductor for those who wanted him removed from office. Mark Wickham had made the mistake of alienating the wrong people over a long period of time, and as a result he was destined to pay a high price.

In fact, the recommendation to sack the chief had been made to council in the previous June. Then, the Waterworks and Fire Brigade Committee had reported that, 'following reorganisation, we hoped the steps taken would have led to a better state of affairs in so important a department of the corporate service', but they regretted that the measures had produced no lasting improvement. They felt bound to propose that a new Superintendent should be appointed and that Mr Wickham should be subordinate to the new officer. The new Superintendent should be, 'a skilled Fireman, and not more than forty-five years old, and would have a salary of £9 per month, with residence, fuel, light, and uniform cloth-ing'.[17] So far, so good. But when an astute council member did some quick mental arithmetic and concluded that, with the creation of a new rank (that of Mark Wickham's subordinate position as Brigade Foreman), it would incur an expenditure of a further £120 per year, the proposal stopped dead in its tracks. The council, who never wasted an opportunity to exercise their penchant for parsimony, referred the whole matter to yet another sub-committee. And then, in rapid succession to the courthouse blaze, came the fire at the Clarence Hotel, and Mark Wickham found himself once more in hot water.[18]

Injuring his shoulder at a house fire in Gillabbey Street on Saturday 4 April, he applied for, and was granted, sick leave by the City Engineer (his immediate superior in the corporate hierarchy). The engineer put Sgt Michael Ryan in temporary charge of the brigade. At 2.45a.m on Monday 13 April, the stillness of the night sky over the city was shattered by a resounding explosion – almost certainly heard at the fire station over on Sullivan's Quay – and, in minutes, the Clarence Hotel on the recently-renamed 'Parnell's Place' was one mass of flames. As the owner, Mr O'Mahony, his wife and family, and several guests made good their escape, 'much difficulty was experienced in getting an invalid lady, a boarder in the hotel, out of the building as the fire had taken complete possession of the hotel. A chair was quickly procured and the lady was safely removed'.[19]

In his report on the fire, Sgt Ryan stated that the alarm was given at 3a.m. The members of the brigade turned out immediately, with hose carriage, fire reel, and fire escape. On arrival, they found the whole southern portion of the building on fire from the basement right through the roof. The fire was spreading northwards and the firefighters turned their attention to cutting off the fire from the adjoining houses. The water supply was excellent and three lines of hose were made down. Then, wraith-like, out of the miasma of smoke and steam enveloping Parnell Place, appeared the figure of Mark Wickham, his arm in a sling.

As the firemen went about their business under the Sergeant's directions, the fire chief ordered them to ignore Ryan and obey him instead, and, according to the City Engineer, 'interfered with the man in charge in a highly censurable manner, and one that might have had serious consequences as a result of contrary orders being given'.[20] While the whole sorry *contretemps* was being played out, the old building, burning like matchwood, was reduced to a smoking ruin. The cause of the fire was attributed to an escape of gas in the dining room resulting from rats gnawing through a gas pipe. Rats had been known on past occasions to gnaw through lead pipes in order to obtain water; on this occasion, they chewed through the wrong pipe and, finding no water, wandered off leaving gas to escape to eventually cause an explosion and fire.[21]

The Superintendent was ordered to resume his sick leave until an inquiry into his conduct was held. Their patience finally exhausted, the Waterworks and Fire Brigade Committee convened to consider the motion of Cllr Julian 'that the Fire Brigade be disbanded'. Cllr Crean seconded: if they wanted 'to have a proper and efficient Brigade' ,the present staff should be dismissed and they should start from scratch.[22] After a lengthy debate during which depositions on behalf of Mark Wickham were heard from the Mayor and Dr Dunlea, the recommendation of June 1890 was adopted: the chief would be demoted and his position advertised in 'the principal Fire Brigades of the United Kingdom'. The proposal was rubber-stamped by council on 29 May 1891, some eight years after the first recommendation that he should be replaced.

After a reasonably auspicious start, the fire brigade had gradually lost the confidence of the general public to a point where, in the words of Cllr Kelleher, it had become 'the laughing-stock of the police and the entire people'.[23] Drastic measures would be needed from the new incumbent to restore the esteem in which it had once been held. Just as the tenure of office of the most famous Chief Officer of the London Metropolitan Fire Brigade – a Corkman – was drawing to a close, a former London fire officer arrived in Cork to take up his new appointment. His name was destined to become a household one for two generations of Corkonians.

9

O Captain! My Captain! – The Long Reign of Alfred Hutson

'Mr. Hutson has maintained an admirable discipline and system of drill and other duties, and completely overhauled and improved our Fire Brigade'.

(Alderman Henry Dale, Chairman, Waterworks and Fire Brigade Committee, Feb. 1892).

'Captain Hutson, who made Cork Fire Brigade'.

(The *Sunday Graphic,* 11 May 1930).

In times past, when a principal officer of a fire brigade was required to adopt a hands-on approach to operational firefighting, it was inevitable that his character should manifest a decisive influence upon the morale and outlook of the brigade. To the extent that this is true, it is perhaps invidious to single out a particular officer as the personification of an era. Nevertheless, the very length of Alfred Hutson's tenure of office – thirty seven years (he was seventy nine when he retired on 1 March 1928) – his reputation, and the panache with which he led his men, entitle him to this honour which no one is likely to begrudge him.

Always presenting a trim military appearance, Capt. Hutson (he was invariably referred to as 'Captain', rather than his official designation of Superintendent) set his stamp upon the spirit and administration of the brigade, and, to judge from the succession of stolid bewhiskered faces whose level gaze meets one's own in numerous, long-faded photographs, he seems to have moulded the very appearance of its members at the same time. Never a man to lead from behind, throughout his long service he was fully operational at the side of his men with an almost cavalier disregard for danger and his own well-being.

Hutson's talents lay in the accretion of small details: his almost intuitive grasp of the 'mind' of a fire, his ability to manage men, his concise planning, and his apparently genuine empathy with every member of the brigade, which, in time, would embrace permanent, auxiliary, and volunteer cadres.[1] It is not surprising that a number of important milestones in the history of Cork Fire Brigade are associated with the protracted period of service of this energetic officer. Over time, these included:

The establishment of numerous street fire-escape stations.
Life and accident insurance on members (1891).
The launching of the Cork Volunteer Fire Brigade (1892).
The building of a new central fire station on Sullivan's Quay (1893).
The setting-up of the Widows' and Orphans' Fund (1897).
The opening of sub-stations at Shandon Street (1899) and Grattan Street (1906).
The inauguration of the fire brigade ambulance service (1902).
The commissioning of a steam fire engine (1905).
The introduction of the first breathing apparatus (1914).
The acquisition of the first motor tender (1921) and the first motor fire pump (1923).

Alfred James Hutson was born at Streatham, Surrey, on Good Friday, 14 April 1849, and went to sea at the age of fifteen with the British Merchant Navy. By the age of twenty-two, he had achieved Warrant Officer rank and had served on a number of vessels. On 20 September 1871, he presented himself at the Metropolitan Fire Brigade Headquarters, Watling Street, in London for interview by the redoubtable Capt. Shaw as a candidate for the Recruits' Class. If his prospective chief had not quite reached the apogee of his fame, he was well on the way. In the five years since the formation of the MFB, Shaw had succeeded in having twenty-six new fire stations built and, building on the foundations laid by his illustrious predecessor, Braidwood, had moulded his brigade into an elite firefighting force, the envy of the world's fire services.[2]

Fred Hutson's one-on-one encounter with the renowned fire chief was as a result of Shaw's insistence on evaluating each potential candidate for the brigade himself. The would-be recruit had to have a naval background and be under twenty-five years old. He had to be, 'stout, strong, healthy-looking; of general intelligence, and be able to read and write: and to have to produce certificates of birth and testimonials as to character and service'.[3] Having been measured, he then faced the daunting Escape Test, which required him to raise, single-handed, an old-fashioned wheeled fire escape by the head with the tackle reversed. This was the equivalent of lifting a straight 150kg. Successful, he was then subjected to a rigorous medical examination by the brigade surgeon. Only then, upon receiving a positive result, was he admitted to the Recruits' Class at Station B23, Grand Junction Wharf, Tudor Street, Whitefriars.

Shaw placed great emphasis on training and education, and in this respect was extremely ahead of his time. Previously, it was believed that firefighters should receive only the minimum of training before becoming operational.

Raising a wheeled escape by the head with the tackle reversed. This test of strength was the equivalent of lifting a straight 150 kg.

Firefighting, it was propounded by the old-fashioned fire officers, was an inexact science to be learned by experience on the fire ground. Shaw would have none of it. He wrote:

> The importance which I attach to a sound system of training will probably be understood, when I state my conviction, founded on what appears to me the clearest and most positive evidence, that some of the greatest losses by fire which the world has experienced, have been owing to want of skill on the part of firemen. I consider a proper system of training, *before attending fires*, the only true method for making men real firemen.[4]

During his training period, Probationer Fireman Hutson was required to live at the training school, and recruits were not allowed to attend fires, for, according to Shaw, 'nothing is so destructive of sound education in this way as permitting men to attend fires before they know how to handle the appliances properly'.[5] In February 1872, at the end of the first phase of his basic training, he was subjected to a series of tests, including a written examination, the results of which have survived:

Dictation: Good.
Letter: Good.
Petty cash: Fair.
Arithmetic: Good.
Pay sheet: Good.
Reading: Very good.
Result: Passed.

His certificate was signed by the Chief Officer, Capt Shaw, and he was posted to Station D38 (Kennington, the district headquarters for 'D' District south of the River Thames), as a fourth-class fireman, registered number 349.[6] Hutson now embarked on a rigid routine with a minimal amount of leave. As a single man he was required to live in dormitory accommodation provided at the station. Later, he would serve at Station D42 (Deptford) and Station D43 (Old Kent Road). His final posting was at Brigade Headquarters, Watling Street, in 'B' District, which covered the City. Here he renewed his acquaintance with Capt. Shaw for whom he would continue to nurture a deep regard all his life, evidenced by the annual ritual of the sending of boxes of shamrocks from Cork to his former boss for St Patrick's Day (which were always acknowledged), and the christening of his second son Eyre Massey. During his time in the MFB, Alfred Hutson recorded that he had fought many of the great fires which plagued London, not least those involving huge warehouse complexes in dockland. He estimated that he had attended over 1,600 incidents during his service.

Within a few short years, the ever-ambitious young man had again moved on to become fire engineer to the General Steam Navigation Company where, besides having the responsibility of attending to all the fire appliances on board upwards of eighty large steamships, he, 'attended to the whole repairs to Fire Plant at Irongate Wharf, St. Katherine's Wharf, Blackwall Pier, the Dry Dock at Deptford and at a large works where over 800 men were employed'.[7] With all this responsibility one wonders where on earth he got the time for courtship and marriage, but marry he did, to Elizabeth Jane (*née* Costin). They were married at East Ham Parish Church on 23 November 1873. Their first son (also named Alfred James) was born at Deptford the following year.

Fireman Alfred J. Hutson, Metropolitan Fire Brigade. (Courtesy of Raynor de Foubert).

THE BRIGHTON VOLUNTEER FIRE BRIGADE.

By 1891, as we have seen, the authorities in Cork had decided to advertise for a new fire chief. Sixteen applications were received by Alexander McCarthy, the Town Clerk, for the position. The temerity of some of the applicants in putting themselves forward for a position as a principal fire officer beggars belief. A few had only the most tenuous links with the fire service, others, none at all. The full list, with occupations, is as follows:

1. Alfred Wylde, Superintendent, Southampton Docks Fire Brigade.[8]
2. Charles G. Smith, Superintendent, Rathmines Fire Brigade.
3. Charles Magnusson, First-class Fireman, Metropolitan Fire Brigade.
4. John Smith, First-class Fireman, Metropolitan Fire Brigade.
5. William Johnston, First-class Fireman, Metropolitan Fire Brigade.
6. William Nagle, Slater.
7. Charles M. Bennett, Fireman, Dundee Fire Brigade.
8. John Fleming, Fireman, Paisley Fire Brigade.
9. Ernest Hincks, Lieutenant, Chester Volunteer Fire Brigade.
10. Robert Seward, Second Officer, C.C. Steam Packet Company.
11. Alfred J. Hutson, Superintendent, Brighton Fire Brigade.
12. William J. Cross, Mechanical Engineer, Salford Fire Brigade.
13. James Gray, Inspector, Mutual Insurance Corporation, Glasgow.
14. John McNamara, Armourer, Cork.
15. James F. Quinlan, Shipwright, Cork.
16. Timothy Connolly, Sanitary Sub-Officer, Cork.

Numbers 6, 8, 10, 15, and 16 were declared disqualified. Numbers 11, 1, 4, 5, 14, and 7 were selected as the most eligible.[9] The name of Alfred J. Hutson appeared on the list as 'Superintendent of Brighton Fire Brigade'. Strictly speaking this was incorrect. The reality was that, in 1891, there were two fire brigades operating quite independently of one another in Brighton. The official one, run by the Brighton police force, and the unofficial one, made up of part-time, unpaid volunteers, dependent on the largesse of the townspeople for its upkeep. The latter was Hutson's brigade, and, in any event, neither was he its Superintendent (a rank which did not exist in the volunteer brigade), but its Station Master (the Victorian equivalent of Station Officer) – the one and only paid position in the outfit. For all that, there is no doubt that Alfred Hutson was very highly thought of in all quarters in Brighton and came to Cork armed with an impressive CV and references.

The Brighton Volunteer Fire Brigade was formed in 1867, following dissatisfaction by the townspeople with the firefighting arrangements organized by the police. The police (who had previously held undisputed control at fires) resented the intrusion of these new interlopers and decided to completely disregard them.

Matters came to a head when the volunteers were first to arrive at a big fire in Preston Street. They were about to get a jet to work on the first floor and had already placed a man in position at the top of a ladder when the police arrived and pulled the fireman down, insisting that they should be the first to carry a hose into the building. The volunteers remonstrated with the police, regained their equipment and carried on, ignoring the police objections.[10] This unsatisfactory state of affairs was partly resolved by swearing in the volunteers as borough constables. Henceforth, they would technically be under the control of the senior police officer at the scene of a fire. This is the situation that the twenty-six year old Alfred Hutson found himself in when he arrived in Brighton in 1875 to take up the position of Station Master of the Brighton Volunteer Fire Brigade.[11] It is a measure of the esteem in which the volunteer brigade was held that, in 1875, they could afford to build a new fire station, at Duke Street, and employ the services of a full-time, paid fire officer, all from voluntary subscriptions and fees received from attending fires with no subvention from any official quarter.[12]

The annual report for the brigade for 1875 was presented at its A.G.M. in January 1876 and states, *inter alia*:

> In order that everything shall be kept in a state of real efficiency a Station-master has been engaged, who has several years in the London Fire Brigade, and having the best possible recommendation, was selected out of over 230 applicants for the post.

Station Master Alfred J. Hutson,
Brighton Volunteer Fire Brigade.
(Courtesy of Raynor de Foubert).

Though nominally subordinate to the volunteer Captain and Lieutenant of the brigade, Hutson was, *de facto*, in charge of its day-to-day running.

Not content with his achievements on the operational side of the service, he also turned his attention to the question of the passive fire defence of buildings, a discipline not fully understood by many architects or builders, and certainly not enshrined in much legislation. Hutson delivered a paper (translated into French) at the International Fire Brigade Congress held at Caen, France, in September 1890, entitled 'On the Construction and Protection of Public Buildings, Mills, Factories, Hospitals, and Places of Public Amusement and Interest', dealing at some length with the 'desirability of Exterior Protection versus Interior Protection, also with so-called fireproof buildings, etc'. In the same year, he won First Prize and Medal at the Health Exhibition at Brighton for his innovative project, 'Illustrating the utility of Fire Engines in removing foul gas and poisonous matter from sewers, mines and wells, and for rescuing persons from same when employed therein'.

During the early 1880s, Station Master Hutson's quick thinking was responsible for saving the life of the engineer in charge of the steam fire engine. While working on a fire at nearby Hove, the uniform of the engineer, Louis Victor Lacroix, was inadvertently sprayed with burning naphta. In a trice, his clothing flared up. Hutson, working a branch nearby, saw Lacroix's predicament and instantly turned the water on him. The journal *Fire and Water* opined that, without this action 'the consequences would have been very serious'.[13] Fred Hutson's sojourn in Brighton was not without at least one other claim to fame: for five years he was in charge of the renowned Hodge's Manual, arguably the most celebrated and certainly the most ornate fire engine in the United Kingdom and possibly the world.

Frederick Hodges was the wealthy philanthropic owner of one of the largest gin distilleries in south London, replete with a purpose-built fire station, engines, and equipment. To the growing band of fire buffs in London – including the Prince of Wales, the Duke of Sutherland, and the Earl of Caithness – Hodge's Distillery became a convenient stopping-off point for discussing the finer points of fire engineering; and, no doubt, for sampling the excellent liquid refreshments provided by their host.

Hodges extended his firefighting service to anyone who requested it outside of the confines of his distillery. Between 1851 and 1862, it was estimated that his brigade had attended over 500 fires including some of the greatest conflagrations of the age. The story goes that, in recognition of this, the grateful citizens of south London suggested having a whip-round to present him with a tea service. Much to their dismay he told them that a new fire engine would be infinitely more preferable. Whatever the truth of the matter, the resultant manual engine, built by Merryweather in 1862, must have almost bankrupted the area; the engine cost some £300 and the decorations twice that.

The manual fire engine presented to Frederick Hodges in 1862. Alfred Hutson, while Station Master at Brighton, had charge of this famous appliance from 1875-1880. (*ILN*, 20.09.1862)

It was made to the design of Italian Signor G.M. Casentini and was capable of discharging 140gpm while being worked by thirty men. On each side of the superstructure were six panels in which were placed bronze *bas-reliefs* of firemen's helmets and axes. The main shaft passed through the mouth of a golden dolphin and the driver's seat, richly ornamented, displayed the motto, '*Publicae Utilitate*' (Public Utility). The driver's footboard was supported by a bronze dragon.[14]

Frederick Hodges took part in the inaugural ceremonies for the Brighton Volunteer Fire Brigade in 1867, and displayed his famous 'testimonial' manual fire engine on the occasion. Seeing that the brigade could not rise to the cost of a new engine, he generously provided them with his engine on permanent loan. There it remained until 1880 when, for whatever reason, Hodges took it back and sold it. (On 9 July 1877, Hodges called unexpectedly on Hutson and made the following entry in the Visitors' Book, 'The above was very pleased to find his old Testimonial kept in such perfect order'). Since then, practically every history of the fire service that has been written has included the obligatory picture of the legendary 'Hodge's Manual', now beautifully restored and on display in the Museum of London. Few if any, however, refer to the thirteen years it spent fighting fires in Brighton in the charge of Station Master Hutson.

It is not clear how Alfred Hutson got to hear about Cork Corporation's quest for a new fire chief. His small, part-time Brighton unit hardly qualified as one of 'the Principal Fire Brigades of the United Kingdom'. He probably came across the advertisement in one of the service journals or perhaps through a tip-off from Capt. Shaw, his erstwhile boss. In any event, on Wednesday 1 July 1891, the officials of the Cork Waterworks and Fire Brigade Committee saw before them a medium-sized, stocky, dark-haired man with Mephistophelean eyebrows, moustache, and goatee beard (made fashionable by Shaw), well turned-out and with a southern English accent.[15] By the time the lengthy interview concluded, they were more than impressed. It was clear to them that this man thoroughly knew his business. The committee made its recommendation to council in the following terms:

Left: Alfred J. Hutson shortly after his appointment as Superintendent of Cork Fire Brigade in 1891. (Courtesy of Raynor de Foubert).

Below left: An illuminated address presented to Alfred J. Hutson by the 'Officers and Men of the Brighton Volunteer Fire Brigade' in July 1891. This was one of three such addresses presented to Hutson upon leaving Brighton to take up his Cork appointment. (Courtesy of Raynor de Foubert).

Below right: The silver helmet presented to Alfred J. Hutson by his Brighton colleagues in July 1891. The inscription on the peak reads, 'Presented to A.J. Hutson by the officers and men of the Brighton Volunteer Fire Brigade as a token of their esteem after 16 years' service July 1891'. (Courtesy of Raynor de Foubert).

Mr. Hutson's testimonials and previous record are of an exceptionally creditable and meritorious character. A lengthened interview more than convinced
[us] that in appointing Mr. Alfred J. Hutson we have secured for the city the
services of a man possessing in a marked degree all the qualities of skill, experience, energy, and high personal character, which we have long desired to see
combined in the head of the Cork Fire Brigade. The Committee anticipate
from his appointment a complete transformation of the Brigade in point of
discipline and efficiency.[16]

Cllr Julian moved that Alfred Hutson be appointed, Mayor Daniel Horgan seconded, and the motion was carried. Cork had a new fire chief.

Returning to England to settle his affairs, Hutson was the recipient of
three illuminated addresses: from Brighton Corporation, Brighton Volunteer
Fire Brigade, and the inhabitants of Brighton (signed by more than 100 of the
town's Irish community). He was also presented with a principal officer's silver-
plated fire helmet, suitably inscribed on the peak, which he wore operationally
throughout his long service in Cork.

He had been an unassuming but energetic member of the Brighton Society
for the Provision of Free Dinners to Poor Children, and was both surprised
and embarrassed when the Mayor presented him with a special gold medal for
his endeavours. Hutson would continue his extra-curricular work for deprived
children through his involvement with the Cork children's excursions.[17]

The new Superintendent was formally introduced to the members of the
brigade by Mayor Horgan on Friday 7 August 1891. A spokesman for the men
articulated their disquiet on hearing that the chief was to have arbitrary powers
of dismissal, and suggested that any disciplinary matter should be the subject
of a proper investigation. Hutson assured them that all serious charges would
be referred to the Waterworks and Fire Brigade Committee for arbitration. He
settled in, with his family, to temporary accommodation at 38 Great George's
Street. Once again, Cork Fire Brigade was off the ground. Almost immediately,
the task of restoring its self-esteem began.

One of the first matters to secure his attention was the whole approach to
training. Henceforth, morning parade would be at 7a.m., followed by drill class,
and a firm new regime was put in place. Some weeks later, the chief was ready
to show off the brigade with their newly-acquired skills:

At seven o'clock yesterday morning the members of the Fire Brigade were
put through some interesting drill performances at the Municipal Buildings,
under the direction of the new Superintendent, Mr. Alfred J. Hutson. Since
Mr. Hutson has been placed in charge of the Brigade he has shown the greatest
activity in respect of its reformation in many points … his efforts in this direction so far seem to have not been unfruitful, and judging from the exhibition

given yesterday morning at the Cork Exchange it must be said that distinct improvement was noticeable in the general discipline of the men, and the different exercises were gone through with accuracy and despatch.[18]

A large number of spectators had assembled on Albert Quay, where, four years earlier, the astonished crowd had gaped and gasped at the disgraceful conduct of the truculent firemen during the blaze at McCarthy Brothers. On this morning, the new fire escape was wheeled from Grand Parade to the scene of the 'assumed fire' in the Municipal Buildings and immediately raised against the building. Nine men who had been lying on the roof were 'rescued', in turn, by the 'fireman's lift' method. The chair knot system was then demonstrated and five more men were quickly lowered to the street. The display concluded with a show of high-powered water jets being 'sent flying over the clock tower, the whole operation being performed in a remarkably short time'. A gratified *Cork Examiner* concluded:

> It will be seen that attention was first directed to the saving of life process and the next consideration was the property. The drill proved highly successful and reflected credit alike on the energetic Superintendent and the Brigade.[19]

The exercises, which involved both the permanent and auxiliary staffs, were observed by the Mayor, Ald. Dale (Chairman of the Waterworks and Fire Brigade Committee) and members of the city council, all of whom expressed complete satisfaction at the proceedings. Within a month, however, a fire on French's Quay had concentrated the fire chief's mind on the urgency of putting an effective life-saving system in place.

'WHERE'S THE ESCAPE?' A NEAR BRUSH WITH TRAGEDY.

Jerome J. Hegarty's brush factory stood on French's Quay. In the normal course of events, by 6.30p.m. on a winter's evening all the employees would have gone home. On the evening of Monday 21 September 1891, however, three girls and a man were working after hours to fulfil a special order. The young women were busy at their work in the top loft when their male colleague decided to light an extra paraffin lamp. As he did so, it exploded in his hands, and, burned and shocked, he threw it down the stairs where it landed on some bales of coir, the fibre obtained from the husk of coconuts and used in brush, rope, and matting manufacture. The fibre immediately blazed up, setting the stairs on fire. Thick volumes of oily, black smoke coiled up the stairs. The employees were trapped:

> These came to the window of the topmost loft, which is very high and from which smoke was issuing, screaming loudly, their cries being responded to

by a large number of their relatives and friends below, who besought them to wait for a moment and the Escape would arrive. One of the girls betrayed signs of losing her presence of mind and jumping into the street, and, observing this, two or three men swarmed up a chain which hung from the top of the building, and reached the girls, whom they had almost forcibly prevent from doing themselves injury.[20]

Someone ran to the fire station on Sullivan's Quay, a short distance from the scene of the outbreak, and there they met Capt. Hutson chatting with his 'number two', Mark Wickham, now Brigade Foreman.[21] The two men, assisted by Turncock Pat Higgins and ex-Sgt Ryan (who had retired a few weeks before), in view of the short distance, decided to pull the hose reel manually to Hegarty's. A line of hose was at once laid down, and, a side door having being forced open, the fire was attacked:

> The crowd, which now assumed very large proportions, became almost frantic with excitement, and cries of 'Where's the Escape?' were heard on all sides, while those in the loft became gradually more terrified, and to all the ten minutes that elapsed before the flames were subdued seemed almost years. At length Mr. Hutson was seen in the loft, and dispelled the fears of those in the street … the women were then brought down in a very frightened condition and were cordially received by their relatives. It was fully a quarter of an hour after the flames had been extinguished that the Escape was brought from the Grand Parade. The cause of the delay is not apparent, and in ordinary circumstances the Escape can be brought the distance mentioned in five minutes, whereas it took almost half an hour in the present instance. Some men should be in charge of it on the Parade, as at a moment's notice it is not always possible to have sufficient assistance immediately on the spot to roll such a heavy article with anything like reasonable celerity.[22]

At this stage, the brigade had only two escapes: the Clayton escape located at the toll box at St Luke's Cross, and the new Jessop Brown escape positioned on the Grand Parade. The new fire chief responded to criticism of the delay in procuring the escape by stating that, in his opinion, there was no necessity for it. Retorted the *Cork Examiner*, 'However this may be, it was brought to the scene by the members of the Brigade'.[23] The only casualty was John Fitzgerald of Keyser's Hill whose face was badly burned. Hutson had learned his lesson.

Directly as a result of this incident, it was decided to expedite the manning of the city-centre escape station and that a suitably functional, yet ornamental, shelter be built for the fireman on duty. Within a few years, the city would be ringed with so-called 'escape stations'.

Vigilantly Zealous for the Preservation of Life: The Street Fire Escape Stations

'The 'Fireman's Rest' is one of the most comfortable out-stations
in the Kingdom'.

(Capt. Hutson, 1894).

'The 'Fireman's Rest' is the worst station in the city'.

(Fireman Aherne, 1911).

When Mark Wickham arrived in Cork in 1877 to set up the brigade, he found that the saving of human life from fire, despite the many sanctimonious pronouncements to the contrary, had never been regarded with any sense of urgency. Indeed, an atmosphere of near-fatalism prevailed; if one had the misfortune to be trapped in a fire, one's number was as good as up. For the establishment, the protection of their fine Monster Warehouses, full of all manners of luxurious commodities, from the ravages of the 'all-consuming element' was paramount. Poor Mrs Murphy, who lived with her children in a top-floor room of a dreary tenement on the Marsh, would have to take her chances should a fire break out on a floor beneath her. If they perished, it would really be too bad; but there would be no high-powered delegations of merchant princes marching on the Municipal Offices looking for answers.

Neither the insurance brigades nor the Waterworks Brigade regarded it as any of their business to attempt the rescue of people from fires. While these 'fire-fighters' tried to tackle the actual blaze, it was entirely left up to the initiative of bystanders or the police to use any means at their disposal – builders' ladders, ropes and so forth – to try to save people from perilous situations. The one and only piece of life-saving equipment the council had ever bought (in 1858) lay disused and rotting, never having been used, not even on drill, let alone at a fire.

Within the limited confines of his budget, Supt Wickham tried to redress this appalling situation and persuaded the council to purchase new equipment. This included new rescue lines and the brand-new Clayton 60ft telescopic escape. Wickham, himself an expert in their use, drilled his men with the equipment until they could practically use it with their eyes shut. The preservation of human life was, for the very first time at fires in Cork, to take precedence over the saving of property. A number of standard builders' ladders were also acquired, in sizes ranging from 20 feet through 50 feet. These were placed at numerous locations throughout the city and suburbs to be used by the police or citizens to attempt rescues while the fire brigade was on its way. Over a period of time they were placed at: Drummy's Lawn (Shandon), Union Quay RIC station, Blair's Hill, Cottage Row (Madden's Buildings – Watercourse Road), Lower Glanmire Road, St Luke's, Sunday's Well, Tivoli, Sawmill Street, Mahony's Avenue, Corcoran's Quay, O'Leary's Lane (Bandon Road), Phair's Cross, College Road RIC station, Military Road, Wolfe Tone Street, and Hansboro' (Wellington Road).

Initially, the one and only serviceable fire escape was kept in the yard of the fire station at Sullivan's Quay, and in the event of it being required anywhere in the city it had to be trundled laboriously through the streets to the fire ground, helped by the hastily-recruited supernumeraries. If for example, the escape was required for a rescue at the top of Shandon Street, one can well imagine the considerable time that elapsed before its arrival. In March 1891, a new telescopic escape was bought from Dublin manufacturers Jessop Brown at a cost of £65. Wickham's plan was to relocate the Clayton escape from the fire station to the Fr Mathew Statue on St Patrick's Street (always referred to in the council minutes as the 'Mathew Statue') and keep the new Jessop Brown one at Sullivan's Quay, but his demotion intervened. Now, it would be up to the new incumbent to formulate his own plans.

The city had by now expanded out to the four points of the compass (rural district areas outside the borough boundary were, technically, no concern of the city fire brigade, and a county fire service did not exist), and Hutson set about locating at least one escape or fire ladder in each ward, or in contiguous wards. Wheeled escapes were located at the following venues (date of installation in parenthesis):

Sullivan's Quay (at fire station) (1877)
Grand Parade (junction of Great George's Street) (1891)
St Luke's Cross (at toll booth) (1891)
Roman Street (opposite North Chapel) (1892)
Nelson's Place (junction of Lavitt's Quay) (1894)
Sunday's Well (St Vincent's chapel yard) (1895)
Courthouse (Great George's Street) (1895)
Shandon Street (northern end) (1896)
Henry Street (junction of Adelaide Street) (1900)
North Infirmary yard (Roman Street escape transferred) (1898)
St Patrick's Street (Fr Mathew Statue) (1900)

Rocksavage (junction of South Terrace) (1900)
Grattan Street (at fire station – Henry Street escape transferred) (1905)
Blackpool (opposite RIC barracks) (1915)

With the acquisition of the brigade's first escape-carrying motor appliance, a Merryweather *Albion*, in 1930, the long era of the street escape stations came to an end. What is surprising is that it took Cork Fire Brigade so long to acquire a vehicle capable of carrying a fire escape when the technology had been in place since 1890. It is amazing that the manufacturers of such vehicles were practically on the brigade's very own doorstep, and that the volunteer fire brigade of Passage West, a small estuarine township eight miles south of the city solely dependent on voluntary donations, had acquired the first of two such appliances in 1904.[1] A horse-drawn vehicle capable of carrying a 50ft wheeled escape had been invented in England in 1890, but it was not until the end of the century that they were first introduced in London by the Chief Officer, Commander Sir Lionel de Latour Wells, CB, RN (rtd). Their introduction enabled many street stations to be closed: a horsed escape (known as an Escape Van) could now arrive at a fire far quicker than the old static escapes could be pushed through the streets with the often dubious help of passers-by.

At about the same time that the 'vans' were being instituted in London, the Chief Officer of Dublin Fire Brigade, Capt. Thomas Purcell, was using his engineering skills to design something far more advanced.[2] This was the 'Aerial Telescopic Extension Ladder' (also horse drawn). With added extensions it could reach a height of some sixty-six feet, one of the first-ever turntable extension ladders in Europe.[3]

Locally, Capt. Edwin Roberts, founder and driving force behind the much-respected Passage West Volunteer Fire Brigade, with his engineering background created his own bit of service history with his invention of a 'Combined Fire Escape, Hose reel and Pump'. Not alone did Roberts' apparatus carry an escape, but also its very own fire pump, something neither the Dublin nor London appliances did. It was built to Roberts' design by the firm of George Nason and Co., South Gate Bridge Carriage Works, on French's Quay, a stone's throw from the city's Central Fire Station. The *Cork Examiner's* report on the apparatus which appeared on 12 October 1904 is worth reproducing:

The apparatus has been on view during the past week at the South Gate Bridge Carriage Works. It consists of a novel combination of a fire escape, hose reel and manual fire pump mounted on a high two-wheeled trap, to be drawn either by one or two horses, or, if necessity arises, it can be wheeled by hand. One of the principal features of the machine is that it carries all the fire appliances and life-saving gear on the carriage, and these occupy but very little space. There is also room on the machine for firemen. Then there is a powerful fire pump, which will enable the brigade to cope with fires which may occur outside the

radius of the water mains. Through this can be pumped water from any adjacent stream or well and delivered to a fire through a line of hose carried on a
reel under the driver's seat. The pump is detachable from the machine, which
enables it to be removed to the nearest source of water supply. The escape is
composed of a braced telescopic set of ladders, which will reach a distance [*sic*]
of forty feet. These can also be readily detached from the carriage.

The escape was also built by Nason's to the design of Capt. Roberts. Later, a
second 'Combination' was also built by Nason's for Roberts, and these, along
with their 'Jumper', gave Passage West VFB the edge on their city counterparts
when it came to mobile apparatus. That the Cork brigade, with its hilly top-
ographical area of operations, eschewed such labour-saving and much faster
machines is inexplicable. But shun them they did and for almost half a century,
fire escape stations with the firemen running through the streets pushing their
escapes in front of them were as much a feature of Cork street life as the high-
collared, spike-helmeted policeman on point-duty or the shawled spratt-seller
at the corner of Parliament Bridge.[4]

'Horsed escapes' of the Passage West Volunteer Fire Brigade complete with portable pumps,
pictured on 'Lifeboat Saturday' 1911. The appliances were made by Nason & Son, South gate Bridge
to the design of Capt. Edwin Roberts. Pictured on the appliances, from left, are: Vol. Firemen Dan
Mulcahy, Dan Ahern, P. Fahy, and C. Callaghan. The gentleman with the epaulettes is the Chief
Officer, Capt. R.E. Roberts. Middle appliance: Vol. Fm. P. Fitzgerald and J. Payne. Righ appliance:
Vol. Fm. Dan Spillane, Dave Splaine, Joe Ahern, and Dan Donahue. Note that the French-style
Adrian brass helmets worn by the firemen. (Courtesy of Richard I. d'Esterre Roberts).

Cork firemen manually trundling a wheeled escape through the city's streets at a time when the volunteer brigade in Passage West had two mobile escape units.

During the long span of their existence, the escapes were a nightly point of reference for troops of youths hanging out and for courting couples ('meet you at the escape at half-seven – there's a great follyer-upper on at St Mary's Hall').[5] They were frequently blown over in storms and badly damaged, sometimes beyond repair. They were wheeled about and damaged by youths, until they were chained and locked in position, the key being deposited with some local stalwart such as the parish priest (the chaining of them led to an outcry). They were scorched and blistered at fires, caught in tram tracks, hit off the overhead tram wires, and during the Troubles, commandeered by Crown forces, and others, who used them during various operations.[6]

Notwithstanding, many Corkonians owed their lives to the street escapes and the fire brigade members who used them. When the brigade's first DP appliance ('dual-purpose' meaning it had an escape-carrying as well as a pumping capability; later renamed PE, meaning 'pump-escape') was acquired in 1930, all the street escapes were withdrawn. Now, the rescue ladders could reach any part of the city within minutes of an alarm being raised. The shelter which had been used by the firemen on escape duty in St Patrick's Street was left *in situ*, however, and for a short time continued to be used by personnel of the tramway company. One year later, the trams disappeared from the streets of Cork, and henceforth the shelter was the sole domain of the city bus staff. It was a landmark which commanded the northern end of St Patrick's Street from 1904 until its unceremonious removal in 2002, and for generations of Corkonians it was as well known as the Berwick Fountain or the National Monument. Almost from day one it was never far from controversy; and it was detested by the firemen.

'NICELY FITTED INSIDE AND OUT': THE FIREMAN'S REST.

> 'The smell on Patrick's Bridge is wicked,
> How does Father Mathew stick it?
> Here's up 'em all, said
> The Boys of Fair Hill'.

The boys of Fair Hill may have ruminated long and hard on the age-old question, but in reality of course the good Father's patina-coated nostrils were quite oblivious to the offensive malodours which frequently wafted off the nearby River Lee. On the other hand, the olfactory nerves of the flesh-and-blood fireman, on his lonely vigil duty at the Fireman's Rest in the lee of the statue, were not.

Foley's figure of the 'Apostle of Temperance', Mangan's Clock and the Fireman's Rest were a trio of Victorian street furniture which stood sentinel over the northern limits of Cork's city centre. Here, Cork history has been made for over 200 years, and towards it Corkonians spontaneously gravitate in times of trouble or jubilation. Mutely, the trio witnessed the passing parade of pompous potentates, artful artisans, charabancs of chancers and charlatans, courtiers and clerics, and the good, the bad, and the ugly. They were present when poor Mother Ireland suffered her prenatal trauma during the birth of our nation. Sadly, only the first two landmarks now remain, for during the revamp of the city's main thoroughfare in the early 2000s, it was decided that the Victorian 'Rest' was out of synch with the ambience of the (largely Victorian) streetscape and was removed.

In August 1891, Capt. Hutson had placed the Jessop Brown fire escape on the Grand Parade at its junction with Great George's Street. This he considered the optimum location for the equipment due to its proximity to the city centre and the high, inhabited buildings in the vicinity. But practically from day one its location proved disputatious. The city's Superintendent of Lighting complained that it obstructed the light coming from the nearby street lamp. The *Cork Examiner* lamented that it was the focal point for gangs of teenagers who, nightly, 'are to be found disporting themselves on the ladder and shrouds of the escape. Last night between 8.30 and 10p.m there were upwards of 20 young men on it. Do the police ever turn the crowds from off it? Apparently not'.[7] In the wake of the fire at French's Quay it was decided to proceed with the manning of the escape station, and the City Engineer, Mr M. J. McMullen, BE., was asked to provide a shelter of an 'ornate character' at a cost not exceeding £60. The shelter – for evermore to be known as the Fireman's Rest, (the term was emblazoned along the ridge of its roof on an iron scroll) was made by the famous 'Saracen' ironworks of Walter McFarlane and Co., Glasgow.[8] One of the auxiliary firemen was upgraded to the permanent staff, and the 'Rest' became operational on Monday 9 May 1892. It had a direct telephone link to both to

the fire station and the chief's residence. The responsibilities of the duty fireman were clearly detailed in brigade regulations (when a fireman took charge
of an escape he became its 'conductor'):

RULES FOR THE ESCAPE CONDUCTOR.

* Upon going on duty, the Conductor is to examine the condition of the
  ladders, ropes and other accoutrements, and see that the whole are clean
  and in good condition, and fit for immediate use.

* The Conductor will be held responsible for the appearance and sound condition of his Escape, and will be required to pay for any damage that may arise
  from his carelessness or inattention. The Escape is to be thoroughly cleaned at
  least once a week, and the wheels taken off and greased once a month.

* While on duty, the Conductor is on no account to leave his station, or to
  enter any public house or other building. The watch-box is provided as a
  protection against inclement weather, and must not be used by any person
  but the Conductor; nor are the doors to be closed when the Conductor is
  within, as he is expected to be vigilantly zealous for the preservation of life
  and ready to give immediate attendance whenever required.

WHEN CALLED TO A FIRE.

* When called to a fire the Conductor will immediately obtain the assistance of three or more persons as may be required (police constables to be
  preferred), and losing no time in starting, proceed with his Escape to the fire;
  on the way he will explain as well as he can the nature of the assistance to be
  rendered, particularly cautioning them to let no person ascend the Escape
  save the Conductor; he should be careful to see that his drop-line is correct.

* On arriving at a fire the Conductor is to place his Escape in the most advantageous position, allowing no person to touch it beyond those he has selected,
  one of whom is to be stationed at the lever while the Conductor ascends the
  ladder; the whole attention and utmost energy of the Conductor is to be
  given to the preservation of life; and having ascertained beyond a doubt that
  the inmates are out of danger, and that no further service is required of him,
  he must take his Escape back to the station with all reasonable speed.

* If from the particular construction or situation of the house on fire, the
  Escape cannot be available, the Conductor resigning it to the charge of a
  police constable or other responsible person will make the best of his way
  to the roof of the adjoining house, or otherwise take such steps as are most
  likely to rescue the lives in danger, availing himself of the short ladder,
  ropes, drop-line, crowbars, etc. If in a narrow court try and render assistance from the opposite window by placing the short ladder across.

View of St Patrick's Bridge and Lavitt's Quay showing the Fireman's Rest on the quayside opposite the Opera House. (Courtesy of Michael Lenihan)

* The great variety of circumstances attending a fire render it impossible to lay down any precise rules; much will always depend upon the coolness, presence of mind and skill of the Conductor, whose chief aim must be the saving of life. It is also necessary that the Conductor make himself acquainted with the neighbourhood of his respective station, and with all the fire hydrants.

* While the observance of these rules will be strictly enforced, every encouragement will be given to the Conductor to perseverance in good conduct; and the Committee will never allow vigilance and efficiency to pass unrewarded.

* If taken suddenly ill while on duty, the Conductor must send a messenger to the fire station. Upon no pretence whatever will absence from duty without the Superintendent's knowledge be permitted.

[The penultimate rule would later attain a particular poignancy, as we shall see.]

The denizens of Cork city centre could now sleep contented in their beds, secure in the knowledge that the streets below their windows were patrolled by vigilant policemen, ever-alert to spotting a fire in its early stages; while the fireman in the 'Rest', sipping his beefy Bovril while studying form in the sports pages of the *Echo*, constantly practised his 'vigilantly zealous' mode. But, naturally, not everyone was happy with the new arrangement.

Ald. O'Brien said he heard for a fact that the Fireman's Rest was costing £200 a year to run, and if that were so, it should be closed down at once. Patiently, the City Treasurer enumerated the actual cost:

Salary for one fireman: £46 16s.0d.
Uniform for above: £5 12s.9d.
Gas: £9 0s.0d.
Total: £61 8s.9d.[9]

Then, in April 1893, Mr M.D. Daly, prominent Cork businessman and director of Alexander Grant and Company ('Drapers, Milliners, and Carpet and General Furnishing Warehousemen') waited on the Mayor to object to the position of the Fireman's Rest. It was, he maintained, obstructing the view of their handsome new shop front at 17-18 Grand Parade. They wanted it moved without delay. Capt. Hutson and the City Engineer visited the site and agreed to shift it twenty feet to the south, provided that Grant's paid the cost. The next deputation to arrive at the Municipal Buildings was from the residents of Grand Parade. They said they were quite happy with the position of the 'Rest', thank you very much, and objected vociferously to any suggestion of its relocation, even by twenty feet. For the next twelve months the debate batted to and fro, until, in March 1894, the City Fathers, with some reluctance, pronounced that the shelter would be moved to the junction of Lavitt's Quay and Nelson Place, opposite the Opera House. Then, of course, the inevitable happened.

'I NEVER SAW MORE MERITORIOUS CONDUCT': DISTRICT INSPECTOR CREAGHE, RIC, ON AUXILIARY FIREMAN JAMES KEATING.

Wearily, Father O'Sullivan closed his breviary, somewhat later than usual, his office at last finished. A passage in the Canticle of Simeon troubled him, and he made a mental note to discuss it with his spiritual director. And on this evening of Saturday 22 June 1895, he had also reflected at length on the heroic lives of the two sixteenth-century English Catholic martyrs, Thomas More and John Fisher, whose special day it was.

He stepped to the window of his cell in the Augustinian Priory on Great George's Street intending to open it more fully on this sluggish, mid-Summer's night. It was still light, but he saw that the lengthening evening shadows were embellished by another, more dazzling glare. And then, a shrill, horror-filled scream ripped through the still air. For a moment, confused, he thought it was just another street row. Then he noticed the flames lighting up the street and heard the breaking of glass. A young woman was on the street in her night clothes. 'Dear God, help us!' she screamed, 'people are dying!'

Fr O'Sullivan felt a moment of panic. He seemed to be the only person in the world able to help. Never had he seen such a fire! Flames, fed by exploding barrels of paraffin, paint, turpentine, and great quantities of matches were leaping out of the broken windows and coiling up the front of Lavallin's Oil and Colour Stores; the roaring, crackling noises growing louder by the second. Then he remembered his *confrère* who occupied a nearby cell. Dressing hurriedly, both men ran across the road to the scene of the fire, where, assisted by passer-by Robert Bullen, they, 'exerted themselves most strenuously in rescuing most of the inmates'.[10] But not all.

Meanwhile, over on Sullivan's Quay, Capt. Hutson and his men had just arrived back at the fire station having spent all that evening tackling a serious fire at McNamara's Corn Stores on Copley Street. Hardly had they drawn up, when a breathless runner brought word of the drama unfolding on Great George's Street. The brigade arrived on the fire ground in less than three minutes and at once got to work. By now, the ground, first, and second floors were heavily involved. The wheeled escape, which had been located only yards from the scene, but now stationed on Lavitt's Quay on the northern periphery of the city centre, was sent for. After what seemed like an eternity to those watching (the brigade was first alarmed at 10.05p.m. and the escape arrived on site at 10.20p.m.), the apparatus arrived in the charge of Auxiliary Fireman James Keating, its conductor. Keating at once ascended the escape and gained admission to the burning building from the roof of an adjoining house. His eyes burned in the pitch-darkness. His first breath caught in his throat as if his windpipe was blocked. The *Examiner* narrated how:

> Having no light, and with clouds of smoke and steam making the search still more difficult, Keatinge [*sic*] groped his way through the rooms. After a most desperate search, in which he had to fight the flames, the plucky fireman found Mrs. O'Connell lying under a table … Keatinge succeeded in bringing her safely down the escape, and the immense crowd cheered him loudly.[11]

The senior police officer at the scene, District Inspector Creaghe, later testified that, 'he never saw more meritorious conduct. Fireman Keating brought Mrs. O'Connell down the escape as gently as it possibly could be done'.[12] Keating, having deposited his charge into the care of many willing hands, then re-ascended the escape and once again entered the blazing building to continue the search for the remaining occupants, but , unbeknown to him, the house was empty. The women who had been trapped above the fire, a Mrs O'Keeffe, and a Madame Bridau who resided on the third floor had before the escape arrived, got out through an attic window onto the roof and gingerly made their way along the parapet to a skylight where they were helped in. Nobody thought of informing the brigade of this, and Keating and his colleagues were subjected to further unnecessary gruelling punishment before they could declare the building empty. The *Cork Examiner* documented how, 'When at last the flames were finally extinguished the crowd cheered the Brigade'[13] Sadly, Mrs O'Connell, who, it emerged, was profoundly deaf and therefore unable to hear the cries of alarm, succumbed to her ordeal in the early hours of the morning.

A week later, a deputation led by Fr O'Sullivan and Mr Hart, the Manager of the Queen's Old Castle department store, waited on the members of the Waterworks and Fire Brigade Committee to deplore the dearth of fire escape facilities in their neighbourhood. Neither, they said, were the hydrants in the area sufficient and telephonic communications were non-existent. As a result of their complaints, new hydrants were laid down, Great George's Street RIC station was linked to the fire station by telephone, and a new Merryweather 'Improved Telescopic Escape', to command a height of 60 feet was purchased at a cost of £74. The escape was stationed inside the railings of the courthouse on Great George's Street. Cork now had three escape stations.

The Cork electric tramway system came on stream in December 1898 under the style of the 'Cork Electric Tramways and Lighting Company Limited'. The hub of the service was the Fr Mathew Statue in St Patrick's Street.[14] To facilitate the officials of the tramway company, a small ticket office was positioned on the southern side of the statue. Following the fatal fire at Alcock's shop (further up the street) in November 1900, the company was approached with a view to allowing the duty fireman at Lavitt's Quay (where the Fireman's Rest was located) the use of the ticket office during the hours of 11p.m. to 7a.m. The escape would be wheeled into position at the statue for the night. In the morning, it would revert to its station at the Fireman's Rest. Permission was duly granted (in all the brigade's dealings with the tramway company over a period of thirty-three years they were always met with the utmost courtesy and consideration), and a fireman began night-duty at the ticket office in February 1901. Three years later, in February 1904, again with the company's agreement, the Fireman's Rest and escape were moved from Lavitt's Quay to St Patrick's Street, where the 'Rest' permanently supplanted the small ticket office. Electric lighting and a telephone were installed and from then on, barring a period during the Troubles of 1920-21 (when the city centre escapes were relocated) until 1930, the Fireman's Rest was used by the tramway personnel by day and the fire brigade by night.[15]

Above left: The wheeled fire escape stationed at the Cork Courthouse on Great George's Street. (Courtesy of Cork City Libraries)

Above right: The Fireman's Rest and wheeled escape at the Fr Mathew Statue, St Patrick's Street. (Courtesy of Tim Cadogan)

Captain Hutson (seated left, wearing képi) pictured with brigade members at drill class in 1894. The permanent members at this time comprised Capt. A.J. Hutson, Brigade Foreman Mark Wickham, Turncock Patrick Higgins, and four firemen: William Gloyne, Keane Mahony, Philip Lecane, and James Barry.

In February 1894, Capt. Hutson reported to the service journal *Fire and Water* in the following terms:

I am sending you a picture of the men mustered for 7 a.m drill. We usually go through our drills before breakfast, as I like to break the back of the day's work early so that the station is clean and all the gear likewise for the day. Our telephone system at the station [this is a reference to the newly-built fire station on Sullivan's Quay] is now complete, and is like an exchange, as we can switch on to lines running to any part of the city and outlying towns such as Queenstown, Blarney, Midleton, Douglas, etc; all Police Stations and also the Municipal Buildings and Barracks, are in direct communication with us. We have a very nice view of the River Lee, as it runs close by the door. The men have three rooms each provided with all conveniences in the new Station.

We have a central street station [the Fireman's Rest, then on the Grand Parade] now with fire escape, hose, standpipes and other gear. It is very nicely fitted inside and out; in fact, I think it is one of the most comfortable outstations in the Kingdom. There is a good water service with plenty of hydrants in the city, but in some instances the mains have been laid too great a distance for their size.

The men are all thoroughly equipped, and I can muster, with the paid, auxiliary and volunteer staff, close upon thirty men in a few minutes. A night turn-out takes about 2 ½ minutes with men fully dressed and horses out.

Hutson may have considered the 'Rest' 'one of the most comfortable outstations in the Kingdom', but it was certainly the most unpopular duty with the firemen.

The Fireman's Rest escape station at the Fr Mathew Statue. Note the levers of the wheeled escape, just out of the photograph, on left. The iron scroll on the roof of the shelter reading 'Fireman's Rest' (reversed in the picture) may be seen. (Courtesy of *Irish Examiner*, ref: 121).

Generally, a man did night-duty a month about; but in 1911, Fireman Timothy Ahern, requesting a change of roster, claimed that he had been on night-duty at the 'Rest' without a break for a period of one year and eight months. The Fireman's Rest was, without doubt, he said, 'the worst station in the city'.[16] The firemen complained that the unheated shelter was injurious to their health and that the iron walls 'sweated' due to the condensation of vapour. In winter, this 'sweat' froze on the walls, making the 'Rest' like the inside of a refrigerator. Furthermore, due to the Brigade Order stating that the door was to be left open at all times regardless of weather conditions, they often came off their tour of night-duty half-dead from the cold. (In addition to the Fireman's Rest, two other escape stations were manned: Henry Street and Shandon Street. In both cases the firemen were accommodated in nearby houses.).[17]

Arguably the saddest chapter in the story of the Fireman's Rest occurred in 1897. On the evening of Wednesday 17 November, Fireman James Barry arrived at the 'Rest' on Lavitt's Quay to relieve the duty officer, Mark Wickham. On entering the shelter he found him lying on the floor in a collapsed state. He was immediately removed to his residence at 24 Sullivan's Quay but, sadly, never regained consciousness.

The 'late and first Captain of Cork Fire Brigade' was fifty-nine years old and had served in Cork for just over twenty years.[18]

Working in Harmony under Intelligent Direction: The Cork Volunteer Fire Brigade

'It would afford a good deal of amusement and healthy exercise'.

(Alderman Dale, Chairman of the Waterworks and Fire Brigade Committee, on the proposed volunteer fire brigade, April 1892).

'I am quite sure that the young men of Cork will take this up in the same spirit which distinguishes them always, and will carry it out with great efficiency'.

(Mayor Daniel Horgan, May 1892).

Capt. Hutson's letter to the journal *Fire and Water* in 1894 is revealing on a number of counts. Amongst other things, it mentioned that, in the two and a half years he had been in Cork, a new fire station had been built and that the brigade now consisted of, in addition to paid and auxiliary staff (the auxiliaries were also paid, perhaps 'whole-time' would have been a more apt definition of the former appellation), a volunteer cadre. He details the type of direct communication the fire station had with other public bodies such as the RIC and the army at Victoria Barracks, a telling snippet of information in the light of happenings yet in the distant future.[1] Perhaps most remarkable of all, he contends that a night turn-out, with a muster of thirty men and horses, takes only two and a half minutes, surely a remarkable achievement by any standard.

To assert that the members of the Waterworks and Fire Brigade Committee and the council in general were delighted with their new fire chief is no exaggeration. An examination of their minute books during Hutson's early years reveals that such is the case. Thus, it came as a complete shock to them when, in February 1892, just six months into his Cork appointment, he announced his intention of applying for the position of 'Superintendent of the Dublin Metropolitan Fire Brigade', a vacancy created by the retirement of Supt John Boyle.[2] The salary for the post, with emoluments, came to £500 a year, a considerable improvement on his Cork salary of £108. Copies of Testimonials were carefully drawn up, including references from Ald. Henry Dale, JP (Chairman of the Waterworks and Fire Brigade Committee, MD of Richard Clear and Co. and MD of the Cork Cold Storage and Warehousing Co), M.J. McMullen (City Engineer), William Harrington (of the well-known Cork chemical firm), John Horgan (manager of the Cork Opera House), Canon O'Mahony (Administrator, North Cathedral), Br M.T. Moylan (Superior, North Monastery), and Dr Richard D'Alton (Hon. Surgeon to the fire brigade). The City Fathers needn't have worried; Hutson was informed by the Dublin authorities that he was debarred on age grounds; he was then forty-three. The ever-ambitious fire officer made once last attempt at moving up the service ladder; in March 1899 he applied for the post of Superintendent of Belfast Fire Brigade. He was unsuccessful. The position went to a London fire officer.[3]

The confidence Cork Corporation had in their principal fire officer is perhaps best illustrated by the fact that Cllr E.J. Julian, who, only twelve months before had proposed that the fire brigade be disbanded, now proposed that they embark on a costly project: to build the municipality's first-ever dedicated fire station.

'ON THE BANKS OF MY OWN LOVELY LEE': SULLIVAN'S QUAY FIRE STATION.

In May 1892, the City Engineer, Mr M.J. McMullen, was asked to report to the Waterworks and Fire Brigade Committee on the most suitable site on which to build the new fire station. He submitted three proposals:

* On the site of the existing 'station' on Sullivan's Quay, which then consisted of little more than an open yard with out-buildings.
* At 20 South Mall, the site of the Municipal Offices before their relocation to Albert Quay.
* Adjacent to the Municipal Buildings, facing onto Albert Quay.

Submitting a plan and elevation of the proposed station, he estimated that to erect the building on Albert Quay would cost £2,500, while it could be built at Sullivan's Quay for around £1,500. The site on South Mall being ruled out, it was decided to proceed with the Sullivan's Quay site. The building of the complex, to include 'a suitable residence for the Superintendent' (next door, at 23 Sullivan's Quay), was confirmed by council on 22 July 1892.[4]

The bank of the river that is now Sullivan's Quay is one of the oldest and most historic areas in Cork. As far back as the ninth century, the marshy bank along the south channel was used as a dock by the Vikings. John Carty's map of 1726 shows the area is by then 'made ground' and is called Roch's Key. Smith's map of 1750 refers to the same location as Sullivan's Quay. Both men were local merchants. And Sullivan's Quay was the place originally chosen for the building of the Capuchin Friars' new church to replace their 1771 chapel in Blackamoor Lane (subsequently built on Charlotte Quay; now Fr Mathew Quay).

In August 1892, the tender of builder Stephen J. Scully in the sum of £1,775 was accepted, and the corporation raised a loan on the Munster and Leinster Bank of £1,600, 'payable over twenty years by continuous equal half-yearly instalments, with 4% interest on the balance of principal due from time to time'. (An extraordinary meeting of the Board of Directors of the bank had to be convened to consider the loan).[5] Upon examining the drawings, the Cork Stonecutters' Society, ever-vigilant to maximize their members' input on local building projects, immediately objected to the proposal to use terra cotta in the arches and corbels of the new station. They requested that Cork limestone should be substituted, and with the support of Cllr Eugene Crean MP, they won their case. The limestone, however, added a further £40 to the contract price.

It was clear from the building on Sullivan's Quay the fire brigade was not consulted with regard to its requirements. For a start, the station was provided with only a single bay, which meant that the appliances had to be parked one behind the other, and exit, of course, in a similar manner; which was a major drawback.[6] Another critical shortcoming was the lack of a drill yard and training tower, a prerequisite for every fire station. This lacuna meant that with the exception of basic ladder and other drills, more advanced training had to take place at a variety of locations around the city, most notably at the Municipal Buildings. This deficiency would remain until the opening of the new Central Fire Station at Anglesea Street in 1975.

The period for completion of the station expired on 28 March 1893, and the City Engineer had to explain to council that the works were delayed by bad weather and the inclusion of limestone in the facade. In August 1893, a Mr Dee was awarded the contract for supplying and fitting all the blinds which came to the grand total of £10.6s.3d, and Mr J. Murphy got an order to paint the words 'Fire Station' across the front gates. Two large lamps, at front and back, were erected, and the National Telephone Company installed a large alarm bell on the front gate at a rent of ten shillings a year. A member of the public making a 'running call' would press the bell-push to alert the dutyman in the watchroom within. The corporation was approached by the Insurance Company of Hong Kong with an offer to insure the premises at a very attractive premium, but they were politely informed that all corporate insurance business was already under contract to the Royal Exchange Assurance Corporation. Notwithstanding this rebuttal, the Hong Kong company generously made a donation to the funds of the volunteer fire brigade – the only insurance company to so do.[7]

Each married member was provided with three rooms, an unimaginable luxury in a city where many thousands of families occupied just one room. (Nearby, 25 Sullivan's Quay was rented at a cost of £25 a year for some staff who could not be accommodated in the new station). Unlike Dublin's new Central Fire Station, which was officially opened in 1907 amid great pomp and ceremony, the commissioning of the Cork station seems to have been rather a muted affair. The members appear to simply have vacated their quarters at the Fire Brigade Residence and moved in. Likewise, Capt. Hutson and his family transferred from the house on Great George's Street. The *Cork Constitution* for 19 August 1893 carried the following account:

> The City Fire Brigade.
> Occupation of the New Station.
> Yesterday morning the new station which has been erected on Sullivan's Quay, at a cost of £1,800 for the City Fire Brigade, was certified as completed, and the building was taken over from the contractor by the City Engineer, Ald. Dale and Mr. P.H. Meade, on behalf of the Waterworks Committee. The structure which is built of red brick, and faced with limestone, has been turned out in a most creditable manner by Mr. Stephen Scully, contractor.
>
> The Fire Station is not what could be termed a big building, but when compared with the former dingy habitation of the firemen, it is a magnificent structure. The ground floor, of course, is set apart for the various appliances of the Brigade, while the upper floor consists of apartments for the very efficient Superintendent and his staff. This is the first time that the entire staff have been accommodated with residential accommodation at Head Quarters, and the advantages of such an arrangement are too obvious to need recapitulation. Suffice it to mention that the most modern improvements in the art of fire extinguishing have been introduced by the Corporation, and for the purpose of summoning the men together, the tinkle of the telephone bell has been found

The Central Fire Station Sullivan's Quay, taken during the early 1920s. Built at a cost of £1800, it became operational in 1893 and closed in 1975.

to be more efficacious than the hoarse roaring of the foghorn. Three rooms have been allocated to each of the married men, and two to each single fire-man, while Captain Hutson has set apart for his use a handsome suite of rooms. It has been arranged that the fire apparatus on being brought back from a fire shall be taken through a back entrance of the building, and then after the cus-tomary cleaning up, run into position in the front of the premises to be ready to run out at a moment's notice. Altogether the Corporation may be congratu-lated on this the latest addition to the civic establishment.

In January 1894, each member was issued with a half-ton of coke as, 'on going into the new station, they have had to keep up fires to dry out the walls, etc., during the past quarter'.[8]

THE CORK VOLUNTEER FIRE BRIGADE.

Hutson now turned his attention to the paucity of staff. He still had only four whole-time members, the Brigade Turncock Pat Higgins, and the six auxilia-ries. To a large extent, he had succeeded in having the order rescinded whereby the firemen were expected to perform a range of extra-curricular activities unrelated to their fire brigade duties and they were at last available on-station to respond immediately to emergency calls. He also knew that any increase in the whole-time staff had been ruled out for the foreseeable future. But at really big fires, a total complement of ten was far from ideal, and he had dispensed with the doubtful services of the next-to-useless, untrained supernumeraries. What better solution to the problem than a corps of idealistic young volunteers, who would, importantly, require no pay? After all, had he not been Station Master of the Brighton Volunteer Fire Brigade for sixteen years, where the scheme, by and large, had worked well?

Hutson ran the idea by the members of the Waterworks and Fire Brigade Committee on 12 April 1892, and once it became clear that the new unit would cost the ratepayers absolutely nothing it was enthusiastically received. Applicants should be over twenty-one and under thirty, and would have to pro-duce the consent of their employers to join. The Chairman, Ald. Dale, thought that, 'a good many young men of the city would be glad to join a Volunteer Fire Brigade. It would afford a good deal of amusement and healthy exercise, and training that might be of great use in after life'.[9] The newspapers devoted many column inches to the proposed unit, the *Cork Examiner* weighing-in behind the idea with a sympathetic editorial:

The want of such a force must have long been apparent to everyone ... the Fire Brigade has for some time shown remarkable efficiency, but it is scarcely equal to the demands which might be made on it under certain conceivable circumstances. In the case of a very large and really serious fire the services of a band of volunteers working in harmony, and under intelligent direction would be of inestimable value. The public will wish the project every success.[10]

Capt. Hutson was determined that his volunteer corps would be organized, well trained, and under his control. They were not simply a gaggle of immature young men swanning around town in their shiny helmets and spotless uniforms. On their very first night of induction, training was held at the Municipal Buildings. Hutson had one or two surprises up his sleeve for the apprehensive young recruits, such as jumping from the equivalent of a second-storey window into a canvas sheet. The *Cork Examiner* described how:

> A large canvas jumping-sheet ... was held a short distance off the ground by a number of firemen and others, and the volunteers ... representing persons escaping from a burning building ... jumped from the landing at the door of the Council Chamber into the sheet, a distance of some twenty feet. Two members of the Fire Brigade showed how to do it, then a volunteer followed after some hesitation, and his jump was loudly applauded. Quite a number then went through the same exercise in safety. In the jumping exercises, it may be mentioned that two Pressmen distinguished themselves.[11]

'Jumping Sheet' Drill. The officer would give the command, 'Taut Sheet!' as the 'victim' stepped out into space. The firemen were regularly drilled in this procedure.

Two weeks later, Mayor Daniel Horgan called a meeting at his chambers to put the volunteers on a formal footing. The meeting aroused great interest, with twelve Aldermen and Councillors and a large number of prospective recruits attending. The Mayor said he was glad to see so many young men present. He thought that:

> A Volunteer Fire Brigade would make the city a safer place in every sense of the word. The regular Brigade frequently was called to fires outside the city, and … they were not bound to attend, and it would be most injudicious to leave the city unprotected; but by the co-operation of the Volunteer Brigade, they would always be able to leave a reserve in the city. He was quite sure that the young men of Cork would take this up in the same spirit which distinguished them always, and would carry it out with great efficiency.[12]

Ald. Dale proposed that the name of the new corps be formally known as the Cork Volunteer Fire Brigade with the Mayor *ex-officio* President. This was seconded by Cllr Julian and carried unanimously.[13]

After six weeks of intensive training, the fire chief was confident enough in his new charges to suggest that they should be entered in the fire brigade competitions to be held in Brighton in conjunction with its volunteer brigade's twenty-fifth anniversary on Bank Holiday Monday, 27 June 1892, and that the city should bear the greater portion of the cost of the trip. A few short years back, such a proposal would have been met with incredulity and regarded as nothing less than a frivolous waste of corporate funds. Now, however, Richard Cronin, Vice-Chairman of the Standing Committee, thought the idea was an excellent one:

> The men [would obtain] a knowledge of the numerous fire appliances in use, and the experience the brigade would gain would bring credit to the city. Such competitions were very popular in America, the Colonies and in England; and next year, they hoped to have a large meeting of firemen in the city which would, doubtless, attract a great crowd, the city would be benefited, and the inhabitants would have the satisfaction of knowing that they had a fire brigade second to none in the country.[14]

There was only one dissenting voice. Mr Twomey asked where the money was going to come from, adding, 'they were going to great expense in order to make property more secure for the Insurance Companies, who would not give one shilling towards the expenses'. Mr Cronin, however, said they were bound to give the brigade every encouragement, and permission was granted to partake in the competitions.[15]

A grant of £9 was allowed Capt. Hutson, who selected the following personnel to accompany him: Turncock Pat Higgins, Aux. Fm. Keating, his son Aux. Fm.

Alfred J. Hutson, Jnr, Instructor to the volunteers; three members of the volunteer brigade, including M. J. Mahony who would later be elected their Chief Officer, [16] and Volunteer T. Quill. The unit acquitted itself very well, returning from the competitions with two first-class, and one third-class, prizes. While in England, the group visited James Compton Merryweather, at his world-renowned London fire engine factory, where they had their picture taken with him.

Meanwhile, in Cork, the rest of the volunteers were having their first experience of tackling an actual fire. On the evening of Wednesday 29 June 1892, fire broke out on the top floor of the eastern wing of the 'Lunatic Asylum'.[17] The blaze was promptly tackled by the 'Asylum Fire Brigade' and in twenty minutes the city fire brigade was on the scene accompanied, for the first time, by five volunteer firemen and 'rendered considerable aid towards checking the fire, which, if suffered to rage, would certainly have had disastrous results'.[18] Again, at 4a.m. on 8 July, the volunteers were in action alongside their regular colleagues at a fire which occurred on the premises of T. Lyons and Company, 55 St Patrick's Street. The firm penned a glowing letter of thanks to the council

Photo of Cork members taken at Greenwich, London on 30 June 1892. Following Cork's participation in Brighton Volunteer Fire Brigade's twenty-fifth anniversary of fire brigade competitions, the Cork party were guests of J. Compton Merryweather at his Long Acre works. Front row, from left: A member of Cork Corporation, James Compton Merryweather, Capt. A.J. Hutson, Merryweather staff member, ditto, Cllr William Kinmonth. Back row, from left: Michael J. Mahony, T. Quill, a Cork volunteer fireman, Turncock Patrick Higgins, James Keating, and Alfred Hutson, Jnr.

Obverse of hallmarked silver medal presented by Merryweather and Sons for fire brigade competitions, engraved, 'One Man Drill-Cork-1891'.

for affording the citizens, 'such protection in case of fire' and the City Fathers' preened their feathers with self-satisfaction.[19] Ald. Dale said the fire brigade had rendered a great saving of life and property; there was a considerable quantity of 'inflammable goods' in the shop and if the fire had been allowed to spread the result would not bear thinking about. Cllr Julian concurred, adding that since Capt. Hutson had come to the city there had been no serious fire. The chief, he said, 'did not give fire a chance at all. They, one and all, expressed themselves satisfied, and more than satisfied, with the work of the brigade'.[20] These were the first of many such incidents which the Cork Volunteer Fire Brigade attended over the course of the next few years.[21]

On 29 August 1892, the members of the volunteer brigade assembled at the Municipal Buildings to draw up formal rules and regulations for the corps and to elect officers. M.J. Mahony was unanimously elected Chief Officer; F.J. Murphy, First Officer; Joseph Hosford, Second Officer; and A. St J. Wolfe, Third Officer. C.J.L. Thompson was elected Hon. Secretary; Cllr E.J. Julian Hon. Treasurer; and A.J. Hutson Jnr., Instructor. Dr D'Alton agreed to act as Hon. Surgeon. The committee members were Messrs Knox, Wolfe, Kinmonth, Butt, Elmes, and Murphy.[22] The scheme was proving so successful that Capt. Hutson suggested that the corporation should settle Merryweather's bill for the volunteers' personal equipment of helmets, belts, and axes which amounted to £38.0s.6d, 'in view of the valuable assistance rendered by them'. The City Fathers agreed, and later settled the account for their uniforms as well.

On 12 June 1893, the group was off on its travels again, this time to compete at the International Fire Brigade Congress and Tournament in Islington, London. Along with Capt. Hutson, the team consisted of M.J. Mahony (Chief Officer Cork Volunteer Fire Brigade), Volunteers Murphy, O'Sullivan, and

McNamara, and Auxiliary Fireman Keating. Once again they distinguished themselves, returning with a bevy of medals which were presented to them by the Mayor at a civic reception on 28 June 1893. And some weeks later, Cork would play host to its very own Fire Brigade *Fête* for which Hutson had been putting the organization in place for some time.

By 1896, the volunteer firemen appear to have lost the initial fire in their bellies, the scheme, apparently, having run its course. There is little in the official record to indicate what led to its demise, but part of it may be that the perceived 'thrill' and 'glamour' of firefighting had long dissipated, in the aftermath of one too many gritty, sleepless nights suppressing other people's fires for no reward and precious little thanks. Additionally, the volunteers were only allowed time off work at the sufferance of their employers, whose initial enthusiasm for the project no doubt began to pall as their businesses were affected by lost man-hours, including sick-leave taken as a result of injuries and illness in the aftermath of fires. Neither are there any hints as to the attitude of the regular firemen towards them, but it is probably safe to assume that it was no different than the position of professionals and amateurs towards one another in many walks of life: one of mutual distrust and barely-concealed disdain. A last ditch attempt to resuscitate the corps was made early in 1896 when, 'the following gentlemen [offered] their services as volunteer firemen: H. Dawson, J. Wilson, P. Bateman, J. Patterson, D. Casey, C. Murphy, J. Roche, and R. Elmes'.[23] Although their offer was accepted, no more was heard of it. In theory, Capt. Hutson's idea was fine, but as in many such schemes the one factor that cannot be reckoned with probably eventually sealed its fate: the vicissitudes of human nature.

THE FATE OF THE GRAND FÊTE:
WINTRY WEATHER AND A FLAMING FIRE.

By August 1893, Alfred Hutson, veteran of so many fire brigade tournaments and *fêtes* in England, felt ready to mount such an occasion in his adopted city.[24] The annual field day of the Cork Amateur Athletic and Bicycle Club was scheduled to be held at the Agricultural Society grounds, Cork Park (situated behind the South Jetties; Centre Park Road now runs through the site) on Bank Holiday Monday, 7 August, and a 'Grand Fire Brigade *Fête*' would be held in conjunction with it. The *fête* was well advertised, with British fire journals announcing that:

> As this is the First Demonstration of its kind ever held in Ireland, every Fire Brigade in the World is asked to take part, so as to make it in every way a great success. Special Excursions will be run in connection with the Fete from all parts of the United Kingdom.[25]

This, of course, was pure hyperbole, but the Great Western Railway Company, in conjunction with travel agents Thomas Cook, agreed to run a special excursion from London at a return fare of £1.9s.0d. As well as the usual assortment of fire brigade drills, 'Horse, Galloway and Pony Racing' and 'All Kinds of Gaelic Sports' were on offer. All the fire brigades in the world didn't turn up (fortunately!), but ones from Brighton, Stoke-on-Trent, and Stafford did. Sadly, the Cork entrants, although fresh from their successes at the London competitions, were unable, on their home ground, to emulate their earlier achievements: the English firemen swept the boards on the day.

It seemed as if the day's events were doomed to failure from the word go. Early on the Sunday morning, when many of the entrants were arriving in Cork and would have expected to be greeted by Capt. Hutson and his staff, a large, unoccupied building under renovation in Thomas Street (near the Mercy Hospital) went up in flames. As the firemen advanced cautiously up the burning staircase, the weakened, burning structure over them collapsed with a resounding crash, injuring the fire chief and Fireman Barry. A short time later the whole party wall collapsed, causing great panic among the residents of the adjoining houses who, fearing for their lives, fled into the street in their night attire. Although injured, the men remained on the fire ground until the operation was complete. The fire was eventually subdued at around 7a.m, damping down and turning over accounting for some additional hours.[26]

On the Bank Holiday, a day of atrocious weather, the day's events began with a parade of more than sixty fire brigade members progressing through the city streets with their engines and appliances, starting out from Sullivan's Quay and finishing at the Agricultural Grounds. (James Compton Merryweather had sent from London, on loan, a 'First-class Manual Engine', and the CFB manual was completely refurbished for the occasion by Messrs Morgan McSwiney at a cost of £5). The *Cork Examiner* commenting on the parade thought that 'the sight was a very pretty one', although quite what the thoughts of three-score burly, wax-moustachioed firemen were on being described as 'very pretty' has, alas, not been recorded. Notwithstanding the awful weather conditions, Corkonians in their thousands turned out to hand over their sixpences and shillings admission charge, swamping the grounds with their large numbers and completely overwhelming the stewards on duty. The press noted that in spite of the terribly adverse conditions, the programme of events was adhered to rigidly.[27]

The Fire Brigade *Fête* was held in the Judging Arena, the competitions including 'One-man Manual Engine Drill', 'Two-men Drill', 'Three-men Manual Engine Drill', 'Six-men Turn-Out Wet Drill', and drills involving the wheeled fire escapes. The works fire brigades of some Cork companies competed in the 'Drill for Local Firms' section with the following results:

First prize: Murphy's Brewery (Messrs O'Leary, Twomey and Martin).
Second prize: Beamish and Crawford's Brewery (Messrs Kenneally, Lynch and Cherlotte).
Third Prize: Dwyer and Company (Messrs O'Callaghan, Troy and Drury).

In the public fire brigades' section, Brighton and Stafford scooped most of the honours, the 'Six-man Fire Escape Drill' being a typical event. For this the crew was required to 'Run 50 yards and get to work with Kingston fire escape; rescue two persons from top of [specially-constructed high platform] stage. Time taken from signal to start to second person being placed on the ground'. Brighton won this in a time of seventy-five seconds, the first prize consisting of six medals presented by Ald. Horgan and Julian, and J.C. Merryweather. Between events, the vast concourse of people was entertained by the Band of the Shropshire Regiment who played suitably stirring martial airs, including the Grand March '*The Fire Brigade*' by Charles d'Ace (which had first appeared in *Boosey's Military Journal* in 1886), ably supported by the Greenmount Industrial School Band under the baton of their conductor Mr J.F. Lynch.

Despite the inclement circumstances the whole experience was voted a great success, but the foul weather was to play a role in one final sad epilogue before the curtain came down on the day's proceedings. As the evening drew to a close and everything was being taken down and tidied away, a Mr O'Herlihy, a carman employed by carriers Pickford and Company, was tasked with collecting the cases of empty bottles from the hospitality marquee. His float got stuck in the muddy ground, and as he was striving to work it free, he slipped and fell. The horse, startled, moved off and the wheels of the dray passed over him. The misfortunate man died instantly.

EARLY FIRE EXTINGUISHERS.

Fire is all-powerful and all-consuming. It gives us light and heat and helps to sustain life. In contrast, in seconds, it can take life and cause untold misery and destruction. It seems certain that no sooner had early man gained an uneasy mastery over fire, than he was forced to devise ways and means of suppressing it whenever it threatened to spread beyond bounds. 'Fire', as the saying goes, 'is a good servant but a bad master'.

The first attempt at marketing a portable fire extinguisher went with a bang – literally. And for a very good reason; the main ingredient was gunpowder. Ambrose Godfrey, a London chemist and *protégé* of Lismore-born Robert Boyle, son of Richard Boyle the Earl of Cork, and renowned Father of Chemistry, had noticed that whenever a fire broke out, the scarcity of water meant that by the time fire engines were in place, even the smallest blaze could develop into a conflagration. Just as a candle can be blown out, he reasoned that larger flames could also be blown out if one were to blow hard enough: thus anticipating, by over 200 years, the famous Red Adair's use of explosives to extinguish flaming oil gushers. In 1723, he described his invention in a paper entitled *An Account of the New Method of Extinguishing Fires by Explosion and Suffocation.*

His 'machine' – the term 'fire extinguisher' lay in the distant future – consisted of a sealed wooden barrel of water with additives, a mysterious concoction which in the flim-flam language of the day he cryptically described as 'An Enemy of Fire'. On top was a lined tin cover protecting a fuse 'garnished with Wildfire',[28] which led down a tube to a pewter sphere containing gunpowder. To use the device, the fuse was lit and the barrel thrown into the burning room where it exploded: instead of scattering shrapnel, like a bomb, it was supposed to drench the contents with the abstruse 'Enemy of Fire'. At least, that was the theory. The trick was to ensure that everyone was out of the house first and to move pretty rapidly when the fuse was lit. Although Godfrey's 'Machine' was still being sold in the 1760s, in time, interest waned and the invention passed into the great limbo of forgotten things.

The *Cork Mercantile Chronicle,* in its edition of 16 December 1805 (at a time when Madame Tussaud, in person, was displaying her famous waxworks in George's Street), brought its readers' attention to the very latest in fire extinguishing technology. This device was particularly suited to quenching fires in chimneys and consisted of:

> Several joints, which being put together as it is elevated in the chimney, when it has gained its proper altitude, by means of springs, the whole expands after the manner of a parachute, and sweeps down every particle of the soot before it. The construction is such, that it may be effectually applied to extinguish fires in chimneys which frequently happen through the carelessness, &c, of servants.
>
> In how many instances might fires of this nature be extinguished, by the application of such machines? In the first alarm, all is confusion and terror, and long before the engines can possibly arrive, the flames have communicated themselves to the whole dwelling. When this invention becomes duly patronized and publicly known, no family should be without such a machine. And numbers of poor unhappy boys, instead of contracting internal disease and exterior decrepitude, may be trained to the navy [or] may recruit our armies ...

The latter was a reference to the so-called 'climbing boys' employed by chimney sweeps, who were small enough to clean chimneys from the inside. As may well be imagined, the work was filthy and dangerous, and the boys suffered from burns, deformed joints and a form of testicular cancer caused by the carcinogenic chemicals in the soot. An Act of 1788 had forbidden climbing boys to be under eight years old but lacked enforcement. One way or the other, for the little boys the choice appears grim: risk scrotal carcinoma and almost certain death, or become a powder-monkey in His Britannic Majesty's Navy's sea-battles against Napoleon.

THE CORK AUTOMATIC FIRE EXTINGUISHER.

An early Cork-made automatic fire extinguisher was demonstrated at the National Exhibition held in Cork in 1852. The venue for the exhibition was the Corn Exchange, where the City Hall now stands. Sir John Benson was commissioned to design the exhibition buildings, which extended up as far as SS Joachim and Anne's Home on Anglesea Street. The idea for the exhibition had grown out of a visit to the Great Exhibition at the Crystal Palace in London the previous year by a group of influential Cork businessmen, which had included the ubiquitous John Francis Maguire. Exhibitions were a prominent feature of mid-nineteenth century life. Like the 'bread and circuses' of the ancients, they tended to divert the masses, temporarily at any rate, from more pressing problems such as poverty, unemployment, and disease.

The ultimate object of the Cork National Exhibition was that people could wonder at, examine at close quarters, and purchase Irish-made goods. In the aftermath of the horrors of the Great Famine, it would give a much-needed boost to local, and it was hoped, national industry. The exhibition was a great success. In the three months of its existence almost 140,000 people flocked through its doors.

Having earlier appeared in the *Practical Mechanic's Journal* (vol. III, April 1850-March 1851), the 'Working Model of an Automatic Fire Extinguisher' was fully described in Maguire's book on the exhibition, *The Industrial Movement in Ireland as illustrated by the National Exhibition of 1852*. It was devised and demonstrated by Osborn Marmaduke Bergin, an accountant and local agent for the National Assurance Company of Ireland, scion of the well-known Cork Congressional family that would one day produce the noted Irish scholar, Prof. Osborn Joseph Bergin.

Designed to protect fire hazards such as ovens, stoves, kilns, boilers, and drying-chambers, essentially it consisted of a tank full of water fixed over the risk, having a discharge pipe at the bottom. The flow of water in and out of the tank was controlled by a series of valves which terminated in a fuse cord:

> From the fuse cord hung a number of short strings within an inch of the surface of the oven. Being of an inflammable nature, the strings ignite at once the moment the contents of the oven take fire and blaze up. The flame is communicated to the fuse cord, which burns through, relieves the weight on the lever, by which means the valve is opened, and the water rushes down upon the contents of the oven.
>
> The chief value of this contrivance consists in the fact that it is self-acting, and consequently comes into operation just at the required moment when the fire in a building is in an incipient and smouldering state, and at a time when one gallon of water would prove more efficient than hundreds at a subsequent period of conflagration.[29]

The 'Self-Acting Fire Extinguisher' invented by Marmaduke Osborn Bergin and demonstrated at the National Exhibition at Cork in 1852. Bergin was the Cork Agent for the National Assurance Company of Ireland with offices at 7 George's Street. (Courtesy of the Mitchell Library, Glasgow.)

Bergin's invention contained features which were not dissimilar in essence to systems marketed by Mather and Platt and others more than a century later. Although primarily intended as an automatic device, it could also be operated manually when staff was on the premises. Although Bergin's fire extinguisher found high praise from various scientific bodies, it is not clear to what extent, if at all, it was commercially exploited.

Cork's early automatic fire extinguisher was exhibited and demonstrated in a transept off the Southern Hall of the exhibition building, practically on the spot where the Fire Brigade Headquarters on Anglesea Street was erected in the 1970s.

By the late nineteenth century, chemical extinguishers were widely available but their high price prohibited them from having mass appeal. For example, the small-est size of Miller's extinguisher in 1890 cost £1.1s.0d or almost half the fire chief's weekly salary. Thus, the extinguisher manufacturers' marketing strategy was almost exclusively directed at the business community, institutions, and the gentry in their fine Palladian mansions. Frequently, the Mayor, prominent politicians, business leaders, and the fire chief were invited to attend demonstrations of extinguishers (invariably, for reasons best known to the vendors, referred to, with a whiff of the exotic, as *'L'Extincteurs'*), thus bestowing on the proceedings a veneer of legitimacy and apparent endorsement of a company's product: not always warranted.

One such early portable fire extinguisher was demonstrated at the Munster

Model Farm in January 1877. This was 'Dick's New Patent Chemical *L'Extincteur*', for which the Cork agents were Thompson Brothers of 4 Winthrop Street. William Boyle, Inspector at the Model Farm, in a letter to the *Cork Examiner* testified that he had witnessed 'three large fires lighted in an open space extinguished with surprising rapidity'.[30] The prices of Dick's appliances in an advertisement in Capt. Shaw's book *Fire Protection* (1876) match exactly those in an advertisement inserted in the *Cork Examiner* by Thompson's on 18 April 1878. Dick's No.4 *Extincteur* ('most useful in dwelling-houses') cost £5.5s.0d, the equivalent of six and a half times an ordinary fireman's weekly pay. Translate that into modern currency and one gets an idea of just how expensive these appliances actually were. The No.6 *Extincteur* came highly recommended for use, 'on basement floors and by the Fire Brigades or wherever the men in charge are skilful, strong and have been practised in their use'. According to the *Cork Examiner* advertisement , it contained '640 pints carbonic gas to each charge'; small wonder the apparatus had to be carried on one's back! In spite of these drawbacks, it appears to have worked admirably well. When Inverary Castle went on fire in October 1877, the Duke of Argyll wrote to Thompson Brothers extolling the virtues of Dick's extinguishers which, he said 'arrested the fire at various points where it was about to gain access to new divisions of the building'.[31]

Not all fire extinguishers were as competent. One gadget of dubious efficacy was the so-called 'fire bomb', the Harden 'Star' Fire Grenade. This American invention sold in its hundreds of thousands all over the Americas and Europe,

A Harden 'Star' Fire Grenade, described as, 'glass globes of about four inches in diameter, filled with a chemical fluid which generates enormous volumes of extinguishing gas when brought into contact with fire'. In reality, the contents comprised simple chemicals such as saltwater, bicarbonate of soda and muriate of ammonia. The grenades first appeared about 1868 and had lost their appeal by the early 1900s.

and was demonstrated by local agents Robert Day and Son of St Patrick's Street on 6 June 1885.[32] The display was held in the yard of the fire station on Sullivan's Quay before 'a large number of gentlemen, including the Mayor, Alderman Scott, Mr. M.D. Daly, T.C., Mr. James McMullen (City Engineer), and Superintendent Mark Wickham'. The military were represented by Colonel Shuldham and Capt. Sarsfield. The *Cork Examiner* explained its modus operandi:

> Wood screens, about 8ft x 6ft, coated with tar, and sprinkled over with paraffin … were erected in the yard of the Fire Brigade Station. These were set fire to, and more oil squirted on the flames, making the heat so intense as to compel the spectators to retreat five or six yards, and when the fire was at its height the operator threw one of the grenades at the base, smashing the glass in the throw, and the moment the contents of the jar were liberated the fire was completely extinguished. Many orders for the grenade were booked on the spot from the gentlemen present. From what we have seen of the grenade, we should say that no house ought to be without a few of them, as a better safeguard against the devastation of a dwelling-house, or even a business premises by fire – if the conflagration be observed at an early stage – could scarcely be conceived. The grenade is a small glass flask containing a pint of chemical fluid (made up of alum, ammonia, and some other ingredients), harmless to the taste, and not injurious to either flesh or fabric. The flask is hermetically sealed, and only needs to be broken at the base of the fire in order to extinguish it momentarily. If one grenade does not accomplish the entire work, a second or third application will suffice. The grenades are only 45 shillings a dozen.[33]

What the onlookers, and probably Day, did not realize is that pre-burn time was always kept to the bare minimum. Before the fire had an opportunity to really take hold, the demonstrator invariably battered the 'crib' with grenades so the flames were quickly extinguished: rather like the snuffing out of a candle. The vendors of the grenades maintained that their principal value lay in protecting small enclosed spaces. They claimed that carbonic acid gas was given off in sufficient quantity to subdue any reasonable fire. In such cases, the grenade would not be required to actually be thrown at the fire, but simply suspended from the ceiling in a wire cage. When fire broke out in an enclosed brick store in the basement of one school, the entire contents were destroyed. After the fire was extinguished by the fire brigade, a cage with two broken grenades was found hanging on the wall. Like many such inventions of the Victorian era, they were next to useless. A well-aimed bucket of water would have achieved an equal, if not better, result at no cost.

In an entirely different category was 'Miller's New Patent Concussion Fire *Extincteur*'. Following a demonstration in January 1890 at the Cork Exchange yard by Mr A. Gordon of 26 St Patrick's Street (the representative of William Miller of Glasgow), so impressed were the members of the Waterworks and Fire Brigade

Committee that they bought a number of them for the brigade. They remained in service for many years and in an age before fire appliances were fitted with pumps and hose reel tanks, incipient fires were invariably tackled using these 'chemical *extincteurs*' with remarkable efficiency. No longer would small fires have to be drowned with a deluge of water from a jet drawn directly from the mains. A small hand-cart was made up by the foreman carpenter of the corporation, and by this means the extinguishers were conveyed to the scene of a fire.[34]

By modern standards the capacity of the extinguishers was prodigious. The largest size, costing £5, ejected forty-eight gallons of 'effervacing fluid' a distance of some fifty feet, the medium sixteen gallons and the smallest, eight gallons. By comparison, a present-day standard water extinguisher has a capacity of two gallons. So convinced was Supt Mark Wickham and the elected representatives of their worth that they took the unusual step of approaching the County Inspector of the RIC with a request to allow them install Miller's extinguishers in each city barracks a remote distance from the fire station. They would be available to members of the public should fire break out in a neighbourhood. Hesitant at first to get involved, the police officer was won around having requested, and witnessed, a demonstration. Thus, while city-centre barracks were not equipped with the appliances, outlying stations at Sunday's Well, Shandon Street, Clarence Street, St Luke's, and Lower Glanmire Road were. The total cost of the appliances and spare charges, including those supplied to the brigade, amounted to £47.[35]

While the percentage of fires tackled with these barrack-based extinguishers is unknown, there is little doubt that numberless incipient fires were quickly dispatched with them during the succeeding thirty years. One of the earliest successes occurred next to the fire station. When fire broke out at Sullivan's Quay CBS school, the Brother Superior quickly and efficiently doused the flames in less than three minutes using his newly-acquired extinguisher.[36] Countless small boys from Cork's south side were, without doubt, decidedly unimpressed.

In the Line of Fire: Around the Clock with the Brigade

'Firefighting is a hazardous occupation in which death and injury are not infrequent. Its paramilitary character registers the necessity for self-control, orderliness and obedience both to protect the individual [firefighter] and sustain him/her in the primary work groups through which his/her dangerous duties are performed'.

(David Englander in *Forged in Fire: The History of the Fire Brigade Union*).

By the last quarter of the nineteenth century, the days when the dangers facing Cork's firefighters were confined solely to burning carbonaceous materials were well and truly over. Increasingly, the use of an ever-growing range of deadly chemicals was added to the lethal cocktail of dangerous substances with which they were expected to deal in the course of their duties, wearing only the most basic of protective clothing and without the security of breathing apparatus. Although concern was expressed from time to time about the dangers posed to firemen's health by toxic fumes, effectively nothing was done to lessen the risk. Not until 1914 did the brigade acquire its first rudimentary breathing apparatus, this was the 'Eed's Smoke Helmet', which, it was hoped, would afford the men some small modicum of protection.

Francis Guy's quaintly-titled *Descriptive and Gossiping Guide* (Cork, 1883) lists the following Cork firms as being involved in the manufacture, or selling, of chemicals:

W. and H.M. Goulding, St Patrick's Street and the Glen.
Scott and Co., Millfield Chemical Manure Works.
Thomas R. Lester, St Patrick's Street.
Wm. Harrington and Son, 80 St Patrick's Street.

Among the many potential hazards which lurked in these gloomy Victorian business houses, often stored in less-than-ideal conditions awaiting the unwary fireman, were ones like:

Hydrocyanic acid (aka Prussic acid): 'Extremely poisonous; a few breaths will cause unconsciousness, followed by death'.

Camphor: 'Vapours form flammable and explosive mixture with air; toxic'.

Ethylene chloride: 'Vapours are anaesthetic; inhalation will lead to unconsciousness'.

Cadmium: 'Will ignite when exposed to flame in the form of dust. The metal, when heated, emits very poisonous fumes'.

Oil of Vitriol (Sulphuric acid): 'Deadly dangerous. A splash on the skin has a powerful corrosive action causing great pain and severe burns. Inhalation of vapours leads to rapid loss of consciousness with damage to lung tissue'.[1]

Capt. Hutson did not have long to wait before his first encounter with chemicals in Cork.

10A.M. 24 NOVEMBER 1891. FIRE AT THE SHANDON CHEMICAL WORKS, COMMON'S ROAD.

In the early 1880s, William, Ignatius, and Stanley Harrington established the firm of Harrington Brothers and acquired over two acres on the Common's Road on which they built their Shandon Chemical Works.[2] The works were renowned as the only makers of 'fire red' colour anywhere in the United Kingdom, and they were the only Irish producers of their distempers and varnishes. They were also among the principal suppliers of inks and colours to the printing industry. Like the nearby flax mills of the Cork Spinning and Weaving Company, the site was carefully chosen, not for any lofty philanthropic ideal of creating employment in a community where unemployment was rampant, but in order to avoid the payment of rates to Cork Corporation, for both sites lay outside the borough boundary. This seemingly crafty decision proved to be something of a Pyrrhic victory over the corporation, for it later cost both companies dearly; the city trunk main with its fire hydrants ended at the start of the Common's Road, an appreciable distance away. When fire broke out (on a number of occasions) in both premises, great delay was experienced before effective firefighting water was brought to bear, leaving the concerns greatly exposed to having their businesses wiped out.

One of the earliest recorded fires involving chemicals occurred at the Shandon Chemical Works on the morning of Tuesday 24 November 1891. The *Cork Examiner* outlined the sequence of events:

What narrowly missed being a disastrous fire broke out yesterday morning at Harrington's Chemical Factory, Blackpool. A two-storey building in which was stored numerous jars of chemicals was observed to be burning. The alarm was immediately raised, and in a few minutes the hands employed in the place turned out, and vigorous efforts were made to subdue the fire.

The City Fire Brigade was communicated with, and were in attendance without loss of time. All efforts were now directed to confining the fire … and in this the Brigade were successful. In the apartments in which the ignition took place were carboys of vitriol and some nine or ten jars of various acids. To the rear was a shed containing a large quantity of chemicals, and were it not for the promptitude with which the burning was encountered the results must have been very serious. During the fire a good deal of coolness and bravery were displayed by those engaged in extinguishing it. At imminent risk to life, they seized many of the jars of acids, the baskets around which were blazing and bringing them from the burning premises carried them to safety.[3]

Apart from the fire danger, the firefighters who moved the acids were in mortal peril, for carboys which have become heated frequently crack. The fire was traced to the overheating of a flue which ran underneath the sheet-iron floor of the chemical store.

This was the recently-appointed fire chief's first major incident in the area, and he was not best pleased to discover that the city fire hydrants stopped short a significant remove from the fire ground. At the December 1891 meeting of the Waterworks and Fire Brigade Committee, he urged that the main be extended beyond the borough boundary for the protection of these important industries. His recommendation was not acted on, and in 1894 over 600 people found themselves out of work at the flax mills when the brigade again experienced great difficulty in sourcing a water supply when a major fire broke out there.

Early view of the Shandon Chemical Works, Common's Road.

12.40A.M. 26 DECEMBER 1892. BRIGADE ALMOST WIPED OUT AT MURRAY AND CO., GUNSMITH'S, ST PATRICK'S STREET.

The dangers posed by the collapse of buildings and falling masonry are well known to members of the fire service. A firefighter working in a structure weakened by fire has to be ever vigilant to the suddenness and sometimes unpredictability with which such collapses occur. Thus, throughout firefighting operations, it is essential that close watch is maintained to ensure that dangerous conditions which may lead to the collapse of a building are not set up. For instance, heavy machinery on the upper floors of a building is liable to prove a great danger in the event of weakening of the walls or supports, and water must be removed from upper floors as soon as possible. A few inches of water spread over a large floor area can weigh upwards of several tonnes, and together with goods and machinery, may load the structure beyond its capacity. Walls may fail in a building for a variety of reasons. In buildings having steel joists, for example, failure may occur through the expansion of the joists in the course of the fire pushing the walls sufficiently out of the perpendicular to cause them to collapse.

One such collapse of falling masonry at Christmas 1892 very nearly accounted for the deaths of the entire permanent staff of the brigade.

The brigade was called to Murray's, Gunsmiths, at 12.40a.m. on St Stephen's Day, 26 December and on arrival in the near-deserted St Patrick's Street found the whole area illuminated by the dancing flames from the blazing premises. They 'got to work with all dispatch, and quickly extinguished the outbreak'.[4] What happened next very nearly 'dispatched' the fire chief and his crew. Damping down and turning over on the ground floor, and no doubt quietly congratulating themselves on their efficient 'save', by the dim light of his hand lamp Capt. Hutson noticed a sudden movement out of the corner of his eye. There was a quick series of sharp cracks, then a wrenching, screeching noise. Shouting a warning to his men, they barely had time to run for their lives when the upper floors, carrying hearth, mantelpiece, and chimney, fell into the shop in a terrific avalanche of concrete, steel, brick, and plaster. It was all over in a split second. Miraculously, all escaped unharmed.[5]

2.30A.M. 17 MAY 1893. FATAL FIRE AT CROSS STREET: BALES OF STRAW STORED IN BEDROOM LEAD TO OUTBREAK.

Cross Street is a short street running down the eastern side of the Cork Courthouse, connecting Liberty Street with Washington Street, which was Great George's Street before 1917.

Sometime after 2.30a.m. on 17 May 1893, Constable John Foster heard 'a noise as of a fire' coming from Cross Street. Investigating, he found a Miss Sheehan and several of her family evacuating a four-storey house, let out in apartments, which was on fire. Told that a sixty-year-old woman, Mary Shanahan, who lived in the attic, was trapped, and now joined by Constables Wellwood, Smith, and Kearney, he made several plucky attempts to get up the stairs to rescue the misfortunate woman, but the heat and smoke drove him back every time:

> He then went to the Fireman's Rest, and with the assistance of Constable Wellwood and some Firemen brought the fire escape up to the scene of the fire. Captain Hutson arrived with the Brigade [from Sullivan's Quay] almost immediately.[6]

Capt. Hutson later deposed that the brigade was alarmed at 2.45a.m. and arrived on the fire ground in three minutes: a time corroborated by Miss Sheehan, who ran, barefooted and clad only in her night-dress, to Sullivan's Quay to summon the brigade.

The escape was quickly pitched to the roof and Auxiliary Fireman James Keating effected an entry through the skylight and dropped down into the room below. The opening up of the skylight made conditions marginally more tolerable for the crew battling their way up through the blazing house. Sadly, their efforts proved too late for the poor woman trapped by the fire. When Auxiliary Fireman Keating reached her, she had already become the victim of smoke inhalation.

At the inquest, the Coroner thought that 'recognition should be taken of the action of the constables and the Fire Brigade at the fire that night'.[7] (It wasn't). The fire had started in the bedroom below the attic, and was caused when bales of straw, stored up against a disused fireplace, were ignited by a spark escaping from the common flue which also served the ground-floor kitchen range. The *Cork Examiner* observed that:

> Great assistance was rendered in the subduing of the fire by some members of the Volunteer Fire Brigade Corps who were present. There were ten persons sleeping in the house when the fire originated, and considering the nature of the building, it is providential that nine of them escaped.[8]

6 A.M. 4 DECEMBER 1893. ELEVEN LIVES SAVED AT 18 KING STREET AS PETROLEUM DRUM BLOWS UP.

About 6 o'clock yesterday morning a fire of a very serious nature broke out in a house in King Street. The house is occupied by Mr. O'Connor, and in the lower portion of it he carried on a provision business. In the shops were several drums of petroleum, and the fire was the result of one of these barrels igniting in some way.[9]

The manner in which the barrel took fire cannot clearly be ascertained, but a girl employed as a servant by Mr. O'Connor states she had just returned from the 'Examiner Office' having obtained the supply of papers for the day, and was about lighting the fire in the kitchen when a frightful explosion took place in the shop. A stream of liquid flame rushed in through the door leading from the shop, and but for her instant flight upstairs she would have been enveloped in flames. She immediately alarmed the other occupants – ten in all – and all rushed for the staircase to make their escape, but this was impossible as the staircase was found to be one sheet of flame.[10]

The terrified occupants now made their way to the front windows and managed to alert the neighbours to their plight. A Mr Wilkie ran to the burning building with a ladder, and he was soon joined by a number of men, also bearing ladders, employed in nearby firms F.H. Thompson and the Clyde Shipping Company. By means of these private ladders, all were brought to safety before the arrival of the fire brigade. The *Cork Examiner* took up the story:

> Meanwhile, the alarm was conveyed to King Street Police Station and one of the policemen ran over to the Fire Brigade Station and the Fire Brigade staff turned out immediately, bringing with them a horse hose reel and life lines. Two lines of hose were brought to bear, and with a good supply of water the fire was quickly got under control.
>
> A large crowd of the neighbouring householders was now present, and considerable excitement prevailed, as it was known that at the rear of the house are the extensive stores of Sir John Scott and Mr. R. Scott, the roofs of which are covered with tarred felt, and close to these are large stores, in which is stored a quantity of paraffin and other highly inflammable oils; but by 8a.m., owing to the strenuous efforts of the Fire Brigade under the command of Supt. Hutson, the fire had been extinguished. The shop, stocked with provisions, toys, etc., was destroyed by the fire.[11]

On the following day at the weekly meeting of the Waterworks and Fire Brigade Committee, the fire chief praised the timely rescue intervention of Messrs Daniel O'Connell, Daniel Mooney, and Patrick Gorman, all employees of the Clyde Shipping Company, who, he said, without doubt were responsible for saving the lives of those trapped. The chairman, Ald. Dale, thought some recognition should be made of their heroic conduct, and it was unanimously agreed that two guineas, along with a Letter of Commendation from the council, be given to each man. However, at the following week's meeting, Dale said it had been brought to his attention that a further six men, employed by Thompson's, had also rendered valuable aid and their actions ought to be recognized too. On the suggestion of Ald. Crean, the arrangement made at the previous meeting was cancelled, and each of the nine men was paid £1 instead.[12]

The *Cork Examiner*, in a follow-up editorial, noted the efficiency of the brigade had improved 'and not before it was time'. However, it went on:

> The reformation had not been carried out without increasing the burthen of the ratepayer, and there seems to be fair grounds for asking has he got value for his money? It is, of course, a great improvement to know that he is safer from fire than he was, but he probably thinks something more is due to him. If his premises are now less exposed to risks from fire than they were, why, he may well ask, should he not expect and get some reduction in insurance rates he pays now from the rate charged when the old and incompetent Fire Brigade was his sole protection?
>
> And while we are on the subject it seems to us that our police force might be made more available in case of fire than it is at present. The sum Ireland pays for her police is no small one, and justifies her in trying to get as much value for it as possible. We think there should not be much difficulty in the way of the Constabulary providing that in all populous centres the policemen should get a course of training similar to that which our Volunteer Fire Brigade now gets the benefit of.[13]

7P.M. 4 SEPTEMBER 1894 AND 2P.M 20 JULY 1897. THE GREAT FIRES AT BLACKPOOL FLAX MILLS.

> May Sunbeam (the old flax mill)
> Rain and smoke on Spangle Hill!
> (*The Rancher's Curse*).

The Rancher was a character on Cork's north side, who, when he failed to gain a seat on the city council during an election in the 1940s, composed his lengthy *Rancher's Curse* in which he castigated all and sundry who he considered had not voted for him. Among the many who gained his displeasure were William Dwyer and the employees of his great Sunbeam complex. His imprecation on Sunbeam ('the old flax mill') eventually came to pass in September 2003 when the complex was gutted in the most extensive area of fire seen in Cork since the destruction of the city centre during the Troubles of 1920. The Rancher may not have been aware of it but the flax mills had previously suffered two serious fires, in 1894 and again in 1897.[14]

The Cork Spinning and Weaving Company (of which the Chairman was John Francis Maguire) built their Millfield mills between the years 1864 and

1866 on a site containing a disused distillery and a flour mill. Because the site lay just outside the jurisdiction of Cork Corporation, no rates were payable to them. Neither, however, was the site serviced by town's mains nor fire hydrants, which ended a considerable distance away. Unlike English flax mills, where single-storey structures were the rule rather than the exception, the Cork mills were fashioned on those of Ulster where multi-storey buildings were favoured. Indeed the mills, a five-storey brick structure, were designed by Belfast architects Boyd and Pratt. The operation of the mills was a direct 'cog' of that appertaining in the north, and to this end, Ulstermen were employed in managerial and supervisory roles.

The company traded indifferently throughout its early years – no-one could have foreseen the fall-off in demand for Irish linen in the lean years following the American Civil War – and in 1871, it closed its doors and was sold off for £19,000. Some years later it re-opened, but failed again in 1885 and remained closed for four years. The new owners decided to grow their flax locally, employing the European system under the supervision of a Dutch expert, and finally the business began to prosper. Some 200 acres were rented locally to accommodate the growing of flax.

The Blackpool Flax Mills, the scene of major fires in 1894 and 1897. In September 2003, the Sunbeam complex on the same site, was gutted in the most extensive area of fire Cork had experienced since the destruction of the city centre in December 1920.

The first serious fire broke out at the Blackpool Flax Mills at 7p.m on Tuesday 4 September 1894. With the greater majority of the 800-strong workforce gone home for the evening, the clerks were still at their counters in the office when a glare was noticed coming from the drying room.[15] The drying room lay directly over the boiler room, which had been only recently extended and was connected to the main five-storey block via a chute, which conveyed the yarn from the reeling room to be dried.

A workman made an attempt to enter the drying room but soon beat a hasty retreat. The place was blazing, emitting volumes of heavy smoke for which burning flax is renowned. An attempt was made to lay on a line of hose from 'a pump working in connection with the machinery, but the flames continued to increase'. At 7.30p.m. the fire brigade was called, fully half an hour after the fire was discovered, and, as the *Examiner* narrated:

> The Brigade arrived soon afterwards under the command of Captain Hutson, who now turned his attention to getting a supply of water from the city mains. The nearest hydrant, however, lay about a mile away at the beginning of the Common's Road. He made the connection, but the supply fell short, and more [hose] had to be telephoned for to the Central Fire Station at Sullivan's Quay.[16]

With no firefighting water available, the fire continued to grow out of control. The flames from the blazing drying room now ran up the chute to the main building where they set fire to the roof. It looked as if the entire complex was doomed when several workmen took matters into their own hands. Armed with saws and hatchets, they began to hack away at the foundations of the chute in order to bring about its collapse, but:

> The fire overcame them and they had to retreat. People were beginning to have a very gloomy hope of the main building being saved, when, suddenly, the chute having burned itself out, fell to the ground, and the communication between the conflagration and the main building ceased.[17]

There was, however, still the small matter of the roof fire in the main building which still posed a significant threat. Suddenly:

> A constant stream of men with buckets of water could be seen going up and down the long flight of stairs leading to where the roof was on fire – about 90 feet high – and this continued until the safety of the large building was assured.[18]

Presently, the brigade's manual fire engine (a legacy of the insurance brigades' era, gifted by the REA in 1888) arrived in the charge of Brigade Foreman Wickham (the former fire chief), and this was worked from the River Bride by a large contingent of troops drawn from the York and Lancaster Regiment under their officers who, it was noticed, were still wearing their mess dress under their greatcoats.

The drying room and boiler house were completely wrecked, the fire causing some £5,000 worth of damage, the *Examiner* reporting that:

> The entire machinery must remain at a standstill for some six weeks ... and although 200 ... can resume work, the remainder, about 600, will be thrown out of employment. That this will press heavily on the workers will easily be understood, and we fear great distress amongst them will be the inevitable consequence. It is most unfortunate that just when the enterprise of the gentlemen who sunk their money in this speculation showed promise of bearing fruit this blow should have fallen on the company.[19]

The fire fiend struck hard again at the flax mills less than three years after the first outbreak. On this occasion the fire broke out in the extensive stores complex containing over 9,000 bales of flax and tow (short length fibres). Each bale weighed up to 200lbs and was loosely packed as was the norm, thus facilitating rapid spread of fire over the bales. The stores, part of the old distillery, extended right up against the workers' houses on the Mallow Road, which were now in grave danger. The factory proper was some 100 metres from the fire zone, but still too close for comfort.

The fire was well established when first discovered around 2p.m on 20 July 1897, a Monday. All the workers quickly evacuated the plant save one man, who, working in a remote corner of the upper floor, had failed to hear the alarm. Not realizing the building was on fire until the flames actually curled along the ceiling over his head, he quickly made his escape by lowering himself from a window onto the roof of the manager's house, which adjoined the stores, and thence to the ground. This time, the factory owners were prepared, and the works fire engine was speedily set to work from the mill's well, augmented by water drawn in large buckets from the nearby mill stream. Then, disaster struck.

The over-exuberant handling of the fire engine by the many willing hands caused the crank-pin to fracture, and the men holding the branchpipe could only watch helplessly as the water fell away to a trickle and then stopped altogether. Any ground gained was lost as the extinguished material dried out from the immense heat and once more burst into flames.

> Captain Hutson and his full staff of men, with a plentiful supply of hose and the manual engine, arrived about 2.30p.m. The fire had by then been burning over half an hour, and the large amount of tow and flax was one blazing mass, sending out an almost unbearable heat. Captain Hutson directed his attentions to the saving of the labourers' dwellings on the Mallow Road, and to prevent the spread of fire to the residences of Messrs MacIlroy and Campbell,

the managers. Two lines of hose were made down from the manual engine, which was worked from the mill stream by some 30 strong Blackpool men. Thus the labourers' dwellings were saved.[20]

Not without some sacrifice, however, as the house nearest the burning stores had to be partially demolished in order to create a fire break.

One more danger to concentrate Hutson's mind was the possibility of a collapse of the walls. Water played on absorbent substances, like flax, presents a twofold risk. Firstly, that it will cause them to expand considerably and, if they are tightly packed, it may force out the walls or displace columns and, secondly, that all water so absorbed cannot be cleared and is added to the floor loading. In fact, a wall did collapse, seriously injuring one of the workmen, Jeremiah O'Keeffe of Waggett's Lane, who, with several of his colleagues injured to varying degrees, was removed to the North Infirmary.

The bill for the firefighting operation, submitted to the directors of the flax mills, amounted to £48.2s.0d.[21]

During the course of operations at the flax mills, several lengths of old leather hose had leaked. The fire chief had had to press into service every single length of hose in his possession, including stuff normally marked as 'condemned', given the distance from the mains. This led to stinging criticism about aspects of the brigade's equipment. He recommended the urgent acquisition of 600 feet of the best modern fire hose, and McGregor's of Dundee tendered successfully for the supply of their *Rob Roy* brand at 10½d per foot. The new hose was made from flax.[22]

7 P.M. 9 OCTOBER 1895. TIME RUNS OUT AT THE STANDARD WATCH AND CLOCK COMPANY.

The iconic, red-brick, Rapunzel's tower-like building, standing on the corner of Bridge Street and Camden Quay, was erected after the previous building was gutted in a spectacular fire on the evening of Wednesday 9 October 1895. The outbreak started in that portion of the premises occupied by the Standard Watch and Clock Company. The *Cork Constitution* for the following day outlined what had happened:

A most disastrous fire occurred last evening at 10, Bridge Street, corner of Camden Quay, the house occupied by the Standard Watch and Clock Company, who have only been a short time occupying it. The fire was first discovered about 7 o'clock by Mr. Uppington, a resident on the premises, who when going out noticed the workshop (which looks out on the quay) in flames. He immediately gave the alarm, and had barely sufficient time to convey his sisters, who lodged in the upper rooms, out of the house.

The Fire Brigade man in charge of the escape at Lavitt's Quay [the Fireman's Rest] was very quickly on the scene. Meantime, the Fire Brigade were called from the King Street Police Barracks and Captain Hutson was very quickly in attendance with the hose reel and several men. By this time the flames had complete hold of the upper rooms, but two lines of hose were quickly at work, one on the quay front and the other was brought to the top of the escape and played on the roof. At this time there was great fear of the fire spreading to the adjoining houses, but Capt. Hutson's admirable arrangements, together with a good supply of water, averted the danger. The house was completely gutted and … the stock which consisted of clocks and jewellery, was completely destroyed, the wooden frames of the clocks being burnt off and the works twisted into the most fantastic shapes.[23]

Two elderly ladies, cut off on the upper floor of an adjacent premises and who seemed in great danger for a while, were rescued 'by members of the Volunteer Fire Brigade at so much risk to their own lives.'[24] The watch company relocated across the street to the corner of Bridge Street and St Patrick's Quay to a premises henceforth known as the Standard House, and the new building erected on the site of the burnt premises was later occupied by the Camden Hotel.

12.30A.M. CHRISTMAS DAY 1895. A VALLEY OF TEARS: BLACKPOOL DEVASTATED IN THE GREAT FLOODS.

'Ite, Missa est', intoned the bishop.

'Deo gratias', came the chanted reply, unbidden, from the lips of the congregation thronging the cathedral. Taking up the chalice and covering it first with the veil and then the burse, the bishop descended the altar steps, genuflected reverently, and, led by the altar boys and the priests of the Chapter, processed to the sacristy. The warm organ tones barrelled off the vaulting and the lights from hundreds of tapers were reflected in the windows as the choir stridently sang the Adeste Fideles.

That Christmas Eve of 1895, the North Chapel had never looked lovelier: the beautiful arrangements of flowers so attractively displayed by the ladies' committee, the lights, the singing of the choir under their master and organist, Herr Swertz. And, in deference to him, this night they had made a very credible attempt to sing a verse, in his own language, of that most beloved of all Christmas carols, Stille Nacht. *But the warm glow within, suffused by the soft lighting and sacred music, belied the atrocious weather on the outside. Now, as the people shuffled out into the blackness, they braced themselves to face the full force of the torrential rain as the storm reached its apogee.*

For Cork, it was the worst of all barometric combinations: day after day of unrelenting, monsoon-like rain coupled with a hurricane-force, south-east gale

howling up from the harbour. For five days and five nights the rain had buck-
eted down mercilessly, driven by the gale-force winds. In the city centre, whole
streets were torn up where the currents were fiercest. The bursting of water pipes
added to the general misery. At the Lower Park (now the area around Centre Park
Road) the buildings of the Agricultural Society were under five feet of water.
Neither did the south-west escape. One eye-witness, William Hosford, testified
seeing the houses in the 'back village of Glasheen' inundated to a depth of several
feet, forcing the occupants to flee for their lives, the aged and infirm having to
be carried on men's shoulders, 'the cause of all this being the insufficiency of the
gully where the College and Magazine Roads converge to carry the volume of
water supplied by the Glasheen stream'.[25] But it was Blackpool, with its network
of channels and rivulets coming from Goulding's Glen, the Kilnap Stream, and
the Killard River (aka the Bride), all now raging torrents, that bore the brunt of
the onslaught. Hitherto, the bulk of the Killard River had been distributed and
retained in Inchcamane bogs, but following the construction of new drainage, all
the water was now diverted into the Blackpool River.[26]

The fire brigade had responded with alacrity as soon as its help was requested
by the RIC at Blackpool. With the Mayor, the fire chief, and a number of
firemen on board, the horse-drawn jumper managed to get only as far as Pine
Street where they found the depth of water was already approaching five feet.
With terrific velocity, the water rushed from the adjoining lanes and byways,
tearing up the soil in all directions. Laboriously, the rain-sodden little party
succeeded in reaching the corner of Lady's Well Brewery, and with the water
fast approaching the horse's withers, were forced to a halt. Turning around,
they galloped along Camden Quay, up Roman Street (where they liaised with
North Parish curate Fr Magner and a party of volunteer helpers) and down
Clarence Street until, finally, they arrived at Blackpool Bridge. The scene that
greeted them was one of utter devastation. The rescuers at once set to work, up
to their waists in water, removing people to the upper storeys of the flooded
houses which were all but ruined.

In Cottage Row, off Madden's Buildings, it was reported that an old man was
in imminent danger. The rescuers made their way, half swimming, to the house,
and discovered the infirm misfortunate lying in his bed, terrified and exhausted,
with the rising flood waters swirling around him. Their timely intervention
undoubtedly saved his life. In the house of Mr Rooney, in Great Britain Street,
the water raced in from Barrett's Tannery, and by the time firemen were tasked to
break down the boundary wall to relieve the pressure of water, Rooney's yard was
flooded to a depth of eight feet. On the Common's Road, the adjoining fields
were submerged to the extent of several feet and the houses were under water
with the torrents rushing down from Farranferris and Spangle Hill. In one case
so fierce was the current that a man had to remain for hours with his back against
the door, clutching his children in order to save their lives.[27]

In the days following the deluge, there were many tales of narrow escapes. In a house jutting into the Killard River on Wherland's Lane lived Mrs Hicks and Miss Nagle. The latter occupied the ground floor, while Mrs Hicks lived upstairs. There was a separate door from the street to both the upper and lower apartments, so that there was no interior connection between upstairs and downstairs.

Both women retired to bed as usual on Christmas Eve, but in the early hours of the morning, Mrs Hicks was awakened by a neighbour calling out, warning her about the rising floods. Simultaneously, Miss Nagle awoke to find the water coming into her bed. There was no possibility of escape via the lane, which by then was a virtual river. She stood on the bed with the water lapping around her bare feet and began shouting loudly for help. Mrs Hicks heard her cries from overhead, and, with great presence of mind, started hacking away at her bedroom floor in order to make a hole into the lower room. For her part, Miss Nagle frenziedly tore at her ceiling, and at length the two women had opened an aperture big enough for her to pass through. By catching on to the bedstead above and with the help of Mrs Hicks she managed to squeeze herself through the flooring joists. There they remained, marooned, but safe and dry at least, until the flood waters had subsided.[28]

Christmas Day brought no respite for the hapless people of Blackpool. If anything, conditions were even worse. In the house of a poor woman near Harrington's Chemical Works, the waters had reached such a height that she could only save herself by clinging to the rafters. Two men on horseback, Cornelius Mullane and John Mahony, were told of her plight and at once set off to her assistance. But the horse jibbed at crossing the raging torrent, and only with the utmost coaxing did the men manage to make it cross to the house. There they plucked the petrified woman to relative safety, but, 'just when the torrent of water threatened to overcome them, three men named Dan Mahony, John Ryan and John McCarthy, rushed into the water, almost up to their necks, and enabled the horsemen to land the woman in safety'.[29]

The Mayor, P.H. Meade, having worked tirelessly since the beginning of the emergency, had one more important duty to perform on Christmas Day, which he intended to carry out come hail, rain, or shine. That was the Annual Poor Children's Christmas Dinner at the Municipal Buildings. The hour fixed for the dinner was 1p.m., but from 10a.m:

> The streets were in possession of the mites [all 2,000 of them], many of them bareheaded and barefooted who flocked from the lanes and alleys and obscure quarters of the city. For them the blustering weather and drenching rain had no terror, inured as most of the ill-clad and ill-fed army must have been to the toils and adversities of the battle for existence in their wretched homes. [The children] received a substantial plate of meat, with buns, cakes, sweets, oranges and minerals.[30]

They were waited on by an army of helpers, led by Sir John and Lady Arnott and the Revd Canon Maguire. Each child received a toy bought with the proceeds of the *Evening Echo* Toy Fund.

By Saturday 28 December, the floods had all but disappeared, but 'traces of distress and suffering ... and scenes of unparalleled poverty and misery are to be witnessed on all sides'.[31] Now the clean up and relief operation began in earnest. The Mayor, Frs Magner and Barrett, council members, corporation staff, the Sick Poor Society, and the people of Blackpool themselves all played their part in distributing coal, clothes, blankets, bedding (the latter being supplied free by the Munster Arcade and the Queen's Old Castle department stores) to those hardest hit by the worst floods Cork had experienced in living memory. The gentry too were not backward in coming forward. Lady Arnott and her daughter, the Pikes of Bessborough, and others all worked assiduously in helping to distribute the much-needed relief.

Only when the reports from the various areas were collated did it become clear that the emergency had not passed without loss of life. Four unfortunate souls perished during that awful Christmas: William Wool, found drowned off Gillabbey Street; Edward Rogan, drowned off Pope's Road; Catherine Lambert, found drowned off the Common's Road; and an un-named mother of five who was found dead in Wherland's Lane.[32]

The fire chief and his small staff had worked well under the adverse conditions considering their limited equipment, and their response was later lauded by Mayor Meade who:

> Thanked the men of the Fire Brigade for their conduct. He had no hesitation in saying that the exertions of Captain Hutson and his men were most creditable, and he did not believe that too much could be said of them. The Captain and his men were up to their waists in water on Christmas morning.[33]

The people of Cork in general, and Blackpool in particular, were glad to see the back of Christmas 1895. It was one that would not be quickly forgotten.

Any reprieve for the hard-pressed firefighters was short-lived. Their sodden uniforms were hardly dry when the General Alarm sounded throughout the fire station at 6.30p.m. on that New Year's Eve. On foot of a delayed call to the Vulcan Foundry on Lapp's Quay, owned by partners McLean and Parkes, they responded with two hose reels, the wheeled escape from Sullivan's Quay, and the escape from Lavitt's Quay. The great glare in the frosty winter sky could be seen all over the city. The fire, concentrated in the pattern room, was well established, with the roof in some places having already fallen in. The brigade's immediate priority was to save the part of the plant consisting of the erecting shop and machine room, and also the adjacent Cork Harbour Board premises. Three good jets were soon brought to bear, the excellent supply of water being augmented by the fourteen-inch main from the Western Road.

A large number of people flocked to the scene, who, however, watched the efforts of the firemen in a most orderly manner. The firemen worked admirably under Captain Hudson [*sic*] and ... they extinguished the flames in a very brief period of time.[34]

The damage, confined almost exclusively to the pattern room, was said to be 'considerable'. By the early years of the twentieth century the Vulcan Foundry had ceased operations and for a time was used as a coal store.

VISITING FIREMEN AND THE FLAG FIASCO.

As Alfred Hutson's reputation grew, the authorities in towns and cities all over Munster – Bandon, Clonakilty, Clonmel, Fermoy, Kanturk, Lismore, Midleton, Queenstown, Skibbereen, Youghal, and Waterford – all sought his advice on how best to organize their own fire protection. Limerick, too (under its Superintendent, Alfred Wylde, a contender for the Cork vacancy in 1891 when Hutson was successful), with its whole-time brigade and steam fire engine, sought the Cork chief's guidance on how best to emulate the Cork model. In each and every case, permission was granted for Hutson to travel, his hosts covering his expenses. Bizarrely, even American foreign policy advisors appear to have been interested in the fire protection of Cork! In 1892, Hutson was directed by the council to reply 'to the queries from the Department of State, Washington, USA, relative to building construction and precautions against fire'.[35]

His name had also become very well known on the international Fire Brigade Congress circuit. As well as attending at several in UK cities, he had also received invitations from the Belgian Government to their National Fire Brigade *Fête* in July 1892 and from the British Consul at Rouen to the Congress there in May 1896. Also in 1896, Hutson had sought permission to attend the Great International Fire Tournament and Exhibition in London. On this occasion, the corporation was unable to see its way to granting permission, prompting the following remarks – which may indicate the man's popularity among his peers – in the next edition of *The Fireman*:

> The Cork Town Council has refused to allow their Brigade to attend. It is hoped, however, that Chief Officer Hutson will be able to run over in an unofficial capacity. The gathering will not be complete without him.[36]

In the event, Hutson did not get to 'run over' to London, but a group of Canadian and US fire officers attending the Congress decided to extend their visit to include Ireland. Their visit, indirectly, almost scuppered Alfred Hutson's career in Cork.

Chief E.S Hosmer of the Lowell Fire Department, who led a delegation from North America on a visit to Cork in July 1896. (Courtesy of Susan Fougstedt, Pollard Memorial Library, Lowell, Mass.)

Following fact-finding visits to London and other English brigades (with which, by and large, they were singularly unimpressed), they went over to Paris for a few days. They found the French organization far too militaristic for their liking (the *Brigade de Sapeurs-Pompiers* was, and still is, since Napoleon Bonaparte's time, an integral part of the French Army), and they quickly hurried off on the next leg of their tour. They arrived in Cork on 4 July 1896. Chief E.S. Hosmer of Lowell, Massachusetts, recounted their European experiences to the Massachusetts's Firemen's Association at their annual convention the following September. His remarks contribute an interesting perspective on how an outsider viewed the state of the Cork Fire Brigade at the end of the nineteenth century:

At Cork we were heartily received by Chief Hutson, and in the afternoon he gave us a pleasant ride on one of those back-breaking instruments of torture called a jaunting car. We visited the Blarney Stone where it cost us a shilling to go on top and kiss the Stone, and another shilling to get down again. Sunday afternoon the Chief took us out to the Park, where we saw a hurling match, and in the evening we took another enjoyable ride in the suburbs.

Monday morning the Mayor [Sir John Scott] invited us to remain and partake of a banquet in the evening, which he desired to give in our honour, an invitation which we were reluctantly obliged to decline for lack of time. We had our photograph taken with the Mayor at the Chief's headquarters.

The Brigade here is not very large, which the Chief accounted for by saying that they do not have many fires, and a large force is not necessary. He has a few permanent men, the remainder being Corporation employees. The apparatus at headquarters consists of one horse, one two-wheel hose reel, one two-wheel hose cart drawn by hand, one manual fire engine and one fire escape.[38] There are two manned escape stations on the streets the same as in London. They have no [steam] engine, the Chief stating that the water pressure is sufficient to cover everything, and they don't need one. The alarm system is by telephone, and very little of that. There are small standpipes and hydrants the same as in London.

That night we stayed in Glengarriff, the next night in Killarney, and from there we went to Dublin where we received a royal welcome from Chief Purcell … I hope I have given you a fair idea of what they have in the Old Country, so far as our observations extended. But as an American, I cannot refrain from saying in conclusion that the idea I have heretofore entertained, inspired possibly by a spirit of patriotism, has been solidified into a conviction by my observation abroad – and that is, that this hustling, bustling progressive Yankee nation of ours has, and will always have, the most complete and efficient system of fire fighting on the face of the earth.[39]

The party from North America was shocked at the smallness of the Irish and British fire brigades, the size of the water mains, the inadequacy of the telephone system, and at 'so meagre and inadequate a fire service'.[40] Street escape stations and wheeled escapes were unknown in Canada and the US, and they were highly critical of a system whereby these heavy ladders had to be manhandled through city streets, which they considered archaic and unnecessary in the light of new technology. American rescue ladders (notably, the 1888 Hayes 55ft Aerial Ladder built by La France) were mounted on mobile apparatus which, of course, were considerably faster in arriving on a fire ground.

The visitors' sojourn in Cork had been a pleasant diversion, for a few days at least, for Hutson and his staff. In every way he regarded it as an unqualified success. As they departed, various small 'keepsakes' were exchanged between host and guests, as is the norm on such occasions, including apparently, the gift of a flag (of uncertain provenance) from the North Americans. Hutson folded it carefully and placed it in a drawer with some other knick-knacks, and promptly forgot all about it.

The subsequent fall-out from this seemingly innocuous gift unequivocally serves to give the lie to the notion that the vast majority of the population of late Victorian Cork was completely at ease with itself and its place within the British Empire. And, darkly, it reveals a spiteful undercurrent of xenophobia among a small number of public representatives towards the fire chief, which, reprehensibly, appears to have been motivated by his English pedigree. It propelled him into the limelight of controversy, and very nearly cost him his job.

In 1898, a committee was established in Cork to explore ways and means of ensuring that the one hundredth anniversary of the 1798 Rebellion would not pass unnoticed. It was decided that a monument – later to be known as the National Monument – should be erected, which would also serve to commemorate the subsequent risings of 1803, 1848, and 1867. A site was selected near the river's edge on Grand Parade, close to where the equestrian statue of King George II once kept its lonely vigil. The committee made its plans and fundraising began.

A great demonstration in connection with the laying of the foundation stone was planned for Sunday 2 October 1898, and Capt. Hutson was approached by the Centenary Committee with a view to the fire brigade assisting in the erection of decorations on the Grand Parade. Hutson readily agreed, releasing fire escapes and men for the purpose, and the firemen enthusiastically threw themselves into the work. At the Berwick Fountain, two fire escapes were placed so as to form an arch of banners and streamers. The chief was also notified by the Mayor that the brigade should be officially represented at the ceremony.

On the Sunday morning, as thousands began to throng the Grand Parade, some of the firemen thought it a shame that the fire station – situated directly across the river from the monument site – looked so bare, and suggested to the chief that it too, should be bedecked with flags and bunting. Hutson consented, 'provided they had any to spare', and then he remembered The Flag.

The fire chief later said that he had been told on good authority that the flag had connotations with Brian Boru and the ancient tribes and clans of Ireland and he thought it was, therefore, a most suitable banner to display on the day that was in it. Many thought it was some sort of Canadian flag: to others, it looked suspiciously like the Royal Standard. There were dark whisperings that, looked at in a certain light, it even resembled the Union Flag. Whatever it was, as it fluttered cheekily from the fire station in the soft south-westerly zephyr, the general consensus on the Grand Parade was that great provocation was being afforded the Nationalist community of Cork on this, their special day. Fuming, members of the organizing committee marched off in high dudgeon to confront the Mayor, Patrick Hagin Meade, who quickly sent flunkies scurrying over the South Gate Bridge to have the offending banner removed. They wanted Alfred Hutson's head on a plate.

Despite a full statement from the bewildered chief that no offence was intended, and if, inadvertently, the flying of the flag had offended anyone, he apologized profusely, the debacle dragged on at both meetings of the full council and the Waterworks and Fire Brigade Committee for over two months, occupying numerous column inches in the newspapers. The council received a memorial signed by twenty-five 'Citizens and Ratepayers' referring to, 'the action of Capt. Hutson in hoisting a British (i.e. Canadian) standard on the day of laying the foundation stone of a monument to the [national] heroes

... and in the name of the people of Cork we demand an apology'. In the event of the chief refusing to apologize, they requested 'an alternative course be adopted'.[41] Stormed Cllr Barry:

> No official of the Corporation should dare presume to flaunt a rag that is disagreeable to his fellow-men. We have a sense of our own, and we can understand what is offensive and what is not, and the sooner this gentleman, or any other gentleman who comes here from another country and takes upon himself to be offensive to the citizens ... the sooner he is brought to his facings the better for himself. If I thought I would have any support, I would certainly move Captain Hutson's discharge.[42]

Cllr O'Shaughnessy said he had:

> read the history of Ireland, in fact he had three works on it at home, and he never heard a word about Brian Boru's Castle 'til a gentleman from Brighton came over to teach him. They could not expect any national feeling from Captain Hutson.[43]

The Mayor, Ald. Dale and others spoke in Hutson's defence. Cllr Scully said he, 'knew Captain Hutson since he came to Cork, and he believed he would cut off his right hand before giving offence to anybody'.[44] But some seemed bent on humiliating the fire chief in public. The Mayor addressed Hutson saying:

> You explained to me that your action was due to pure inadvertence; that it was not your intention to give pain or offence to any of your fellow citizens, and that if you hung out any flag or emblem that was displeasing to them you are sorry for it. Is that what you say?
> Captain Hutson: 'Yes, sir'.
> Alderman E. Fitzgerald: 'I object! He said that in a whisper!'
> Councillor J. Banks: 'What nonsense!'
> The Mayor: 'Say it loud, Captain'.
> Captain Hutson, in a loud tone: 'Yes, sir. I regret it'.
> The Mayor: 'That finishes it, and I hope, Captain Hutson, it will check your ardour in the future'.[45]

For Alfred James Hutson it had been a salutary lesson. As he left the council chamber, only the vein that pulsed in his forehead betrayed the storm in his heart. In future, he would keep his distance at all political demonstrations, irrespective of shade.

Ironically, the outpouring of invective against him was not matched with largesse for the monument project and it almost foundered through general apathy and lack of funds. The foundation stone lay on the Grand Parade, half-forgotten, the site derelict and weed-strewn. In 1902, the project was resurrected under the aegis of the Cork Young Ireland Society, fund-raising recommenced in earnest, and a contract was signed with Ellis's for £2,000. The fifteen-metre-high monument, described as Early Irish Gothic was designed by D.J. Coakley and executed by sculptor John Francis Davis who carried on a sculpturing business at Sunset Terrace, College Road. The central figure of 'Erin' is flanked with statues of Theobald Wolfe Tone, Michael Dwyer, Thomas Davis and O'Neill Crowley. More than forty names are etched on the monument, all of them men bar one, Anne Devlin.

The National Monument was unveiled on St Patrick's Day in 1906 by the famous Fenian and Rosscarbery native Jeremiah O'Donovan Rossa. The Grand Parade was thronged to capacity for the ceremony, with sections from all walks of life from the city and county marching in the huge procession.

Cork Fire Brigade was not represented.

Níl aon Tinteán mar do Thinteán Féin: Station Life and Conditions *c.* 1900

'The Fire Station ... is a magnificent structure. The most modern improvements in the art of fire extinguishing have been introduced.'

(*Cork Constitution,* August 1893).

'Home' to members of the fire brigade on the cusp of the new century was usually a three-roomed apartment over, or adjacent to, the Central Fire Station on Sullivan's Quay, or over the recently-opened Shandon Fire Station.[1] This is where the fireman could retire to when he was neither on duty nor on watch, but 'on call'. Almost akin to a soldier living in barracks, here he lived with his wife and children with no front door to call his own. A man's 'quarters' were rooms sharing a common landing or corridor with other families. Washing, showering, and laundering facilities were shared.

The men were under service-type discipline all the time.[2] The Superintendent, under authority vested in him by the council, had the right to call on any man's quarters, day or evening, to inspect the facilities and ensure the place was being maintained to a certain standard. Generally, the wives kept to themselves, but in such a confined community it was inevitable that personal and professional matters became common property and everyone knew everyone else's business. The majority of drills were conducted by Hutson in the narrow lane behind the station, and on occasion, if he was 'smartening up' or 'dressing down' a man on parade, a wife might suddenly appear out of nowhere, taking a short cut to her apartment: a discomfiting situation for all concerned. The children enjoyed each other's company, playing in the small station yard or in the narrow maze of streets in the vicinity. Children, being children, of course, could not always be kept away from the appliances and equipment, and if they were shooed out of the appliance room by the dutyman, their mothers might take umbrage. Invariably, the boys received their education at the nearby Christian Brothers, the girls either at the

Mercy Sisters in St Marie's of the Isle/St Aloysius' in Sharman Crawford Street or at the Presentation Sisters in Douglas Street. The fire chief's family was Church of England. The Protestant schools were St Nicholas', Cove Street and Christ Church, South Main Street (primary), and Cork Grammar School and Rochelle (secondary). In addition to the fire chief and his family, the 1901 Census reveals the following members in residence, with their families, at fire stations:

Sullivan's Quay station:
Patrick Higgins (Chief's Assistant) and Firemen Philip Lecane, James Keating, William Gloyne and Charles McCarthy.
Shandon station: Firemen John Murphy and James Lyons.

The total strength of the brigade, including auxiliaries, in November 1900 was sixteen.

Members of the brigade worked twenty-four hours a day, with only short-leave periods granted by the Superintendent. This harsh regime was ameliorated to a degree in 1890, when following a submission from the four permanent members, they were allowed a day's leave of absence in turn. This meant that they had one Sunday off a month between 8a.m. and 8p.m. for the winter months and between 8a.m. to 10p.m. for the summer months.[3] The firemen were allowed to take breakfast and lunch in their quarters with their families, two at one hour, and two at another hour, 'each man to enter in the book

FIG. 1.

"Kingston" Escape ready for running.

Illustration of a William Rose 'Kingston' wheeled escape, similar to the pattern stationed at Shandon Fire Station. Capable of being operated by one man, it could reach a height of forty feet.

provided for the purpose in the station the time of his leaving and returning'. Curiously, all were required to partake of the evening meal in the station mess.

THE TURN-OUT.

Each apartment was fitted with an alarm bell over the door, with a further bell outside on the landing or corridor. On receipt of an emergency call, the dutyman in the station watchroom would trip the General Alarm switch into the down position on the bell board, an action which would set every bell throughout the station and quarters jangling; hence the fire brigade expression 'the bells went down' for a fire at such-and-such an address. Later, with the advent of electric lighting, emergency lighting was fitted throughout the premises, which, by night, was operated simultaneously with the bells. Thus, all parts of the station – apartments, corridors, stairs, landings, and engine room – were lit up like a Christmas tree at the flick of a switch.

On arriving in the engine room, the firemen would be met by the duty-man calling out the fire address from the watchroom steps. Typically, a day time turn-out took one minute, by night two minutes. One never knew, day or night, when the jarring, clanging of the bells would ring out for a fire or other incident. The small children, woken from their sleep by the bells and lights in the middle of the night, would run to their bedroom windows overlooking the quay, eyes wide with wonder and trepidation at their daddies turning out, brass helmets gleaming in the soft glow of the gas lamps, the horses prancing and whinnying with anticipation. With a crisp 'walk on!' and a shrug of the reins from the drivers, the horses would begin their journey with a brisk canter, developing into a full gallop as they were given their heads.

If the job had periods of *ennui* and tedium there was also the animation and excitement of the fire ground and the knowledge that one was performing a worthwhile, humanitarian service, respected and appreciated by the vast majority of the populace; the indiscretions of the early years by now a distant memory, unknown to a younger generation. After hours, there was the camaraderie of the recreation room, sitting around a blazing fire, yarning, reading, or enjoying a game of billiards, chess, or cards (playing for money was, officially at any rate, prohibited under brigade regulations), more often than not some men from the locality making up the numbers at a card school or at the billiard table. On the wall, portraits of Eyre Massey Shaw, St Barbara, Patroness of Firefighters, and national hero Robert Emmet benignly looked down.[4]

MORNING DRILL CLASS.

The day began at 7a.m. when the men paraded before Capt. Hutson to be given their daily orders. Street closures, fire mains out of commission, exceptional fire hazards in port or in town, or a myriad other matters which might impinge on the work of the brigade were brought to the members' attention. This was followed by a period of routine maintenance, checking, and repairing the equipment, cleaning and polishing the appliances, mucking out the stables and looking after the horses, and generally ensuring the station passed muster.

After a short 'stand-to' period for breakfast, the firemen assembled again for drill class. Here they were put through their paces in the various evolutions, with rescue

Left: The brigade horses were stabled at the rear of the Central Fire Station. With the inauguration of the Fire Brigade Ambulance Service in the early 1900s a third horse was acquired.

Below: An 'ambulance' used by the fire brigade to convey accident victims to hospital. From 1893 one was located at the Central Fire Station with another at the Fireman's Rest.

procedures high on the agenda. (The auxiliaries drilled on Saturdays). The men were drilled in 'pitching' a wheeled escape to any particular window in a building in double-quick time, until they could practically do it in their sleep. They knew how to climb the escape smoothly and efficiently, left hand and left foot, right hand and right foot in order to avoid body sway, grasping the rounds (not 'rungs') and never the strings (not 'sides'), palms down with the thumbs under the rounds.

The firemen were taught not to watch their feet but to look slightly upwards in the direction of the climb. The escape, they knew, should be pitched to the extreme side of a window, normally to the right (unless the wind was blowing smoke and fire to that side), thus enabling the rescuer to use his right hand, the stronger and more useful, to grasp the round and assist him in lifting the rescued person on to the ladder.

The use of knots and lines formed an important part of the drill syllabus. The firemen were expected to be able to make and identify numerous knots and hitches, blindfolded, each with its own particular use on the fire ground. Examples included 'hoisting hose aloft by means of a line, utilizing a rolling hitch and a clove hitch', or the method used to secure a line to any round object, the 'round turn and two half-hitches'. Some men excelled in making a 'Turk's Head', a complicated ornamental knot used as a finial on bell cords, etc.

In addition to the longer rescue lines carried on the escape boxes and horsed hose-reels, each member was issued with a 40ft 'personal line' of tanned manilla, which he carried suspended from a swivel hook on his uniform belt. In the event of having to search a room from the head of an escape, he would first attach his personal line to an adjacent round before entering the burning building. The forty feet of line allowed just enough leeway to search a floor of an average-sized house. In dense smoke (without breathing apparatus his only protection being a wetted kerchief hastily tied across his mouth and nostrils, and useless where there was oxygen deficiency) he could then make his way back along the line to the relative safety of the escape.

In the event of a casualty being found and the stairs impassable, the fireman would have to execute a 'carry down', the so-called 'Fireman's Lift'. The unconscious person would be pulled to a kneeling position, the fireman smartly positioning his right knee between the patient's legs, and, bending over, allow the weight to fall evenly balanced across his shoulders. (A modified version was used where the patient was a woman to 'protect her modesty'). While descending the escape, the fireman had to take particular care to prevent the feet or head of the rescued person riding over the guy-wires; and he had to remember that when stepping off the escape, on reaching the ground, when the casualty's head is over the rescuer's left shoulder, to step off to the right and turn left about immediately; in that way, any possibility of the rescued person's head striking the large escape wheel would be avoided.

THE JUMPING SHEET.

Where time or circumstance did not permit a rescue by conventional means, the jumping sheet was introduced. The men were drilled regularly in its use in Blackamoor Lane at the rear of the Central Fire Station. Early jumping sheets consisted of a circular canvas sheet with a diameter of ten feet, fitted across the diameter with two two-foot strengthening bands of similar material and a three-foot circular centre piece. The circumference was strengthened by a line sewn in the canvas and was fitted with twenty-four hand beckets spaced about twelve inches apart.

Mary Ann Bogan of Warren's Place offered to make twelve sheets at a cost of £2.6s.8d each, but Abraham W. Sutton and Co. undercut her with their tender of £2.5s.0d and their proposal was accepted.[5] During 1893, new jumping sheets were provided at RIC stations at Sunday's Well, Blackpool, Shandon, St Luke's, and Lower Glanmire Road, as well as at the Central Fire Station and street escape stations. Later, in the aftermath of a number of incidents in which people actually jumped from buildings on fire (some with fatal consequences), the number of sheets was considerably increased. By August 1901, in addition to the police stations mentioned, the following were equipped: Bridewell, Great George's Street, Tuckey Street, College Road, Blackrock Road, Union Quay, and King Street. The fire chief further reported to his committee that 'jumping sheets are kept at the fire stations on Sullivan's Quay, Lavitt's Quay, Shandon St and Henry St'. He sought, and received approval, to install sheets at the *Cork Examiner* office, the *Cork Constitution* office, the GPO, the North and South Infirmaries, the Blind Asylum, the Women's and Children's Hospital, the Mercy Hospital, and the Eye, Ear and Throat Hospital.[6]

The fire brigade could rarely muster enough numbers of its own to operate a jumping sheet effectively on the fire ground (a minimum of fourteen was required), so the assistance of as many policemen and civilians as possible was needed. The sheet was held close into the building from whence the rescue was to be effected; where time permitted, occupiers of nearby houses would be requested to place mattresses, large cardboard boxes, etc., under the sheet to help soften the impact of the jumper's fall. Those gripping the sheet were instructed to lean well back so that the impact of the jumper striking the sheet did not result in the canvas sagging and hitting the ground. The misfortunate victim would be advised to try to fall as a dead weight rather than to actually jump. Jumping into the sheet resulted in the same effect as a springing body bouncing off a trampoline – sometimes with dire consequences.

Nor was the operation without its danger to those at ground level. There are reports of jumpers missing the sheet entirely and hitting one or more persons on 'sheet duty'; the height of the building being in direct proportion to this possibility. The officer in charge of the sheet would watch the victim intensely. At the moment he or she stepped out into space, the order 'Taut sheet!' would be given. All gripping the sheet would then lean back, arms straight, and looking dead ahead, not up, to lessen the possibility of whiplash to themselves.

For many years, with the auxiliary staff making up the numbers, the firemen acted as 'live' casualties on jumping sheet drill, stepping off a ledge from one or other of the windows at the rear of Sullivan's Quay fire station from a height of some 25 feet. Following a fatal accident to a member of the UK National Fire Service in the 1940s, the use of live casualties was discontinued, a twelve-stone sandbag being substituted. Jumping sheets are no longer carried on modern fire appliances.

FIRST AID.

Members of the fire brigade were regularly lectured on 'First Aid to the Injured' by Dr Richard D'Alton, who had, in October 1891, at Capt. Hutson's suggestion consented to be the brigade's Hon. Surgeon.[7] Two years later, Hutson was granted permission to 'establish a branch of the St John Ambulance Society in connection with the paid, auxiliary and volunteer' cadres in the fire brigade: over forty years before a division of the St John Ambulance Brigade was formally established in Cork, in 1934.[8] Thus began a long association between the fire brigade and St John's, which continued unbroken until 1966 with the establishment of the Ambulance Training School at Phoenix Park, Dublin, under the auspices of the Department of Health.

Textbooks used were the standard publications of the St John Ambulance Brigade, but in 1902 the fire service would have its own dedicated first aid book, *First Aid in the Fire Service* by William Ettles, MD. The subjects covered included:

> The structure and functions of the human body.
> Haemorrhage, or bleeding.
> Dressings and bandages.
> Fractures and dislocations.
> Burns and their management.
> Insensibility, or unconsciousness.
> Poisoning.
> Asphyxia, or suffocation.
> Transport of the injured and sick.
> Preparing for reception of a case of accident.

The methods of artificial respiration used were Howard's Method, Laborde's Method, and the much-favoured Silvester Method. (The *Cork Examiner* carried a report on a man who had been drowned in New York and taken to the City Morgue. Some time later, on vital signs being noticed he was successfully resuscitated using the Silvester Method.[9]) In times of emergency, the community naturally gravitated towards the local fire station, the perception being that 'the firemen will know what to do'. Thus, when small Johnny fell off his 'steering car' and suffered a nasty graze to his knee, the first port of call was invariably the fire station. It was the focal point in the neighbourhood for folk requiring dressings for minor cuts and grazes, for each station maintained a well-stocked first aid box. Similarly, at a time when telephones were few and far between, people urgently requiring a doctor or clergyman knew they would always be facilitated at their local fire station with its round-the-clock watch.

In 1890s Cork, no dedicated public accident ambulance service existed. In the event of an accident, the misfortunate person was dependent on the goodwill of a passing carter, or a policeman commandeering a 'jingle' to transport him or her to either the South or North Infirmaries. The fire chief sought to address this by the purchase of a number of 'ambulances as used by the St John Ambulance Association'.[10] These ambulances (called 'litters') were little more than covered stretchers fitted with pneumatic tyres – such was the definition of an ambulance then – but the contraptions were regarded as 'state of the art' in 1893 and two were supplied to the fire brigade, being located at the Central Fire Station and at the Fireman's Rest on the Grand Parade. A major improvement came in 1902, with the inauguration of the Fire Brigade Ambulance Service. In that year, the brigade's first horse-drawn ambulance was placed 'on the run', operating out of the central station. Cork Fire Brigade would continue to provide the accident ambulance service for the city, and a large portion of the county, until 1978 when its functions were transferred to the Southern Health Board Ambulance Service.

Capt. Hutson's first annual report showed that, in 1891, the brigade had responded to 96 alarm calls. This had increased to 121 in 1892, fallen back to 97 in 1893, and then risen, year on year, for 1894 (104), 1895 (151), and 1896 (174). His sixth annual report, presented on 6 January 1897, records that of the 174 alarms, 66 were to serious fires. Four fires were 'county calls' (i.e., to addresses outside the borough boundary), including ones at 'the Right Reverend Bishop O'Callaghan's Palace, Farran Ferris', and 'the Rev. Mr Ruby's, Brighton Villas, Western Road'. Both of these places have long been incorporated into the city. Six people lost their lives 'by coming into contact with fire' during the year and false alarms amounted to five. A number of fires were caused by the 'excessive heat' of July. By 1901, the number of calls attended had jumped to 209.

Included in the more notable incidents during those years were:

13 AUGUST 1896: 9 P.M. SERIOUS FIRE AT MESSRS J.M. TWOMEY,
KNAPP'S SQUARE, OFF CAMDEN QUAY – ASSISTANT COLLAPSES
AND DIES:

About nine o'clock last night a fire broke out in a store belonging to Mr

J.M. Twomey, 2 Knapp's Square. A quantity of hayseed and corn was in the store, at the rear of which were stables in which were eight pigs and five horses.

When the brigade reached Patrick's Street, their progress was blocked by the large number of people attending the bands which paraded in the city. They, however, proceeded down Bowling Green Street, and reached the scene of the fire by a circuitous route. The fire escape was brought from Lavitt's Quay... and the fire was got under control.

During the course of the fire, a man named Daniel Field from Curry's Rock was helping to remove some sacks from the burning stores when he collapsed. Capt. Hutson and the firemen immediately went to his aid, placed him on the jumper between two members, and conveyed him to the North Infirmary, a short distance away. Sadly, he died about ten minutes after admission.[11]

Earlier on the same day, a great fire broke out in the town centre of Kinsale during which six houses in Market Street, McCarthy's Stores, Acton's Hardware and Oil Shop on Long Quay, and Ahern's Piggery on Short Quay were all destroyed in a conflagration which broke out around midnight:

> The bells of the Parish Church and Friary were rung, and thousands of persons attracted by the noise of the ringing bells ... made their appearance on the scene, but despite all their efforts and those of the Inniskilling Fusiliers under Col Crawford, the Coastguards and Naval Reserve – the water supply being very deficient – in less than two hours ... the whole block presented a mass of ruins. The loss attained by the conflagration amounts to about £6,000.[12]

> The CFB was not requested to attend.

8A.M. 3 AUGUST 1897. MAJOR FIRE AT MESSRS JOHN WALLIS AND SONS, MERCHANT'S QUAY – FIRE CHIEF INJURED:

> Unless attended by loss of life, the outbreak could not have been of greater gravity, for the large building was completely burned to the ground, while the adjoining store of Messrs Hayes suffered to a considerable extent. The destroyed premises runs from Merchant's Quay back to Fisher's Lane a distance of about 100 feet.[13]

During the course of the operations Capt. Hutson was injured by falling glass. While inspecting the third floor of Hayes' premises, he found it necessary to get on to a window sill commanding a view of the loft. Whilst so engaged the roof of the blazing building gave way, showering him in shards of large fragments of glass. He lost a large quantity of blood and was removed to the North Infirmary. His injuries necessitated him being laid up for a month.

7.15P.M. 16 JUNE 1898. MAJOR FIRE AT MESSRS POPE'S TIMBER YARD, BANDON – FIRE ENGINE KEEPER DROPS DEAD FROM SHOCK.

One of the biggest fires seen in the south of Ireland in the late nineteenth century occurred on the evening of 16 June 1898. The fire, which broke out at the Timber Yard and Corn Stores of Pope's in Bandon, resulted in the complete destruction of the extensive premises with damage estimated at the then enormous amount of £10,000.

The outbreak in the complex, situated in a densely-housed locality, was initially attended by the fire engine of the 17th Lancers under their NCOs:

> having come with the most praiseworthy despatch. Their engine was placed on Market Quay, just opposite the burning premises, and only separated from them by the Bridewell River, a shallow stream, which, happily, afforded a sufficient supply of water. The presence of an immense crowd of spectators, aghast with terror and excitement at the heaving sea of fire within the timber yard, produced indescribable confusion.[14]

Presently, the efforts of the military were joined by the Ballymoden fire engine:

> which forms part of the fire-extinguishing apparatus of a rather poorly-equipped fire brigade which was established in the town a year or two ago through the exertions of a prominent local gentleman. When the excitement and confusion was at its height an incident occurred which gave a tragic horror to the whole scene. Someone called out that the boiler of the steam engine [of the timber yard] was sure to burst, and the local engine was brought to the spot … the old engine failed utterly, and Mr. John W. Sullivan, a much-respected old gentleman, who was in charge of it, dropped dead from shock.[15]

It soon became apparent that the reason the engine would not deliver was because the suction strainer was not under the surface of the water. When this was rectified the machine worked admirably. After some consultation:

> The heads of the Police and some of the principal residents sent an urgent telegram to Cork asking to have the Fire Brigade sent out. On receipt of the telegram, Captain Hutson, with three men and a manual engine, immediately proceeded by road to Bandon, and reached the scene at 11 o'clock. Captain Hutson and his men rendered valuable aid, going heartily with the many other willing hands in their effort to save property and to prevent the possibility of the loss of human life.[16]

Mr George Pope later wrote to the Mayor of Cork, P.H. Meade, 'congratulating the citizens of Cork on having such a capable body of men and such an efficient officer', and testified that the Cork unit refused much-needed refreshments and insisted on remaining at their posts until 8a.m the following morning when the danger had subsided.[17]

The bill for the services of the brigade amounted to £21.7s.6d of which ten guineas was lodged to the credit of the Widows' and Orphans' Fund.

3 OCTOBER 1898. SERIOUS FIRE AT MESSRS ADAMS CORN STORES, QUEEN STREET – ASSEMBLY ROOMS NARROWLY ESCAPES DESTRUCTION:

To the Fire Brigade, under Captain Hutson, all praise is due for the promptitude with which they responded to the alarm, and the effective manner in which they coped with a fire which threatened at one time to assume epic proportions.[18]

The Assembly Rooms, which adjoined the Corn Stores, narrowly escaped being the scene of a mass tragedy. An industrial exhibition in the Rooms had just concluded and the crowd dispersed before the fire was discovered, otherwise 'many lives might have been lost in the stampede which is characterized by such occasions'.

2P.M. 30 NOVEMBER 1898. SERIOUS FIRE AT MESSRS JAMES MURPHY-CONNOR AND CO., WINE AND SPIRIT MERCHANTS, DEANE STREET – PREMISES DESTROYED:

The Fire Brigade were at once communicated with, but when they arrived they found that the flames had already made considerable progress throughout the three-storey premises. The fire had now eaten its way into the timber loft of Mr T.W. Magahy, Organ Builder, Lower George's Street … the flames were spreading in two different directions, threatening to envelope the adjoining properties of Messrs James Ogilvie and Co., the butter stores of Mr R.M. Keatinge, T.C., and the fish stores of Mr Richard Downing, C.H.C.

An element which may be counted as having had much to say to the wonderful progress which the blaze had made was the rather fresh breeze which prevailed at the time. Mr Magahy was successful in saving a quantity of materials, but nothing was rescued from the establishment of Messrs O'Connor [*sic*] except the books.[19]

PAY AND CONDITIONS.

Fire brigade members' pay compared very favourably with that of other public servants, for example, that of an RIC man or a national teacher. Artisans such as masons, bricklayers, plasterers, carpenters, and painters each earned 5s 9d per day. Assuming a six-day week, this translated into a wage of £1.13s.9d per week.[20]

In November 1900, the four permanent members – Firemen Gloyne, Lecane, Barry, and McCarthy, as well as Patrick Higgins – applied for an increase in pay in the usual manner by way of a 'memorial', or petition, to the Waterworks and Fire Brigade Committee. In an age before collective bargaining or National Wage Agreements, each section was responsible for negotiating its own pay deals and the firemen would closely watch developments in other fire brigades. An increase of two shillings a week each to the four firemen and three shillings and sixpence to Higgins was sanctioned.[21] This gave the firemen a weekly rate of £1 12s 0d, plus the added bonuses of emoluments such as accommodation, fuel, lighting, and uniform. In 1880, these were calculated by the City Treasurer to be worth £24 a year, or 9s 5d extra a week. Additional allowances were also payable. For example, Higgins, who as well as his other duties had special responsibility for the care of the horses, was paid an extra shilling per week, and the escape conductors at Lavitt's Quay and Henry Street received an extra two shillings per week. This put a Cork firefighter ahead of a policeman with twenty years' service who had £1 7s 0d per week, and on a par with a principal teacher who earned between £1 5s 0d and £1 12s 0d per week. In return, fire brigade personnel had to endure the socially-isolating, always-on-call duty system.[22]

The remuneration for the eight auxiliary firemen (whole-time occupations and pay in parentheses) was as follows:

Aux. Fm. J. Keating (Lamplighter @ £1 per week) – auxiliary @ 2s. p.w. with rooms, fuel, and gas.
Aux. Fm. T. Healy (ditto) – auxiliary @ 2s. p.w. only.
Aux. Fm. E. McCarthy – ditto.
Aux. Fm. J. Reardon– ditto.
Aux. Fm. J. Murphy (Sanitary Sub-Officer @ 18s. p.w.) – auxiliary @ 2s. p.w. only.
Aux. Fm. J. Hutson – auxiliary @ 2s. p.w. only (resides with Superintendent).
Aux. Fm. M. Higgins – auxiliary @ 2s. p.w. only ('no residence provided').
Aux. Fm. T. O'Leary – auxiliary only with rooms provided, but no pay.

In 1899, auxiliaries not provided with official accommodation were granted an allowance of 2 shillings per week.[23]

Capt. Hutson, who had been appointed in 1891 at a salary of £9 per month received his first rise in February 1896 when his pay was increased to £13 per month, a very substantial rise in the context of the time, after the secretary of the Waterworks and Fire Brigade Committee had checked on the salaries of principal officers of fire brigades in similar-sized cities across the UK. He found that Southampton paid its Chief Officer £114 per annum; Bolton £134; Cardiff £160; and Blackburn £200. In November 1896, Hutson's salary was further increased by £20 per annum to £176. By comparison, in 1900 a Head Constable of the RIC had £104 per annum after six years' service.

What would these wages have bought? A good suit could be had for around £1 15s 0d, tea ranged from 2s. to 3s 8d per pound, and coal (with which the firemen were provided) was about £1 1s 0d per ton. The fireman on his Sunday off could take his family on an excursion to Killarney on the train – the return adult fare was 3s 6d. While there, he might decide to have a hot toddy or two to fortify himself against the bracing Kerry air; whiskey cost from 16s. to £1 per *gallon*. A farm of 76 acres at Cloyne, Co. Cork was sold for £385.[24]

THE WIDOWS' AND ORPHANS' FUND.

The idea of a Fire Brigade Widows' and Orphans' Fund was first mooted in December 1896 by Capt. Hutson.[25] Its primary function was to alleviate hardship on members, or their widows and children, faced with sudden or unexpected expenses occasioned by the death of a spouse or child. He proposed that the fund be supported by monies received for the services of the brigade outside the borough. After the corporation had deducted the actual cost of the service to it, any surplus would be credited to the fund. (This meant, in effect, that 'the client' was subsidizing the fund.)

His recommendation received a sympathetic hearing, and he was requested to submit examples of how the scheme worked in other cities. The systems operating in Dublin, Manchester, Bradford, Bolton, Southampton, Birmingham, Cardiff, and Liverpool were duly delivered to the 'Joint Committee formed outside the Corporation' for their deliberation in early 1897.[26]

The first lodgement into the fund was made after the great fire at Blackpool Flax Mills in July. In October of the same year, cheques for 10 guineas and £37 12s 0d were received from the insurers 'for hire of the Manual Fire Engine and services of Brigade' at the flax mills fire. After the City Treasurer had deducted the corporation's expenses, the balance was lodged to the credit of the fund with the Munster and Leinster Bank. The first grant from the fund was made on 18 August 1897. When the widow of Aux. Fm. Michael McCarthy, 'whose death she attributed to the severe cold he contracted on night-duty' (at the Fireman's Rest) applied for a grant, she was awarded £5.

Funding came, not only from the 'Out of Area' calls endowment, but from a variety of sources. The insurance companies, business people whose property had been saved by the brigade, even members of the RIC made a donation to the fund on at least one occasion.[27] The fire chief also tried to swell the coffers of the fund by raising its profile among the general public, but with limited success. Over-ambitiously booking the Opera House for two nights in December 1896 with a 'Variety of Entertainments' programme, that included the St Nicholas Gymnastic Team ('Dumbbell, horizontal bar, and parallel bar exercises'), lance and sword exercises by the 12th Royal Lancers; lightweight and heavyweight boxing exhibitions, and the Band of the 2nd Leicestershire Regiment, the *Cork Examiner* diplomatically reported that 'the entertainment merited larger patronage than was accorded it, especially in view of the charitable object in whose interest it was promoted'.[28]

Intended for the benefit of fire brigade members, their widows and children, over the years the original rules had gradually become blurred to the extent that, for example, even the family of the man who looked after the fire extinguishers at the City Hall successfully applied for a grant from the fund on his death. In 1916, the City Solicitor raised the thorny question as to whether the fund had ever been placed on a proper legal footing. He pointed out that when the scheme was started there was no local government audit of the corporate accounts, and consequently the validity of the resolution passed by council in setting up the fund went unchallenged. Further, he suggested that perhaps all monies received for the services of the brigade for duties outside the borough formed part of the corporate revenue and therefore should be placed to the credit of the City Improvement Fund. (Between the start-up of the Widows' and Orphans' Fund in 1897 and July 1916 sixty-two payments were made totalling £343.5s.3d). His suggestion that the facts be laid before a Senior Counsel for advice as to how to proceed was accepted, and on 21 November 1916, he was able to lay before council the proposed new scheme, which was subsequently adopted. Applications to the re-constituted fund would henceforth be adjudicated on by a sub-committee consisting of three elected representatives from the Waterworks and Fire Brigade Committee and two members of the brigade. The Widows' and Orphans' Fund provided a much-needed service during the brigade's formative years when conditions were relatively harsh. With the passage of time and the vast improvement in conditions of service the need for the fund diminished until, during the 1980s (many members by then not even being aware of its existence), the long-dormant fund was eventually wound-up.

Prior to the existence of the occupational pension scheme, a member might receive a gratuity from the corporation, recommended by the Waterworks and Fire Brigade Committee, but this was purely on a grace and favour basis. When, in September 1891, Sgt Michael Ryan resigned due to 'defective eyesight from injuries received at a fire', he was awarded a gratuity of £40 and an illuminated address, the Town Clerk advising that the council had 'no legal powers to grant a superannuation or any pecuniary grant to an employee in the same capacity as Sgt. Ryan served in'.[29]

14

Fortune Favours the Brave: Some Profiles in Courage

'They did their duty in a most humane, creditable and courageous manner. They saved lives and property'

(Coroner William Murphy on Firemen Peter Murphy and Martin Higgins, 28 November 1900).

Prior to the establishment in 1947 of *Cómhairle na Mire Gaile* (the State's Deeds of Bravery Council) [1] the authorities in Cork regularly turned to two UK-based organizations for the recognition of outstanding acts of bravery. These were the Royal Humane Society (hereafter, RHS) and the Society for the Protection of Life from Fire (hereafter, SPLF). Between the establishment of the fire brigade in 1877 and the turn of the new century, several awards were made to fire brigade members by these bodies. During the latter half of the nineteenth century, awards for the RHS were processed locally by Messrs Tomkins of Winthrop Street, whose premises, as noted, were severely damaged by fire on 27 December 1850 [2]

The first member of the fire brigade to receive an award from the RHS was thirty-four-year-old Fireman Michael McCarthy for a rescue from the River Lee on 4 May 1882. The casualty was a schoolboy, Mark Wickham Jnr., none other than the ten-year-old son of the Superintendent of the brigade, Mark Wickham. The *Cork Examiner* for 5 May 1882 reported :

Rescue from Drowning.
Michael McCarthy, a Fire Brigade man, at the Sullivan's-quay Station, yesterday evening, about half-past six o'clock, saved the life of a child who fell into the water there. There was a very rapid current at the time, and the child was brought by it under a boat, beneath which the fireman gallantly dived and succeeded in grasping it and bearing it to shore.

Fm. McCarthy was duly awarded the Bronze Medal of the RHS.

Obverse of the bronze medal of the Royal Humane Society. (Courtesy of Dr R. Willoughby.)

Some ten months later, on 30 March 1883, McCarthy was again in the river attempting to save a little boy. On this occasion, the lad, who lived in Kift's Lane, was seen to fall into the river at the City Club at around 1p.m. He was borne rapidly along by the current towards Parliament Bridge where his predicament was observed by a Dr H. Townsend who immediately entered the river in a bid to save him. By this time Firemen McCarthy and Michael Thompson, dashing along the quayside, had reached the scene. Both entered the water, but Thompson seems to have been the principal rescuer, for the minutes of the Waterworks and Fire Brigade Committee for 9 April 1883 read:

Fire Brigade Superintendent reporting that on 30th March Fireman Michael Thompson jumped into the river near Parliament Bridge, and with the assistance of Dr H.R. Townsend rescued from drowning a boy named Murray who had accidentally fallen into the river. Letters from Dr Townsend, Messrs Conway and Barratt bearing testimony to the courage and gallantry displayed by Thompson on the occasion. Ordered, that copies of the Superintendent's report and of the letters referred to be forwarded to Mr Valentine Tomkins with a request that he would bring Thompson's conduct under the notice of the Royal Humane Society.

For whatever reason, no award seems to have been bestowed on this occasion, but on 30 June 1887:

> At 11.10p.m. Dominick Horgan under the influence of drink fell off Sullivan's Quay, into the Lee at Cork. Fireman Michael Thompson (38) who was from 15 Sullivan's Quay jumped fully clothed into the river and held the man up. A rope was lowered to them which Thompson tied around the man's waist and he was then hauled up to the quay.

The society approved the award of its Bronze Medal to Fireman Thompson at its committee meeting on 28 July 1887.

THE ROYAL SOCIETY FOR THE PROTECTION OF LIFE FROM FIRE.

Principally due to the indifference of the insurance fire brigades in saving life from fire, a body styling itself the Society for the Prevention of Loss of Life by Fire was formed in 1829. It collapsed five years later through lack of funds. On 22 March 1836, the Society for the Protection of Life from Fire was formally launched in London. In the following year, Queen Victoria agreed to be its patron, and from 1843 onwards it was allowed to use the prefix 'Royal'. It was supported by voluntary contributions, and provided and maintained fire escapes and men in London and various large provincial towns throughout the UK, including Dublin where it was known as the Irish Society for the Protection of Life from Fire.[3] On the death of Queen Victoria in 1901 when her son (the erstwhile volunteer fireman), King Edward VII, was approached to continue the royal patronage of the society, he declined, on the basis that, with the proliferation of public fire brigades, the organization had lost its principal *raison d'etre*. Henceforth, it reverted to being simply the Society for the Protection of Life from Fire. The exigencies of time and two world wars have meant that many of the Society's records have been lost or destroyed.

In the closing years of the nineteenth century, two notable fires occurred in Cork resulting in the conferring of awards on a policeman and two firemen. The first broke out in December 1898 and is one of the incidents for which the Society now has no official record.

A TRAGEDY OFF BLARNEY STREET.

On Friday 30 December 1898, Mrs Nora McGrath, a widow, and mother of six-year-old Willie, was up early. At 8a.m. she gave him his breakfast, and ensuring – as she thought – that the child was safe and secure, left her house at 6

Reverse of the bronze medal of the Royal Society for the Protection of Life from Fire. (Courtesy of Dr R. Willoughby.)

Vincent's Place, off Blarney Street, to go to work, intending to return about noon. The last image she had of her little son was of him sitting up in bed, happily playing with his gaily-decorated soldier's drum, his Christmas present from Santa. Her cursory 'safety check' around the bedroom had failed to pick up on the box of matches, lying, ominously, on the mantelpiece shelf.

At about twelve o'clock, with the Angelus bells ringing out across the city, Constable John West, attached to Shandon RIC Station and who lived nearby, was on beat duty when a woman came running up to him reporting a house on fire with a child trapped inside.[4] At the subsequent Inquest Constable West deposed that:

> He ran up and struck at the door [of the bedroom] which opened, when he was met with a gush of smoke and flame. He got a shock, and was thrown back against the wall. He went half-way down the stairs to get air, but came back and went into the room, but he was again overcome by the flame and smoke, which was so thick that he could not see anything. He ran down the steps to recover himself, and when he returned he went into the room again … he then found himself surrounded by fire. Then hearing a slight noise from the corner – just like a gasp – he went towards the direction of the sound, feeling the ground with his hands and found the little boy with fire on each side of him. At this

time he was quite overcome, but he caught the little boy … and carried him outside. When he got to the door some persons caught him [the policeman] and held him, as he was falling and [feeling] faint at the time.[5]

Cons. West's tunic and trousers were seen to be badly scorched and both his hands burned. The fire brigade under Capt. Hutson arrived promptly and quickly extinguished the fire. The child was removed to the North Infirmary but died from horrific burns within a short time. At the meeting of the Waterworks and Fire Brigade Committee on 4 January 1899 Capt. Hutson lavished praise on Cons. West's courageous conduct and recommended him for an award from the RSPLF, and on the following 22 March at the Police Office the Resident Magistrate, on behalf of the society, presented West with its silver medal and a purse of money.

The decision to open a fire station in the Shandon area was as a direct result of this fire tragedy.

A NIGHTMARE ON ST PATRICK'S STREET: TUESDAY 27 NOVEMBER 1900.

The cat stopped dead in the middle of the gloomy street and, for a brief moment, suspiciously contemplated the two pairs of eyes watching her from the recessed doorway before padding off into the night. Except for the hissing of the street gas lamps, not a sound was heard. To a casual observer, the street looked deserted. The only give-away was when one of the policemen – both dressed from head to toe in bottle-green uniform – drew deeply on the cigarette cupped in his right hand and the tiny bull's-eye of light reflected in his pale face. Constables Martin and McBride, on beat duty from Tuckey Street RIC station, were allowing themselves a brief respite, from what otherwise had been a tedious night, before their 3.15a.m. rendezvous with the beat sergeant at Woodford Bourne's corner. More than half-way through the night's shift, their talk was of the big parade at Union Quay on the previous Saturday before the newly-appointed Inspector-General of the RIC, Col Neville Chamberlain [6] and of Christmas, now less than a month away. Bill McBride finished his cigarette, stubbed it out underfoot, and with a sardonic chuckle remarked, 'Ah well, Jim, as the man said, a policeman's lot is not a happy one!', recalling that the funeral of the great Sir Arthur Sullivan himself would take place that very day in London. The two men continued on their beat up Marlborough Street, Martin changing step to keep correct pace with his burly colleague. As they reached its junction with St Patrick's Street, James Martin came to an abrupt halt. He was the first to see the eerie glow, something altogether different to the usual dancing shadows of the night. Even as he watched, aghast, the glow brightened and then he saw the flames. 'Oh my God, Bill', he gasped, 'Perry's is on fire!' The two policemen quickly decided on a course of action. Martin would run to the nearby offices of the Cork Constitution newspaper at 40 Marlborough Street to alert the fire brigade while his colleague would hasten to the scene of the fire.

He later would recall that:

> I dashed into the '*Constitution*' Office and said 'Oh, God, Perry's is on fire;
> send for the Brigade', because I was so confused and excited that I thought it
> was Perry's that was on fire. Constable McBride ran down to the burning and
> I ran round and met the other men at the corner of Cook Street on the Mall
> – Constables O'Sullivan and O'Malley. When we got back there was nobody
> at the fire except Constable McBride and Mr Dawson, from the '*Constitution*'.
> At this time we did not see anybody at the windows, so we tore down the
> shutters under 74, hoping to get upstairs, but we found the entrance to the
> stairs and the whole shop a mass of flames. We then tore down the shutters
> under No.75 and pulled away the iron bars with our hands, but we found that
> we could not get into the place.[8]

Glancing up, to their horror they saw a man gesticulating at the third-storey
window.

Con Fleming, a tobacconist, with shops in Winthrop Street and George's
Street, his wife, who ran a millinery business on the premises, and family consisting of two boys and two girls, their nurse and maid occupied the two topmost
floors of Messrs Bernard J. Alcock, grocers and wine and spirit merchants at
Nos 74 and 75 St Patrick's Street. A four-storey building with a frontage of
some 56 feet, it was an impressive Victorian business premises.[9] Mr and Mrs
Fleming slept on the second floor with one of the boys. The boys, Cecil (9) and
Leo (6), now that they were getting that bit older, had baulked at occupying
the same room as their sisters and the two young women in the nursery on the
floor above, so the parents had agreed to allow them sleep in their bedroom, in
a separate bed, on alternate nights. Tonight was little Leo's turn.

The premises of
Alcock and Co.,
74-75 St Patrick's
Street *c.*1900.

Fifteen minutes after midnight, Con Fleming had made his way down through the darkened premises, turned off the gas at the meter in the hall, and gone immediately to bed. On the top floor Cecil, Ivy (4), Grace (2), and Nurse Margaret McCarthy (18) and Julia Donovan (20) slept soundly.[10] Then:

> My wife shouted out 'Con, Con'. I jumped up, and the first thing I saw were huge flames shooting up outside the large glass window. I said, 'My God, the house is on fire'. I ran through the corridor to the front window and shouted for help. The first person I saw was a policeman who was running towards the house. My wife was with me, and the child was left behind. I thought I would be able to go back for him. I lost my head, but I did not think it would be so serious. I tried to go back. The place was full of thick smoke. I tried to get up to the nursery, but it was impossible. I would be suffocated. For the time I was at the front window the smoke increased greatly. Mrs. Fleming also tried to go upstairs, but I told her that there was no possible chance of doing so. The people in the street told us to jump for our lives.[11]

Meanwhile, over at the Central Fire Station the General Alarm was clanging stridently, alerting the members to the outbreak. The dutyman at Sullivan's Quay, in turn, notified by telephone, the fireman-in-charge at the Fireman's Rest on Lavitt's Quay to take his escape to a fire on St Patrick's Street. Fireman Jim Barry at once began trundling his wheeled escape, in the 'bridged' position, up Nelson's Place, left into Academy Street and right into St Patrick's Street, a journey of only a few minutes, while Capt. Hutson and his station party quickly prepared the horses for turn-out (including the brand-new Jessop Browne four-wheeled hose reel purchased at a cost of £30 only a few weeks before), and set off at a gallop. The time was 3.10a.m., and the fire brigade was headed for Perry's, not Alcock's.

Events at Alcock's were now unfolding rapidly. The commotion in the street, and the incessant blowing of policemen's whistles, had alerted the staff sleeping on the upper floors of Grant's Department Store just across the street. Locked in for the night, with access to neither keys nor telephone, to their consternation they realized that their only role would be as reluctant spectators of the drama being played out before their very eyes. One quick-witted staff employee, appreciating that people might begin to jump before the arrival of the fire brigade, began throwing out bedding to the crowd below.[12]

As the moon rose dully through the pall of smoke, a mass of burning material, whirled along by the convection currants from the blaze, was seen to land on the tower of nearby Ss Peter and Paul's Church. It seemed that this would be engulfed too. The fire continued its capricious leaps. A brand landed on Lipton's Tea Warehouse next door and wisps of smoke soon issued from the rear of the building. As the pace of the fire increased, the conflagration lit up the sky almost to the brilliancy of daylight; 'from any part of the city it could be seen from the red glare in the sky that a fire of tremendous magnitude was in progress'.[13]

The Flemings, perched on the second-floor window sill, had by now given up all hope of being able to get back into the building to save little Leo. They knew well, too, that their three other children and two employees were trapped on the floor above them with no hope of rescue via the stairs. In one last moment of anguish they made the decision to jump:

> The people in the street told us to jump for our lives. I got my wife by the hands and dropped her down onto the facia, and then she jumped down into the street. The police caught her below. She got hurt in the first fall. In the jump she escaped unhurt. I tried to go back again to the bedroom, but I found it was no use, and then I had to jump in the same way as my wife into the street.[14]

Seconds later, there was a collective gasp from the crowd when there was a sickening thud, as another body hit the pavement. Julia Donovan had thrown herself from the top-most window and, 'struck the centre of the blanket with her feet, and the force of it knocked five of us down. She went through it as through tissue-paper'.[15]

The police quickly commandeered a pony and trap and, with Cons. Martin driving, set off for the North Infirmary with the misfortunate girl moaning quietly in the back. There she remained critically ill with serious spinal injuries. Then, 'Captain Hutson and the members of the Fire Brigade arrived, and were received by loud cheering from the crowd who realised that relief had come'.[16] In spite of being initially directed to the wrong address, just over three minutes had elapsed since the brigade had been alerted.[17]

On seeing the predicament of those at the window some fifty feet above the ground, Fm. Barry now made a quick decision, which flew in the face of all his training. He decided to 'run' the escape straight up the wall of the building on its head-iron and rollers, the rest of the crew winding feverishly on the extend-ing gear. Such a manoeuvre was fraught with danger as the escape might come to rest with either its carriage wheels or lever wheels off the ground. In such a position, when a weight – such as a person stepping out on to the head of the escape – was transferred on to it, the jolting of the apparatus thus balanced, might cause the chocks to become displaced and the drop-bolts not to hold. If that happened, the escape might 'take charge' and, running back, spill anyone on its upper extensions onto the ground. Only in the most extreme circum-stances, where actual seconds, rather than minutes, counted, should a wheeled escape be operated in such a manner. Thankfully, on this occasion, Barry's ini-tiative was rewarded and the escape held firm.

Auxiliary Firemen Peter Murphy and Martin Higgins mounted the escape and were climbing rapidly even before it had come to rest, and in a trice were at the window. Nurse McCarthy's cool demeanour now came into its own. Calmly remaining at her 'post of danger'[18] (the actual window frames were on fire) she handed the three brave little children to the firemen, one by one, who brought them swiftly to ground level, each time passing through 'a regular sea of fire' for, by now, the entire facade of the building was engulfed.[19] Mr R.O'Donovan of the *Cork Constitution* later deposed that 'he thought the fire escape could scarcely survive in the fire. Fireman Murphy certainly showed extraordinary heroism because he passed through the flames'[20] The fire chief, realizing that all on the ladders were in mortal danger of being roasted alive, quickly ordered a spray branch to be directed as a protective barrier over them. This action helped to cool them and save them from the worst effects of the heat and flames, and provided a breathable atmosphere in their immediate vicinity. Only when the last of the children was safely on the fire escape did Maggie McCarthy step out into the waiting arms of Aux.Fm. Higgins, who brought her safely to the ground.

But the firemen's work was still far from over. There was still the question of the missing child and the fire, now seriously threatening Lipton's, English's, Thompson's, and Ss Peter and Paul's, to be brought under control. And a wave of anxiety was spreading over the crowd for the safety of W. Harrington and Son Ltd., druggists and chemical purveyors, at No.80, many fearing the consequences should these premises become involved and wondering aloud where the fire would be stopped.

Murphy and Higgins now made a last-ditch attempt to rescue little Leo, last seen on the second floor. Quickly attaching a life-line to the escape, they entered the room without the luxury of any kind of breathing apparatus and were immediately choking in a cloud of smoke.[21] The whole room was engulfed in flames. Hot tongues, like some evil animal, licked the walls, then billowed back across the ceiling. Dropping to their hands and knees, they crawled slowly forward, making a mental note of features which might assist them in retracing their route to safety. Murphy was in front, his free hand lightly clenched, back uppermost, feeling for obstructions. But there was no way of seeing whether there was anyone still alive in the building let alone trying to rescue them. No human being could have survived the appalling conditions. There was a crash of falling timber. The suffocating heat was getting to them now, on the backs of their necks, burning their ears. With great regret, they decided on the futility of the effort and made their way back out onto the ladder. Hardly had they done so when the dreaded 'flashover' – the bogey of all firefighters - took place. Everything in its path was instantly incinerated. All further attempts at rescue, or of saving Alcock's, were abandoned. The strategy now was to stop the spread of the conflagration along the street.

With his men braced against the kick of the hoses, their black shapes clearly silhouetted against the red glow, Capt.Hutson brought six powerful jets to bear on the fire from St Patrick's Street, Paul Street, Ss Peter and Paul's Place, and

Conjectural image of the drama unfolding at the fatal fire at Alcock's in the early hours of 27 November 1900.

even from the interior of the church itself. In spite of the best efforts of the fire brigade, Thompson's and Lipton's were badly damaged. Ss Peter and Paul's however, escaped practically unscathed, but it had been a close-called thing; some of the stained glass windows melted so intense was the heat. By six in the morning, the fire had died and the glow disappeared from the street. Later that morning, the badly-charred remains of the missing child were found by John Twomey, foreman carpenter with the corporation, who was in charge of a gang clearing away the debris. The body, still in its metal bed, was found at the rear of the ground floor, having fallen with the upper floors as they collapsed. It was covered with rubble. So extensive was the destruction that the cause of the fire was never established. Suspicion fell, however, on the cookhouse of Thompson's Restaurant situated at the back of the block of buildings.

The *Cork Constitution* in its editorial on 28 November praised the brigade for the manner in which the rescues were effected and the conflagration tackled, but asked:

> Can nothing be done to diminish the danger attendant upon sudden outbreaks of fire? In London, and in other cities, the first person who notices an outbreak of fire can not only apprise the Fire Brigade of the fact, but locate the fire, by the simple process of breaking a pane of glass in the nearest Fire Alarm apparatus.

It urged the corporation to give serious thought to installing such a system in Cork, and also asked that the practice of erecting shutters on shop windows by night should be abolished in favour of wire guards. It transpired that policemen on the beat had passed the building only some twenty minutes earlier when the fire must then have been raging within, but were unaware that anything was wrong due to the shutters being up. Finally, it exhorted anyone sleeping on the upper floors of buildings to keep a coil of rope in the bedroom capable of reaching to the ground.

The council only briefly considered the proposition to install a street fire alarm system. Apart altogether from the initial hefty cost of installation, the system worked on a closed-circuit requiring an expensive continuous flow of electric current day and night. The scheme was perfectly reasonable: a system of alarm pillars erected on the pavements at key points about the city, each pillar housing a telephone as well as an alarm handle. All an alarmist had to do to notify the fire brigade of an outbreak was to pull on the handle. This action immediately registered at a Central Fire Station, identifying the location of the alarm pillar (not the address of the fire). Policemen on the beat were issued with a special key by which they could also access the telephone housed on top of the pillar. As far back as 1880, however, when the system was first introduced to London, Capt. Shaw had warned:

> We have received [numerous] false alarms, many of which were, without doubt, wilfully raised. Thus it will be seen that the great advantage of the system has not been obtained without harassing the men and casting doubt on the value of all messages received by these instruments. This has been the experience of all places which have adopted the system of street fire alarms, but I had great hope that in a city such as London, we should have been free from an annoyance which, if persevered in, must eventually force us to discontinue what ought to be a very great improvement.

In 1897, such was the scale of their nuisance value, the Metropolitan Fire Brigade briefly considered adapting their alarm pillars by fitting a device which would grab the alarmist's hand and detain him or her until the brigade's arrival.[22] Wisely, the idea was quietly dropped.

Despite these reservations, Dublin saw its first street fire alarms installed in 1903; an initial scheme consisting of twelve pillars, all located on the city's north side. The system was never adopted in Cork.

If the heroes of that awful night to remember were Aux. Fm. Murphy and Higgins, the heroine was, undoubtedly, young Margaret McCarthy. In the days and weeks following the fire, letters to the newspapers lauding her courageous action took up many column inches. A 'Maggie McCarthy Fund' was launched, the first contributors being some English and Irish commercial travellers who,

while staying at the Victoria Hotel, had a grandstand view of the whole gripping spectacle as it unfolded. To kick-start the testimonial they donated £5. Just
over a week later, and with many weeks to go, it had grown to just under £60
with subscriptions flowing in from all over County Cork and beyond, including a shilling from 'A Coward'.

The bravery of Peter Murphy and Martin Higgins was not forgotten. Both
were awarded the Bronze Medal of the RSPLF. The awards were made by Lord
Mayor Edward Fitzgerald on behalf of the Society in open council at the City
Hall on Friday 22 March 1901, who said:

> He never discharged a duty with more pleasure than he now did in present-
> ing the two young firemen with those medals. He congratulated them on the
> heroic manner in which they had acted on the occasion. They ought [to] be
> proud of those medals all their lives, and while hoping that both lads would
> long be spared to their families and the city expressed the belief that they
> would act again similarly should the occasion arise.

'The Rescuers and the Rescued' pictured in the aftermath of the fire at Alcock's. Front row, from left: Fireman James Barry, Cecil, Ivy, and Grace Fleming with their nursemaid Margaret McCarthy. Back row from left: Auxiliary Firemen Peter Murphy and Martin Higgins.

It was a fulsome tribute from a man who, in a moment of frustration some ten years before, had been among the City Fathers that had suggested the fire brigade should be disbanded. It was perhaps final proof, if any was required, that the brigade under Alfred Hutson's tutelage had finally 'arrived'.

In the weeks following the fire, the fire chief and the city engineer, Mr Cutler, were tasked to carry out fire safety audits of 'all the large warehouses in the city', and across County Cork too there was a flurry of activity as communities reviewed their scanty fire protection arrangements, the experience of Queenstown (Cobh) being fairly typical. When their 'splendid fire escape' was extricated after 'a considerable time' from its location in the Town Market yard with the object of extending it against a nearby building:

> A greater surprise awaited those who assembled to witness the experiment. Although a number of men laboured energetically under the direction of the Engineer ... the escape could not be put up to the house. In fact, nobody seemed to know anything about it, and general merriment varied the operation.[23]

Had anyone learned anything?

Conclusion

It is almost inconceivable that the great fires which devastated Cork in times past could ever occur again. Today, within minutes of an alarm being raised, state-of-the-art fire appliances, manned by highly-trained crews, are on site to launch an immediate attack on an outbreak.

Fire remains, as it has been throughout the ages, a hard-working and adaptable servant when suitably confined and controlled. When uncontrolled, it becomes a devastating menace. Constantly we hear of fresh methods, of improved processes, and new materials, many of which bring with them urgent demands for careful thought about combating the risks inherent in their use. New materials can have a high rate of combustion, a modern process can produce toxic waste, and a new method can be responsible for an increase in the number of accidents if it is not properly controlled. But, 'there is no new thing under the sun' and the danger posed to a community by today's chemical plant was replicated in medieval Cork by the local alchemist. And accidental fires which had their origins in artisans' establishments were responsible for some of the greatest conflagrations in history, including the Great Fire of London in 1666, which consumed more than 436 acres, 13,000 houses, and eighty-seven parish churches.

The Cork Improvement Act of 1852 gave Cork Corporation sweeping powers. For the first time in its history it had the power to strike a rate, but it was the Cork Improvement Act of 1856 that finally allowed the corporation to take over the affairs of the monopolistic Cork Pipe Water Company which had effectively held the city to ransom for years, providing piped water only to those who could afford to pay for it. By 1858, a minor miracle had been wrought in Cork. The new waterworks were finished and water, for the very first time, began to flow into the homes of rich and poor alike. In February 1858, Sir John Benson, the corporation's consultant engineer, reported that 'at every eighty yards hydrants, or 'fire cocks', are being inserted ... for the occasions of fires'. A powerful jet of water could now be projected over the highest building in Cork, on the Grand Parade. Only with the inexorable expansion of the city out into the suburbs, and the mains, in some instances, being laid too great a distance from the reservoirs to provide effective firefighting water did the need for a steam fire engine first become manifest.

In fact, in June of 1859, Benson had reported to the corporation that, 'the insurance engines could be done away with as the hydrants could be used with perfect effect'. This remark was, without doubt, seized upon by the insurance companies who saw in it an opportunity to begin the process of their withdrawal from operational firefighting. Under pressure from their respective head offices in London who had already begun that course of action, a discernible change in their *modus operandi* took place. The development appears to have been a retrenchment to their original position of some sixty years earlier: that fire suppression was, first and foremost, a business arrangement between an insurance company and its client. If you paid for a firefighting service you were entitled to one, if you didn't, you weren't.

As we have seen, two notable fires in Cork City in the early 1860s served to underline their change in attitude, although the criteria they applied are difficult to gauge. When fire broke out in Long's public house on George's Street on 26 February 1861 and a family of seven perished, not one of the insurance brigades responded to the call, even though the fire address was but a short distance of all three engine houses: the REA (South Mall); the Atlas (Cook Street), and the West of England (Anderson's Quay). The building was insured, but not, apparently, with any of them. And when fire engulfed the West Wing of Queen's College in May 1862, only one insurance engine responded, the REA, and then only after a lapse of over two hours. On this occasion, the premises were not insured at all. The dates are significant. In London, in 1861, the greatest conflagration the metropolis had witnessed since the Great Fire of 1666 occured. The huge claims bill of £2.5 million brought the whole insurance industry to its knees. Thus began the process of the withdrawal of the insurance companies from fire suppression, a process that would culminate in Ireland in the following year with the establishment, by Act of Parliament, of the Dublin Fire Brigade, and in Britain, in 1866, with the creation of the Metropolitan Fire Brigade.

In Britain, the iconic figures of Braidwood and Shaw would become the benchmarks by which all succeeding fire chiefs for years would be judged. Ireland produced no such charismatic figures, although Cork City parliamentarian and founder of the *Cork Examiner,* John Francis Maguire M.P., well travelled man–of–affairs, thoroughly versed in the many developments being introduced across the water, bravely attempted to mark his own place in local history by harnessing Capt. Shaw's affection for his native place by commissioning him to produce a report on the viability of a fire service for Cork. That audit was compiled in Shaw's parent's home at Monkstown in February 1864. When the City Fathers calculated that the brigade envisaged would mean an additional half a penny on the rates, the report was pigeon-holed, Maguire's efforts being thwarted at every turn. His political detractors, well aware that contemporary legislation contained no element of compulsion, procrastinated year in, year out, until eventually in 1877, did they grudgingly budget to establish a fire brigade for the city, and then only 'if the whole thing could be done for under £500 a year'. Sadly, Maguire did not live to see the project dear to his heart come to fruition; he died in 1872. Thus did the minuscule unit – a 'Thin Red Line' of an officer and four men (a third of what Shaw had envisaged) to serve a population in excess of 80,000 – come into being. It may not have been what was actually required, but it was a start.

As Alfred Hutson left City Hall following his final committee meeting of the nineteenth century, the clock in the bell tower tolled twelve, but on history's clock it was sunset. His lifetime measured the immense rush and sweep of one of history's most remarkable eras of change. His long term of office, from 1891 to his retirement in 1928 at the age of seventy-nine, coincided with a period of momentous transformation, not alone in European history but in Ireland's history as well, incorporating wars, revolutions, and internecine strife. The new Ireland, unimaginable when he was appointed, would be forged through violent struggle, its troubled birth leaving deep scars in a society already over-whelmed by economic disadvantage. Despite such unpromising origins, the Irish Free State not only survived, but developed into a vibrant democracy, one in which the rule of law, parliamentary authority, and the will of the people remained paramount just as supremely cultured nations like Italy and Germany were succumbing to darker systems. And frequently, on a local level, Captain Hutson and the men of Cork Fire Brigade would find themselves at the very epicentre of that history-making epoch.

Appendix 1.

COST OF CORK FIRE BRIGADE FROM 1 OCTOBER 1877 TO 1 JUNE 1880.

Hose: £276 12s.4d.
Escape: £90 0s.0d.
Reel: £52 14s.2d.
Hydrants: £66 1s.6d.
Horse and harness: £59 6s.0d.
Forage: £85 6s.0d.
Repairs: £183 7s.10d.
Misc.: £38 1s.1d.
Rent and rates: £138 9s.0d.
Gaslight: £84 14s.9d.
Coal: £49 13s.0d.
Clothing: £176 13s.0d.
Staff: £744 15s.11d.
Supernumeraries: £60 1s.0d.

Total: £2096.10s.1d.

Average cost of house, fire, light and clothing, viz:
£60 a year for Superintendent.
£120 a year for staff of five men.
£24 each, or nearly 9s.5d per week.

Signed: John Cahill,
Treasurer's Office,
Municipal Buildings.
June 15, 1880.

Appendix 2.

CORK FIRE BRIGADE SCALE OF CHARGES.

For a distance not exceeding three miles from the Fire Station, Sullivan's Quay, and for a period not exceeding four hours from the time the Brigade leaves to the time of returning to the Station:

Attendance of Superintendent: £2 2s.0d.
Do. Foreman: £1 10s.0d.
Do. Turncock: £1 1s.0d.
Do. Firemen (each): £0 7s.6d.
Use of Fire Engine: £10 10s.10d.
Hose reel and hose: £5 5s.0d.
Horse: £1 1s.0d.
Damage to Engine, hose and appliances – The actual cost of making good.

Additional charge when the above-mentioned limits of time or distance are exceeded:

* For every mile or part of a mile beyond the three-mile limit – one-fifth of the foregoing charges.

* For every hour or part of an hour in excess of the four-hours limit – one-fourth of the foregoing charges.

All such charges to be paid to the City Treasurer, at his office, Municipal Buildings 26 February 1896.

Appendix 3.

NOMINAL ROLL OF MEMBERS OF CORK FIRE BRIGADE 1877-1900.

Mark Wickham (Supt): 12 October 1877-18 November 1897 (dis).

John Walsh: 15 November 1877-19 November 1883.

Patrick Ellard (1): 15 November 1877-6 January 1879.

James Sheriff: 15 November 1877-19 October 1878.

Michael McCarthy (1): 15 November 1877-31 March 1884.

John Sullivan: 23 October 1878-6 January 1879.

Michael Ryan (Sgt 27 July 1888): 6 January 1879-19 August 1891.

Michael Thompson (Sgt 27 July 1888): 6 January 1879-18 May 1891 (dis).

Jeremiah Crowley (Turncock): 13 May 1879-20 February 1894 (dis).

Patrick Ellard (2): 23 July 1883-?

Thomas Wiseman: 23 July 1883-29 September 1884.

William Gloyne: 8 January 1884-December 1913.

Keane Mahony: 15 October 1884-November 1900.

Michael McCarthy (2): 20 August 1888-April 1897.

William Purcell: 20 August 1888-22 June 1892.

James Keating: 20 August 1888-26 August 1912.

Nicholas Butler: 20 August 1888-22 June 1892.

John Murphy: 20 August 1888-March 1913.

Philip Lecane: 20 August 1888-January 1919 (dis).

Patrick Higgins (Turncock): 12 October 1888-24 February 1926.

Thomas Healy: 20 July 1892-12 January 1927 (dis).

Patrick Fox: 20 July 1892-31 August 1892.

Alfred J. Hutson (Supt): 1 July 1891-23 February 1928.

James Barry: 30 September 1891-July 1905 (dis).

Edward McCarthy: 23 September 1891-?

John Reardon: 31 August 1892-November 1903 (dis).

Timothy O'Leary: December 1897-1 September 1928.

Martin Higgins: December 1897-?

Charles McCarthy: December 1897-?

John Thompson (1): September 1899-April 1900.

John Thompson (2): October 1901-?

James Lyons: September 1899-?

Alfred J. Hutson, jnr: August 1891-January 1900.

J. Ahern: January 1900-?

Peter Murphy: April 1900-?

dis = died in service.

This incomplete nominal roll has been gleaned from the hand-written minutes of the Waterworks and Fire Brigade Committee, now deposited in the Cork City and County Archive. Confusingly, the names of fire brigade members were often transliterated phonetically, as council members pronounced them. Thus Healy is sometimes entered as 'Hailey', Reardon as 'Reardan', 'Riordan' or 'O'Riordan', O'Leary as 'Leary' and Keating with a silent 'e', spelt 'Keatinge'. 'Keane' Mahony is often entered as 'Kean' although he seems to have written his name with an 'e'. No entirely accurate record of members' service during the fire brigade's formative years appears to have survived.

Appendix 4

CHRONOLOGY OF SOME NOTABLE CORK CITY FIRES
(EARLIEST TIMES TO 1900)

Date, Area/Location, Attribution

820, 833, 913, 915, 960, 978, 995, 1013, Cork, Viking raids
1030, Cork, Accident.
1064, Cork, War.
1080, Cork, War.
1087, Cork, Accident
1089, Cork, War.
1127, Cork, War.
1378, Cork, War.
1388, Cork, War.
1612, Cork, Accident.
31 May 1622, Cork (hundreds dead), Electrical storm.
22-29 September 1690, City and suburbs, War.
20 June 1726, St Nicholas' church, Electrical storm.
28 May 1727, South suburbs (117 houses), Accident.
1727, South Chapel, Accident.
2 May 1753, Bowling Green Lane (4 dead), Accident.
6 June 1762, Cat Lane (150 houses), Accident.
10 September 1766, Bandon Rd (74 houses), Accident.
21 June 1770, Hammond's Fields (6 houses), Accident.
6 June 1775, Fair Hill (30 houses), Accident.
28 February 1777, Attiwell Hayes' Malt-Kiln, Accident.
7 December 1799, Red Abbey Sugar House, Accident.
23 August 1800, Cat Lane (50 houses), Accident.
18 November 1802, George's Quay, Accident.
26 October 1807, Lane's Brewery, Accident.

16 October 1808, Chapel Lane (12 houses), Accident.

15 March 1810, Barrett and Keays' turpentine factory, Accident.

1 June 1811, Beamish and Crawford, Mary Street, Accident.

3 June 1820, North Cathedral, Suspicious.

12 April 1840, Theatre Royal, suspicious.

19 April 1840, George's Quay, Accident.

17 March 1848, Lane's Steam Mill, Accident.

11 June 1848, St Patrick's Street/Cook Street, Accident.

24 December 1850, Cork Patent Saw Mills, Suspicious.

27 December 1850, Winthrop Street/St Patrick's Street, Accident.

6 January 1858, Grand Parade, Accident.

26 February 1861, George's Street (7 dead), Accident.

15 May 1862, Queen's College, Suspicious.

10 June 1863, St Patrick's Street, Accident.

11 June 1863, North Main Street (1 dead), Accident.

4 December 1863, Morrisson's Island (1 dead), Accident.

16 October 1874, Daunt's Square/Grand Parade (4 dead), Suspicious.

1 May 1876, Dunbar Street/White Street, Accident.

19 October 1877, Merchant's Quay/North Street, Accident.

22 March 1878, St Patrick's Street/Maylor Street, Accident.

28 May 1883, King Street, Accident.

19 June 1886, Crosse's Green, Accident.

9 February 1887, St Luke's church, Accident.

23 February 1887, King Street, Accident.

27 March 1891, Cork Courthouse, Accident.

4 December 1893, King Street, Accident.

22 June 1895, Great George's Street (1 dead), Accident.

4 September 1894, Blackpool Flax Mills, Accident.

20 July 1897, Blackpool Flax Mills, Accident.

27 November 1900, St Patrick's Street (1 dead), Accident.

The above list is, of course, far from comprehensive. It contains only a minuscule cross-section of noteworthy fires that occurred in Cork city during the period under review. Additionally, in the absence of proper records, it is impossible to quantify the loss of life in fires during the city's early history.

Where 'accident' is given as the likely cause for a particular fire, this is based on the newspaper reports of the day, or, in the case of the early years, from subsequent chroniclers' accounts. No forensic analyses were carried out in the aftermath of fires to determine how they started, and such examinations as did take place were, at best, cursory, with little or no scientific basis. 'Suspicious' means that there was an implication that the fire was started maliciously, although, in none of the cases outlined above, was anybody ever charged in a court of law.

Appendix 5.

Former name: Present name.

Albert Quay: MacSwiney Quay (in front of City Hall).

Anglesea Road: Anglesea Street.

Blarney Lane: Blarney Street.

Brunswick Street: St Augustine's Street.

Charlotte Quay: Fr Mathew Quay.

Clarence Street: Gerald Griffin Street.

Cove Lane: Douglas Street.

Duncan Street: Grattan Street.

Fish Street: Merchant's Street (now extinguished).

Gaol Road: College Road.

Gt Britain Street: Great William O'Brien Street.

Gt George's Street: Washington Street.

George's Street (aka Old George's Street): Oliver Plunkett Street.

King Street: MacCurtain Street.

Maypole Lane: Evergreen Street.

Maypole Road: Evergreen Road.

Mallow Lane: Shandon Street.

Nile Street: Sheare's Street.

Nelson's Place (aka Nelson Place): Emmet Place.

Queen Street: Fr Mathew Street.

Victoria Quay: Kennedy Quay.

Warren's Place: Parnell Place.

Bibliography

PRIMARY SOURCES

MANUSCRIPTS

Cork City and County Archives
PR2, Poer Family Documents, 1703-1908.
U11, Index to Council Books of the Corporation of Cork, 1710-1841.
CPCO1 [CP/C/A], Cork Corporation Council Minutes, 1710-1732.
CPGC [CM/GC], Cork Corporation General Committee 1867-1878.
CP/C/CM/WW/A/, Cork Corporation Waterworks and Fire Brigade Committee
    Minute Books, 1867 -1903, seven volumes.
CPWA, Cork Pipe Water Company, 1768-1877.
U138, Youghal Town Records.
CPPW (CM/PW), Cork Corporation Public Works Committee Minutes 1896-1929.

Representative Church Body Library
05-I, Vestry Minute Book of St Nicholas' Parish, Cork 1721-1787.
05-1, Vestry Minute Book of St Nicholas' Parish, Cork 1788-1808.
05-1, Vestry Minute Book of St Peter's Parish, Cork, 1752-1846.
05-1, Vestry Minute Book of St Paul's Parish, Cork 1796-1926.
385, R. Caulfield, (ed), Transcript of the Will of Ald. John Coppinger, 1637.

Church of Ireland Parish Records (held in Cork)
Vestry Minute Book of St Ann's, Shandon, 1817-1935.
Vestry Minute Book of St Mary's, Shandon, 1814-1975.
Chapter Minute Book of St Fin Barre's Cathedral, Cork 1749-1808.
Vestry Minute Book of St Fin Barre's Cathedral, Cork, 1832-1870.
Chapter Tithe Book of St Fin Barre's Cathedral, Cork, 1771-1776.
Economy Account of St Fin Barre's Cathedral, Cork, 1777-1804.

Cork Fire Brigade (Cork City and County Archives and private)

Cork Fire Brigade Wages Book 1878–1883 (U213).
Superintendent's Rules and Instructions 1877.
Superintendent's Order and Reference Book 1885–1916.

Cork City Library

Report of the Pipe Water Commissioners and list of subscribers, 1809 (R.353.13).
Goad's Insurance Plan of Cork City (1:480), 1897.
Census of Ireland, 1911.
Richard Griffith (Ed), *Primary Valuation of Ireland* 1848-1864.

Cork County Library

Census of Ireland, 1901

The National Archives (Britain)

Returns of members of insurance company fire engine establishments to the British Admiralty for the years 1790-1828 (ADM 7/390)

British Library

Tract on the Great Fire of Cork 1622 (Shelfmark C.32.e.63)

Congregations

Annals of the Ursuline Sisters, Cork, Vol. 1 (1771-1827)
Ursuline Register of Novices, Cork (1771-1978)
Annals of the South Presentation Convent (1771-1892)

NEWSPAPERS

Cork Advertiser 1799-1823 (gaps).
Cork Constitution 1825-1922 (gaps).
Cork Evening Herald 1833-1836.
Cork Evening Post 1767/1769/1781-1791.
Cork Examiner 1841-
Cork Gazette and General Advertiser 1795.
Cork Herald 1870-1874/1896-1901.
Cork Journal 1756-1763.
Cork Mercantile Chronicle 1832-1835.
Cork Morning Intelligencer 1815-1816.
Cork Standard and *Evening Herald* 1837.
Cork Weekly Times 1833-1834.
Hibernian Chronicle 1769-1802.
Munster Advertiser 1839-1841.
New Cork Evening Post 1791-1806.
Southern Reporter 1817-1823 (gaps).

DIRECTORIES

County and City of Cork Post Office General Directory, 1842-1843, 1844-1845.
Cork Directory, 1812, 1817, 1826.
Cork Almanack, 1823,1843.
Guy's County and City of Cork Directory, various dates.
Henry and Coghlan's Munster Directory, 1867.
Holden's Directory of Cork, 1805, 1806, 1807.
James Haly's The New Cork Directory, 1795.
Robert H. Laing's Cork Mercantile Directory, 1863.
Pigot's City of Dublin and Hibernian Provincial Directory, 1824.
Slater's National Commercial Directory, 1846, 1881.
Stratten's Dublin, Cork, and South of Ireland, 1892.
West's Cork Directory 1809/10.

CATALOGUES

McGregor & Co.
Merryweather and Sons.
Shand, Mason & Co.
William Rose & Co

SECONDARY SOURCES

JOURNAL / NEWSPAPER ARTICLES

Coote, W., 'Fire Extinguishing in Ireland,' in *Journal of the Insurance Institute of Ireland,* (1904).
Dudley, R., 'Fire Insurance in Dublin 1700 – 1860' in *Irish Economic and Social History Journal* Vol. XXX (Dublin, 2003).
Fire, various dates.
Fireman, The, various dates.
Fire and Water, various dates.
Fox, J.B., 'Some Notes on the Shaw Family of Monkstown Castle', *JCHAS* Vol. 37 (1932).
Harrison, R.S., 'Harvey, Deaves and Harvey, Merchants', *JCHAS* Vol. 107 (2002).
Hogan, J., 'An Interview', *Dublin University Magazine,* Vol. 35 (Jan-June 1850).
Irwin, L., 'Politics, Religion and Economy: Cork in the 17th Century', *JCHAS* Vol. 85 (1980).
J.C., 'The Wonderful Battell of Starelings Fought at Corke, 1621', *JCHAS* Vol. 2A (1893).
McCarthy, C.J.F., 'The Celtic Monastery of Cork', *JCHAS* Vol. 48 (1943).
McCarthy, C.J.F., 'The Exchange', *JCHAS* Vols. 86/87 (1981/82).
Murphy, M., 'The Working Classes of Nineteenth Century Cork', *JCHAS* Vol. 85 (1980).
O'Brien, J.B., 'Cork Society in the 1850s', *JCHAS* Vol. 101 (1996).
O'Brien, J.B., 'The Council Books of the Corporation of the City of Cork', *JCHAS* Vol. 92 (1987).

O'Mahony, C., 'Industry at Crosse's Green', *JCHAS* Vol.104 (1999).

Ó Murchadha, D., 'The Siege of Cork in 1690', *JCHAS* Vol.95 (1990).

O'Shea, J.J., 'The Churches of the Church of Ireland in Cork City', *JCHAS* Vol.48 (1943).

O'Sullivan, S., 'Old Cork and its Corporations', series in *Cork Evening Echo* Feb. 1975-Jun. 1976.

Simms, J.G., 'Marlborough's Siege of Cork 1690', *Irish Sword* IX, No.35.

PUBLISHED WORKS

Blackstone, G.V., *A History of the British Fire Service* (London, 1957).

Braidwood, J., *Fire Prevention and Fire Extinction* (London, 1866).

Bielenberg, A., *Cork's Industrial Revolution 1780-1880* (Cork, 1991).

Byrne, J., *Byrne's Dictionary of Irish Local History* (Cork, 2004).

Bond, H. (ed), *Fire and the Air War* (Boston, 1946).

Cadogan, T., and Falvey, J, *A Biographical Dictionary of Cork* (Dublin, 2006).

Clarke, Sr U., *The Ursulines in Cork 1771-1996* (Cork, 1996).

Cockerell, H.A.L., & Green, E, *The British Insurance Business, A guide to its history and records* (Sheffield, 1994).

Cox, R., *Oh, Captain Shaw* (London, 1984).

Crowley J., Devoy R, Linehan D, O'Flanagan P (eds), *Atlas of Cork City* (Cork, 2005).

Caulfield, R. (ed), *The Council Book of the Corporation of the City of Cork, from 1609 to 1643 and from 1690 to 1800* (Surrey, 1876).

Coppersmith, Alexander the, *Remarks upon the Religion, Trade, Government, Police, Customs, Manners and Maladys, of the City of Corke* (first published 1737, reprinted by Tower Books, Cork, 1974).

Cody, B.A., *The River Lee, Cork and the Corkonians* (first published 1859, reprinted by Tower Books, Cork, 1974).

Cooke, R.T., *My Home by the Lee* (Cork, 1999).

Cadogan, T., (ed), *Lewis' Cork* (Cork, 1998).

Cleary, R.M., & Hurley M.F., *Excavations in Cork City 1984- 2000,* (Cork, 2003).

D'Alton, I., *Protestant Society and Politics in Cork 1812-1844* (Cork, 1980).

Davis, R.H., *Breathing in Irrespirable Atmospheres* (London, 1947).

ffolliott, R, *Biographical Notices 1756-1827* (n.d).

Fitzpatrick, J.M., *A City of Surprises* (Cork, 2005).

Gamble, S.G., *A Practical Treatise on Outbreaks of Fire* (London, 1926).

Geraghty, T., & Whitehead, T., *The Dublin Fire Brigade: A History of the Brigade, the Fires and the Emergencies* (Dublin, 2004).

Gibson, C.B., *The History of the County and City of Cork* (Cork, 1861).

Gray, W.F., *A Brief Chronicle of the Scottish Union & National Insurance Company 1824-1924* (Edinburgh, 1924).

Hayes, R.J., (ed.), *Sources for the History of Irish Civilization – Articles in Irish Periodicals* (Boston, 1970).

Hawkings, D.T., *Fire Insurance Records 1696-1920* (London, 2003).

Harrison, R.S., *Irish Insurance: Historical Perspectives* (Cork, 1992).

Heiden, van der , J. Snr, & J. Jnr, *Fire Engines and Water Hoses and the Method of Fighting Fires now used in Amsterdam*, (first published in 1690, second edition 1735. Translated into English by L. S. Multhauf and published in USA, 1996).

Henham, B., & Sharp, B, *Badges of Extinction: The Eighteenth and Nineteenth Century Badges of Insurance Office Firemen* (London, 1989).

Herlihy, J., *The Royal Irish Constabulary* (Dublin, 1997).

Herlihy, R., *A Walk through the South Parish* (Cork, 2010).

Holmes, R., *Marlborough* (London, 2008).

Helferty S., & Refaussé, R. (eds), *Directory of Irish Archives* (third ed), (Dublin, 1999).

Henchion R., *Henchion's Cork Centenary Remembrancer 1887-1987* (Cork, 1986).

Holloway, S., *Courage High!* (London, 1992).

Jefferies, H.A., *Cork: Historical Perspectives* (Dublin, 2004).

Johnson, G., *The Laneways of Medieval Cork* (Cork, 2002).

Lenihan, M., *Hidden Cork* (Cork, 2009).

Merryweather, J.C., *The Fire Brigade Handbook* (London, 1911).

Mason, A.E.W., *The Royal Exchange* (London, 1920).

McNamara, T.F., *Portrait of Cork* (Cork, 1981).

O'Shea, J.R., *The Red City* (Cork, 2005).

O'Sullivan, W., *The Economic History of Cork City from the Earliest Times to the Act of Union* (Cork, 1937).

O'Mahony, C., *In the Shadows: Life in Cork 1750-1930* (Cork, 1997).

O'Flanagan, P., & Buttimer C.G., (eds), *Cork: History and Society* (Dublin, 1993).

O'Callaghan, A., *Of Timber Iron and Stone* (Cork, 1991).

O'Callaghan, A., *The Lord Mayors of Cork 1900 to 2000* (Cork, 2000).

Pearson, R., *Insuring the Industrial Revolution: Fire Insurance in Great Britain 1700-1850* (Aldershot, 2004).

Pike, D.R., *Irish Insurance Directory* (Dublin, 1990).

Poland, P., *Fire Call!* (Cork, 1977).

Poland, P., (ed), *The First Five Years* (Cork, 1964).

Pettit, S., *This City of Cork, 1700-1900* (Cork, 1977).

Roetter, C., *Fire is the Enemy* (London, 1962).

Rynne, C., *The Industrial Archaeology of Cork City and its Environs* (Dublin, 1999).

Royal Exchange Assurance Corporation in Ireland from A.D. 1722, The History of, published by the Corporation, 1905, (anon).

Relton, F.B., *An Account of the Fire Insurance Companies, Associations, Institutions, Projects and Schemes Established and Projected in Great Britain and Ireland during the Seventeenth and Eighteenth Centuries* (London, 1893).

Shand, Mason & Co, *Rules and Regulations for Volunteer & Other Fire Brigades* (London, 1890).

Shaw, E.M., *Fire Protection* (London, 1876).

Shaw, E.M., *Fires in Theatres* (London, 1876).

Spalding, T., *Cork City: A Field Guide to its Street Furniture* (Cork, 2009).

Smith, C., *The Ancient and Present State of the County and City of Cork* (Cork, 1815).

Tuckey, F.H., *The County and City of Cork Remembrancer* (Cork, 1837).

Wright, B., *The British Fire Mark 1680-1879* (Cambridge, 1982).

Whitehead, T., *Fire Engines* (Aylesbury, 1981).

Windle, J., *Historical and Descriptive Notices of the City of Cork* (Cork, 1837).

Williams, B., *Fire Marks and Insurance Office Fire Brigades* (London, 1927).

Young, C.F.T., *Fires, Fire Engines and Fire Brigades* (London, 1866).

Yeo, A.W., *Atlas Reminiscent* (London, 1908).

Notes and References

INTRODUCTION

1. The Irish Annalists separated the Norsemen into two distinct groups: the *Lochlainn* (Norwegians) and the *Danair* (Danes). They described the *Lochlainn* as being fair-haired, the *Danair* as dark.
2. The first Viking onslaught on Cork occurred in about the year AD820. Further raids were recorded during the years 833, 913, 915, 960, 978, 995, and 1013.
3. Tuckey, F.H., *The County and City of Cork Remembrancer* (Cork, 1837), p.4.
4. Windle, J., *Historical and Descriptive Notices of the City of Cork* (Cork, 1837), p.6.
5. Revd Canon O'Mahony, 'The O'Mahony's of Kinelmeky and Ivagha' in *JCHAS* Vol.14 (1908), p.17.
6. Twohig, D.C., ed by Cleary, R.M., Hurley, M.F., & Shee-Twohig, E., *Skiddy's Castle and Christ Church, Cork: Excavations 1974-1977* (Cork, 1997).
7. When the walls were new and viewed from afar they would have appeared red and white. It is said that it is from this combination that the traditional Cork colours emanated.
8. Jefferies, H.A., *Cork: Historical Perspectives* (Dublin, 2004), p.71.
9. Cooke, R.T. & Scanlon, M., *Guide to the History of Cork* (Cork, 1985), p.40.
10. O'Súilleabháin, S., *Nósanna agus Piseóga na nGael* (Baile Átha Cliath, 1970).
11. *Ibid.* See also Máire MacSwiney Brugha, *History's Daughter* (Dublin, 2005), p.209.
12. Charter of 12 Edward II, 1318. See O'Sullivan, W., *The economic history of Cork City from the earliest times to the Act of Union* (Cork, 1937), p.288.
13. Geraghty, T., & Whitehead, T., *The Dublin Fire Brigade: a history of the brigade, the fires and the emergencies* (Dublin, 2004), p.1.
14. Webb, D.A, *An Irish Flora* (Dundalk, 1943), p.52; and Mac Coitir, N., *Irish Wild Plants* (Cork, 2006), p.183.
15. I quote just two examples: during the burning of the North Cathedral in Cork on 3 June 1820, and at a fire in Allihies, near Castletownbere, in the early hours of 12 September 1893.
16. McNamara, T.F., *Portrait of Cork* (Cork, 1981), p.8.
17. Stafford, T., *Pacata Hibernia, Ireland appeased and reduced or, an historie of the late Warres in Ireland*, etc. (London, 1633), reprinted Dublin, 1810.
18. Brown, R. & Thompson, W.S., *The Battle against Fire* (London, 1966), p.61.
19. O'Sullivan (1937), pp.50, 51.

CHAPTER 1

1. Sir Richard Cox, *Hibernia Anglicana, or, The Second Part of the History of Ireland* (London, 1689/90), p.39. Cox was Lord Chief Justice of Ireland in the reign of William and Mary, and Lord Chancellor under Queen Anne.

2. *A Relation of the Most Lamentable Burning of the Cittie of Corke, in the west of Ireland, in the Province of Monster, by Thunder and Lightning. With other most dolefull and miserable accidents, which fell out the last of May 1622 after the prodigious battell of the birds called Stares which fought strangely over and neare that Cittie the 12 & 14 May 1621. As it hath beene reported to diverse Right Honourable Persons. Printed this 20 of June 1622, London, Printed by I[ohn] D[awson] for Nicholas Bourne and Thomas Archer, 1622.* (British Library Tract, shelfmark C.32.e.63. Hereafter, *BL Tract*). See also the 'Annals of Cork' section in Dr Richard Caulfield's transcription of the *Council Book of the Corporation of the City of Cork from 1609 to 1643, and from 1690 to 1800* (Surrey, 1876), (hereafter Caulfield, *Council Book*).

3. De Barra, E., *Bless 'em all* (Cork, 1997), p.108.

4. 'They have sown the wind, and they shall reap the whirlwind', Hosea ch.8 v.7.

5. Ditzel, P., *Firefighting in World War Two* (Indiana, 1994), p.98. Other cities would be subjected to massive firestorms as the war progressed, notably Dresden (February 1945) and Tokyo (March 1945).

6. *Ibid*, p.100.

7. 31 May, on the Gregorian calendar adopted in 1752, equates to 11 June.

8. Bond, H. (ed), *Fire and the Air War* (Boston, 1946), p.100.

9. *BL Tract,* p.4

10. More formally, *Feuerschutzpolizei* (*FSchP*), literally, 'Fire Protection Police'. All German professional fire brigades (*Berufsfeuerwehren*) were, in 1938, nationalized and amalgamated into the German police system, being organized in regiments.

11. *Fire and the Air War*, p.100.

12. *BL Tract,* p.4

13. Variously called the 'Royal Street' or the 'Queen Majesty's Street' during the reign of Queen Elizabeth. At the time of the 1622 fire (during the reign of King James) it was referred to as the 'King's Street' or 'His Highness' Street'. Today, the thoroughfare comprises the North, and South, Main Streets.

14. Pettit, S.F, *My City by the Lee* (Cork, 1987), p.37.

15. See Johnson, G., *The Laneways of Medieval Cork* (Cork, 2002).

16. 'James the Shit'.

17. The chroniclers of the Great Fire of Cork mention three churches being within the city. Medieval Cork had three churches at one time: St Peter's, Holy Trinity (aka Christ Church) and St Laurence's, built, apparently, as a chapel-of-ease to Holy Trinity. St Laurence's stood not far from South Gate Bridge on the site now occupied by the former Beamish and Crawford's brewery. However, it is not named in any of the Cork maps of the early seventeenth century, which include the *Pacata Hibernia* map (*c*.1585-1600), the 1602 map (Hardiman collection, Trinity College, Dublin), or Speed's map (1610).

18. Irwin, L., 'Politics, religion and economy: Cork in the seventeenth century' in *JCHAS* (1980), p.7.

19. *Ibid*. Allowing for natural increase, inward migration, and the death toll from the fire, it may reasonably be concluded that the figure lay somewhere close to these two estimates.

20. John Coppinger (aka Copinger: later, Sir John) was High Sheriff of Co. Cork in 1617. On 5 October 1618 he was sworn a Councillor of the City of Cork, being elected Mayor on 1 October 1621. The Mayor and his family all survived the Great Fire. Sir John is mentioned in his father's will (RCB ref: 385) (who himself was Mayor in 1616 and 1619) as having been a severe trial to the old gentleman. Shortly after (Sir) John's marriage to Katherine Russell, he commenced a suit against his father who was arrested and imprisoned in Dublin Castle until he had made provision for his son. Sir John's mother was Katherine Roche of the landed Co. Cork family. The women of the Roche clan were renowned for their pertinacity. In 1644, Viscountess Fermoy was hanged at Cork's Gallows Green for refusing to renounce her Catholic faith (the first recorded execution on the site), and in 1649, Lady Roche, while defending her home, Castletown Roche, against the forces of the English parliament, shot dead one of the soldiers, for which she was subsequently hanged. Blanche, Lady de la Roche, Fermoy (*c.* 1275-1342) was Diana, Princess of Wales, twentieth great-grandmother. Sources: *DNB* (London, 2004), pp.16 and 460; Walter Arthur Coppinger, *History of the Copinger's or Coppingers* (Manchester, 1882).
21. From the French *Garde a l'eau!* – Beware of the water! – A throwback to our Norman ancestors.
22. Caulfield, *Council Book,* p.xxi.
23. *Ibid.*
24. G.V. Blackstone, *A History of the British Fire Service* (London, 1957), p.19.
25. BL *Tract,* p.5
26. *Ibid.*
27. This has variously been identified as Island Negay – a corruption of the Irish *Oileán na nGé* – an island lying between the south channel of the Lee and the south side of the present South Mall, so named after the Brent geese which migrated there from Arctic regions between November and March each year. Its location approximates to the present-day Morrison's Island. See C.J.F. McCarthy, 'When grasshoppers replaced a goddess on the South Mall', *CEE* 12 November 1985.
28. BL *Tract,* p.7.
29. Such a cloud is a phenomenon in the aftermath of a firestorm.
30. BL *Tract,* p.6.
31. Caulfield, *Council Book,* p.xxii.
32. Caulfield, *Council Book,* pp.102-103. The council's choice of date, the Feast of the Nativity of St John the Baptist (24 June), is interesting. The summer solstice was a key date on the pagan calendar, a time of fertility, passion, magic, and fire. St Patrick and the other early missionaries in Ireland adopted the heathen feasts and their adjuncts. It fell to St John's lot to get Midsummer (formerly dedicated to Baal and his fires) as John was regarded as a 'burning and brilliant lamp that precedes the True Light' (i.e. Christ). The Cork Council made it clear that all thatch had to be removed prior to 24 June 1623. Thus, the new Fire Prevention law was to come into effect on a date associated with fire in the public mind: Bonfire Night. Cork pre-empted the great city of London by some forty-four years with its bye-law forbidding thatch as a roofing material, blamed for the rapid spread of fire through the narrow streets.
33. BL *Tract,* p.6.
34. Crowley, J., Devoy R., Linehan, D., & O'Flanagan, P., (eds), *Atlas of Cork City* (Cork, 2005), p.422.

35. *BL Tract,* p.3.

36. Johnson, *Lanes* (Cork, 2002).

37. Jefferies (2004), pp.65, 66, 90.

38. Marlborough's fleet arrived in Cork Harbour on Sunday 21 September, and he entered the city, the victor, via South Gate Bridge on Monday 29 September. John Churchill (1650-1722) was the son of an impoverished English gentleman, Sir Winston Churchill. Following service as Page of Honour to the Duke of York, (later King James II) he secured a commission in the Guards in 1667 and was posted on active service overseas. In 1678, he married Sarah Jennings, a close friend of Princess Anne, James' daughter. He was largely responsible for the destruction of Monmouth's army, which had sought to overthrow James, at the Battle of Sedgemoor in 1685. In 1688, Churchill deserted James and moved his allegiance to William of Orange. It was at this point in his career that he vigorously prosecuted aspects of the war in Ireland, including the Siege of Cork. Following on his wife's loss of the queen's friendship, his position was greatly weakened and he was eventually dismissed from office, accused of corruption. See Richard Holmes, *Marlborough* (London, 2008).

39. 'A description of Cork two hundred years ago', in *JCHAS Vol.III* (1897), p.190.

40. The Religious Society of Friends did not use names for days of the week or months of the year since most of these names were derived from the names of pagan gods. Under the old Julian calendar the year began on 25 March (aka Lady Day); therefore March was the first month and February the twelfth month. When an event occurred in the months of January, February, or up to 25 March, the date was given as, for example, 1748/1749. Such a dating practice satisfied everyone, including the civil authorities.

41. Barclay, J., (ed), *Some Account of the Life of Joseph Pike of Cork, Ireland, who died in 1729* (London, 1837) pp.49-50. Pike committed his memories to paper some thirty years after the Siege. See also C.J.F. McCarthy, 'The Pikes in Cork history', *CEE* 13 March 1973.

42. Ó Murchadha, D., 'The Siege of Cork in 1690' in *JCHAS* Vol.95 (1990), p.5.

43. Red and white, the Cork colours: the 'Blood and Bandage'!

44. For a synopsis of the surviving accounts see Ó Murchadha (1990).

45. Pike account, p.52.

46. By the end of the Siege the defenders were reduced to, 'two small barrels of gunpowder, an hundred of ball at the most, and a good deal of match'. See Simms, J.G., 'Marlborough's Siege of Cork 1690' in the Irish Sword IX, no.35 (n.d), pp.113-123. In the engraving by the Dutch political caricaturist Romeijn de Hooghe (1645-1708) entitled *Innemen van Corck* (the capture of Cork), which appeared in the annual newssheet *Hollandsche Mercurius* in 1691, and which purports to show the city under bombardment, a pall of smoke is seen rising in the vicinity of Skiddy's Castle.

47. Caulfield, *Council Book*, p.326 (29 October 1707). The Williamite forces may well have brought their own portable firefighting appliances with them, for they were well-acquainted with fire engines and their operations. By 1690, the Dutch led the world in fire engine design and advanced firefighting practices, thanks to the Chief Fire Officer of Amsterdam, Jan van der Heiden, a renowned fire engineer. When William of Orange landed at Devon in 1688, included in his ship's manifest were three large fire engines under the personal supervision of Jon Lofting, a fire engine manufacturer. See Holloway, S., *Courage High* (HMSO, 1992), p.21.

48. Wealthy citizens were encouraged to provide the community with leather fire buckets, in much the same way as they might endow a public park with a bench today. The presentation of buckets, and other firefighting equipment, was regarded as a mark of civic-mindedness on the part of a prominent citizen. The Cork Council Book records at least two such endowments: in 1735 a Mr Carré (a member of the Huguenot community) gifted the city with a fire engine, and four years later James Piersey, a prominent wine merchant, provided the corporation with a fire engine and leather buckets. See Caulfield, *Council Book*, pp 541 and 592.

49. The inclement weather had dire consequences for both the Irish prisoners and their guards. According to the Revd Charles Leslie, a Protestant clergyman loyal to King James, 'the Garrison, after laying down their arms, were stripped, and marched to a marshy wet ground, where they were kept with guards four or five days, and not being sustained were forced through hunger to eat dead horses that lay about them, and several of them dyed for want'. The survivors were packed into gaols, houses and churches in such unsanitary conditions that large numbers died. Pike relates that the 'weather was wet and slobbery, the English soldiers as well as the Irish Prisoners, became very sickly and abundance of both sorts died, and the number so great that they buried them together in a hole every day'. (Ó'Murchadha,1990, p.12)

50. Edward Wetenhall (1636-1713) was born at Lichfield, England and educated at Cambridge where he graduated BA (1659) and MA at Oxford (1661). Consecrated COI Bishop of Cork and Ross in 1679 he died in London in 1713 and is buried in Westminster Abbey.

51. James' and William's troops both favoured red coats, red being the colour of the livery of the British monarchy. Shortage of supply, however, made absolute uniformity impossible in the Jacobite army, and coats of other colours were also worn, principally grey/white. The infantry wore broad-brimmed hats, full-skirted coats with wide cuffs, breeches, stockings, and shoes. See Hayes-McCoy, G.A., 'The red coat and the green' in the *Old Limerick Journal* – 1690 *Siege Edition* (Limerick, 1990), pp.9-10; and Carman, W.Y., *British military uniforms*, (Middlesex, 1957).

52. The practical test of coloured uniforms was on the battlefield, where, amid the thick clouds of smoke emitted by the weaponry of the period, uniforms would clearly stand out in their tactical positions. Most of the arms in the Jacobite army were French 'matchlock' muskets. Assuming the Duke of Grafton was standing in or about where present-day Rochford's Lane and Grafton Street bisect, he was well within the range of a matchlock, used by the sniper (supposedly a Cork blacksmith) on the city walls.

53. The senior Irish officers, including Col MacElligott and the Earls of Clancarty and Tyrone were incarcerated in the notorious Tower of London. Tyrone died shortly afterwards, and Clancarty, whose enormous Irish estates numbering some 135,000 acres had been confiscated, escaped to France. MacElligott was released in 1697 when the war with France came to an end, and rejoined the Stuart forces in the service of the French, being made Colonel of the Regiment of Clancarty Infantry. See Simms, *Siege,* p.122; and Childs, J., *The Williamite Wars in Ireland* (London, 2007), p.273.

CHAPTER 2

1. Caulfield, *Council Book,* p.236.
2. 'The windy day is not the day for scallops.' (i.e. thatching).
3. This may also be the legislation alluded to by Anthony Edwards in his *Cork Remembrancer* (1792) when, for 1707, he records 'Fires occasioned by servants, punishable' (p.129), for no other fire legislation is noted in the minutes of Cork Corporation for that year.
4. Caulfield, *Council Book,* p.330.
5. *Ibid,* p.371.
6. *An Act for preventing mischiefs that may happen by Fire. Acts and statutes made in a Parliament begun at Dublin, the twelfth day of November, Anno Dom.1715. In the second year of the reign of our most gracious sovereign Lord King George, before his grace Charles Duke of Grafton, and his excellency Henry Early of Gallway, Lords Justices General and General Governors of Ireland.*
7. The family name is spelled, variously, van der Heiden, Van der Heyde, van der Heijde, van der Heijden, van de Heijden, Van Der Heyden.
8. *Beschryving der nieuwlyks uitgevonden en geotrojeerde slang-brand-spuiten en hare wyze van brandblussen, tegenwoordig binnen Amsterdam in gebruik zynde.* Originally published in 1690, second edition 1735. Translated into English by L.S. Multhauf and published in USA, 1996.
9. The building stood until 1912 when it was demolished and replaced with a primary school. On the gable wall is a bust of Jan van der Heiden, Snr.
10. Geraghty and Whitehead (2004), p.3.
11. Above atmospheric pressure (1 bar).
12. Caulfield, *Council Book,* p.552.
13. *Ibid,* p.601.
14. *Ibid,* p.719.
15. *Ibid,* p.380. Early firefighting appliances were called, variously, 'pipe-engines', 'water-engines', or 'fire-engines'. The latter name stuck.
16. His twin brother reputedly was christened 'Christ came into the world to save'. However, depending on whose version one consults, these names are attributed to either 'Praise-God' Barbon's sons *or* brothers! Many fire service historians opt for the former, including G.V. Blackstone in *A History of the British Fire Service* (1957). Lady Antonia Fraser, on the other hand, in her biography of Oliver Cromwell, *Cromwell: Our Chief of Men* (London, 1973) chooses the latter option, but queries the hard evidence that anyone was so named, implying the story may be merely anecdotal.
17. Michael Hanson in 2000 *Years of London* (London, 1967), ranks Barbon as second only to John Nash as the greatest speculative developer that London has ever seen.
18. This company had no connection with the Phoenix company founded in 1782.
19. Blackstone, G.V., *A History of the British Fire Service* (London, 1957), p.48.

CHAPTER 3

1. Defoe, D., *A Tour Through the Whole Island of Great Britain* (first published 1724; reprinted by Penguin Classics, 1986), p.318.

2. *HC* 18 January 1787.

3. To an even older, Irish-speaking generation, Gallows Green was known as *Fatha na croithe*, 'the green field of the hangings'. See *CE Supplement* 22 September 1888.

4. The fire alarm would have tolled only from Protestant churches. The Relief Act of 1793 (33 Geo.III c. 21) did not repeal the prohibition against bells and steeples on Roman Catholic churches. See Revd Sr C. Meagher, 'Calendar of Bray papers' in *JCHAS* Vol.74 (1969), p.157.

5. The weekly return of deaths in London which began to be published in 1592.

6. A series of legislative enactments passed between 1691 (when Roman Catholics were excluded from Parliament) and 1727 (when they were completely disfranchised). Piecemeal legislative Relief Acts began to emerge towards the end of the eighteenth century, but penal legislation remained in force until the passing of the Catholic Emancipation Bill in 1829.

7. Byrne, J., *Dictionary of Irish Local History* (Cork, 2004), p.318.

8. The 1833 Church Temporalities Act disestablished the parish by abolishing Parish Cess. Subsequently, its local government and health functions devolved to the Grand Jury, later to the Poor Law Union and later still to the County and Rural District Councils under the Local Government Act of 1908.

9. For the list of books consulted see Bibliography.

10. *JCHAS*, Vol. 1A (1892), P.29.

11. St Fin Barre's Cathedral Chapter Minute Book (1749-1808).

12. St Mary's, Shandon Vestry Minute Book (1814-1975).

13. St Paul's Vestry Minute Book (1796-1848). (Ref: RCB 05-1).

14. *Ibid.*

15. *Ibid.*

16. St Peter's Vestry Minute Book (1752-1846). (Ref: RCB 05-1).

17. *CMC* 24 January 1812.

18. At the Easter Monday vestries, the various parish officers were elected and the monies required to be raised on the parish to cover the necessary expenses for the coming year agreed. All residents of a parish had to pay for the maintenance of the Church, upkeep of the parish poor, foundlings, the parish almshouse, and the salaries of the parish clerk, the vestry clerk, the beadle, and the sexton. Additional sums were allotted for the maintenance of the parish fire engine, the engine house, and the Engine Keeper's salary.

19. Cited 2006/12/05 http://etext.library.adelaide.edu.au/d/dickens/charles/d54sb/part 1.html

20. *HC* 18 January 1787. For Cork's First Citizen to accuse the church authorities of being criminally negligent in the provision of adequate firefighting services was a bit rich. In 1781, the corporation had terminated its 'fire service' by abolishing the position of Engine Keeper and transferring its remaining fire engine to St Nicholas's parish. See Caulfield, *Council Book*, 24 July 1781.

21. St Nicholas's Vestry Minute Book (1721-1787). (Ref: RCB 05-1).

22. Revd Sr M. Angela Bolster in correspondence with the author July 2001.

23. O'Connell, W.D., 'Augustinia Corcagiae 1746-1834' in *Analecta Hibernica* No.12 (January 1943), p.165.

24. O'Connell, W.D., *Cork Franciscan Records 1764-1831* (Cork, 1942).

25. 'When a matter is in doubt, side with the tradition'. The story is told of the Protestant clergyman from St Anne's Shandon who called on the Brother Superior of the North Monastery to claim the tithe. The Superior, Br Leonard, flatly refused to pay, whereupon the clergyman reminded him that he had the power to seize the corn growing in the fields around the Monastery. 'You may seize the corn', said Br Leonard, 'but the women in Peacock Lane will thresh it for you on the way out!' See *Meánmain na Mon* (Cork, 1951).

26. This had been invented by Ctesibius some 2,000 years earlier. Examples of early manual fire pumps may be seen at Kinsale Museum and at Charles Fort, Kinsale, Co. Cork.

27. See *CEE* (24 August 1977), 'The days when insurance companies fought the flames'.

28. *HC* 1 December 1800.

29. *CMC* 12 January 1814.

30. Holloway (London, 1992), p.25.

31. *CJ* 14 December 1753. Tuckey's Quay ran along the west side of the present Grand Parade. Nicholas Fitton lived 'at the end of Farrington Lane on Tuckey's Quay'. See *JCHAS* Vol.68, p.98.

32. Caulfield, *Council Book*, p.716.

33. Crofton Croker, T., *Researches in the South of Ireland 1812-1822* (London, 1824), p.187.

34. A 'preventer' was a long wooden pole with a hook on top, usually employed for pulling burning thatch from a roof. On 16 April 1719, the Council Book records that a Mr Wilson is to 'provide six poles with iron crooks to be put in proper places to prevent fire.' This is almost 100 years after the council passed a law, in the aftermath of Cork's Great Fire, expressly forbidding the use of thatch as a roofing material in the city.

35. A dispenser of medicine; a chemist.

36. Caulfield, *Council Book,* p.606.

37. *JCHAS* Vol.11 (1905), p.146.

38. *FDJ* 3 June 1727.

39. *CJ* 15 September 1766.

40. Tuckey's *Cork Remembrancer* for 6 June 1775.

41. For a list of executions carried out in Cork between 1712-1911 (including a number for fire-related offences) see Dr Colman O'Mahony, *In the shadows: life in Cork 1750-1930* (Cork, 1997), pp.329-354.

42. 'Peter's Stocks' may refer to the stocks adjacent to St Peter's church on the North Main Street. Close by St Peter's stood a large Cross where people congregated to hear proclamations and other announcements, and merchants and traders set up their stalls. Thus, by placing the stocks adjacent to a public meeting place, it ensured the maximum humiliation for the hapless offender. The stocks located near Christ Church on South Main Street are preserved in Cork Public Museum.

43. O'Mahony, *In the shadows*, p.64.

44. *Ibid*, p.59.

45. *Ibid*, p.58.

46. *Ibid*, p.59. Salt water contains twice the salinity that the human body can safely digest. It is a caustic brew, consisting of 78% sodium chloride with trace

elements of sulphate, magnesium, potassium, bicarbonate, and boric acid. The high potassium levels leak into the bloodstream and break down the red blood cells, forging the first link in a complex chain that leads to the onset of anaemia, increased physical weakness and, eventually, death.

47. 'Ordered, that £10 a year be paid Nich. Fitton, to keep the city fire engines in good repair, to play them once a month, and attend all accidental fires, to work the engines, and give a bond of £50 for due performance of these conditions'. (Caulfield, *Council Book,* 28 September 1759).

48. Now the Mercy Hospital, Grenville Place.

49. O'Kelly, M.J., 'Wooden water mains at South Terrace', in *JCHAS* Vol.75 (1970), p.125.

50. Fitzgerald, W.A., *Cork City Waterworks 1768-1984: History and Development* (Cork, 1984).

51. *Boyle's Magazine* (8 December 1806) contained a disparaging article on the avariciousness of, 'Mr. Lumley, who unites in his own person the offices of Governor, Treasurer, Secretary and Director' of the Pipe Water Company, and lamented how, 'our streets are regularly torn up ... and afterwards patched up in a most shameful manner'. The practice of digging up the streets to expose the mains in time of fire was prevalent as late as 1858 at least. On 9 January that year, when a fire broke out in Cook Street and no fire plugs could be located, the streets on the South Mall and George's Street had to be torn up in order to access a water supply. (*CE* 11 January 1858).

52. Caulfield, *Council Book,* p.870. Messrs Millerd, Maylor, Morrison, and Wrixon are still recalled in Cork place-names.

53. O'Sullivan, S., 'The long struggle to have a city fire brigade' in 'Old Cork and its Corporations' (series), *CEE* 9 January 1976.

54. See Report of the Pipe Water Commissioners 1809 (Cork City Library ref: R.352.13).

55. *CC* 21 April 1840.

56. *CC* 4 July 1840. Both Deyos' building and his neighbour were uninsured, yet three insurance brigades fought the fire. Some companies who did not maintain brigades had an arrangement to reimburse those who did, who attended at fires in the former's insured properties. The going rate appears to have been £10 per fire.

57. *CE* 28 August 1848. The *County and City of Cork Almanac 1843* (p.66) lists fire plugs at Austen's Lane, Broad Lane and Adelaide Street.

58. See endnote 54, this chapter.

59. Caulfield, *Council Book,* p.965.

60. The city's fire engine had obviously seen better days. On 13 January 1783 the St Nicholas churchwardens were allowed £5.13s.9d for 'repairs to the Fire Engine'; a special shed to house the engine in the churchyard was extra. See St Nicholas's Vestry Minute Book (1721-1787), pp.186-187 (Ref: RCB 05-1).

CHAPTER 4

1. Anon, *The History of the Royal Exchange Assurance Corporation in Ireland from A.D 1722* (London, 1905).

2. A scheme launched in England in 1720 by which the South Sea Company took partial responsibility for the national debt in exchange for a monopoly of trade with the South Sea Islands. The subsequent wild speculation was followed by a massive collapse in the same year.

3. The site near St Anne's, Shandon housed three charities: Skiddy's, Brettridge's, and the Green-Coat Hospital, all of which were administered by the trustees of the Green-Coat Hospital. Skiddy's, 'for the benefit of 12 aged Widows of this City', was founded by Stephen Skiddy (aka Scudamore), by his Will made in 1584. The annuity was paid to 1666 when a third part became 'defalkt' for some years after the Great Fire of London which occurred in that year. In 1717, Captain Roger Brettridge left £33 a year for 'the children of poor Protestant soldiers' and £30 for the support of 'seven old soldiers'.

4. *HC* 25 August 1800.

5. *Annals of the Ursuline Sisters, Volume* 1 (1771-1827), pp.87-91 in original MS, pp 122-126 in transcribed MS. The Ursuline annalist recorded that the nuns first observed the fire, 'on the night of 8th December'. In fact, the fire broke out on Saturday evening, 7 December, being duly reported in the *Hibernian Chronicle* on Monday 9 December. However, if the nuns were reciting Matins, this may well have been early on the morning of 8 December and if, as is likely, the diary was written retrospectively, the sister may simply have got her dates mixed up. Sr M. Magdalene, who caused such amusement on the night of the fire, was the daughter of Edward Clarke and his wife Rose, and was born and baptized Isabella on the island of Madeira. She took the habit of the Ursulines on 24 July 1797, aged twenty-two. She died in May 1830. (See *Ursuline Register of Novices* 1771-1978). Honoria (Nano) Nagle (1728-1784), Cork's own 'Lady of the Lantern', founded nine Cork schools to cater for the needs of Cork's poor and underprivileged. In 1771, she invited the Ursuline Sisters to Cork to join in her work, but not long after a serious problem manifested itself. The Ursulines, being an enclosed Order, were unable to minister to Nano's poor schools located outside the convent grounds; in any event, the Order's gradual interest in the education of the children of the more well-to-do convinced Nano to establish her own Congregation. The foundation of the Sisters of the Charitable Institution of the Sacred Heart of Jesus (reconstituted as the Presentation Sisters in 1802) was the result. At the time of the sugar refinery fire, both the Ursulines and Nano's sisters occupied buildings on the same ground at Cove Lane. Curiously, the *Annals of the South Presentation Convent* 1771-1892 contain no reference to the fire. The Ursuline community moved to Blackrock in 1825. See Sr M. Ursula Clarke, *The Ursulines in Cork since* 1771 (Cork, 1996); and Sr M. Pius O'Farrell, *Nano Nagle* (Cork, 1996).

6. The refinery had previously been in the possession of another Huguenot family, the Randalls. George Randall (1717-1791) was the principal of the concern for a great portion of its existence; it survived his death by only eight years (Richard Henchion, *JCHAS* Vol.74, 1969, p.97). The Perriers were among the leading civic and commercial families in nineteenth-century Cork. Both David and Anthony became Mayors of Cork and both received knighthoods. Sir Anthony (1770-1845) was Treasurer of the Cork Pipe Water Company and in 1823, on the death of Edward Daly, was appointed Agent for the Atlas Assurance Company. In his latter capacity, he frequently superintended the operations of the Atlas Fire Engine Establishment at fires in Cork.

7. Tuckey's *Cork Remembrancer* (1837), p.213. So difficult had it become for the sugar refining industry to obtain adequate cover that, in 1782, it started its own

insurance company: the Phoenix.

8. Anon, The *History of the Royal Exchange Assurance Corporation in Ireland from AD 1722* (Dublin, 1905).

9. Robert Mulock, Comptroller. *A return of the several sums paid at the Stamp Office, for duty on insurance from fire, for the quarter ended 25 March 1822; and by what Offices respectively* (Comptroller's Office, Dublin, 18 July 1822). The lowest duty paid was by the County Fire Office, which submitted £18.4s.0d.

10. Anon, *The History of the Royal Exchange Assurance Corporation in Ireland from AD 1722* (Dublin, 1905).

11. See Alfred W. Yeo, *Atlas Reminiscent,* (London, 1908).

12. 'Last night [21 December 1815], about twelve o'clock, as Mr. Daly, of the Atlas Assurance Office, was coming up Faulkener's Lane he was attacked by five soldiers, who dreadfully beat him and robbed him of his gold watch. He, with difficulty, got home, and his servant went and knocked up Sheriff Evanson, who, accompanied by Mr. Ross, high constable, after searching, found five soldiers rioting near the barracks at three o'clock the same morning ... Suspicions were attached to those men who were then committed to the Bridewell for examination' (in *JCHAS* Vol.1A (1892), P.76). 'Robert Dennis, Jeremiah Sullivan, and Joseph Norton, were indicted for robbing Edward Daly, of the Atlas Office, of his watch and chain and seals. Dennis and Sullivan were found guilty, and sentenced to death, and Norton was acquitted. There were four men hanged this assizes out of the county' (*JCHAS* Vol.2A (1893), p.110).

13. *CMC* 7 January 1814.

14. The Harveys were prominent members of the Religious Society of Friends, commonly known as 'Friends' or Quakers. For further information on the Harvey's involvement with Charlotte Quay see R.S. Harrison, 'Harvey, Deaves and Harvey, merchants: sidelights on Cork's timber trade 1760-1848,' *JCHAS* Vol.107 (2002), p.135. For biographical notes on the Harvey family, see R.S. Harrison, *A biographical dictionary of Irish Quakers* (Dublin, 2008); and R.S. Harrison, *Merchants, mystics and philanthropists: 350 years of Cork Quakers* (Cork, 2006).

15. See Gray, W. Forbes, *The Scottish Union and National Insurance Company 1824-1924* (Edinburgh, 1924), p.141.

16. *Ibid,* p.146.

17. Defoe, D., *A Tour Through the Whole Island of Great Britain* (first published 1724; reprinted in Penguin Classics, 1986), pp.318, 319.

18. The system of part-time service still exists today in the form of the County Fire Service organization. These brigades (known as 'retained' brigades) are largely made up of personnel who make their living outside of the fire service. Only senior staff and key personnel are career officers. Older sons of members of the insurance brigades were probably recruited as 'supernumeraries'.

19. Details of REA Fire Engine Establishment as returned to the Admiralty on 27 October 1812, contained in TNA ADM 7/390, p.42. See also F.B. Relton, *An account of the fire insurance companies, associations, institutions, projects and schemes established in Great Britain and Ireland during the seventeenth and eighteenth centuries* (London, 1893).

20. Pearson, R., *Insuring the industrial revolution: fire insurance in Great Britain* 1700-1850 (Hampshire, 2004), p.79.

21. By contrast, the daily rate for a cabinetmaker in Cork in 1820 was between three shillings and three shillings and fourpence. See Maura Cronin, 'Work and workers in Cork city and county 1800-1900' in *Cork: History and Society* (Dublin, 1993), p.730. Thirty years on the rate had only risen to four shillings a day.

22. Williams, B., *Fire Marks and Insurance Office Fire Brigades* (London, 1927), pp.71-75.

23. H.A. Smith, MA, FCII, MIL., Hon. Secretary and Treasurer of the Fire Mark Circle in a letter to the author 17 November 1977.

24. The Irish police forces up to 1922 were: The Peace Preservation Force (1814), the County Constabulary (1822), the Irish Constabulary (1836), and the Royal Irish Constabulary (1867-1922). See. O'Sullivan, D.J., *The Irish Constabularies 1822-1922* (Dingle, 1999).

25. *CE* 18 October 1861.

26. Cody, B.A., *The River Lee, Cork and the Corkonians* (originally published 1859; reprinted 1974 by Tower Books, Cork), p.122.

27. Young, C.F.T., *Fires, Fire Engines, and Fire Brigades* (London, 1866), p.112.

28. Williams B., *Fire Marks and Insurance Office Fire Brigades* (London, 1927), p.73, *passim*.

29. *CE* 29 May 1861. The streets were not tarmacadamed; they were only dirt roads. When a horse and cart drove over them in fine weather, particularly at speed, clouds of choking dust ensued. The newspapers frequently carried complaints, especially from the business community, about their premises being 'destroyed' by the dust. Reports are extant of the insurance fire engines being appropriated to water down the streets.

30. *CE* 7 December 1863.

31. The Black Jack was a feature on the dinner tables of larger houses since medieval times. A replica of one such vessel may be seen at Barryscourt Castle, Carrigtwohill, Co. Cork.

32. *The Fireman*, April 1955.

33. *Ibid.*

34. *CMC* 19 November 1802. The steam engine installed in Isaac Morgan's, and his partner Mr Terry, flour mill in November 1800, a Boulton and Watt 12hp beam appliance, was notable in that it was the first, and only, ever such engine installed in an Irish flour mill. Contrary to the newspaper report the engine survived the fire, being later sold on to Messrs Roe's Distillery in Dublin. See Colin Rynne, *The industrial archaeology of Cork city and its environs* (Dublin, 1999), p.89.

35. *CMC* 28 October 1807.

36. *CA* 30 January 1812.

37. *CE* 14 May 1860. When, on a bitterly cold February night in 1827, the old Blackrock Castle went up in flames, contemporary reports make no reference to an insurance engine attendance. On this occasion, distance may not have been the deciding factor, but the lack of a water supply. (*CC* 27 February 1827)

38. *CE* 12 August 1859.

39. Merryweather, J.C., *The Fire Brigade Handbook* (London, 1911), p.234, *passim*.

40. *CE* 2 June 1888.

41. De Montbret, C.E.C, *Carnets de Voyage* (extracts). See Ní Chinnéide, S., 'A new view of Cork in 1790' in *JCHAS* Vol.78 (1973), p.1.

42. Whipple, A.B.C, *The seafarers: fighting sail* (Time-Life Books, 1978), pp 24, 25.

43. The nominal rolls of insurance firemen returned by local Agents to the Admiralty are available at the (British) National Archives at Kew: reference PRO ADM 7/370. Early indications were that all firemen employed in these islands were included. However, a trawl through the available records showed that only details of some London companies have survived, thanks, apparently, to the depredations of the 1940 Blitz.

44. In Leith, Scotland. The story had a rather unfortunate sequel. Some days later, when fire broke out in nearby Edinburgh and the alarm was raised, the firemen hesitated in turning out, fearing another ruse by the press gang. The end result was a small fire becoming a conflagration (Blackstone, p.76).

45. See Wright, B., *Firemen's uniforms* (Dyfed, 1991), pp 5-6. G.V. Blackstone, author of *A History of the British Fire Service* (1957) narrates how, following the mutiny on the *Bounty* in 1789 and the subsequent settling on the island of Pitcairn by the mutineers, the island's 'First Citizen' used an insurance fireman's uniform as his ceremonial dress, the implication being that a fireman was impressed in England while wearing his uniform and had thrown in his lot with the mutineers. In an endeavour to determine its authenticity, I contacted the Pitcairn Islands Study Center at Pacific Union College, California, USA. Hereunder is part of their reply, 'This is of great interest, and has caused me to review numerous publications relative to any possible mention of a Pitcairn/British Fire Service connection. I find none. I've particularly reviewed Sven Wahlroos' quite detailed information on each of the mutineers who went with Fletcher Christian to Pitcairn, and find nothing in his writing that indicates a connection with the fire service. In every case Wahlroos gives the England background of each mutineer, and in no case is a fire service past mentioned. I have read that John Adams had a relative in the fire service. But there is no indication that Adams was so connected or that he brought any fire service regalia to Pitcairn. There are numerous mentions of clothing worn on the island (in some cases clothing not worn) starting with Mayhew Folger in 1808 [Capt. Folger, Master of the American sealer, *Topaz*, accidentally came across the island and the surviving inhabitants in February 1808] and right on through the years thereafter. No mention is made, so far as I have read, of any fire service uniform. Herbert Ford, Director, Pacific Union College, 21 January 2002.'
Enquiries to Steve Christian, Mayor of Pitcairn, elicited no response.

46. Williams, B., *Fire marks and insurance office fire brigades* (London, 1927), p.68.

47. They are not to be confused with the metal plaques fixed on properties from 1858 onwards which served to identify the location of nearby fire hydrants.

48. 'Ordered, that the Mayor shall be at liberty to have the names of the different Streets, Lanes, and Alleys, Quays, and passages, printed on boards and put up in such parts of said streets as may be thought necessary by him, and the houses numbered ... as a matter which will be in our opinion a great improvement to this City, and very useful to strangers who resort thereto'. Cork Corporation *Council Book* 8 June 1787.

49. *CMC* 3 January 1803.

50. The Prince Regent, acting in place of his father King George III is probably best remembered in Cork for his gift, in 1818, of a collection of casts executed under the superintendence of the famous Italian sculptor Antonio Canova. Pope Pius VII had sent them to the prince as a gift following British intervention in restoring

treasures appropriated from the Vatican by Napoleon. The prince, without even bothering to open the crates, later gave them to Viscount Ennismore, President of the Cork Society of Arts. They repose to this day in the Crawford Art Gallery. See Peter Murray, *The Crawford Municipal Art Gallery* (Cork, 1991), p.196.

51. 'The Annals of the Ursuline Sisters 1771-1825', pp.335-337 (original MS).

52. This high expense was alluded to by Mayor Barry J. Sheehan during a council debate on the setting-up of the Cork Fire Brigade in September 1877. He recalled when 'the insurance companies had been obliged to keep their own fire engines and men at considerable expense' (*CE* 29 September 1877).

53. McNamara, T.F., *Portrait of Cork* (Cork, 1981), p.74. Francis Johnson (1760-1829) was Ireland's most prolific architect and today his works adorn many locations throughout the country, the GPO in Dublin (1818) perhaps being the best-known example.

54. This was the works fire engine of Wise's Distillery (1779-1920), North Mall.

55. *SR* 5 June 1820.

56. See Cornelius G. Buttimer, 'Early nineteenth century Cork poems in Irish' in *JCHAS* Vol.90 (1985), p.158.

57. *CMC* 5 November 1810.

58. *CMC* 10 June 1811. The short article on the tragedy in Cornmarket Street shared the paper with the news of King George III's seventy-third birthday celebrations which occupied more than twice the space.

CHAPTER 5

1. John Fitzgerald (1825-1910), 'The Bard of the Lee', was born in Hanover Street, and educated at Sullivan's Quay CBS and North Monastery CBS. Following a spell as a chemist's assistant at QCC, he turned his attention to cabinet-making and wood-carving, becoming both craftsman and teacher. An artist of some note, he was also well known for his satirical doggerel on topical issues, such as the lack of firefighting equipment in Cork, which he frequently bemoaned. These lines are taken from an anthology entitled *'Gems of the Cork poets'* published by Barter's of Academy Street in 1857. George's Street is now Oliver Plunkett Street; 'Mr Arnott' (later Sir John) was Mayor of Cork 1859-1861.

2. A native of Co. Sligo, Sir John Benson (1812-1874) studied at the Dublin Society's School of Architectural Drawing. From 1846, he held a succession of appointments in Cork, being made City Surveyor in 1851. As an auxiliary source of power to the giant waterwheels at the new Cork waterworks, Benson recommended a Cornish engine which would be used during dry periods. While his designs were sound, the construction and installation were pronounced faulty. Bitter and prolonged legal battles ensued. The debacle nearly destroyed his fine reputation. He received his knighthood for his work on the Great Dublin Exhibition of 1853. Benson, due to failing health, resigned as City Engineer in April 1873 and died in London on 17 October 1874, aged sixty-two. He is buried in Brompton Cemetery, London.

3. Sir John Arnott (1814-1898) was born in Fifeshire, Scotland. After living for some time in Belfast he returned to Cork where he established a number of businesses. He was the owner of the *Irish Times*, Arnott's department stores, bakeries, a brewery,

and the Passage and Rushbrook Docks. He also had shipping and railroad interests. A philanthropist of note, he donated generously to many causes. He served as a Liberal MP for Kinsale (1859-1863) and during his Mayoralty of Cork (1859-1861) he was knighted by the Earl of Carlisle, the Lord Lieutenant (10 November 1859). He died at his home at 'Woodlands', Montenotte, Cork, on 28 March 1898. 'Woodlands', later occupied by the Crosbie family, owners of the *Cork Examiner*, was burned to the ground by armed men in January 1923 at the height of the Civil War.

4. John Francis Maguire (1815-1872), barrister, eldest son of John Maguire, merchant, represented both Dungarvan and Cork City as a Member of Parliament and was Mayor of Cork on four occasions: in 1853, 1862, 1863, and 1864. A close personal friend of Daniel O'Connell and Fr Mathew, he was a staunch supporter of the Reform Movement and various nationalist policies. In 1841, he founded the *Cork Examiner*, principally to counter the propaganda of the establishment organ, the *Cork Constitution*. He was Chairman of the Cork Gas Consumers' Company and directly responsible for the first Cork International Exhibition in 1853. He established the Cork Spinning and Weaving Mills at Blackpool. Throughout his years in office he championed the cause for the establishment of a city fire brigade, and in 1864, commissioned an audit from his friend, Captain Eyre Massey Shaw, Chief of the LFEE (whose parents lived at Monkstown, not far from Maguire's own home in Glenbrook) on the best way to achieve his objective. Sadly, he died on 1 November 1872 without seeing the project realized.

5. The post of 'Superintendent of the Pipe Waterworks and Inspector of Gas Meters' was advertised by Cork Corporation following on the resignation in March 1860 of the incumbent, John Adams. Adams had resigned in controversial circumstances in the light of allegations made that he had illegally used corporation materials and improperly employed their workers on his farm. John Ring was appointed on a majority vote. Some public representatives, who had their own favourites for the position, objected on the basis that he was over the maximum age of forty-five, but they were over-ruled and he was appointed. In April 1879, Ring, who lived at 10 Dyke Parade, the Mardyke, tendered his resignation due to ill-health and was awarded a pension of $2/3^{rd}$ of his salary: £200 per annum. His successor was James O'Toole. John Ring died on 13 August 1882.

6. 'Malin' refers to Ordnance Survey Datum which is Mean Sea Level at Malin Head, Co. Donegal.

7. *CE* 28 April 1858.

8. Today, there are over 650 kilometres of mains ranging in size from 65mm to 800mm. See Cork City Council, *Water – A Precious Resource* (Cork, 2004), pamphlet.

9. *CE* 3 February 1858.

10. *CE* 13 September 1858.

11. *CE* 8 December 1863.

12. *CE* 12 September 1864.

13. *CE* 24 October 1874.

14. *CE* 16 May 1862.

15. Harrison, R.S., *Irish Insurance: Historical Perspectives 1650-1939* (Cork, 1992), pp 42, 43.

16. *CE* 27 June 1859.

17. Dudley, R., 'Fire insurance in Dublin 1700-1860' in *Irish Economic and Social History Journal*, Vol XXIX (2003), p.49.

18. As late as 1879, the REA was still advertising that it maintained a 'Fire Engine Establishment', although its involvement in operational firefighting had effectively ceased years earlier. (Typically, see advertisement in *CE* 6 October 1879).

19. Franz Liszt (1811-86), performed in Cork between 29 December 1840 and 1 January 1841 when he left for Dublin.

20. Clark, W.S, *The Irish Stage in the Country Towns* 1720-1800 (Oxford, 1965), p.70. 'Theatre Royal' was the most fashionable name for a theatre in the eighteenth and nineteenth centuries, with almost every city and big town having one. The Theatre Royal in Dublin was totally destroyed by fire on the afternoon of 7 February 1880 shortly before the Viceroy, the Duke of Marlborough, and his wife (grandparents of Sir Winston Churchill) were due to attend a charity performance. The fire, in which the manager of the theatre perished and many more were injured, was believed to have been caused accidentally by a boy lighting the gas jets in the Vice-regal box.

21. Clark, p.81.

22. Throughout the nineteenth century, theatre fires were innumerable, often with horrific death tolls. Some examples include: St Petersburg 1836 (800 dead); Karlsruhe 1847 (631); Brooklyn 1877 (283), and the Theatre Royal, Exeter, 1887 (188). In 1884 alone, forty-one theatres around the world were destroyed, killing some 1,200 people. See Cox, p.127, *passim*.

23. Capt Eyre Massey Shaw, *Fires and Fire Brigades* (London, 1889), p.39, *passim*.

24. *CC* 14 April 1840.

25. *Ibid*.

26. *Ibid*. The engineers in charge of the engines were: Thomas Prendergast (Scottish Union), Thomas Cosgrave (West of England), and Denis McCarthy (Atlas). The REA engineer is not named.

27. *Ibid*.

28. *Ibid*. At the City Presentment Sessions held in the following month, John McDonnell, the owner of the Theatre Royal, claimed £4,000 for the destruction of his property, maintaining the fire was malicious. He produced witnesses who testified seeing the theatre burning in two separate areas shortly after the alarm was raised. There were dark suggestions that Frank Seymour (known to Cork wags as 'Scheming Seymour'), owner of the rival Theatre Royal Victoria in Cook Street, had engineered the fire. Nothing was proved and the claim was disallowed. See *CC* 16/19 May 1840. For a detailed account of Cork theatre in the nineteenth century see Nigel Hay (James N. Healy), 'The story of Cork Theatre' (series), in *Cork Evening Echo*, commencing 14 June 1958.

29. Anon, 'The Old George's Street Theatre', in the *Cork Examiner* 26 April 1930.

30. *CE* 18 March 1848.

31. This city block was again destroyed during the Burning of Cork by Crown Forces 11-12 December 1920.

32. *CC* 12 June 1848.

33. *Ibid*.

34. The Wide Street Commissioners were a statutory body responsible for the making, maintenance, and repair of city streets. They were abolished when the Cork Improvement Act of 1852 came into force, by which Cork Corporation assumed full responsibility for all municipal affairs. One of the more enduring legacies of

the commissioners is Washington Street (formerly Great George's Street; renamed in 1917 to mark the United States' entry into the Great War). The *Cork Almanack* for 1823 contains the nominal roll of the Wide Street Commissioners. Among those listed appear the names of Sir Anthony Perrier and his brother, Sir David. Sir Anthony was Agent for the Atlas Assurance Company (and Treasurer of the Pipe Water Company). (See Rowena Dudley, 'Fire insurance in Dublin 1700-1860', in *Irish Economic and Social History Journal,* Vol XXIX (2003), p.48.

35. Herlihy, J., *The Dublin Metropolitan Police: a short history and genealogical guide* (Dublin, 2001), p.70.

36. *CE* 27 December 1850. Cork Patent Sawmills adjoining Harley's Street, between King Street and St Patrick's Quay, stood on the site where the Metropole Hotel was later built. During the 1840s, it was rarely removed from controversy. The steam mills were installed in autumn of 1841 by owners Dr Quarry and John Wilson, resulting in the laying-off of almost 400 skilled sawyers. A number of these decided to take their revenge, and sulphuric acid was thrown in Wilson's face, leaving him with terrible injuries. Those arrested were found guilty and sentenced to transportation, but the charges against them were later dropped. Shortly after, Quarry and Wilson fell out and the partnership was dissolved. On a bleak November's night in 1843, during an altercation on the premises, Dr Quarry was attacked by a party of men in the pay of John Wilson, and died from his injuries. Following a lengthy trial, and an appeal to the Court of Errors in Dublin, the men were discharged. In the early hours of Christmas Eve 1850, the Cork Patent Saw Mills, just nine years after its establishment and so often at the centre of bitter controversy, burned down. The cause was never established.

37. *CE* 27 December 1850. The premises were insured with the Patriotic and National insurance companies. Some insurance companies which did not maintain fire establishments contributed to those that did on a fire by fire basis. The going rate seems to have been of the order of £10 per fire. See *Cork Examiner*, 'Town Council: Report of Fire Brigade Committee', 19 June 1863.

38. *CE* 30 December 1850.

39. *Ibid.*

40. *Ibid.*

41. *Ibid.*

42. *Ibid.* W.J. Tomkins was a Town Councillor for the Glanmire Ward.

43. *CE* 8 January 1858.

44. Constable Phelan died in March 1861 from the injuries he received at Hayden's fire.

45. *CE* 8 January 1858.

46. *CE* 11 January 1858.

47 The Royal Victoria Theatre (aka the Cook Street Theatre) occupied the site of the present-day Joseph Woodward and Sons Ltd, Auctioneers. It stretched practically the whole way back to Marlborough Street. Following the destruction by fire in 1840 of the Theatre Royal, for thirteen years it flourished as Cork's main theatre. The last performance given there was in 1859, after which it was sold and for a time was used by Messrs Lambkin's as a tobacco factory. Woodward's have occupied the building ever since. See Nigel Hay (James N. Healy), 'The Story of the Cork Theatre: its history and traditions', in *Cork Evening Echo* 9 August 1958.

48. *CE* 11 January 1858.

49. *Ibid.*
50. The Secretary of the RSPLF in his Annual Report for 1865 noted that 'there are eighty-five escape stations in London, located half a mile from each other. One notable incident was worth recalling – that of the rescue of 178 men, women and children from the falling building at Westminster on January 26th 1865, all being assisted down the fire escape, and order restored, by the exertions of one man'. See *ILN* 13 January 1866.
51. 12 April 1858. Ebenezer Pike (1806-1883) was head of the old Cork Quaker family with his seat at Bessborough, Blackrock. The Pikes had extensive banking, ship building, shipping, railway, and insurance interests. Glover was Secretary of the Cork Steam Ship Company.
52. This 'old type' hydrant, installed in 1858, is still *in situ.*
53. *CE* 1 March 1861.
54. *CE* 4 March 1861.
55. *CE* 1 March 1861.
56. *CE* 4 March 1861.
57. The number of deaths in the fire at Long's was overshadowed by another local tragedy some five years earlier. On this occasion, a tenement in Penrose's Lane (between North Main Street and Duncan Street) collapsed while a child was being 'waked' in an upper room. Nineteen people died. See *CE* 31 March 1856.
58. Information sworn by Dr Denis Brenan Bullen on 29 July 1862 in *British Parliamentary Papers* (hereafter *BPP*) 1864, Vol.XLVI, 'Depositions taken before the Justices of the Peace, in the Case of the Burning of Queen's College, Cork'.
59. Deposition of Timothy Byrne, Turnkey, in *BPP* 1864, Vol.XLVI.
60. *CE* 15 May 1862.
61. *Ibid.*
62. *Ibid.*
63. *Ibid.*
64. Robert Lowe Stopford (1813-1898) was South of Ireland correspondent and illustrator for the *Illustrated London News.* Oddly, his drawing of the West Wing of QCC on fire, as it appeared in *ILN* 24 May 1862, seems to depict a night scene, whereas, of course, the blaze occurred on a bright May morning.
65. Murphy, J.A., *The College* (Cork, 1995), p.15.
66. 'Ultramontanes' was the name given to those strongly supporting the authority of the papal court over national or diocesan authority in the Roman Catholic Church.
67. Denis Brenan Bullen MD and LRCS Ed. (1823), was the first Professor of Surgery at QCC (1849).
68. For a detailed account of the Bullen/Kane affair see John A. Murphy, *The College,* pp.82-96.
69. *CE* 16 May 1862.
70. Healy, T. M, *Letters and leaders of my day,* (London, 1928), vol.1, pp.15, 16.
71. *CE* 16 May 1862.
72. *CE* 20 May 1862.
73. *CE* 16 May 1862.
74. *Ibid.* John Blyth was Professor of Chemistry at QCC (1849-1872).
75. *CE* 16 May 1862.

76. *WNGA* 29 August 1862. Richard Burke was born at Rehill, between Cahir and Clogheen, Co. Tipperary of 'respectable parents of the farming class'. He had received 'a superior English education', and in 1847 became Clerk of the Clogheen Union where he met his wife, Johanna (*née* McGrath), 'a woman of much intelligence' whose father was a surveyor with Lismore Estates. In 1850, he was appointed Clerk of the Waterford Union and 'with undeniable ability, discharged its duties from that time down to his arrest'. (See *WNGA* 29 August 1862).

77. Murphy, J.A., *The College,* p.85.

78. *CE* 10 June 1863.

79. *Ibid.*

80. Goulding's was insured with the Globe, the Imperial, and the Liverpool and London insurance companies. The adjoining premises were insured with the Globe (Russell's) and the REA (Sheehan's): hence, it is assumed, the attendance of the REA brigade.

81. *CE* 10 June 1863.

82. Broadly speaking, the outbreak of fire in a combustible material without the application of an external source of heat and usually arises as a result of atmospheric oxidation of the combustible.

83. *CE* 10 June 1863.

84. The cast-iron North Gate Bridge, designed by Sir John Benson, was completed in just eleven months. It was opened without ceremony on St Patrick's Day 1864.

85. *CE* 11 June 1863.

86. *CE* 12 June 1863.

87. *CE* 11 June 1863.

88. *Ibid.*

89. *Ibid.*

90. *Ibid.*

91. *CE* 12 June 1863.

92. Hilaire Belloc, *Matilda Who Told Lies, And Was Burned to Death.*

93. *CE* 19 June 1863.

94. *CE* 7 December 1863.

95. *Ibid.*

96. *CE* 8 December 1863.

97. A 'ticket' was a coin-like disc issued to volunteer pumpers on the fire ground. Production of the ticket at the issuing insurance office allowed the pumper to claim the appropriate fee.

98. *CE* 7 December 1863.

99. *Ibid.*

100. *Ibid.*

101. In 1860, a general labourer's wage varied between thirteen shillings and fifteen shillings per week. Assuming (given his relatively young age) Duggan was on the lower end of the scale, this represented about twenty-nine and a half week's wages. (See Maura Murphy, 'The working classes of nineteenth century Cork', in *JCHAS* Vol.85, (1980), p.28.

102. *CE* 9 January 1864.

103. *CC* 29 December 1863.

104. *CE* 28 December 1863.

105. *CE* 19 June 1863.
106. O'Sullivan, S., 'Pioneers of fire brigade – Ring, Maguire, Shaw, Wickham' in 'Old Cork and its Corporations', (series) *Cork Evening Echo*, 9 January 1976. The series ran from February 1975 to June 1976.
107. *CE* 8 December 1863.
108. *CE* 2 December 1863. Shaw's injury at a fire in large livery-stables at Bishopsgate, London, was reported in the *Cork Examiner* on 13 November 1863 in the following terms: 'Captain Shaw procured a ladder … and was in the act of swinging himself upon the flap of the front warehouse when the sudden jerk caused the chains of the flap to give way, and he fell on the end of [the] ladder, a depth of about 16 feet, alighting on it between his legs, fracturing the lower end of the urethra … his injuries are, we regret to say, of a more serious character than has been represented.' The well-known reference to Shaw in Gilbert and Sullivan's operetta *Iolanthe*, in which he is enigmatically described as a 'type of true love kept under', had long been assumed to have been a dig by the waspish Gilbert at Shaw's (alleged) philandering. However, Charles MacMahon Shaw (a distant relative) in his book, *Bernard's Brethern* (New York, 1939), claims that the allusion is to the fire chief's 1863 accident which, he says, 'deprived him of the full powers of his manhood'. Either way, although earning for the fire chief a curious immortality, he was not at all impressed at being apostrophized in this manner. Shaw constantly exposed himself to great danger on the fireground and was seriously injured on a number of occasions. Some years after his retirement his right leg had to be amputated due to thrombosis. Later, his left leg was also removed.

CHAPTER 6

1. *CE* 4 March 1864.
2. *Ibid.*
3. The rates of pay envisaged by both Maguire and Shaw appear to bear little resemblance to what might reasonably have been expected. At a time when wages increased only minimally from decade to decade, when the first permanent firemen were appointed in 1877 their rates of pay were, 1st Class Assistant: 18 shillings per week; 2nd Class Assistant: 16 shillings per week. Additionally, the Cork staff was entitled to 'free apartments, candle and fire- light' as part of their emoluments. By comparison, in Shaw's London brigade, in 1861 the rates were, 'Senior Fireman': 24 shillings and 6 pence per week; 'Junior Fireman': 21 shillings per week.' Deductions were made for rent, surgeon, uniform and pension. (If Shaw had to pay his junior staff 21 shillings per week i.e., £54.12s.0d a year, one wonders where on earth he was coming from in thinking that Cork firemen would accept £5 a year). By comparison, in 1872, following an inquiry into their pay and conditions, a Sub-Constable in the Royal Irish Constabulary had 15 shillings per week (c. £39 per annum), rising to £62 per annum after twenty years' service. However, a policeman's salary was superannuated whereas then, a Cork fireman's was not.
4. *CE* 24 March 1864. Early in 1865, there was yet another scare of fire at the college. On 17 February 1865, a fire was discovered in the Natural History Museum in the east wing, the result of a hearth fire. It was quickly extinguished (*CC* 18 February 1865). When, in 1891, the city's new fire chief, Capt. Hutson, carried out an inspection of the

fire protection arrangements at QCC, he found the hydrants 'set fast, and not capable of working for a considerable time' (WWFBC 16 December 1891).

5. O'Rahilly, R., *A History of the Cork Medical School 1849-1949* (Cork, 1949), p.19; and Rathbone, J., 'Cork's academic luminaries in the early days of Queen's', in *CEE* 11 February 1982.

6. Coote, W., 'Fire extinguishing in Ireland', in *Journal of the Insurance Institute of Ireland,* May 1904.

7. Paragraph 119.

8. In 1866, Charles F.T. Young, chartered engineer and enthusiastic amateur fireman, attempted to establish the level of fire cover in towns and cities throughout the United Kingdom. He sent out over 800 circular letters to local authorities, the results being published in his book *Fires, Fire Engines, and Fire Brigades* (London, 1866).

9. For a detailed account of this unhappy chapter in Cork's history, see Seán Daly, *Cork: a city in crisis* (Cork, 1978).

10. *CE* 27 June 1870.

11. The *Cork Examiner* for 27 June 1870 narrated how, 'Mr. Daly was opposed to employing society (i.e. Union) men, and is not therefore in good grace with a certain party'.

12. See *Borough of Cork Night Watch: Report of Special Committee on the appointment of Chief Constable* (Cork, 1870).

13. 'Police Fire Brigades' were common throughout Britain at this time, and survived well into the twentieth century.

14. *Borough of Cork Night Watch: Report* (1870).

15. At this time the RIC did not patrol by night. Their paramilitary character precluded them from being a preventative force.

16. *Borough of Cork Night Watch: Report* (1870).

17. *CE* 17 October 1874.

18. *CE* 20 October 1874.

19. *Ibid.*

20. No investigation was carried out into whether there was any substance in the threats made by the two soldiers. Arraigned on the theft of the clothing from the shop, Patrick Murray was found guilty and sentenced to four months' hard labour, while Thomas Peterson was discharged.

21. *CE* 20 October 1874.

22. *CE* 17 October 1874.

23. Joseph William McMullen acquired the mills from Joseph Dunlop in 1854.

24. Rynne, C., *The industrial archaeology of Cork City and its environs,* (Dublin, 1999), p.92.

25. *CE* 2 May 1876.

26. The City Club on Grand Parade was later the headquarters of the Legion of Mary (*Dún Muire*) in the city. It was later occupied by various financial institutions.

27. *CE* 2 May 1876.

28. *Ibid.*

29. *CC* 2 May 1876.

30. WWFBC 9 January 1877.

31. *Ibid.*

32. WWFBC 19 February 1877.

33. One of their children, also Mark (born Dublin 1872) married Hannah Donovan in Cork in 1894 where they set up business. Both he, his wife, and a number of their children were heavily involved in the nationalist movement in the early years of the twentieth century. Wickham's Oil and Lamp Store at 8 Merchant's Quay was closed by military order and Mark was interned both in Wakefield and Frongoch Camp in Wales, the so-called 'University of Revolution', where future leaders of the movement, including Michael Collins, were also incarcerated. In 1921, he was again interned, this time on Spike Island in Cork Harbour. He died in Cork in 1928. For a detailed account of the Wickham family tree and their involvement with Sinn Féin and the Irish Volunteers, visit http://freepages.genealogy.rootsweb. com/~bwickham/wickgen.htm. See also Bureau of Military History Witness Statement WS 558 for statement of Mark Wickham (grandson of the fire chief), Company Officer, 'B' Company, 1st Battalion, 1st Cork Brigade 1917-1921.

34. The big whiskey blaze at Laurence Malone's Bonded Warehouse in Chamber Street in the heart of Dublin's famous Coombe occurred on 18 June 1875. The fire brigade was criticized for not applying water to the burning building immediately on arrival, but Capt. Ingram's tactics were proved to be correct. The burning whiskey would have merely floated on the water, carrying the fire to nearby buildings and causing gas explosions in the sewer network. Instead, Ingram ordered the streets to be dug up and the sewers stopped to prevent the flow of burning liquor. Some four hours after the fire started, the brigade mounted a great barrage of jets, but by this time the warehouse and ten adjoining tenements were gutted. Nevertheless, it is estimated that the fire would have reached conflagration proportions were it not for Ingram's stratagem. See Geraghty and Whitehead, *The Dublin Fire Brigade* (Dublin, 2004).

35. WWFBC 23 February 1877.

CHAPTER 7

1. The Cork Improvement Act 1868 (310 & 320 Vic.C.xxxiii), p.114: 'The Corporation may for the Purposes of this Act appoint an Inspector of Fires (herein-after called "the Inspector"), who shall be responsible to the Corporation for the Maintenance of the Fire Brigade and Fire Establishment by this Act authorized in a complete state of Efficiency, and for the good Conduct of the Firemen appointed by him, and he shall make Provision for securing a speedy Attendance of Firemen with Engines and their Appurtenances, and with Fire Escapes and other Impliments, on every Alarm of Fire within the Borough, and he may send such of the Engines under his Charge with their Appurtenances, and such of the Firemen appointed by him as he can spare, beyond the Limits of this Act for the purpose of extinguishing Fire'.

2. WWFBC 16 October 1877.

3. In England, cities comparable to Cork in area and population had the following whole-time firemen (in parentheses): Bolton (20), Bradford (21), Leicester (33).

4. The Opera House replaced the Athenaeum which had been constructed from materials salvaged from the Fine Arts Hall of the National Exhibition held in 1852. The acoustics of this building, however, proved unsuitable for musical performances, hence the decision to erect the new building.

5. The reformed corporations had an ambivalent relationship with allegiance to the British monarch. In 1887, when Victoria celebrated her Golden Jubilee, the corporation issued the following statement, 'That this Corporation decides to place on record its most emphatic condemnation of the action of those members of Council who took upon themselves to supersede the authority of the Mayor, by hoisting on the flagstaff of the Mayor's office, and on the Grand Parade Market, black flags on the occasion of the Queen's Jubilee' (*CE* 29 June 1887).

6. When stationed in Dublin, Mark and Mary Wickham had already buried three of their children: Catherine (two months), Marianne (four years) and Esther (eighteen months).

7. *CE* 20 October 1877.

8. *Ibid.*

9. As outlined by Chief Officer J.G. O'Kelly BE in a presentation on the history of Cork Fire Brigade to Cork Rotary in 1953.

10. See Laing. R.H., (ed), Cork General Directory 1863.

11. Nearby stood the site originally chosen by the Capuchin Friars for their new church, to replace the 1771 chapel in Blackamoor Lane (aka the 'Back Lane', which runs parallel to, and behind, Sullivan's Quay) built by the famous Capuchin priest Fr Arthur O'Leary. As far back as 1853, the corporation had taken a lease on the ground (comprising an area of some 200ft by 150ft) from the Warren Estate with a view to eventually erecting a new City Hall there.

12. William Clayton, Camden Street, Dublin patented his telescopic fire escape in 1874 and became a renowned manufacturer of these appliances.

13. The first faltering steps at acquiring telephonic communication for Cork Fire Brigade had been made in 1879 when proposals were received by the corporation from John Ahern of Manchester and G. Percival of Cork to connect the municipal offices (20 South Mall), the waterworks, and the fire station by means of a loop. Ahern quoted £73 for the work and Percival £58. Both proposals were rejected, the committee 'not agreeing as to the necessity of the work'. (WWFBC 7 October 1879).

14. See *The Fireman,* February 1878.

15. The Dublin Fire Brigade continued to wear the red shirts into the 1930s. They were withdrawn in Cork in 1894.

16. With the introduction of scientifically-designed Personal Protective Equipment (PPE) in the 1990s, firefighters' personal axes were consigned to history.

17. *The Fireman,* and *Journal of the Civil Protective Forces of the United Kingdom,* was a monthly journal published by Merryweather and Sons Ltd.

18. Young (London, 1866).

19. Jessop Browne's Wheel and Wagon Works, 104/105 Great Brunswick Street (now Pearse Street), Dublin, was founded in 1822 by William Browne.

20. The coach building firm was founded in 1860 by James Johnson. The name survives in the transport business in Cork to this day in the form of Johnson and Perrott Motor Group (JPMG), a partnership first established in 1910 and now owned by the extended Whitaker family.

21. Councillor Creedon at Cork Corporation Improvement Department meeting 1 March 1878.

22. *CE* 23 March 1878.
23. In the aftermath of the fire, the council made overtures to the insurance companies to acquire one of their engines, none of which had appeared at a fire for years. The companies refused the request.
24. *CE* 23 March 1878.
25. WWFBC 2 April 1878.
26. *Ibid* 29 March 1878.
27. *Ibid* 5 April 1878.
28. *CE* 30 March 1878.
29. WWFBC 14 November 1882. In April 1885, this duty was extended to St Patrick's Bridge also; one fireman to be on duty at each bridge.
30. When Charles Stewart Parnell paid an unexpected visit to Cork in the early hours of the morning of 30 November 1890, the Mayor instructed the fire chief to dispatch two firemen (on foot) to the houses of council members all over the city requesting them to meet 'The Chief' at Glanmire Road Railway Station. Councillor Julian objected to the depletion of the fire staff in this way and an order was issued directing the brigade 'never to leave the station in a body again … save … to attend a fire or perform other legitimate duty' (WWFBC 3 December 1890).
31. Hibernia Buildings was rebuilt after the fire.
32. Although sprinkler systems had been commercially available since the early 1860s, their introduction had been met with a deal of apathy by owners of property who were reluctant to incur the initial considerable expenditure, over and above insurance, for security from a chance destruction of their premises, especially as the feeling existed in their minds that they might as well have their goods destroyed by fire as by water, whilst the spread of fire to adjacent premises was no business of theirs.
33. *CE* 28 May 1883.
34. Indeed, Fr Mathew's campaign had been launched on 10 April 1838 in the very shadow of the premises that would become the future fire station.
35. The fire service was far from being unique in this regard. Other public bodies such as the police had a similar problem. In his book *The Bulkies: Police and Crime in Belfast 1800-1865,* Brian Griffin asserts, 'drunkenness was the most common disciplinary problem affecting the Irish Constabulary and the Dublin Metropolitan Police, as well as the British police forces.' In a survey of offences committed by the Belfast police between 1850-1859, Griffin states that drunkenness accounted for 444, or 38.4 per cent of total offences.
36. WWFBC 23 July 1883.
37. See O'Mahony, C., 'Industry at Crosse's Green', *JCHAS,* Vol. 104, (1999).
38. *The Fireman,* 1 June 1897.
39. Gamble, S.G., FSI, AMICE, MIFireE, *A Practical Treatise on Outbreaks of Fire* (London, 1926).
40. *Ibid.*
41. See Hurley, M.F., & Sheehan, C. M., *Excavations at the Dominican Priory, St Mary's of the Isle, Cork* (Cork, 1995).
42. *CE* 21 June 1886.
43. *Ibid.*

44. *Ibid.* The fire chief, throughout this lengthy narrative, was not once referred to by his official title but by his surname. This may, or may not, be indicative of how far the brigade had fallen in the public's esteem by then, or it may simply suggest that the particular (anonymous) reporter was personally antagonistic towards him.

45. *Ibid.*

46. CE 23 June 1886.

47. CE 21 June 1886. More correctly, The Liverpool and London and Globe Insurance Company (1864-1919). In 1919, the company was acquired by the Royal Insurance Company.

48. *CE* 26 June 1886.

49. *Ibid.*

50. *Ibid.*

51. *Ibid.*

52. WWFBC 26 August 1886.

53. There was no legal requirement on local authorities to provide fire services until the passing of the Fire Brigades Act 1940.

54. When the author joined the fire brigade in 1964 many of the older parts of the city were still served by three-inch spurs.

55. WWFBC 11 July 1887.

56. *Ibid* 25 July 1887.

57. See O'Shea, J.J., 'The churches of the Church of Ireland in Cork City', *JCHAS*, Vol.48 (1943).

58. *Irish Builder*, No.14 (1873).

59. Furnace rooms had long been recognized as the starting point for fires in churches. It was recommended that such rooms be of brick construction with concrete ceiling and entered only from the open air. If this was not practicable entry should be through self-closing fire-resisting doors in order to restrict the spread of fire should it commence in the furnace room. See *The Fireman*, 1 March 1881, p.150.

60. *CE* 24 February 1887.

61. *Ibid.*

62. *Ibid* 25 February 1887.

63. It was the second major fire at Browne's in a decade. On the night of Friday 21 September 1877, just weeks before the fire brigade was formed, the complex was gutted. Unlike the 1887 fire when the blaze broke out after the workers had left the premises, the night millers were still on duty and the mill working when the earlier fire was discovered about 11p.m. They were locked in (as was the custom) and had to break down a gate opening onto St Patrick's Quay in order to escape the flames. This took some time and meanwhile the inferno spread with terrifying rapidity. Two workers had to actually run through a virtual wall of fire and were dreadfully burned about the head, torso, and arms. (*CE* 22 September 1877).

64. *CE* 30 May 1887.

65. *Ibid.*

66. WWFBC 31 May 1887.

67. Henchion, R., *Henchion's Cork Centenary Remembrancer 1887-1987* (Cork, 1986).

CHAPTER 8

1. Kipling lost no time in putting pen to paper. His (to quote the *Cork Constitution*) 'vigorous poem' first appeared in the *National Observer* and was reproduced in full in the (pro-Unionist) *Cork Constitution* on 9 April 1891, but was not published in the *Cork Examiner*. Actually, the rousing cheer from the crowd on seeing the Union Flag enveloped in the flames was premature. By some extraordinary quirk of fate it was not burnt, although the flagpole itself was. The flag was retrieved on the following day by County Surveyor, Mr Samuel Alexander Kirkby, who confirmed this in a letter to the *Cork Constitution* on 6 April 1891, 'Your many readers will be interested to learn that I took the Union Jack [*sic*] which floated over the Courthouse and was supposed to have been burnt at the recent fire, from the cornice at the east end of the building practically intact'. S.A. Kirby (1845-1927) served in Cork county 1874-1909. See, Brendan O'Donoghue, *The Irish County Surveyors 1834-1944: A Biographical Dictionary* (Dublin, 2007), pp 226-230.

2. See the *Irish Penny Magazine,* 6 April 1833. The late Mr T.F. McNamara (Cork City Architect and author of *Portrait of Cork*) contended that there was much confusion regarding the identity of the actual architect. It was common then, he asserted, for architects to undertake the building of works they did not design and design works they did not build. On all the information available to him (1981), he concluded that the courthouse was designed by Kearns Deane and the Pains were the contractors.

3. See Collins, J.T., 'Seat of Law through the Passing years', in *Cork Evening Echo* 9 May 1955. In light of subsequent events the Cork stonecutters' insistence on the non-use of terra cotta seems justified, but for a different reason. A report submitted to the United States' Government following the Great Fire of Baltimore (1904) contained the following, 'both stone and terra cotta suffered severely. The effect of fire on terra cotta was a surprise; it was thought that architectural terra cotta was reasonably fireproof, but it failed completely at this conflagration. It cracked and fell to pieces, and the heat seemed to destroy its texture; in some cases it became soft and pliable. More particularly was this so with projecting and highly ornamental work'. (See *Fire and Water,* January 1910, p.176).

4. Lost in the fire were early municipal books, charters, and important documents relating to Cork Corporation. Fortunately, Dr Richard Caulfield had transcribed the proceedings of council meetings which he published in 1876 as *The Council Book of the Corporation of the City of Cork 1609-1643 and 1690-1800*. In the 1950s, an Index to the council books from 31 October 1710 until 25 October 1841 was acquired by historian John J. O'Shea, and in 1983 an original volume of council minutes covering the period October 1710-September 1732 surfaced, leading to hopes that other material would come to light.

5. *CE* 28 March 1891.

6. *Ibid.*

7. Eugene J. McSwiney (1866-1930) lived at 16 Grattan Street behind the courthouse. His works were exhibited at the Royal Academy and the Royal Hibernian Academy.

8. *CE* 28 March 1891.

9. *Ibid.*

10. Twelve months earlier, on Friday 28 March 1890, the courthouse had experienced another alarming outbreak. While engaged at a serious fire at McSweeny's leather stores on South Main Street, the fire chief was informed that the courthouse was

on fire. The *Cork Examiner* for 29 March documented how, 'The Brigade divided their forces, leaving a couple of men in charge of McSweeny's, while Captain Wickham with his best men proceeded up Liberty Street to the Courthouse. At the north-western corner ... the flames had taken possession ... it was after 11p.m when the fire was discovered, and in less than half an hour it was completely extinguished.'

11. Sir Edward Fitzgerald (1846-1927), building contractor, Lord Mayor of Cork in 1901, 1902, and 1903, was something of a local character and was variously known as 'Up with the shafts!' or 'Ate the mate!' (Eat the meat). The former soubriquet resulted (or so the story goes) from a time when, building houses for the local authority, a contractor would only receive his first payment on satisfactory completion of the chimney shafts. Thus, when his workmen moved onto a building site, their first order from 'Fitzy' would be 'Up with the shafts, lads!' His other, more well-known, epithet resulted from the period when he was Lord Mayor. The great Cork International Exhibition (1902-1903) held in the Park on the Mardyke (later to be named Fitzgerald's Park in his honour) was his brainchild, and King Edward VII and Queen Alexandra visited there and dined in the Shrubbery House (now Cork Public Museum) on 1 August 1903. Noticing that the queen was only 'picking' at her sumptuous meal while pretending to eat (as royalty, apparently, are wont to do), he is reputed to have gently admonished her to 'at least eat the meat, Ma'am, eat the meat!' See Mary O'Leary, 'Social Change in Currykippane 1885-1935' (Unpublished MA thesis, University College Cork, 2002).

12. This unfounded proposition grew legs as news of the fire circulated. The *New York Times* (28 March 1891) recounted how, 'While the Judge was summing up ... the Court House was set on fire and a scene of alarm and confusion followed'.

13. *CE* 3 April 1931.

14. The only fire engine the brigade possessed was the manual engine received from the REA in 1888 (an 1858 model).

15. Eugene Crean (1854-1939) lived at 3 Douglas Street, Cork. A carpenter by trade, he was President of the Cork United Trades Workers' Association. Elected nationalist MP on an anti-Parnellite ticket for Queen's County in 1892 and 1895. Elected nationalist MP for SE Cork 1900, he retained his seat to 1918. A member of Cork Corporation, he was elected Mayor in 1899, the last incumbent to bear the title, from 1900 it became 'Lord Mayor'. President of Cork County Board GAA 1890/1891. See Tim Cadogan and Jerh. Falvey, *A Biographical Dictionary of Cork* (Cork, 2006) p.66; and *The Catholic Who's Who and Year Book* 1916 (Dublin, 1916), p.102.

16. *CE* 1 April 1891.

17. WWFBC 11 June 1890.

18. In 1891, also, the Dublin Fire Brigade was experiencing its own set of traumatic circumstances. In May of that year, Inspector Doherty and Fireman Burke were killed during dramatic rescue attempts at a fire in Westmoreland Street. The incisive O'Meara Report into the working of the brigade was adopted in September 1891.

19. *CE* 13 April 1891.

20. WWFBC 15 April 1891.

21. *CE* 14 April 1891.

22. WWFBC 23 April 1891.

23. *CC* 16 April 1891.

CHAPTER 9

1. In an interview in December 2008 with Jim Murphy, whose late father, Stn. O. Daithi Murphy, served under Alfred Hutson from 1912 until the chief's retirement in 1928, I asked him what his father had thought of Hutson. He replied, 'He adored him'.
2. See John B. Nadal, *London's Fire Stations* (Huddersfield, 2006).
3. Eyre Massey Shaw, *Fire Protection. A Complete Manual of the Organization, Machinery, Discipline, and General Working of the Fire Brigade of London* (London, 1876), p.304. This naval heritage is still reflected in some of the vernacular of the fire service: 'crew', 'mess', 'watch', etc. Victorian fire stations were akin, according to one commentator, to 'ships on dry land; and the men were as isolated as if they were at sea'.
4. *Ibid,* p.306.
5. *Ibid,* p.305.
6. The MFB was, at this time, organized in four districts: A, B, C, and D. A, B, and C were north of the Thames; D district, with seventeen fire stations, covered the entire area south of the river. Barring a short sojourn at Brigade Headquarters at Watling Street, all Hutson's London service was spent in D district.
7. Alfred James Hutson, 'Qualifications', 6 January 1888. (Personal CV).
8. Alfred Wylde was appointed Superintendent of Limerick Fire Brigade in 1893. Alexander McCarthy served as Town Clerk to Cork Corporation from 1859-1901. His father, also Alexander, was Town Clerk 1845-1859.
9. WWFBC 24 June 1891.
10. See 'Captain Silverthorne's tomfoolery, or, how the Brighton Volunteers made good' in *The Fireman,* November 1954.
11. The 1881 Census of England reveals the following persons occupying 4 Duke Street (as well as Station-master Alfred J. Hutson): James S. Fleetwood (20), Alfred J. Hutson (6), Elizabeth J. Hutson (26), Elizabeth J. Hutson (1), James W. Hutson (3), Emily Symonds (18), Henry J. Yorke (19). The Census for 1891 records (again in addition to the Station-master): Elizabeth J. Hutson (33), Alfred J. Hutson (16), James C. Hutson (13), Elizabeth L. Hutson (11), Ethel C. Hutson (9), Gladys M. Hutson (6), Beatrice M. Hutson (4), Mable M.M. Hutson (1), Margaret E. Costin (20), Henry T. Bowles (48). Note the variations in the two censuses, including the entry on Mrs Hutson (who should, by now, be 36) entered as being 33.
12. See *A Ten Years' Record of Fire Brigade Competitions,* (Birmingham, 1888).
13. See *Fire and Water,* 1 March 1893, p.5.
14. *ILN* 20 September 1862.
15. Hutson was nicknamed 'Bloody Blazes' due, apparently, to his penchant for the use of fruity words of command on the fire ground.
16. WWFBC 29 July 1891.
17. The annual Cork Poor Children's Excursion to Youghal was inaugurated in 1893 during the Mayoralty of the popular and highly-esteemed Augustine Roche (1849-1915) of Douglas Street, a prominent wine and spirit merchant. From the start, members of the fire brigade, encouraged by the involvement of the chief, were identified with the movement, giving up their (limited) time off to help out in a variety of ways.
18. *CE* 28 August 1891.
19. *Ibid.*
20. *CE* 22 September 1891.

21. There are no clues in the surviving records of the fire brigade as to the nature of the relationship between Mark Wickham and the man who supplanted him. It appears to have been, at the very least, a cordial but workmanlike one, for between his taking office in 1891 and Wickham's death in 1897, Hutson seems to have had no cause for complaint during what must have been a difficult time for the former fire chief.

22. *CE* 22 September 1891.

23. *Ibid.*

CHAPTER 10

1. Originally, a yearly grant of £10 was provided by the Local Government Board towards the upkeep of the Passage West Volunteer Fire Brigade. Because of misuse of the fire equipment by employees of the District Council who, on account of the grant, insisted that they had the right to remove it, without prior permission of the brigade, for flushing out drains, sewers, etc., the volunteer firemen resigned *en masse* in December 1903. In July 1904, a committee representing local business and civic interests was formed to reconstruct the brigade. They prevailed on Capt. Roberts to continue on as fire chief, and henceforth they would rely solely on voluntary subscriptions. The brigade was disbanded at the outbreak of the First World War in 1914 when Capt. Roberts, a reservist officer, was called up and several members joined the Royal Navy and British Army.

2. Thomas Purcell was born in Kilkenny in 1851 and qualified as a civil engineer. Prior to his appointment as Chief Officer of the Dublin Fire Brigade he was manager of the Shannon Foundry and Engineering Works. An enthusiastic volunteer fireman, he won the Silver Medal of the RSPLF in 1876 for his extraordinary bravery at a house fire in Kilkenny. According to Geraghty and Whitehead (2004, p.87), his appointment to Dublin was 'an outstanding choice. Over the next twenty-five years he proved to be the most inspiring, innovative, and forward-looking chief in the brigade's history'.

3. Geraghty and Whitehead, p.107.

4. In June 1913, the corporation was approached by the London firm of Henry Simonis and Co. who offered to sell them a second-hand 'London pattern' four-wheeled escape van, complete with 50ft wheeled escape. Their offer was declined.

5. The Roman Street escape was originally planned to be stationed at St Mary's Temperance Hall (now long demolished) opposite the North Chapel. However, when Capt. Hutson reported to his committee that the cost of a plinth and iron railings to protect the escape would cost £35, the location was changed.

6. 'Curricle' pattern and 'sliding-carriage' fire escapes were developed, in the early 1890s, in response to the advent of electric tram systems. Upright escapes were no longer desirable due to the melange of electric wires criss-crossing busy city streets. (See Merryweather, J.C., *The Fire Brigade Handbook,* 2nd ed, London 1911, p.184). With the coming on-stream of Cork's electric trams, Capt. Hutson drew attention to the necessity of acquiring a number of the new escapes, suggesting that the tramway company might make a contribution towards their purchase. (WWFBC 9 May 1899). The company paid £100 towards the £190 cost of two new Merryweather 80ft 'Improved Sliding-Carriage Telescopic Pattern' escapes. (WWFBC 5 December 1900). Another serious problem for the firemen was

the danger of electrocution: they were authorized to cut the wires in time of emergency. Asked for their advice, the tramway company declined but agreed to furnish the City Engineer with all relevant technical data: he, in turn, could advise the brigade. The engineer reported that, 'the current pressure in the trolley wires of electric tramways in the city has been limited by the Board of Trade to 500 volts, so as to prevent fatal accidents from the passage of current through the body; but that a shock might be received by firemen when cutting the wires, which might cause them to fall from a height and so prove fatal'. (WWFBC 4 December 1899).

7. *CE* 24 August 1891.

8. Walter McFarlane's 'Saracen Ironworks' was Glasgow's biggest and most widely-known foundry. See Tom Spalding, *Cork City: A Field Guide to its Street Furniture* (Cork, 2009), pp78, 79.

9. WWFBC 28 March 1893.

10. *CE* 24 June 1895.

11. *CE* 25 June 1895.

12. *Ibid*. District Inspector Philip Crampton Creaghe (RIC registered number 38313) was transferred to Cork from Midleton in 1892. His service in Midleton had been marred by controversy. He was the officer-in-charge of the RIC in the town on the evening of 1 November 1888 when a twenty-five year old local man, Patrick Aherne, was bayoneted to death by the police. During some local disturbance, Aherne had innocently emerged from his home to see what the commotion was, not realizing that the RIC was clearing the street with fixed bayonets. Creaghe was later appointed a Resident Magistrate, retiring in 1916. See Jim Herlihy, *Royal Irish Constabulary Officers* (Dublin, 2005), p.107; and Jeremiah Falvey, *The Chronicles of Midleton* (Cork, 1998), p.78.

13. *CE* 24 June 1895.

14. For the definitive history of Cork's trams see Walter McGrath, *Tram Tracks through Cork* (Cork, 1981).

15. During August 1920, the escapes at the Fireman's Rest and the Courthouse were badly damaged when commandeered by the British military. After repair, they were placed in Conway's Yard (Oliver Plunkett Street) and the yard of the Imperial Hotel (Pembroke Street). There they remained until after the Troubles.

16. WWFBC 21 November 1911.

17. In August 1897, the widow of Aux. Fm. Michael McCarthy was awarded £5 from the Widows' and Orphans' Fund following on the death of her husband, which 'she attributed to the severe cold he contracted while on night-duty' at the Fireman's Rest. (WWFBC 18 August 1897). And in November (in the wake of the Inquest into the death of Mark Wickham), Coroner Murphy wrote to the Waterworks and Fire Brigade Committee 'that in the evidence given to him, the Rest was ... unhealthy and injurious to the men who occupied it owing to the walls sweating in cold and damp weather'. The City Engineer suggested that the interior of the 'Rest' should be coated with cork paint 'so as to prevent the walls weeping'. (WWFBC 24 November 1897). On 14 November 1900 Capt. Hutson reported to the WWFBC that 'Fireman Kean Mahony, station watchman at the Fireman's Rest, Lavitt's Quay, had become insane and suggesting that his sister be appointed in his place. Recommended, that the suggestion be adopted, Mahony's sister to be paid for the duty eight shillings per week'. This is the one and only reference to the

recommendation in the committee's minutes and it would appear that nothing ever became of it. When, just two weeks later, a major fire broke out in Alcock's on St Patrick's Street and a number of daring rescues was effected, Fireman Jim Barry was the escape conductor at Lavitt's Quay. The first female firefighter to be appointed to the brigade was Ff. Irene Wallace in November 1995.

18. *CE* 19 November 1897.

CHAPTER 11

1. Arguably the most pressing call ever made on the 'hot line' between the fire brigade and Victoria Barracks was on the night of 11 December 1920, when Capt. Hutson urgently requested the assistance of the barrack engines and fire picket during the burning of the city centre by Crown forces. His call went unanswered.

2. John Boyle was a Superintendent in the Dublin Metropolitan Police attached to the mounted unit at Kevin Street station, at a time when the DMP had responsibility for fire engines and fire escapes. He became Superintendent of the DFB in 1882 (when sixty-three years of age), retiring ten years later.

3. WWFBC 28 March 1899.

4. Denis Sullivan owned all the lands from Sullivan's Quay (named after him) to Greenmount. He lived at 'The White House' in Cat Lane.

5. WWFBC 12 July 1892.

6. In 1938, a second bay was added to accommodate the ambulance section. When the building, no longer a fire station, was renovated by developers in the 1980s, the facade was restored in a style faithful to the original.

7. WWFBC 28 June 1893.

8. WWFBC 10 January 1894.

9. *CE* 13 April 1892.

10. *CE* 14 April 1892.

11. *CE* 10 May 1892.

12. *CE* 24 May 1892.

13. *Ibid.*

14. *CE* 9 June 1892.

15. *Ibid.*

16. Michael Joseph Mahony was a native of Grenagh, Co. Cork. He was married to Cissie (*née* Twomey, of Twomey's Bakery, Shandon Street), and they had ten children. An employee of Messrs John Daly and Co., mineral water manufacturers of Caroline Street, he later became its Managing Director. He excelled at sports of many codes. On the night of 11/12 December 1920, when word of the burning of the city centre was brought to him, in defiance of the military curfew, he and the Managing Director of Newsom's went into town to check on their respective premises. There they met Capt. Hutson who hastily pressed them into service on the 'business end' of a fire hose. Between them they are credited with saving from total destruction the Victoria Hotel and Woolworth's. He died in 1952 at the age of ninety-six.

17. When originally commissioned, the great complex on the Lee Road was named the Eglinton Lunatic Asylum after the Lord Lieutenant.

18. *CE* 30 June 1892.

19. WWFBC 12 July 1892.

20. *Ibid.*

21. In the course of an address to Cork Rotary in 1953, Mr J.G. O'Kelly, BE, Chief Officer, Cork Fire Brigade, asserted that he had been told by a former member (then still living and who had served under Capt. Hutson) that, in addition to the volunteer brigade, a separate corps was raised from among students at Queen's College, Cork. The old gentleman had referred to these student-firemen as 'cadets', and even provided details of their uniform: tunics piped with green braid to distinguish them from the regular fire staff. I have come across no mention of such a unit in the WWFBC records.

22. *The Fireman,* October 1892.

23. WWFBC 29 January 1896.

24. A letter from Alfred Hutson appeared in *Fire and Water* journal on 1 April 1893 (p.29, extract), 'The scenery around here is very beautiful, and I hope all the old Brigades will take this opportunity of kissing the Blarney Stone ... Brigades can leave any part of England on Saturday and arrive in Cork on Sunday morning before breakfast. As this is the fifteenth competition I have arranged, besides taking part in some forty or fifty as a competitor, I think we may safely guarantee that this one will be properly carried out'.

25. *Fire and Water,* 1 April 1893.

26. The fire was discovered to have originated in joists which ran into the chimney flue of the house next door. Trimmer joists were often not used and the flooring joists projected into the brickwork of the chimney, or were laid immediately below the hearth. In the former case the breaking away of the pargeting in the chimney exposed the ends of the joists, which then smouldered and charred, and if sufficient oxygen reached them, burst into flame.

27. *CE* 8 August 1893.

28. 'Wildfire' was also known as 'Greek fire'. A highly-flammable composition of doubtful origin, it probably contained sulphur, naphta, and quicklime. Godfrey died on 15 January 1741 and his business passed to his sons, Boyle and Ambrose, the eldest being named after his erstwhile mentor, the Earl of Cork. See G.G. Bickers, 'He put fires out with a bang' in *London Fireman,* (September 1967), pp 6-8.

29. Maguire, J.F., *The Industrial Movement in Ireland as illustrated by the National Exhibition of 1852* (Cork, 1853), pp.151-152.

30. *CE* 15 February 1877.

31. *CE* 14 November 1877.

32. Robert Day (1836-1914), Alderman, Cork Corporation 1880; High Sheriff of Cork 1893. Day's of 103 St Patrick's Street specialized in saddlery, along with angling and sports equipment. Firefighting equipment was an unusual line for them, although Robert's in-laws owned the hardware firm of Robert Scott and Company, which may explain his involvement in this line of business. President of both the Cork Cuverian Society and the Cork Historical and Archaeological Society, he ranked as one of the foremost antiquarians and collectors of antiquities in Ireland.

33. *CE* 8 June 1885.

34. WWFBC 19 March 1890.

35. WWFBC 4 June 1890.

36. WWFBC 26 February 1890.

CHAPTER 12

1. The Institution of Fire Engineers, *Chemical Fires and Chemicals at Fires* (London, 1934).
2. The firm of Harrington and Goodlass Wall (HGW) was established in 1922. Today, occupying the same site is ICI Dulux Paints Ireland Ltd.
3. *CE* 25 November 1891.
4. *CE* 27 December 1892.
5. Ironically, it was falling masonry that, sadly, claimed the life of Cork Fire Brigade's first fatal casualty. Auxiliary Fireman Michael O'Connell was fatally injured during the course of firefighting operations in Kilmallock, Co. Limerick, on Wednesday, 16 May 1928.
6. *CE* 18 May 1893.
7. *Ibid.*
8. *Ibid.*
9. 'Petroleum' in this context refers to mineral oils used in lamps, rather than petroleum spirit (i.e. petrol) used in internal combustion engines.
10. *CE* 5 December 1893.
11. *Ibid.*
12. WWFBC 13 December 1893.
13. *CE* 7 December 1893.
14. The full text of Jerry McCarthy's (The Rancher) *Curse* is available at the Local History Department, Cork City Library. See also John R. O'Shea, *The Red City* (Cork, 2005), p.209.
15. Drying rooms in flax mills were notorious as points of ignition for destructive fires. Mechanical driers frequently overheated and the flammable dust and fluff lying on the floor, roof beams, and machines all added up to a considerable fire hazard. See *Manual of Firemanship Part 6C: Practical Firemanship III*, (HMSO, 1984), pp.76, 77.
16. *CE* 5 September 1894.
17. *Ibid.*
18. *Ibid.* Even if the brigade had had sufficient hose to lay down a line from the Common's Road hydrant, they still could not have brought a jet to bear on the burning roof from that source alone. A fire at such a height, assuming the use of a one-inch nozzle, would have required a minimum pressure of some 5.3 bar (80 psi), not factoring in the considerable friction and other losses. This kind of pressure and volume was simply not available from the small, end-of-main, spur. With the arrival of the manual engine on the fire ground, operating from the open source, firefighting operations were largely independent of the unreliable hydrant system.
19. *CE* 5 September 1894.
20. *CE* 20 July 1897.
21. A formal Scale of Charges for the attendance of the brigade at incidents outside the city limits was first published in January 1896. (See Appendix 2).
22. Up to the mid-1870s most of the delivery hose for fire brigade use was made from copper-riveted leather, then flax hose began to overcome the prejudice of the old-fashioned fire officers and gradually found favour. Alfred Hutson, while stationed in Brighton, was among the first in England to introduce the new, more efficient, delivery hose. This was at the major fire that destroyed the Clarendon Hotel in 1882.
23. *CC* 10 October 1895. The current building was used as a bank since 1924 and was originally a Munster and Leinster Bank branch, later AIB.

24. S. Spiro of the Standard Watch and Clock Company in a letter of appreciation to Alex McCarthy, Town Clerk, 15 October 1895.

25. *CE* 1 January 1896.

26. *CE* 27 December 1895.

27. *Ibid.*

28. *CE* 31 December 1895.

29. *CE* 28 December 1895.

30. *CE* 27 December 1895.

31. *CE* 28 December 1895.

32. *Ibid.*

33. *CE* 1 January 1896.

34. *Ibid.*

35. Cork Fire Brigade Superintendent's Order and Reference Book, 6 April 1892.

36. *The Fireman*, 1 July 1896, p.7.

37. *Ibid.*

38. In 1898, a second horse was acquired for the brigade. A bay mare was purchased from Michael Ahern of Minane Bridge at a cost of £25, 'having been examined by Mr. Hoare, V.S., and certified sound' (WWFBC 4 May 1898). Timothy Lynch of Barrack Street was awarded the contract for supplying the horses' fodder: 11s 8d per barrel for white oats and 5s 6d per cwt for bran. Hay was carted from St Finbarr's Cemetery to the fire brigade stables. The horses were insured with the City of Cork Horse Proprietors' Insurance Society for £1 per annum. (See David R. Pike, *Irish Insurance Directory*, Dublin, 1990, p.42).

39. *The Fireman*, 1 January 1897.

40. *Ibid.*

41. WWFBC 16 November 1898.

42. *Ibid.*

43. *Ibid.*

44. *CE* 3 December 1898.

45. Town Council minutes 2 December 1898. Mayor Meade was well-disposed towards Hutson and the brigade. Following a fire at his Barrack Street premises, he spoke in 'laudatory terms to the services rendered by Supt. Hutson and the Brigade ... and presented a cheque for £20 to be distributed amongst the staff'. (WWFBC 10 June 1896).

CHAPTER 13

1. Following a fire at St Vincent's Place, Blarney Street, on the morning of 30 December 1898 in which a little boy lost his life, the fire chief explored the possibility of opening a station to cover the Shandon area. He identified suitable premises at the top of Shandon Street for which the landlord, John Twomey, would accept a yearly rent of £28. He suggested that two additional auxiliaries be recruited, thus freeing up two trained members to occupy the new station. His suggestions were approved, and on Monday 13 November 1899, Shandon Fire Station became operational with Auxiliary Firemen John Murphy and James Lyons in occupation. The National Telephone Company established a link with the central fire station at Sullivan's Quay at a charge of £1.15s.0d per annum ('half the rental charged to an ordinary subscriber'), but this was by way of a loop

through Shandon RIC station, an unsatisfactory state of affairs as delays were inevitable. In August 1900, a direct line was approved provided, 'the cost did not exceed a further £1.10s.0d per annum'. Number 120 Shandon Street remains today largely as it appeared over 100 years ago. From a cursory examination of the outside of the building one can immediately see that it was never a fire station in the true sense of the term. 'Fire post' is probably more accurate. The fire escape and hose reel were housed in a short passage at the side of the building. No transport of any kind was available to the two members on duty. When a fire call was received the escape and reel had to be trundled manually through the streets to the outbreak. It has, of course, to be borne in mind that the north side in 1900 was a fraction of the size of what it is now and consisted largely of the areas surrounding Blarney Street, Shandon Street, and Blackpool. Shandon fire station became non-operational in May 1925.

2. Although the brigade's first dedicated Discipline Code was not compiled until 1943, disciplinary regulations had existed since its earliest days. Supt Wickham had issued his 'Rules and Instructions' and these were expanded upon during Supt Hutson's term of office. Hutson (like the majority of his contemporaries) was affiliated to the National Fire Brigades Union (NFBU). In the absence of governmental standards in matters relating to uniform, rank-markings, terminology, drills, parades, service routine, etc., the NFBU had been singularly successful in winning almost universal acceptance for the standards it promulgated. The NFBU Handbook contained a Discipline Code which appears to have been adapted by small brigades (such as Cork) without their own formal code. A truncated version of the Code is as follows:

> Smoking in the street when on duty in uniform is forbidden. Gambling and unseemly conduct is strictly prohibited at stations. Intoxicating liquors are not to be brought into the business portions of station premises. Any neglect of duty will be dealt with by the Chief Officer as the case demands. When the Chief Officer of the Brigade, Members of the Council, Chief Constable, or Superintendent of Police, enter the Station, members of the Brigade will stand to attention, and when passing them in the street will salute them.

3. WWFBC 22 October 1890.
4. St Barbara, an early Christian martyr, was regarded as the Patron Saint of those in hazardous occupations such as artillerymen, miners, and firefighters. In recent years she has fallen somewhat out of fashion. Many now regard St Florian, another Christian martyr, as Patron of the Fire Service.
5. WWFBC 28 March 1893.
6. WWFBC 14 August 1901.
7. WWFBC 21 October 1891.
8. WWFBC 9 November 1893.
9. *CE* 25 July 1896.
10. *CE* 16 November 1893.
11. *CE* 14 August 1896.
12. *Ibid.*
13. *CE* 4 August 1897.
14. *CE* 18 June 1898.
15. *CE* 17 June 1898.

16. *CE* 18 June 1898.
17. WWFBC 29 June 1898.
18. *CE* 5 October 1898.
19. *CE* 1 December 1898. Murphy-O'Connor's, 'Wine merchants to the clergy and gentry of southern Ireland', were progenitors of the well-known dynasty of medical doctors and Roman Catholic clergymen, of whom Cardinal Cormac Murphy-O'Connor, the former Archbishop of Westminster and Primate of England and Wales, is a member.
20. See Cronin, M., 'Work and workers in Cork City and County 1800-1900' in *Cork: History and Society* (Dublin, 1993).
21. WWFBC 30 January 1901.
22. For rates of pay in the RIC see Jim Herlihy, *The Royal Irish Constabulary* (Dublin, 1997). For rates of pay in the DFB see Geraghty and Whitehead, (Dublin, 2004).
23. WWFBC 4 April 1899.
24. *CE* 26 May 1900.
25. WWFBC 2 December 1896.
26. WWFBC 10 February 1897.
27. WWFBC 6 October 1898.
28. *CE* 17 December 1896.
29. WWFBC 2 September 1891.

CHAPTER 14

1. *Cómhairle na Mire Gaile*, the Deeds of Bravery Council was established in 1947 to provide for suitable recognition by the State of deeds of bravery. The State has not instituted specific bravery medals for the various 'Front Line' emergency services. Members of these organizations can, and have been, endowed with awards from *Cómhairle na Mire Gaile*. (The Scott Medal, awarded to *Gardaí*, endowed by wealthy Canadian philanthropist Walter Scott in 1924, is not a State award. It has, however, been the practice for Ministers for Justice to make the formal presentations at an annual ceremony). See Wing Commander Éamonn O'Toole, *Decorations and Medals of the Republic of Ireland* (London, 1972).
2. William J. Tomkins was a member of the Cork City Record Jury and a Town Councillor for, variously, Glanmire Ward and North-East Ward. Between 1856 and 1877, he recommended seven Silver Medals and fifty-one Bronze Medals for conferring. Later, his son Valentine became the local Hon. Rep. of the RHS.
3. See Geraghty and Whitehead, pp.27, 30.
4. Constable John West, registered number 49131, a Kerryman, joined the RIC on 24 April 1882.
5. *CE* 2 January 1899.
6. Col. Sir Neville Chamberlain is generally regarded as the inventor of snooker. See Jim Herlihy, *Royal Irish Constabulary Officers* (Dublin, 2005), pp.89-94.
7. The hardware warehouse of John Perry and Sons Ltd stood at the corner of St Patrick's Street and French Church Street, the site of the present-day *Moderne* fashion store. Its postal address was 89 St Patrick's Street. The author is unable to reconcile how, if the policeman was standing with his colleague just across the street (at the top of Marlborough Street) as he testified, he could have determined that it was Perry's that was on fire when the actual premises involved, Alcock's, at

Nos 74/75, was approximately 100 metres up the street, and around a bend, to the left of them.

8. *CE* 29 November 1900. From the deposition of Cons. James Martin at the Inquest on 28 November 1900.

9. Now occupied by Mothercare. Alcock's reopened on the same site on 19 October 1901.

10. Contemporary accounts refer to Margaret McCarthy as 'nurse'. It is not clear, however, whether Ms McCarthy was a trained (medical) nurse in the present-day accepted sense of the term, or a 'nursery maid'. In view of her young age the former is unlikely.

11. *CE* 29 November 1900. From the deposition of Cornelius Fleming at the Inquest on 28 November 1900.

12. After some time, Grant's staff managed to make their way out onto the street where they assisted in whatever way they could.

13. *CE* 28 November 1900

14. *CE* 29 November 1900. From the deposition of Cornelius Fleming. In the aftermath of the fire jumping sheets were installed at the following locations: Fireman's Rest (Lavitt's Quay), Central Fire Station, and at the following RIC stations: King Street, Blackpool, Shandon, Sunday's Well, Great George's Street, Blackrock Road, Bridewell, and St Luke's.

15. *Ibid.* Deposition of Cons. Martin.

16. *CC* 27 November 1900 (special city edition).

17. *CE* 29 November 1900.

18. *CE* 1 December 1900. As described by Revd Michael O'Flynn, Administrator, Ss Peter and Paul's Church.

19. *CC* 28 November 1900.

20. *CE* 29 November 1900.

21. In 1900, the brigade possessed no breathing apparatus of any kind. Although rudimentary forms had been available for many years, (including a version developed by the noted Carlow-born scientist Professor John Tyndall), the instructions to Cork firemen while working in smoke were to apply to the face, 'a wet silk handkerchief, a wet worsted stocking, a wet sponge, or any wet flannel substance folded'. Wet cloths removed some of the larger particles when smoky air was inhaled, but gave no protection against asphyxiation from oxygen deficiency or excess of carbon dioxide, or poisoning from excess of carbon monoxide, and tended to give a false sense of security. Some of them thought the mark of a good fireman was the amount of punishment he could endure in a smoky building. Such firemen, known as 'smoke-eaters', were often condemned to a retirement plagued by emphysema, chronic bronchitis, or worse. Not until 1914, was a number of Eed's smoke helmets purchased. As these were not self-contained, they were of very limited use. The first truly self-contained BA sets (Siebe, Gorman 'Salvus' models) were not acquired by the CFB until 1934.

22. *The Fireman*, 1 May 1898, p.217.

23. *CE* 1 December 1900.

Index

Adams, John, 102
Admiralty, British, 78, 91
Aegis Fire and Life Ins. Co., 97
Alcock, Bernard J. and Co., (fire) 282, *passim*
Alleyn, John, 41
Amsterdam, 39
Anne, Queen, 38, 46, 78, 90
AOH Hall, (fire) 110
Arnott, Sir John, (Mayor) 102, *passim*
Atlas Assurance Co., 63, *passim*
Augustinians, 32, 53

Baddeley, William, 170
Bagwell, Phineas, 59
Bandon, 272
Barbon, Nicholas, 43, *passim*
Barry, Fm. James, 224, *passim*
Beamish and Crawford, (fire) 127
Belfast, 149
Bennett, Thomas, 50, 77
Benson, Sir John, 102, *passim*
Bergin, Osborn Marmaduke, 238
Blackpool, 254
Blackpool Flax Mills, (fires) 249, *passim*
'Black Jacks', 85
Blewit, Thomas, 50
Blyth, Dr John, 130
Bolster, Sr Angela, 53
Boyle, Robert, 236
Boyle, Supt John, 225
Braidwood, Supt James, 39
Brandy Lane (explosion), 100

Breda, HMS, 36
Bretridge's Hospital, 66
Bridewell, the, 61
Brighton Volunteer Fire Brigade, 204, *passim*
British and Irish United Fire Ins. Co, 70
British Commercial Life and Fire Ins. Co., 97
Browne, Bishop, 47
Browne, Edward, (Mayor) 38, 43
Browne's Mills, (fire) 187
Browne, Thomas, 56
Buckley, Jeremiah, 87
Bullen, Prof. Denis Brenan, 129, *passim*
Bullen, Robert, 220
Burke, Br James Dominick, 161
Burke, R.C., 111
Burke, Richard, 130, *passim*
Byrne, Capt., 164

Caledonian Ins. Co., 63, 95
Callaghan, Daniel, 72
Cantillon, Head Cons., 175
Carroll, Joshua, 72
Carson, Edward Q.C., 196
Casentini, Signor G.M., 207
Cat Fort, 31, 81
Cat Lane, (fires in) 57, 68
Christ Church (aka Holy Trinity), 47, 54, 63
Churchill, Brig. Charles, 32
Churchill, John, Earl of Marlborough, 30, *passim*

City Basin, 61, 103
Clarence Hotel, (fire) 198
Clarke, Sr M. Magdalene, 69
Clayton, Messrs, 165
Clear, William, 73
Cogan, Arthur, 141
Cómhairle na Mire Gaile, 278
Connors, John, 77, 140
Coote, William, 148
Coppinger, John jnr (Mayor), 23, *passim*
Cork Electric Tramways and Lighting
  Co, 222
Cork Fire Brigade (now Cork City Fire
  Brigade), 160, *passim*
Cork Gas Consumers' Co., 119, *passim*
Cork Improvement Acts, 102, *passim*
Cork Pipe Water Co., 60, *passim*
Cork Public Museum, 96
Cork Saw Mills, (fire) 116
Cork Steam Ship Co., 123
Cork Stonecutters' Society, 193
Cork Volunteer Fire Brigade, 229,
  passim
Cornmarket Street (tragedy), 101
Cosgrave, John, 77
Costin, Elizabeth Jane, 203
Courthouse (Gt George's Street), 192,
  (fire) *passim*
Courthouse (Main Street), 56
Cove (Queenstown/Cobh), 70, 90, 290
Cramond, Ensign William, 31
Crawford Art Gallery, 71
Creaghe, D.I. Philip Crampton (RIC),
  220
Crean, Ald. Eugene, MP, (Mayor) 197,
  passim
Crosse's Green (fires), 60, 111
Crowley, Jeremiah (Turncock), 181
Cunningham, Messrs John F., (fire) 163

Dale, Ald, Henry, 210, *passim*
D'Alton, Dr Richard, 270
Daly, James, 77
Daunt's Square (fire), 152, *passim*
Day, Messrs Robert, 240
De Montbret, Charles Etienne
  Coquebert, 90

Deyos, Joseph, (fire) 63
Dick's fire extinguishers, 239
Dobbin and Ogilvie's, Messrs, (fire) 175
Dorman, Thomas (Mayor), 86
Dublin, 38, *passim*
Dublin Fire Brigade, 108, 225
Dublin Ins. Co., 70
Dublin Metropolitan Police, 115, 149
Duggan, Jeremiah, 140
Dunbar, William, 155
Dunscombe's Marsh, 37, 43, 47

Eagle Ins. Co., 70, 97
Elizabeth Fort, 81, 113
Evory, Robert, 71, 98,
Exchange, the, 43, 56

Fair Lane (fires), 58
Farren, Ald., 41
Fenn's Marsh, 37
ffranklyn, Mayor, 38
Fireman's Rest, 217, *passim*
Fire Marks, 94, *passim*
Fire Office, the, 44, *passim*
Fire Office's Committee (FOC), 186,
  passim
Firestorm, Cork (1622), 18, *passim*
Fitton, Nicholas, 55, 61, 103
Fitzgerald, Ald. Sir Edward, (Lord
  Mayor) 197, *passim*
Fitz Patrick, John Roche (Mayor), 28
Fleming family, 283, *passim*
Flint family, 153
Franciscans, 32, 53
Friendly Society, the, 65
Fuller, Ald. William, 56

Gamble, Sydney Gompertz, 179
Garde, Joseph, 50
Gaven, Luke, 66
Geany, Thomas, 140
Geary, Francis, 50
General Ins. Co. of Ireland, 70
Gifford, Robert, 151
Ginkel, General, 32
Globe Ins. Co., 70
Glover, L.W., 123

Goddard, Ald., 38
Godfrey, Ambrose, 236
Goold, Edmond, 63
Goulden, Cons., 131
Goulding, Messrs W. and H.M., (fire) 132
Gray, W. Forbes, 74
Guardian Assurance Co., 71
Guardian Royal Exchange, 71

Hall, H. Ernest, 186
Hall, Messrs R. and H., 140
Haman's (aka Hammond's) Marsh, 37
Hamburg (firestorm), 19, *passim*
Hancock, W.N., 107
Hand-in-Hand Fire Office, 65
Harden fire grenade, 240
Harris, Eustace, 74
Harrison, Richard, 41
Harvey, G.N., 74
Harvey, Thomas, 74
Hawkes, Messrs, (fire) 54
Hayden, Messrs, 118
Heiden, Jan van der, 39, *passim*
Henderson, Alex, 74
Hewitt's Distillery, 116
Hibernia Buildings (fire), 175
Hibernian Ins. Co., 70
Higgins, Aux. Fm. Martin, 285, *passim*
Hill, W.H., 187
Hodges, Capt. Frederick, 206, *passim*
Hogan, John, 71
Hosmer, Chief E S, 259
Hope Fire and Life Assurance Co., 97
Horgan, Daniel (Mayor), 209, 221
Horses, fire, 87, *passim*
Hudson, Jemmy, 49
Hussey and Townsend, 71
Hutson, Supt Alfred J, 200, *passim*

Imperial Cinema, (fire) 110
Ingram, Capt. Robert J, 157, 166
Insurance Co. of Hong Kong, 227

James I, King, 23
James II, King, 30, *passim*
Jessop Browne and Co, 170
Johnson, James, 170

Johnston's, Messrs, 105, 141
Jones, Ald. John, 153

Kane, Sir Robert, 126, *passim*
Kavanagh, William, 153
Keating, Aux. Fm. James, 186, *passim*
Kellett, Henry, 72
King's German Legion, the, 71
Kinsale, 36
Kipling, Rudyard, 192
Kirkby, Samuel, 196

Lane, Abraham, 72
Lane, Denny, 120
Lane's Porter Brewery, (fire) 86
Lane's Steam Mills, (fire) 112
Large, William, 73
Lavallin's Oil and Colour Store, (fire) 220
Lee Cinema, (fire) 110
Leslie, James Edward, 71
Leslie, John, 71
Limerick, 28
London, 38, 39, 43, 66, 77
London Fire Engine Establishment, 107, 137, 144
Long's Public House (fire), 124
Lumley, William, 73
Lynch's Oil and Colour Warehouse, (fire) 173
Lyons, Denis, 153

McBride, Cons. William, 282
McCarthy, Alex jnr (Town Clerk), 157, 173
McCarthy, Bros, (fire) 190
McCarthy, Margaret, 288, *passim*
McDermott, Mary, 157
McElligott, Col Roger, 31, *passim*
McFarlane, Messrs Walter, 217
McLean and Parkes, (fire) Messrs, 257
McMullen, Joseph William, (fire) 155
McMullen, M J (City Engineer), 217, 226
McSwiney, Eugene, 195
Maguire, John Francis (Mayor), 102, *passim*

Mahony, M J (Chief Officer, CVFB), 231, *passim*
Majendie, Col V.D., 174
Mansion House, the, 61, 64
Marlborough, Earl of (see also John Churchill), 30, *passim*
Martin, Cons. James, 282
Meade, P.H. (Mayor), 256, *passim*
Metropolitan Fire Brigade, 201, *passim*
Millerick, Martin, 124
Minerva, 71
Monaghan, Chief Officer Liam, 61
Morgan, Isaac, (fire) 86
Morrison's Island, 84, 139
Murphy, Aux. Fm. Peter, 285, *passim*
Murphy, Bishop, 100
Murphy, Edmund, 117
Murray, Messrs (fire), 246

Nagle, Nano, 68
Nason, Messrs George, 214
National Ins. Co. of Ireland, 71
National Monument, 261, *passim*
National Telephone Co,. 227
Newsham, Richard, 53, *passim*
Night Watch, the, 151, *passim*
North Cathedral, 98, 187
North Cork Rifles, 144
Norwich Union, 78, *passim*

Oates, John, 40
O'Callaghan, Mary, 152
O'Grady, Revd Fr W.J., 100
Opera House, (fire) 110
Ó Séagha, Labhrás, 99
O'Sullivan, Revd Fr William, OSA, 220

Pacata Hibernia, 15, 21
Pain, James and George R., 193
Parnell, Charles S., 162
Passage West Volunteer Fire Brigade, 214, *passim*
Patriotic Assurance Co. of Ireland, 108
Pavilion Cinema, (fire) 110
Pay and Conditions, 274
Penal Laws, 47
Perkins, Jacob, 89

Perrier family, 51, 63, 69, 72, 107
Perrott, Messrs Richard, 127
Peter's Tower, 25
Phelan, Cons, 118
Phoenix Assurance Co., 95
Phoenix Fire Office, 45
Pike, Ebenezer, 123
Pike, Joseph (1690), 31
Pike's Marsh, 37
Pope John IX, 15
Pope's, Messrs, (fire) 272
Potter, Sub-Inspector, 164
Power and Gamble, Messrs (fire), 139
Protector Fire Ins. Co, 95
Pudding Lane (London), 43
Purcell, Capt. Thomas, 214

Queen's College, Cork, (fire) 126, *passim*
Queen's Old Castle, 117

Red Cow, the, 32
Reeves, Thomas Somerville, 73
Reidy, James, (fire) 120
Ring, John, 102, *passim*
Roberts, Capt. Edwin, 214, *passim*
Roberts, William, 170
Roe, Head Cons., 124
Rogers, Tom, 117
Royal Exchange Assurance Corporation, 50, *passim*
Royal Humane Society, 278, *passim*
Royal Irish Constabulary, 149, *passim*
Royal Society for the Protection of Life from Fire, 278, *passim*
Royal Victoria Theatre, 120
Rowland, Samuel (Mayor), 46, 60
Ryall, Dr, 126
Rycot, Col, 35

St Anne's, Shandon, 47, 98
St Dominick's Mill, (fire) 179
St Fin Barre's Cathedral, 47, 50, 57
St Francis' church, (fire) 187
St John Ambulance Brigade, 270
St Luke's church (St Luke's Cross), (fire) 187

St Mary's (Pope's Quay), (fire) 187
St Mary's, Shandon, 48, 50
St Michael's church (RC) (fire), 187
St Nicholas' church, 47, 52, 63, 187
St Paul's church, 43
St Peter's church, 47
St Sepulchre church, 47
St Werburgh's church (Dublin), 53
Scottish Union Ins. Co, 63, *passim*
Scravemoer, Gen., 32
Scully, Stephen J., 227
Sellers and Pennock, Messrs, 89
Sexton, Mons. Patrick, 99
Seymour, Frank, 111
Shandon Chemical Works (fire), 244
Shand, Mason and Co, 169
Shaw, Capt. Sir Eyre Massey, 39, 110,
    143, *passim*
Shea, William, 135
Sheehan, Barry (Mayor), 159, 164
Shinkwin, Austen, 95
Skiddy's Hospital, 66
'Smoke Silver', 13
South Chapel (St Finbarr's South), 155,
    187
South Sea Bubble, 66
Standard Watch and Clock Co, (fire)
    253
Stopford, Robert L., 128
Sun Fire Office, 63, 66
Sweeney, Edward, 52

Tettau, Gen., 32
Theatre Royal (Cork), (fire) 108, *passim*
Tholsel, the, 22, 28
Tóirpín, 14
Tomkins, Messrs W.J., (fire) 116
Tooley Street (London), 108
Townsend, S.P., 74

United General Gas Lighting Co, 119,
    passim
Ursulines, 68, 96

Victoria Hotel, 113
Vikings, the, 10, *passim*
Vize, Ralph, 56

Walker, Robert, 106, 138
Walker's Distillery, 86
Washington Cinema, (fire) 110
Waterworks 'Fire Brigade', 105, *passim*
Wesley, Revd John, 281
Westminster Fire Office, 66, 70
West of England Ins. Co., 63, *passim*
Wickham, Supt Mark, 157, *passim*
Wide Street Commissioners, 63, 115, 119
Widows' and Orphans' Fund, 276
Wise's Distillery, 99
Wrixon, Ald., 62
Wurtemberg, Duke of, 35

Young, Charles F T, 81

Pat Poland served with Cork Fire Brigade for over thirty years. He holds an MA degree from the School of History at University College, Cork. A member of Cork Historical and Archaeological Society, the Cork South Parish Historical Society, and the Fire Mark Circle, his articles on fire service history have appeared in local, national, and international publications. He was a contributor on the widely-acclaimed documentary *The Burning of Cork*, screened on RTÉ 1. He is currently researching the post-1900 story of the great fires of Cork and those who fought them.

He and his wife, Elaine, have four grown-up sons and live in East Cork.